BLACK WOMEN IN
UNITED STATES HISTORY

Editor

DARLENE CLARK HINE

Associate Editors

ELSA BARKLEY BROWN

TIFFANY R.L. PATTERSON

LILLIAN S. WILLIAMS

Research Assistant

EARNESTINE JENKINS

A CARLSON PUBLISHING SERIES

See the end of this volume for a comprehensive
guide to this sixteen-volume series.

Quest for Equality

THE LIFE AND WRITINGS OF MARY ELIZA CHURCH TERRELL, 1863-1954

Beverly Washington Jones

CARLSON
Publishing Inc

BROOKLYN, NEW YORK, 1990

See the end of this volume for a comprehensive guide to the sixteen-volume series of which this is Volume Thirteen.

Library of Congress Cataloging-in-Publication Data

Jones, Beverly Washington, 1948-
    Quest for equality : the life and writings of Mary Eliza Church
Terrell, 1863-1954 / Beverly Washington Jones.
        p.   cm. — (Black women in United States history ; v. 13)
    Includes bibliographical references
    ISBN 0-926019-19-8
    1. Terrell, Mary Church, 1863-1954. 2. Afro-Americans—Biography.
3. Social reformers—United States—Biography. 4. National
Association of Colored Women (U.S.)—Biography. 5. Afro-Americans–
–Civil rights. 6. United States—Race relations. I. Title.
    II. Series.
    E185.86.B543 vol. 13
    [E185.97.T47]
    973'.0496073 s—dc20
    [973'.049607302]
    [B]   90-1396

Typographic design: Julian Waters

Typeface: Bitstream ITC Galliard

The index to this book was created using NL Cindex, a scholarly indexing program from the Newberry Library.

This book was originally written as a Ph.D. dissertation in 1980 at the University of North Carolina, It has been edited for publication. Mary Church Terrell's *Selected Essays* are gathered together here for the first time.

Printed on acid-free, 250-year-life paper.

Manufactured in the United States of America.

Contents

MARY CHURCH TERRELL: SELECTED ESSAYS

To my husband, Ray,
my three children, Garry, Michelle and Ingrid
and to my sister, Lillie W. Williams

List of Illustrations

All illustrations are courtesy of the Moorland-Spingarn Research Center, Howard University, unless otherwise noted.

Introduction

One response to the civil rights movement of the 1950s and 1960s was the publication of a number of studies of the black experience. Unfortunately many of these works provided only limited information on the role of the black female. The biographies that have been published are generally confined to such notables as Phillis Wheatley, Sojourner Truth, Harriet Tubman, and Mary McLeod Bethune. Many black women leaders remain virtually unknown, their accomplishments forgotten.

This study documents the unique accomplishments of one of the foremost twentieth-century black woman leaders—Mary Eliza Church Terrell. For more than sixty-six years she was an ardent champion of racial equality. In the late nineteenth century, she was one of the most articulate and best educated black women in America—probably the only one who spoke three languages fluently. Few flaws in black-white relations escaped her notice or her outrage. Among the things she protested were lynching, disenfranchisement, segregated public accommodations, and employment discrimination.

As a lecturer who understood the nature of discrimination, Mrs. Terrell became nearly as well known in Europe as she was in the United States. She was determined that the entire world should know her native land for what it really was. Though she spent much of her time exposing and denouncing racism in all its forms, she worked equally hard in the effort to devise means to improve the lot of her people, especially women. Mrs. Terrell was one of the founders and the first president of the National Association of Colored Women, one of the early organizers of the National Association for the Advancement of Colored People, a member of the black vanguard that promoted political activity among blacks, and a fighter for women's rights. She also worked assiduously to combine her numerous community and civic activities with her role as a wife and a mother.

Her zeal and energy were matched by her uncompromising and unequivocal stand on every cause she advocated. Mary Church Terrell never hesitated to criticize Southern white liberals or Northerners or members of her own race, when she was convinced that their positions were not in the best interest of mankind. She was never reluctant to summon to the cause of human equality anyone and everyone whom she believed could serve.

Mrs. Terrell's importance as a suffragist and a race spokeswoman lies in the racial ideology revealed in her writings, speeches, and direct action strategies. Her life provides a vivid kaleidoscope of black-white interactions in the post-Reconstruction period, World War I, the Depression and New Deal, World War II, and on into the 1950s, an era that marked the advent of the second Reconstruction. Mary Church Terrell represents a transitional figure who encompassed in her life both the nineteenth-century woman who sought the basic meaning of life in the home and the twentieth-century "New Woman." As a race leader she is also transitional, having begun in the nineteenth century as one whose ideology was a blend of interracial dialogue and moral suasion, and having ended in the twentieth century as one who advocated a militant legalism and the use of such direct action tactics as picketing, boycotting, and sit-ins.

ONE

Choices

"A White Woman has only one handicap to overcome—a great one, true, her sex; a colored woman faces two—her sex and her race. A colored man has only one—that of race."[1] This penetrating statement was made in 1890 at the National Women's Suffrage Association convention in Washington, D.C., by Mary Eliza Church Terrell, one of the earliest college educated American black women. It reflects the major social issues that vexed Terrell during the mature years of her life. Only after she resolved how to deal with these handicaps for herself was she able to analyze the larger social issues and to implement measures designed to ameliorate the dual problems—sexism and racism—common to all black women.[2]

The oldest child of Louisa Ayers and Robert Reed Church, Sr., Mary Church Terrell was born September 23, 1863 in Memphis, Tennessee.[3] The Memphis she was born in had been founded in 1819 as a port city on the Mississippi River by Andrew Jackson and James Winchester, both of whom had been generals in the War of 1812, and John Overton, a retired Chief Justice of the Tennessee Supreme Court. The city was built on the fourth of a series of hills known as the Chickasaw Bluffs that towered over one hundred feet above the river. Jackson, who later became the seventh president of the United States, remarked that "this is the only site for a town of any magnitude on the Mississippi, between the mouth of the Ohio and Natchez."[4]

By 1830 the Bluff city had an unsavory reputation as a tough and uninviting place to live. Human and animal waste cluttered the streets and alleys. Sanitation was such a problem that most travelers recalled the smell as the most memorable part of their visit. Eli Whitney's invention of the cotton gin in 1793 made profitable the opening of land in Mississippi, Alabama, Arkansas, and Texas to large-scale cotton growing and production burgeoned. Memphis became one of the central collection and distribution centers for cotton and other commodities produced in the South. By 1850, the city was the largest inland cotton market in the world. With this new wealth and the emergence of a responsible mercantile class, Memphis gained some degree of social stability.

By 1860 Memphis was the sixth largest city in the South and was described as the "Charleston of the West." The 1860 census counted 22,623 residents—11,803 native whites, 4,159 Irish, 3,882 blacks, 1,412 Germans, 522 English, 140 British-Americans, 120 French, 113 Scots, and 472 of other foreign stock.[5]

During the Civil War, the economic prosperity of Memphis continued unabated. Few Southern towns suffered as little from the four years of war as did Memphis. The war brought no extensive military action to the Bluff city. The Battle of Memphis was a short-lived naval engagement on the Mississippi that ended with a federal brigade taking possession of the city. The Union forces used Memphis as a center from which to continued their successful campaign to control the Mississippi River and to operate against the Confederate forces in western Tennessee and northern Mississippi. It also served as an important commercial center. During the Union occupation, Memphis succeeded in maintaining trade and communication with the lower South, and served as an warehousing center for most of the contraband trade between the North and the South. Even cotton, despite efforts of the Confederate government to suppress trade with the enemy in this commodity, continued to play a significant role in the city's economic life.[6]

Mary Church grew up in Memphis during a postwar decade in which whites, and especially the Irish who were the largest of the foreign-born white groups, viewed the proliferating black population with alarm. While the increase in the white population was moderate during the 1860s, blacks moved into the city in large numbers—first as refugees during the war and then as freedmen afterward. By 1870 the black population had increased to 15,471 while the white population had increased only to 24,755.[7]

On one hand, the Irish were particularly disturbed by possible competition for jobs from freed blacks. Although the Irish immigrant vigorously asserted the supremacy of his white blood, he had to compete with blacks for jobs at docks and warehouses and in "pick-and-shovel gangs." On the other hand, increasing black visibility and mobility provoked whites to push for a return to the order and ideology of the Old South. That ideology depicted an organic society in which blacks and whites had clearly defined roles, blacks being by nature subordinate. In the antebellum world, black subordination had been guaranteed by the institution of slavery. After emancipation, whites resorted to violence in an attempt to maintain black subordination and to remove black labor competition for jobs. Racial antagonism reached a violent and lurid climax on May 1, 1866 when working class whites, mostly Irish, indulged in a two-day orgy of rioting that resulted in the death of forty-six blacks and the wholesale destruction of property. Three of the forty-six killed were women.[8]

The Memphis Riot, commonly referred to as the "Nigger Riot," "Irish Riot," and "Massacre" by the nation's press, became the subject of a Congressional investigation.[9] The background of this event is an appropriate beginning for analyzing nineteenth-century race relations in Mary Church's Memphis.

Reconstruction for Memphis, although short, was tragic for blacks. Since western Tennessee had been under Union control prior to the issuance of the Emancipation Proclamation, the institution of slavery was not abolished until February 22, 1865, by the ratification of an amendment to the state constitution. In spite of the passage of this legislation, whites, especially the Irish, continued their drive to subjugate the freedman. On June 5, 1865, a Union convention in Nashville passed the so-called "Disfranchisement Act" that denied the vote for five years to Confederates who had aided the rebellion and for fifteen years to those of high rank.[10] This policy enabled the newly arrived and heretofore uninfluential Irish to become a politically powerful group. They took an active interest in politics and by May 1866 controlled nearly all of the offices in the city government. During the period of their political hegemony, the Irish joined with others to petition the War Department to remove black troops from the occupation forces in the city because of their alleged assaults on white women.[11]

According to the findings of a Congressional Committee, the delay in discharging 4,000 black troops in the spring of 1866 started the actual conflagration. During the few days of idleness before their formal discharge, the troops allegedly harassed the Irish, who lived in close proximity to Fort Pickering where the men were stationed. Allegedly, several black soldiers became intoxicated, and the police force, 90 percent Irish, attempted to arrest them for disorderly conduct. This incident escalated into a mass conflict in which the Irish, joined by other whites, fought against blacks.[12]

The Congressional Committee, dominated by Radical Republicans, attached political significance to the riot. Unable to prevent the restoration of Tennessee to independent statehood, the Radicals saw the Memphis Riot as a way to discredit President Andrew Johnson's reconstruction policy and possibly effect the mid-term Congressional elections (mid-August-September

1866). The committee concluded that "the state of things in the city of Memphis is very much as it was before the breaking out of the rebellion. There will be no safety to loyal men either white or black, should the troops be withdrawn." Agreeing with these conclusions, the Tennessee General Assembly passed the Metropolitan Police District Act that placed Shelby County under state police protection.[13]

Under the unionist government blacks became an aggressive minority in politics. Suffrage was granted in 1867. This offered a wide opportunity for black participation and leadership. By 1868, they had been active in the county and state conventions of the Republican Party and held several important offices in the party's organization.[14]

Socially, the Freedman's Bureau and various benevolent societies aided in the establishment of schools for black children. In 1867, the legislature passed a general school law that required boards of education to provide schools for blacks.[15]

From 1867 to 1869, blacks continued their drive to overcome the heritage of slavery and to protect their gains, particularly the rights of suffrage, office holding, and education. However, On October 4, 1869, the conservatives (the Democratic Party) won control of the state and made white domination absolute. Thus, Mary Church grew up during a postwar decade in which race relations in Memphis were at first strained by conflict and violence and then by white domination and black subordination.[16]

The yellow fever epidemics of the 1870s had a profoundly disturbing effect on Memphis society. The first siege of fever in 1873 engendered a cautious attitude among inhabitants that was detrimental to the economy. Many residents were eager to sell their houses and lots and flee the city. The total value of taxable property dropped from thirty million in 1874 to twenty million in 1878. With the outbreak of yellow fever epidemics in 1878 and 1879, many of the well-off left the city, most never to return. By 1880 the city had no deeply entrenched social aristocracy of either race and thus was open to the rise of men who could establish their position on the basis of wealth rather than tradition. Mary's father, Robert Reed Church, came to prominence in this environment.[17]

Robert Reed Church, "Bob" as he was commonly called by both blacks and whites, provided a life of ease and luxury for his family. He had been born a slave in 1839 in Holly Springs, Mississippi. As a youth, he worked as a cabin boy on Mississippi River steamboats owned by his white father. After the Civil War, Church settled in Memphis. He began as a saloon

Robert Reed Church, Sr., Mary's father, was an influential businessman in Memphis. In 1900, he was considered the richest black man in Memphis and was frequently described as the first black millionaire in the South.

keeper and soon acquired a hotel. Working quietly with the required amount of obsequiousness within the framework of the white power structure, he became a prominent businessman. In the riots of 1866, he nearly lost his life when he was shot in the back of the head and left for dead on the floor of his saloon. He recovered and continued to acquire Memphis real estate. During and after each yellow fever epidemic, Robert Church added substantially to his real estate holdings. In 1891, he built a large auditorium that became the city's leading meeting place for black organizations and was, at the time, the largest theater for blacks in the United States. He also developed an amusement park on Beale Street in 1899 that became the black recreation center, and in 1906 opened the city's first—and for many years the only—black bank. By the turn of the century, he was unquestionably the richest black man in Memphis and was touted as the first black millionaire in the South.[18]

Mary's mother, Louisa, had also been born a slave. She was taken away from her mother as a child, became a close companion of her white mistress, and joined the Episcopal Church. She passed for white as a Creole in New Orleans for years. Later, she became the first black woman to operate a successful hair salon in Memphis.[19]

Louisa and Robert Church reared Mollie, as Mary was commonly called, in a sheltered middle-class environment. The Church home at 384 South Lauderdale Street was a large, spacious, white two-story dwelling that consisted of a living room, parlor, dining room, kitchen, sitting rooms, bedrooms, bath, and sleeping porches. In the rear of the home were a carriage house and servants' quarters.[20] The Churches attempted to obliterate any trace of their former status as slaves. Her father, who was "so fair that no one could have supposed that he had a drop of African blood in his veins," did not mention his white father and told Mollie only about his mother, who was simply called Lucy.[21] Lucy was purported to have been a Malay princess and only fourteen years old when brought to the United States from the island of Santo Domingo. She worked as a seamstress and was never treated as a slave or required to do menial chores. Mollie's mother's comments on slavery were brief, but benevolent. She stated that "her mistress taught her how to read and write, but also had given her lessons in French."[22] Even her wedding trousseau had been bought in New York by Laura, her mistress's daughter. It was only through her maternal grandmother, Lisa, that Mollie was able to see the darker side of slavery. Aunt Lisa, as she was called in the community, detailed the atrocities and

Mollie, as Mary Church was nicknamed, at about age six, when her parents separated, later to be divorced. Her mother, Louisa, moved with Mollie to New York, where she established a successful hair styling business.

brutalities slaves suffered. Shocked by her words, Mollie cried because "it nearly killed me to think that my dear grandmother, whom I loved so devotedly, had once been a slave."[23]

It was, of course, impossible for Mollie's parents to create a perfectly protected and roseate world for her. She had her first encounter with racism in 1868 at age five on a trip with her father to Cincinnati, Ohio. While her father was socializing in the "smoker," the railroad conductor attempted to remove her forcefully from the first-class coach. Bob Church had to draw his pistol to stop the conductor. Mollie, perceiving the conductor's actions as indicative only of her misbehavior, sought an explanation from her mother. Continuing to protect her daughter from the outside world, Louisa Church explained that "sometimes conductors on railroad trains are unkind and treat good girls very badly."[24] The Church's world functioned to isolate Mollie from the realities of being black in a white world, but, of course, the isolation could not be complete.

But Mollie's seemingly immutable world was soon to be radically transformed. In 1869, when she was six, her parents separated and later became divorced. Mollie's mother, Louisa, sold her shop in Memphis, moved to New York, and established a successful hair business. She decided not to enroll her daughter in the "segregated" schools of New York but rather in an integrated "model school" connected with Antioch College, in Yellow Springs, Ohio.[25] This transition was traumatic for Mollie. She began to understand that her race rendered her inferior in the eyes of the whites. In spite of her wealth, she now experienced the full and direct effects of racism.

Through the study of history at Antioch, particularly the history of the Civil War and the Emancipation Proclamation, she learned that she was a descendant of "these very emancipated slaves." Initially, this knowledge was traumatic, but it later became a significant source of strength for Mary. She concluded that the slavery of her people gave them a common bond with humanity. She theorized that "no race had lived upon the face of the earth which has not at some time in its history been the subject of a stronger. Holding human beings in slavery seems to have been part of the divine plan to bring out the best there is in them."[26] This approach to slavery became the catalyst that led Mary to a pursuit of academic excellence. She vowed to show those white girls and boys whose forefathers had always been free that she was their equal in every respect. Psychologically, Mary prepared herself to counteract racial discrimination. When ridiculed by a group of white classmates about her complexion, she proudly remarked, "I don't want my face to be white like yours and look like milk, I want it to be nice and dark just like it is."[27] When invited to perform in the school's play the role of a black servant, who made a mockery of the English language, she adamantly refused to disgrace her race.

The Antioch experience prepared her for the intellectual challenges she was soon to face at Oberlin College Academy and Oberlin College. Oberlin, Ohio, situated in the northern part of the state, had been the hub of anti-slavery activity during the middle decades of the nineteenth century. Prior to the Civil War, runaway slaves found aid in Oberlin for their journey to Canada, and those who wished to remain in the town were relatively secure from slave-catchers. The pre-Civil War period also saw faculty members, students, and alumni of Oberlin College actively involved in the anti-slavery movement. As a part of their interest in blacks, in 1835, two years after Oberlin College was founded, its leaders decided to accept students of all races.[28] Mary's student days provide a microcosmic glimpse of the situation after emancipation in a college traditionally friendly to blacks.

From 1875 to 1880 at Oberlin Academy and from 1880 to 1884 at Oberlin College, the period in Mary's development from adolescence at age twelve to adulthood at age twenty-one, she continued her effort to prove the intellectual capabilities of blacks generally and black women especially by enrolling in the classical rather than the literary curriculum. The literary curriculum at Oberlin Academy, usually taken by women, was completed in one year with the nominal reward of a certificate; while the classical curriculum, generally pursued by men, took an additional year, culminating with a two-year diploma. She was chided by her friends, who asked, "Where do you think you will find a colored man who knows Greek?" Mary proved her exceptional abilities when, out of a class of forty men, she was chosen to read a passage of Greek before the English writer, Matthew Arnold.[29]

Mary's achievements at Oberlin College were numerous. She was freshman class poet, a member of the honorary literary society, and Aeolian Society Editor of the Oberlin Review. Her academic achievements and social affiliations, however, did not protect her entirely from the effects of racism. She was denied the position of Senior Poet Exhibitionist, which she felt that she deserved, and her application for a summer job as a private secretary was rejected by middle-class whites as soon as they realized her race. Mary's experiences suggest that after the Civil War Oberlin College may have exhausted some of its traditional interest and enthusiasm in working and fighting for the freedom of blacks.[30]

Mary graduated from Oberlin in 1884.[31] As a college graduate and a black—a minority within a minority—she decided to teach, one of the few professions then open to women. Her aspirations were postponed for a year because of the adamant opposition of her father, who insisted that she return to Memphis to live with him. Emulating the Southern aristocratic tradition, he refused to allow his daughter to work. She spent a year keeping house for her father until he re-married. During that year Mary was restless. In her own words, "I could not be happy leading a purposeless life, where I could not put my college education, that had taken pains to acquire, to good use."[32] Defying her father's threats of disinheritance, Mary, accepted, in 1885, a position at Wilberforce University, a predominantly black institution in Ohio. Now twenty-two years old, she launched a career that she felt would enable her to reach the youth of her race, especially women. In 1887, she moved to Washington, D.C., to teach Latin at M Street Colored High School, where she met her future husband, Robert Heberton Terrell, then Chairman of the language department. Happily, Robert Terrell knew Greek.

In 1888, after a reconciliation with her father, Mary accepted his invitation to finance two years of travel and study in Europe. Two years of freedom in Switzerland, Germany, and France promoted intellectual and physical growth, but they also spawned tensions and anxieties in her life. She was faced with a choice between a European world with considerably less racial discrimination, a world where one was judged on the basis of ability not color, as against an American world, where she would be a "marginal" person, living on the same caste level as the less fortunate members of her race. A radiant woman with Italian complexion and Caucasian features, Mary Church could have faded into whiteness, "passed" and lived without suffering racial discrimination. She had precisely such an opportunity. She was offered marriage proposals from a German baron, an American student, and a successful businessman. One day in Berlin, while looking at the American flag, she was inspired to return to the United States. Later she stated the reason for her choice:

> It is my country; I have a perfect right to it and I will. My African ancestors helped to build and enrich it with their unrequited labor for nearly three hundred years. . . . I knew I would be much happier trying to promote the welfare of my race . . . working under certain hard conditions, than I would be living in a foreign land where I could enjoy freedom from prejudice, but where I would make no effort to do the work which I then believed it was my duty to do.[33]

Mary (Mollie) Church, at Oberlin College in Ohio, where she was a
student from 1880 to 1884. She specialized in classical languages and
received her bachelor's degree in 1884. She was the freshman class poet,
a member of the honorary society, and Aeolian Society Editor of the
Oberlin Review.

A similar choice was made by one of Mary's contemporaries, William Edward Burghardt Du Bois, then a recent graduate of Harvard University. After traveling and studying in Europe from 1892 to 1894 on a grant from the Slater Fund, Du Bois vowed to return to the United States "to put my new knowledge to use for the advancement of my people." According to Elliott Rudwick, one of Du Bois' biographers, even though "the European experience made him feel more human, he was still an American Negro and never in his life could he forget the implication of this fact."[34] In many other ways, Mary's and Du Bois' life were parallel. Both were born in sheltered family and community environments that initially rendered them relatively oblivious to their racial backgrounds—Du Bois in Great Barrington, Massachusetts, and Mary in Memphis, Tennessee. Both were educated at predominantly white universities with excellent reputations in the academic world. Both were mulattoes. Though they developed different strategies to elevate the black race, each was a champion of black equality.

Over the ensuing sixty-four years, this refined, cultured, and intelligent woman strove to implement her goal—the elevation of her race. Before engaging totally in this racial crusade, however, her desires and hopes as a woman had to be satisfied. Returning from Europe, she resumed her teaching career in Washington. In 1891, she declined a position as a registrar at Oberlin. Had she accepted, she would have been the first black in the United States in such a position. She chose, rather, to marry her M Street Colored High School colleague Robert H. Terrell, the first black person to graduate from Harvard University. Mr. Terrell later became the first black to serve as Judge of the Municipal Court in the District of Columbia. Married women were not allowed to teach and Terrell resigned herself to the pursuit of the "cult of true womanhood" by being a devoted wife.[35]

However, several factors, both internal and external, caused an upheaval in Terrell's life, an upheaval that was taking place in the consciences, thoughts, feelings, and self-conceptions of many American women at the time. Externally, changing economic conditions in the late nineteenth century were rendering traditional ideas about women's nature and role inadequate. The new technological time-saving inventions—factory-produced clothing, commercial laundries, prepared foods—provided leisure for the middle-class woman. Evidence from contemporary sources indicates that many women were questioning and rejecting old standards and trying to define new ideas and life styles better suited to their altered culture and new aspirations.[36] Often these involved abandoning the purely domestic life and going out into

Mary Church Terrell in her wedding gown, 1891. Because her husband also taught at M Street Colored High School, she was required to resign her teaching position there when she married.

the world to do good works. Robert Wiebe, a specialist in turn-of-the-century American history, found these changes common not only among women but also among middle-class groups of many kinds. He writes that "between 1895 and 1915 about every group within the middle class experienced its formative growth toward self-consciousness."[37]

Her personal situation also caused Mary Church Terrell to call into question women's orthodox role. Her late marriage at the age of twenty-eight provided her with a period after physical maturity and before marriage in which she experienced a very high degree of independence. Also, her maternal desires were shattered by the death of each of her first two children shortly after birth. And, she simply was not domestic. In her autobiography, she tells of walking "ten miles" between the cookbook and the bird she was roasting in her first attempt at preparing Thanksgiving dinner. Finally, her educational experiences fostered a sense of confidence and worth both as a person and a woman. All of these factors intensified latent characteristics of independence, confidence, and venturesomeness that could not be contained in a domestic life.

These aspirations and ideas came to be incorporated in the idea of the "New Woman." Journalists seized the term in the 1890s to try to describe changes that they sensed were taking place among women, changes important not so much in women's actual situations as in their outlooks and expectations. These contemporaries never interpreted the New Woman as an objective historical reality. She was an ideal that, like most ideals, meant different things to different people. More recently, historians have begun to analyze the emergence of this feminine ideal.[38] The New Woman was self-reliant. She was physically vigorous and energetic. She was well-educated. She was eager for direct contact with the world outside of her home. She held independent views. She wanted to play an active role in solving social problems that had previously been left to the male. Above all, she made a choice to break the Victorian model for her sex and move out into the world.

Mary Church Terrell was the apotheosis of the New Woman. She was determined to make her life useful and complete. The women's club movement of the late nineteenth century became a major vehicle through which Mary Church Terrell fulfilled her desires for herself, her sex, and her race.

TWO

The Women's Club Movement

After the Civil War, several black women worked independently to improve the status of blacks. Mrs. Frances Jackson Coppin, a graduate of Oberlin, founded Cheyney Training School for Teachers in Pennsylvania, then known as the Institute for Colored Youth, in the 1870s. Mrs. Frances Ellen Watkins, a noted abolitionist and educator, became a prominent lecturer in the South. She spoke in colleges, churches, and homes on such subjects as education, temperance, money, and morality. Years later, black women shifted away from their independent approach and toward the institutionalization of women's clubs that were designed to foster social interaction and self-education. However, in the 1890s, the New Woman eschewed such traditional groups as sewing circles, church clubs, and sisterly orders and organized reform-oriented women's clubs. One of the leading women's associations that sought to combat racial discrimination and to express a sense of identity and solidarity among black women on a national level was the National Association of Colored Women (NACW).

Recently, historians have begun to reexamine the history of women in America. Many of these historians are women working partly to discover the historical roots of their identity. The nineteenth-century women's movement in particular has received a great deal of study and analysis. There have been histories of the suffrage movement and biographies of its leaders. There have been histories tracing changes in the legal and economic status of women, of their struggle for education, and of their position in the family, society, industry, and the professions.[1] These divergent studies have left largely unexplored a salient aspect of the early women's movement—the experience of the black female. The discussion that follows of the NACW makes a contribution to rectifying this situation. Mary Church Terrell was at the center of this organization and its history also helps us understand her life during this part of her career.

The proliferation of black women's clubs and other "self-help" organizations beginning in the early 1890s was a response to the abysmal conditions imposed on blacks.[2] By the end of the nineteenth century the comparative fluidity of race relations in the Reconstruction era dissipated into increasingly rigid discrimination—legally, physically, and culturally. The last decade of the nineteenth and the first years of the twentieth century marked what Rayford Logan, a black historian who has written extensively on this period, has called the "nadir of the Negro," the lowest point of black misfortune. C. Vann Woodward, an authority on Southern history, described the period as the Age of Jim Crow. States enacted Jim Crow legislation that often simply confirmed long-honored customs but stood nevertheless as open and insistent declarations that the South was a white man's country. Specifically, these laws disenfranchised blacks and prohibited racial mixing in public facilities and other spheres of American life.[3] The laws and the widespread desertion by Northern whites from the black cause after Reconstruction forced blacks to embark on several organized efforts for racial betterment.[4] Cast back upon themselves, self-help became the shibboleth that applied to the whole spectrum of black activity. From sisterly organizations and social clubs to reform-oriented women's clubs, black women looked to their own groups as vehicles for advancing the entire race.

The social difficulties that faced black women were also factors in the emergence of reform-oriented women's clubs. Long excluded from the political and business circles of the nation, women felt a timidity in entering these affairs. Affected by a social aura that presumed male superiority and relegated women to a domestic role, black women drew together, organizing clubs around social reforms that would prove their capabilities outside the home. These organizations became both institutions for providing social services for black women and children and laboratories for training women for leadership roles in a society traditionally dominated by males. Fannie Barrier Williams, a noted black club woman and activist, later recalled that the club movement among colored women "has grown out of the organized anxiety of women who have only recently become intelligent enough to recognize their social condition and strong enough to initiate and apply the forces of reform."[5] One of these women was Mary Church Terrell. She became an organizer and the first president of the NACW.

In the early 1890s, black women's organizations spread throughout the country. In the East, the Loyal Union of Brooklyn and New York was organized in December 1892 and the Belle Phoebe League of Pittsburgh was organized in November 1894. In the West, the Harper's Woman's Club of Jefferson City, Missouri was organized in 1893 and the Woman's Club of Omaha, Nebraska was organized in February 1895. In the South, both the Phyllis Wheatley Club of New Orleans and the Woman's Mutual Improvement Club of Knoxville were organized in 1894. In the North, the Sojourner Truth Club of Providence, Rhode Island was organized in 1896.[6]

The establishment of the NACW, the systematizing and unifying of independent clubs, was done under the aegis of the Woman's Era Club of Boston. In the summer of 1894, the Woman's Era Club utilized its journal, appropriately called the *Woman's Era*, to stimulate interest in holding a national convention. The response was positive and many clubs agreed to a convention in 1895. The catalyst that sensitized several lethargic clubs was the disclosure of a scurrilous letter that attacked the morality of black women written by James W. Jacks, president of the Missouri Press Association, to Florence Belgarnie of England, secretary of the Anti-Slavery Society. Jacks stated that "the Negroes of this country are wholly devoid of morality, the women are prostitutes and are natural thieves and liars." The letter was not published in *Woman's Era*, but copies of it were disseminated to leading blacks, both men and women, to gauge their opinions. Numerous mass meetings were held to denounce the scandalous charges of the editor.[7]

Capitalizing on this emotional fervor, the Woman's Era Club convened the first national conference of black women in Boston in July 1895. About one hundred delegates representing twenty clubs from ten states participated in this historic meeting. Mrs. Josephine St. Pierre Ruffin, president of the Woman's Era Club, opened the event and set the tone of the convention. Her stellar address sounded the hope that the women's clubs that had sprung up all over the country would crystallize into a large union and form a national organization. She declared:

> Year after year, Southern [white] women have protested against the admission of colored women into any organization on the ground of the immorality of our women and because our reputation has only been tried by individual work, the charge has never been crushed. . . . It is 'most right,' and our boundless duty to stand forth and declare ourselves and principles to teach an ignorant suspicious world that our aims and interests are identical with those of all aspiring women.[8]

Heeding Ruffin's pronouncement, black women assiduously drafted policies and resolutions essential to the elevation of black people of their sex. The resulting organization was the National Federation of Afro-American Women. There was, however, another organization that purported to be national in scope—the Colored Woman's League (CWL) of Washington. The CWL was not represented at the Boston meeting. Both organizations had as their objective the improvement of the condition of black women. The programmatic emphasis of both concentrated on the cultural development of black women and children. Night schools were established in which classes in literature, language, and other subjects were taught by women volunteers. Mary Church Terrell of the CWL taught a class in German and one in English literature. Kindergartens were also established that provided maternal care to children of working parents.[9]

Realizing the absurdity of two national organizations working for the same objectives the two associations agreed to merge. On July 21, 1896 a committee of seven members from each group met and worked out the union of both organizations into the National Association of Colored Women.[10] Perhaps the most arduous task of the committee was the selection of a president. After numerous ties of 7-7, Mary Church Terrell, at age thirty-three and, incidentally, pregnant, was elected president.[11]

Nine years prior to the establishment of the NACW, in 1997, white women had created their national organization, the General Federation of Women's Clubs (GFWC). While the NACW was similar in function to the GFWC, there were important variations between them in rhetoric and goals—differences that reflected the divergent experiences of women of various middle-class, ethnic, racial, and religious backgrounds.[12] Both organizations provided social services to the community and worked for the betterment of the situation of women, but the black group also worked specifically for the betterment of the members of their race. White women had no need to vindicate their dignity nor did they have the severe problems of racial discrimination that compounded the plight of black women in all aspects of their lives. Black women even encountered discrimination from the GFWC. In 1900, Josephine Ruffin, representing both the black Woman's Era Club and the predominantly white New England Federation of Women's Clubs, thwarted an attempt to bar her from the GFWC convention because she was black. Nevertheless, the convention voted to recognize her as a delegate from the white group, while her credentials from the black group were rejected. At the same convention, Mary Church Terrell, president of the NACW, was denied the courtesy of bringing greetings on behalf of her association because several club members from Southern states objected and threatened to resign from the organization if she were allowed on the floor.[13]

The NACW was fortunate in their choice of Mary Church Terrell as their first president. Shortly after she was elected, her newborn baby died, the third time she had had a child die shortly after birth. Terrell poured her entire energies into NACW activities. In many ways, the organization became a surrogate child for Terrell as she nursed it into one of the most viable social institutions in the black community. Terrell even described the organization as a child:

> So tenderly has this child of the organized womanhood of the race been nurtured, and so wisely ministered unto by all who have watched prayerfully and waited patiently for its development, that it comes before you today a child hale, hearty, and strong, of which its fond mothers have every reason to be proud.[14]

As president from 1896 to 1901, Terrell developed a program that addressed racial problems through the elevation of black women. She believed that the amelioration of discrimination was contingent upon "the elevation of black womanhood, thus both struggles are the same."[15]

With this approach, President Terrell created pragmatic objectives and tactics. These strategies and objectives were at once radical and conservative. The NACW was radically new because it was a national effort exclusively created and controlled by black women. It established the first cohesive network of communication among black women throughout the United States. Its reform emphasis was an assertion of the role of educated women in the drive for social reform. It became a laboratory that fostered leadership skills among its members.[16]

The NACW was conservative in that it aimed not to alter the domestic nature of the social position of its members, but to make them better wives and mothers. It was devoted to the betterment of the entire race, not just the improvement of the status of black women.

The radical nature of the NACW can be seen in Terrell's first presidential address:

> We have become National, because from the Atlantic to the Pacific, from Maine to the Gulf, we wish to set in motion influences that shall stop the ravages made by practices that sap our strength, and preclude the possibility of advancement. . . . We call ourselves an Association to signify that we have joined hands one with the other, to work together in a common cause. We

21

proclaim to the world that the women of our race have become partners in the great firm of progress and reform. . . . We refer to the fact that this is an association of colored women, because our peculiar status in this country . . . seems to demand that we stand by ourselves. . . . Our association is composed of women . . . because the work which we hope to accomplish can be done better . . . by the mothers, wives, daughters, and sisters of the race.[17]

Terrell used several strategies to create a network among black women. First, she established communications by a monthly newsletter, the *National Notes*, to channel information about the programs and objectives of the organization. Each issue contained editorial comments from President Terrell inviting all clubs "with well-defined aims for the elevation of the race" to join.[18]

Second, Terrell organized the biennial conventions in cities with large black populations—Nashville (1897), Chicago (1899), and Buffalo, New York (1901).[19] She highlighted each convention session with such provocative topics as "Modesty in Manners and Dress," "Women and the Work Force," "Purity and the Woman," "Temperance," "Mothers and Children," and "Woman and the Home." Exhibits of paintings and of literature further enhanced the interest of participants in the association's gatherings. The convention sites and the quality of the programs led to an increase in delegates. By 1901 the attendance had increased from 100 to 250 delegates. Of the 250 delegates, there was a larger percentage of women who, in Terrell's opinion, were educated, refined, and cultured. Also by 1901 there were thirty local branches and fifteen federations, each subdivided into twelve "well-organized" departments headed by a superintendent and a committee head.[20]

The creation of a cadre of elite women to head local affiliates was another ingredient in Terrell's network. Ideologically, Terrell's framework of leadership embraced the Talented Tenth philosophy of W. E. B. Du Bois, that maintained that the well-educated, when provided with opportunities to develop their native capabilities, would rise and eventually carry the untalented along with them.[21] The NACW attracted a heterogeneous band of elite women—educators, business women, doctors, etc. From 1895 to 1901, the years that embraced Terrell's tenure as president, of the fifty officers of the national and state affiliates whose educational backgrounds could be determined, thirty had college degrees. Of that number, seven held graduate degrees, and six held professional degrees in medicine or law.[22] To prepare these women for their new leadership role, President Terrell taught a class on parliamentary procedure.

The nation's press helped to promote the development of the network. Its liberal policy of allowing the NACW to place columns in its newspapers widened the public's interest in the club. A "Woman's World" department was established in the *Colored American*, a black newspaper, in Washington, D.C., which highlighted the NACW's concern for the emerging problems of black women.[23] The enthusiastic reports of the conventions in such leading newspapers as the *Boston Transcript*, the *Springfield Republic*, the *Chicago Daily News*, the *Evangelist*, and the *Los Angeles Times* popularized the NACW as the leading organization for black women in the nation. Describing the 1899 Chicago convention, the *Chicago Daily News* commented:

> Of all the conventions that have met in this country this summer, there is none that has taken hold of the business in hand with more good sense and judgement than the National Association of Colored Women, now assembled in this city. The subjects brought up, the manner of their treatment and the decisions reached exhibit wide and appreciative knowledge of conditions confronting colored people.[24]

In analyzing the caliber of leaders, the Chicago *Times Herald* candidly admitted:

> These women were a continual revelation, not only as to personal appearance, but as to intelligence and culture. If by a bit of magic the color of their skin could be changed white, one would have witnessed a convention of wide-awake women, which in almost every particular would compare favorably with a convention of white-skinned women.[25]

Lastly, the programmatic emphasis of Terrell's NACW further contributed to the creation of its national network. By its constitution, the prime objective of the NACW was "to secure harmony of action and cooperation among all women in raising to its highest plane, home, moral, and civil life."[26] Mary Church Terrell, not unlike her black counterpart, Charlotte Hawkins Brown, founder of the Palmer Institute in North Carolina, and her white counterpart, Jane Addams, founder of Hull House in Chicago, maintained that the female's monopoly on virtue obligated her to be the pivotal force in the advancement of society. Unlike Brown, whose educational and social institution fulfilled the needs of a minority of women—the educated—but like Addams, Terrell established an institution that sought to enhance the lives of everyone.

> Believing that it is only through the home that a people can become really good and truly great the NACW had entered that sacred domain, hoping to inculcate right principles of living and to correct false views of life. Homes, more homes, better homes, purer homes.[27]

This conservative ideology could not be called feminist. Terrell's advocacy of the domestic role of the woman did not unequivocally espouse the social equality of women. Yet, in addition to its avowed objective, the NACW succeeded in shifting the interests of its leaders, who were of middle-class status, outside of the home.

Once the institutional structure had been set up and the actual network was underway, Terrell placed less emphasis on what she derided as "paper organization" and more on concrete programs as tools to improve the race through women. Terrell's tenure as president of the NACW was characterized by innovative and progressive programs. She cogently argued for the creation and institutionalization of kindergartens, day nurseries, and Mother's Clubs. She stated that from these institutions "one reaches both the source of many race problems and an intelligent solution of the same, through the home, the family, family life, and the child." Her closing remarks accentuated the sufferings perpetrated upon children of mothers who were wage-earners.

> When one reflects on the slaughter of the innocent which is occurring with pitiless persistency every day and thinks of the multitudes who are maimed for life through neglect, how many there are whose intellects are clouded because of the treatment received during their helpless infancy, establishing day nurseries can seem neither unnecessary nor far-fetched; but must appeal directly to us all.[28]

Terrell's interest in the establishment of social institutions such as kindergartens and day nurseries clearly indicated her awareness of the preponderance of black married women in the work force. In 1890, about 1.2 million women worked as domestics: one-fourth were black, and about 100,000 of that 300,000 were married.[29]

At the biennial convention in Chicago in 1899, Terrell implemented her program. She raised enough money to appoint a kindergarten advisor, whose duty was to "arouse the consciences of . . . women to the necessity of kindergartens."[30] Even before the appointment was made, Terrell's pronouncement on the necessity of kindergartens inspired the Progressive Club of Kansas City to initiate measures to establish a kindergarten in their city. Upon returning from the Chicago convention, the club appointed a committee that persuaded the School Board to appropriate money for the establishment of a black kindergarten. In September 1900, the Board established a kindergarten and employed the first graduates of the St. Louis Normal Kindergarten Training School as teachers.[31] The yearly report of the local clubs given at the Buffalo convention in 1901 indicated that kindergartens and day nurseries had been established in Kansas City, Missouri; Montgomery and Ophelia, Alabama; Charleston and Orangeburg, South Carolina; New Orleans, Louisiana; Galveston, Texas; Washington, D.C.; Philadelphia and Moorestown, Pennsylvania; and Butler, Mission, and Chicago, Illinois.[32]

Financial support for kindergartens and day nurseries came from divergent sources—church donations, state funds, School Board appropriations, and from individual members of the NACW. As president, Terrell donated funds from the proceeds of her pamphlet "The Progress of Colored Women." It was sold to delegates at the NACW's conventions and in 1899 at the 30th Annual Convention of the National American Suffrage Association in Washington, D.C.[33]

The development of Mother's Clubs was an important part of Terrell's program. These clubs functioned as depositories and disseminators of information on the best methods for rearing children and conducting homes. Terrell also hoped that Mother's Clubs would improve the moral standards of the "less favored and more ignorant sisters" because the world "will always judge the womanhood of the race through the masses of our women."[34] Terrell hoped to refute the false accusations that had been applied to black women, the most pernicious of which that black women were promiscuous and thus incapable of monogamy and morality. After the Civil War, some Northern whites placed the blame for a high illegitimate birthrate on black women. One Northern white woman declared:

They are still the victims of the white man under a survival of a system tacitly recognized which deprives them of the sympathy and help of the Southern white woman, and to meet such temptations Negro women can only offer the resistance of a low moral standard, an inheritance from the system of slavery, made lower from a life-long residence in a one-roomed cabin.[35]

How effective were Mother's Clubs? One may suspect that the elite cast of the NACW's leadership minimized the effectiveness of this reform institution. However, Terrell and other leaders were aware that the support of the masses was essential to the success of all of NACW's programs. The Association's motto, "Lifting As We Climb," indicated this awareness. President Terrell declared:

> In no way could we live up to such a sentiment better than by coming into closer touch with the masses of our women. . . . Even though we wish to shun them, and hold ourselves entirely aloof from them, we cannot escape the consequences of their acts. So, that, if the call of duty were disregarded altogether, policy and self preservation would demand that we do go down among the lowly, the illiterate, and even the vicious to whom we are bound by the ties of race and sex, and put forth every possible effort to uplift and claim them.[36]

This statement indicates not only the reasons why the NACW concerned itself with uplifting the less fortunate members of the sex but also reveals the class biases of women elites. Implicitly, Terrell maintains that the leaders, who were not genuinely concerned with the welfare of the masses and did not want to be associated with them, pursued the elevation of the masses of women as a vehicle for enhancing their own social position in society. In other words, modifying the phraseology of Rudyard Kipling, a British poet and storyteller, whose works implied that it was the duty of Great Britain to carry the white man's burden by civilizing backward races, the women elites of the NACW saw the "lowly and illiterate" black women as the "Black Woman's Burden."

In spite of their paternalism, Mother's Clubs became viable institutions in the South. The yearly report of the Tuskegee, Alabama's Mother's Club in 1901 provides a microcosmic view of the approach and methodology of one club. Prefacing its report with the statement that it "had brought the light of knowledge and the gospel of cleanliness to hundreds of poor benighted sisters on the plantation," the club used "heart to heart talks" and demonstrations of new home making techniques. These ideas were called the "A, B, C of living." They spelled out the best ways to "sweep, dust, cook, and iron and clothe children by making or mending clothes."[37]

Because of continuous contact between Mother's Clubs and the masses of women and the rapid loss of jobs held by blacks, Terrell broadened the function of Mother's Clubs to include the social as well as the economic concerns of blacks. She advised the directors of Mother's Clubs to study the labor question, not only as it effected women, but also as it effected men. In addition, she launched a fund-raising campaign to establish schools of domestic science. In 1897, the Phyllis Wheatley Club of New Orleans established a training school for nurses at its public sanitarium. In its yearly report, given at the 1901 convention, the club stated that the municipal government had agreed to appropriate "$250 annually toward its development because of its indisputable proof of its utility and necessity during the yellow fever epidemics of 1898."[38]

Another of Terrell's concern was the impact of city life on the young, specifically single girls who had migrated into urban areas. In her second address, she states that many girls who come to cities without relatives and money become "wayward and fallen." She also lucidly discusses the demoralizing influence of the theater, saloon, and the dance hall on the young.[39]

President Terrell's attempt to confront the ills that flourished in an industrialized and urbanized environment characterized the social welfare and/or social settlement emphasis of the Progressive Era in America. The Progressive Era, the years between the turn of the century and the First World War, was the first reform period of the twentieth century. Many progressives were influenced by the theory of pragmatism that repudiated all fixed doctrines, especially Social Darwinism, which scorned reform efforts as heresy and held fast to the doctrine of the survival of the fittest. This pragmatic philosophy exalted the power of human will—people can shape their own destiny—and led those who were dissatisfied with society to work for change.[40]

As a social-welfare progressive imbued with the theory of pragmatism, President Terrell assisted affiliates in the implementation of measures designed to ameliorate pressing urban problems. In 1896, the Illinois Federation of Colored Women's Clubs opened the Phyllis Wheatley Home for Girls. It provided living accommodations, social facilities, and employment bureaus for girls who found themselves excluded from the YWCA and similar white organizations. The home also operated classes in domestic arts for non-resident women. In 1899, the Chicago Woman's Conference established a "Police and Investigating Committee" to maintain surveillance on all saloons in order to determine the names of children who went in to buy beer. For this herculean task, the committee divided the city into four districts and assigned two members to each. These members were responsible for compiling a record on each child, informing the parents of the child's conduct, and making periodic visits to the home.[41]

Other social-welfare institutions were spearheaded by Terrell. In 1898, the Illinois Federation opened a home for the aged and infirm. By 1900, this institution had thirteen occupants and was administered by a permanent board of trustees. The Alabama Federation organized the Mt. Meig's Institute in 1898 to benefit blacks on plantations in the black belt counties of Alabama. The curriculum of the school addressed the basic needs of the people. Girls were taught everything pertaining to the management of the home, while boys learned blacksmithing, carpentry, and farming.[42]

Though the NACW placed priority upon the creation of a wholesome life for blacks, especially women, President Terrell also pushed for the aesthetic enrichment of black life. She urged the formation of musical clubs believing that "music in colored people was a heavenly born gift that should be cultivated." She also strongly supported temperance organizations because she considered intemperance to be one of the "greatest foes to the progress and development of blacks."[43] Several affiliates of the NACW adapted the methods and specific problems of the national to the special needs of the local communities in which they operated. Clubs in Louisiana and Tennessee took more direct steps toward the eradication of racial discrimination. They petitioned the state legislature to repeal the obnoxious Jim Crow laws and to condemn the barbarity of the convict lease system that made "female prisoners one of its principal victims."[44] The failure of the national organization to address the problem of segregation reveals its conservatism and its reluctance to deal with political issues.

Though Terrell tended to eschew political issues, during her tenure as president the NACW successfully translated its objectives into important reform programs. Here are some statements from the yearly reports of clubs to the NACW in 1897, 1899, 1901:

The free clinic at the New Orleans sanitarium has been visited daily by the poor.

The Woman 's Mutual Improvement Club of Knoxville, Tennessee provides clothing and food for ninety-seven families. Thirty homes, in the alleys and slums, have been visited and this class of people seemed benefitted.

The Ladies Auxiliary of the District of Columbia has done much effectual work in visiting the sick at their homes, the hospitals, and jails, reading to the unfortunate and distributing provisions to those in need.

The Mutual Improvement Club of Selma, Alabama, has paid the tuition of several children of widowed mothers in schools of the city.[45]

Developing kindergartens, nurseries, Mother's Clubs, and homes for girls, the aged and infirm, the NACW emerged as a leading women's organization enhancing of the lives of the masses and also providing a vehicle for the energies of middle-class women. Apart from any of her specific programs, the very existence of the NACW embodied the major strategy of Mary Church Terrell—the creation of an organization of young, educated black women dedicated to the elevation of the race.

The constitution of the NACW prohibited a president from serving more than two consecutive terms, so Terrell stepped down in 1901. In recognition of the immeasurable value of her work, she became the first honorary president for life. For Terrell, it was time to cut the umbilical cord. The NACW had matured into one of the most viable women's associations in the country. For Terrell, her experiences as president were a process of growth. She was now ready to enter the ideological arena of race relations that was dominated by two major figures—Booker T. Washington and William Edward Burghardt Du Bois.

THREE

Interracial Understanding

The ideologies of Booker T. Washington and William Edward Burghardt Du Bois dominated the black world of the last decade of the nineteenth century and the first two decades of the twentieth century. On one hand, in the midst of proliferating discrimination, Booker T. Washington advocated an accommodationist approach of black self-help through industrial education. On the other hand, W. E. B. Du Bois espoused a radical philosophy of struggle to achieve full civil and political rights by open agitation and protest.[1] In spite of the disparity in their philosophies both Washington and Du Bois recognized the essential role of whites in the advancement of the black race. In his famous *Souls of Black Folk* (1903), Du Bois wrote that "while it is a great truth to say that the Negro must strive and strive mightily to help himself, it is equally true that unless his strivings be not simply seconded, but rather aroused and encouraged by the initiative of the richer and wiser environing group, he cannot hope for success." Du Bois's message throughout the book was that blacks "like all backward people need cooperation, leadership, and training from whites" in order to realize "effectual progress."[2] In the same vein, Washington reminded blacks that race advancement was contingent on white cooperation. In his words, "Any movement for the elevation of the Southern Negro needs the cooperation, the sympathy, and the support of the best white people in order to succeed. For whites, after all, control the government and own the property."[3]

During the first three decades of the twentieth century, Mary Church Terrell adopted and refined the Washington–Du Bois theory of interracial cooperation for her own use. She moved from self-help to interracial understanding. From 1896 to 1901 Terrell had defined and developed her role as a "New Woman." By 1901 this role had encouraged a development of purpose, independence, confidence, and vitality in her life as a woman and as a person. She was not skeptical about her ability to function as a leader outside the confines of a woman's organization. Moreover, she was confident enough to transcend the concept of black self-help to a broader ideology.

Terrell advocated education as the way to interracial understanding. She hoped that unbiased research and intelligent dissemination of information to both whites and blacks would spark better cooperation. Her papers indicate that she wanted integration to replace segregation. She never said precisely how this could be done, but her activism in interracial organizations and politics indicates what she considered the essential first steps in the process to be.

Anthropologists have defined race simply and broadly as a biological category based upon genetically transmissible physical characteristics. This scientific definition has little to do with race relations, which is a cultural rather than a biological matter. For practical purposes, the term "race relations" is used here to mean social and cultural interactions between different ethnic and racial groups.[4] This is the way Terrell uses the phrase in her autobiography, *A Colored Woman In A White World*. As early as 1881, her ideas on the matter had begun to crystallize. After developing an amicable rapport with a white classmate at Oberlin College, Mary stated that "there are some white people in the United States too broad of mind and generous of heart to put color of a human being's skin above every other consideration. No one could make this colored girl believe that all white people are innately hostile to her race and that there can be no common ground of understanding and good will between them. . . . It is said that one man can not hate another if he understands him."[5] This attitude was buttressed when Mary accepted an invitation from Mrs. Blanche K. Bruce, the wife of the black Senator from Mississippi during Reconstruction, to attend the Inaugural Ball of President James Garfield in 1881. Witnessing the social mingling of blacks and whites on "an equal basis," Mary was convinced that interracial understanding was possible.[6]

In 1881, Mary had no way of knowing that she would see Washington, D.C., change from a city that sometimes practiced black-white camaraderie to become by 1890 a world capital with a rigid system of segregation. Washington's sobriquet "The Colored Man's Paradise" became a misnomer. Remarking upon its genesis, Terrell stated:

> Whether the sobriquet was given to the nation's capital in bitter irony by a member of the handicapped race, as he viewed some of his own persecutions and rebuffs, or whether it was given immediately after the war by an ex-slaveholder who for the first time in his life saw colored people walking about like freemen, minus the overseer and his whip, history saith not.[7]

In 1904, Terrell examined the transition in a scathing article, "What It Means to Be Colored in the Capital of the United States." "For fifteen years," she wrote, "I have resided in Washington, and while it was far from being a paradise for colored people when I first touched these shores, it has been doing its level best ever since to make conditions for us intolerable."[8] Terrell related how she and other blacks encountered discrimination in housing and in employment. Blacks must protest these conditions. "Colored people should not accept injustice without complaint. . . . They should resort to any subterfuge, using any disguise or playing any trick." However, softening her radicalism, she added, "Provided they do not break the law."

Her instructive pronouncement was not unheeded. In her article, she told of a black woman who wanted to attend a theatrical performance so much that she decided to disguise herself as the nurse of a white child that she knew. She requested Terrell to telephone the ticket office to inquire whether a neat appearing colored nurse would be allowed to sit in the parquet. The reply of the ticket manager was "No." He further commented that "it was a poor policy to employ colored nurses in Washington because they are excluded from every place to which white nurses are allowed to take children for pleasure."[9] This statement explicitly illuminated the ubiquitous color problem that existed in the nation's capital.

Terrell concluded her article with an analysis of the residual effects of segregation—the defection of mulattoes from the race and the fatalistic mentality of black youth. She contended that the exodus of mulattoes to the white race was their way of obtaining economic security. But the forfeiture of one's self respect was a "high price" to pay. The greatest tragedy of discrimination was the sacrificing of "our people on the altar of prejudice."[10] Terrell's appointment in 1895 to the Board of Education of the District of Columbia made her the first black on the board. She had, on many occasions conversed with black youth about their goals. Their collective response indicated the pathological effects of discrimination. Because they were not allowed to compete for jobs, students had no incentive to remain in school, resulting in the "wreck and ruin" of their lives.

In 1895, the emerging black spokeswoman of the twentieth century had discovered that racial discrimination was omnipresent in the South. At the suggestion of Robert Nourse, a well-known lecturer from Falls Church, West Virginia, Mary Church Terrell had launched a career as a public speaker. Her husband was warned by his friends not to allow his wife "to wade deeply into public affairs." They stated that "when a woman became deeply interested in civic affairs, and started on a public career, that was the beginning of a disastrous end."[11] However, Robert Terrell disregarded these warnings and encouraged the public activities of his wife.

From 1895 to 1910, Terrell traveled extensively throughout the South on Jim Crow cars. These facilities lacked sufficient ventilation and food provisions for blacks. Enduring these oppressive conditions on one trip from Washington, D.C., to Fort Smith, Arkansas, Terrell reached her destination ill. In spite of her condition, she fulfilled her lecture engagement because she hated to disappoint her audience.[12] She kept her husband constantly informed about her daily perils. Robert Terrell, on one occasion, took action on her behalf. In a letter to the District Superintendent of the Pullman Company in 1905, Mr. Terrell protested the "deliberate" mistreatment of his wife. He stated that one week before his wife's trip to New York City, she had purchased a ticket for the lower berth near the ladies' lavatory. On the day of her departure, she was informed that some other passenger was given the berth by mistake, and she had to take the one near the men's lavatory.[13]

Enduring the hazards of Jim Crowism in the North and in the South, Mary Church Terrell became a popular lecturer, speaking throughout the United States at Chautauquas, forums, and at universities. Jacob Harris, at the age of ninety-four recalled one of Terrell's addresses, "A Bright Side of a Dark Subject," delivered in 1905 in Atlanta, Georgia. He remembers that Mrs. Terrell gave a well-informed analysis of the progress of blacks after slavery. After her speech, he was fortunate enough to meet her. Mr. Harris found Mary Church Terrell a "very gracious, down-home, and no-put-on person."[14]

After experiencing segregation first-hand throughout the United States, Terrell dedicated herself to implement her gospel of interracial understanding. The underpinnings of her strategy had taken shape during her formative years at Antioch College. Terrell's study of history revealed that an enslaved people can progress.[15] Realizing that it was this concept that was the catalyst for her own academic achievement, she advocated this idea to blacks through her writings and speeches. She believed that racial pride could supplant feelings of racial inferiority if blacks were taught about the accomplishments of their race. Possessing a keen eye for practicalities, she hoped that this pedagogic strategy would transform blacks into exemplary citizens worthy of white support. Terrell also maintained that this goal could only be successfully achieved if whites were educated about black life. It was imperative, according to Terrell, to use education, as a tool of moral suasion, to sensitize

A formal portrait of Mary Church Terrell, ca. 1910.

white consciences to the truth about black conditions. In turn, she hoped that whites would develop positive and sympathetic attitudes to the problems of the black race.

To black people, Terrell played the role of a spokeswoman and educator. Her articles told of the thrifty, industrious, self-reliant, and clean-living blacks, who rose from the depths to the heights by their own means. A typical vignette was her obituary for Paul Laurence Dunbar, a popular black poet of the early twentieth century. She traced his life from the poverty-stricken environs of Dayton, Ohio to his death in 1905. Terrell extolled the determined quest of Dunbar to become a poet in spite of seemingly insurmountable obstacles. Describing him as a "slender colored lad as black as the core of Cheop's pyramid," Terrell ended her article with words that accentuated racial pride and venerated self-respect: "In the flower and fruit of his genius, he has bestowed upon his country and his race an imperishable gift. In grateful appreciation of his services and in genuine affection, Paul Laurence Dunbar lies today enshrined in our hearts as a far nobler mausoleum, after all, than one built of marble could possibly be."[16] To further extol Dunbar's accomplishments, in June 1922, Terrell delivered an impressive commencement address at Dunbar High School in Washington, D.C. She conveyed the message so well that she received several letters from students requesting more information on the achievements of blacks.[17]

Contradicting the contemporary belief that blacks lacked ability to excel in such artistic fields as music, Mrs. Terrell published in 1905 an article on the life of Samuel Coleridge-Taylor, a musician and a conductor. Unfettered by the poverty that pervaded Dunbar's life, Coleridge-Taylor was born in England, "where color constituted no barriers to success," to a "full-blooded African, who was a surgeon, and an English woman." Trained in the best European schools, Coleridge-Taylor unveiled his musical abilities in 1904 in a concert performance in Washington, D.C., that received unprecedented accolades. Terrell interpreted his performance as indicative of the fact that there "is no musical Parnassus too lofty or too steep for colored people to scale."[18]

Terrell wrote numerous articles on pioneer black achievers such as poetess Phillis Wheatley (in whose honor she named her first daughter), scientists George Washington Carver and Ernest Just, and black spokesman Frederick Douglass. Terrell considered Douglass "the greatest man whom this country has produced."[19] As a member of the Board of Education, she presented, in

1897, a resolution to make February 14th, Douglass's birthday, "Frederick Douglass Day" in all public schools attended by blacks. "By establishing Douglass Day," she wrote in her autobiography, "it was the first time a Board of Education in any city set aside a day in which colored people should learn about the career and services of a distinguished man of their group."[20] Perhaps Terrell's Douglass Day inspired Carter G. Woodson to establish Black History Week in 1915. In 1922, Terrell was instrumental in the NACW's establishment of Douglass's home as an historic landmark in Washington, D.C.[21]

Terrell's crusade to extol black contributions to society was threatened in 1923. The United Daughters of the Confederacy petitioned Congress to set aside land in Washington, D.C., for the erection of a monument to honor the plantation Mammy. Igniting a racial controversy, Terrell launched an acrimonious attack upon a movement that she believed would serve as a noxious reminder to all blacks of the major tragedy of a social system that "stripped children away from their mothers."[22]

The monument was not built, but the proposal had given Mary Church Terrell an idea. In 1928, she appeared before the Congressional Committee on Public Buildings and Grounds to request the erection of a memorial building dedicated to the contributions of Afro-Americans. Her request resulted in the creation of a National Memorial Association with Mrs. Terrell as a member.[23] In 1933, she wrote the Phillis Wheatley Pageant that was first performed on May 26 and 27, 1933 at the Booker T. Washington, Jr., High School in Washington, D.C.[24]

As part of her drive to publicize the contributions of blacks and to promote better race relations, Terrell sought to educate white Americans to the truth about black life. One major object of her efforts was the press. Considering the press as a social instrument that shaped public attitudes, standards, morals, and tastes, Terrell began a frontal attack upon several of its policies. She chided the use of the pejorative term "Negro" by both the white and black press. Considering it a misnomer, she ardently argued that "it does not represent a country or anything else nor one single color for it does not describe the various complexions in our group." Therefore, she urged the press to use the term "Colored" rather than "Negro" for it was the "best word in the English language that accurately described the various hues of the race."[25]

She vehemently criticized the white press for publishing stereotypical articles about blacks. Terrell believed the press had "entered into a 'conspiracy of silence' so far as letting the world know about the colored man's point of view." Editors accepted only articles that depicted blacks as "crapshooters," "murderers," "bums," or "buffoons," but rejected all articles that examined obstacles confronted by blacks.[26] Indicative of the press's stance was the fact that only one of Terrell's articles that lucidly analyzed black conditions was in an American magazine. The others were published by the British journal, *Nineteenth Century and After.*

Another direct way to educate white Americans was through her own publications. Her article, "Lynching From a Negro's Point of View," was published in the June 1904 issue of the *North American Review.* She chose this topic both to protest the lynching of her childhood friend, Tom Moss, in 1888, and, to rebut to an "inaccurate appraisal" of lynching by Thomas Nelson Page, an American fiction writer, lawyer, and diplomat, in the January 1904 issue of the same periodical.[27] She refuted the prevalent belief that the majority of blacks who were lynched had committed the crime of rape. She cited statistics that "out of every 100 Negroes, who [were] lynched, from 74 to 85 [were] not even accused of this crime."[28]

Consistent with this contemporary misconception was the belief that mob torture was justified by the diabolical nature of the crime of rape. In her attempt to prove both the savagery and the pervasiveness of mob violence regardless of the crime, Terrell quoted an eye-witness account of the lynching of a black couple in Vicksburg, Mississippi, who were accused of murder, not rape:

> When the two negroes were captured, they were tied to trees, and while the funeral pyres were being prepared they were forced to suffer the most fiendish tortures. The blacks were forced to hold out their hands while one finger at a time was chopped off. The fingers were distributed as souvenirs. The ears of the murderers were cut off. . . . The most excruciating form of punishment consisted in the use of a large corkscrew in the hands of some of the mob. This instrument was bored into the flesh of the man and the woman, in the arms, legs and body, and then pulled out, the spirals tearing out big pieces of raw, quivering flesh every time it was withdrawn. . . . When finally, they were thrown on the fire and allowed to be burned to death, this came as relief to the maimed and suffering victims.[29]

Another misconception was the belief that blacks committed rape because they desired social equality. To disprove this view, Terrell used rapist descriptions from testimonies of eye-witnesses as well as the reports from Southern newspapers. According to her findings, the alleged rapist "was described as being ignorant and repulsive and as near the brute creation as it is humanly possible for a human being to be."[30] In conversations with several "illiterate" blacks, Mrs. Terrell found that they had no idea of what social equality meant nor did they express any desire to implement the idea when explained to them.

Terrell's next article, "Plea for the White South by a Colored Woman," was rejected by several American journals. It is not clear why the *North American Review* refused to publish it. Perhaps it was in response to criticism of the journal for publishing "Lynching." Terrell believed that the rejection of the article by American publishers was due to its "controversial" nature "at a time when Americans were not ready to broadcast their dirty wash throughout the world."[31] In this informative article, Terrell analyzed why Americans should give the prevailing conditions in the South their careful and conscientious consideration. She gave three reasons: the dearth of intellectual activity, the decline of moral rectitude, and the obnoxious treatment of blacks. This emerging race spokeswoman pleaded for the salvation of the South through concerted efforts by the North, East, and West that would instill in southerners "a wholesome reverence for the law."[32]

In her continuing educational campaign, Terrell published in August 1906 "Peonage in the United States: The Convict Lease System and Chain Gangs." She described the convict lease system as "the modern regime of slavery." In this system "thousands of colored people frequently upon trumped-up charges or for offenses that in a civilized community would hardly land them in the gaol, are thrown into dark, damp, disease-breeding cells, whose cubic contents are less than those of a good-sized grave, are over-worked, underfed, and partially covered with vermin-infested rags."[33]

Terrell devotes part of the article to the idiosyncracies of the penal systems. She chided the contemporary contention that the convict-lease system and chain gangs were obsolete phenomena. She proved that not only were both systems viable but that they had now enthralled white women and men as well.[34] Terrell also provides a close analysis of the system in Georgia, the state she considered to be one of its main practioners. The article ends with the hope that this information would arouse just and humane people to concerted action.

In the last years of the second decade of the twentieth century, Terrell developed a penchant for writing short stories. The transition from articles to didactic stories grew from her belief that "the deplorable conditions" that circumscribed black life could be "pictured more vividly and improved more surely through the medium of a short story than in any other way." Her stories were considered by leading journals and periodicals that had rejected her earlier writings. One editor explained that the change was due to the "extrinsic commercial value" of short stories.[35]

Ever mindful of her goal, Terrell's short stories were imbued with the same objectivity and thoroughness that had characterized her articles. Each story depicted true incidents of racial discrimination that had been encountered either by Mrs. Terrell or by others who had told her about the event. Her story, "Aunt Dinah and Dilsey on Civilizing White Folks," satirized the social system in America that heralded black vices and assuaged white defects. In this story, Dilsey, tells her Aunt Dinah about an incident which she overheard while cleaning the table at her employer's, Mrs. Beirut's, home. The incident involved an "ink and water-hurling fight" between two prominent politicians at a committee meeting in Washington, D.C. Dinah's remarks summarize the problem of racial inequity in America. "If a colored man makes a monkey of himself like that, the whole race get a 'black eye' and white folks would be throwing it up to us for the next hundred years."[36]

Terrell wrote four short stories on the ramifications of racism. In the first two, "Apostasy of Aunt Ann," and "Betsy's Borrowed Baby," she analyzed the impact of racism on the lives of a black youth and an adult. Aunt Ann, who had been an active churchgoer for many years, dissociated herself from the church. She was known in the community as a good revivalist, one who could get the congregation to say repeatedly, "Amen." Aunt Ann was begged by Minister Johnson to attend the Sunday revival. She refused because she "could no longer pray to a God that had forgotten the colored people by allowing the Ku Klux Klan to kill her son."[37]

In "Betsy's Borrowed Baby," Terrell examined the experience of a college student on a Jim Crow car. On her way home to Mississippi for the summer, Betsy had to fight off an attempted assault upon her by a white porter. Frightened by the possibility of his success next time, she consented to escort the niece of Mrs. Caldwell, the former mistress of her mother, to Sterling, Ohio. Posing as a maid, she had an enjoyable trip sitting in the Pullman section and even eating with whites.[38]

Terrell discussed the defection of mulattoes from the race in two stories. In "Not Always What They Seem," she describes the life of a couple who were both passing for white without the other being aware of it. Tormented by his dark past, the husband became withdrawn and lethargic. Accidentally, his wife found a letter from his "unknown" mother. She confronts him with the letter. Unable to conceal the secret any longer, he confesses that he had a "drop of African blood." Paradoxically, his wife is relieved and even ebullient. She exclaims, "Thank God, I, too, am colored. My grandmother was a slave."[39] Terrell provides an opposite ending in "The Boulder." The story depicts a love affair between a mulatto, Camille Dupree, and a white man, Arthur Foster. Foster wants to marry Camille but is unable to accept the consequences of his father's threat of disinheritance. However, in a moment of emotional ecstasy, he decides to elope and promises to meet Camille at seven o'clock the next day by the boulder. On the next morning he finds Camille dead. She has left a letter that vividly reveals her inability to forfeit her self-respect. "In death, I am yours, I could not be yours in life. I am willing to sacrifice my life for you, but I could not sacrifice my honor. We have flown in the face of customs and prejudice and we must pay the penalty. Death is the only remedy that can save us both."[40] Despite this tragedy, Terrell ends her story on a positive note. Arthur Foster never forgot Camille and dedicates his life to creating better understanding between the races.

Throughout the first two decades of the twentieth century, Terrell punctuated her writing of articles and short stories with forceful speeches to hundreds of audiences in the United States and abroad. Her addresses abroad were delivered at several women's conferences. In 1904, she spoke at the International Congress of Women in Berlin, in 1919 at the International Congress of Women for Permanent Peace in Zurich, Switzerland, and in 1937, at the World Fellowship of Faith in London. Her performance in Berlin was especially impressive. Speaking fluent German, Terrell was the only American delegate to address the assemblage in a language other than her own. She declared to the attentive audience that

> if it had not been for the War of Rebellion which resulted in victory for the Union Army in 1865, instead of addressing you as a free woman tonight, in all probability I should be on some plantation in one of the Southern states . . . manacled body and soul in the fetters of a slave. And so, as I stand here tonight, my happiness is two-fold, rejoicing as I do, not only in the emancipation of my race, but in the almost universal elevation of my sex. If anyone had had the courage fifty years ago to predict that a woman with African hand in her veins would journey from the United States to Germany to address the International Congress of Women . . . he would either have been laughed out of Court, or adjudged insane.[41]

Terrell's lectures abroad enabled her to meet several prominent individuals. In 1919, she was a guest at the home of Mr. and Mrs. H. G. Wells. She also met Jean Finot, a French editor who was interested in the plight of black Americans; William T. Stead, publisher, and author of *The Americanization of the World*; Samuel Coleridge-Taylor, the musician; and the Countess of Warwick. In 1937 she met Hailie Selassie, the ruler of Ethiopia.[42]

From 1911 to 1913, Terrell was a lecturer at the Brooklyn Institute of Arts and Science. She delivered five lectures on the race problem: "The Bright Side of a Dark Subject," "The Progress of Colored Women," "Uncle Sam and the Son of Ham," "The Strongest for the Weakest," and "Harriet Beecher Stowe."[43] All emphasized the same themes found in her earlier writings.

Terrell promoted interracial understanding not only through her writings and speeches, but also through organizational activities and agitation against racial injustice. The new spokeswoman referred to her role as a "meddler." In an article published in the *Voice of the Negro*, Terrell discussed the "meddler's" responsibility. "In the United States, there is an imperative need of meddlers today—active, insistent, and fearless meddlers who will spend their time investigating institutions, customs, and laws whose effect upon the citizens of any color or class is depressing or bad. The crying need of the whole wide world is meddlers."[44] Mary Church Terrell's activism in the early twentieth century suggests that she was truly a meddler. However, Terrell's role as a meddler threatened the political career of her husband when she attacked the philosophy of Booker T. Washington.

In 1901, Booker T. Washington, at the suggestion of his closest friend in Washington, D.C., Whitefield McKinlay, a real estate broker, had secured the appointment of Robert Terrell to the first federal judgeship held by an Afro-American. Terrell left his position as principal of the M Street High School in Washington to become Judge of the Municipal Court of the District of Columbia.[45] From then on Mr. Terrell's actions identified him as a member of the Tuskegee circle. In 1904, he was among those who defended the Tuskegeean when lawyer Edward Morris of Chicago, in a diatribe before the Bethel Literary and Historical Association, dubbed Washington a "sham and traitor" to the interest of blacks. At a time when the majority of blacks and whites questioned the wisdom of maintaining the amicable relationship between Washington and President Theodore Roosevelt, Terrell wrote an article deifying Roosevelt as a champion of human rights.[46]

Robert H. Terrell was commencement orator at his Harvard College graduation. In 1902, President Theodore Roosevelt (at the urging of Booker T. Washington) appointed him Judge of the Municipal Court in Washington, D.C., the first black to hold this position.

43

In spite of the political alliance between Robert Terrell and Booker T. Washington, Mary Church Terrell took an independent course that was distinctly different from that of her husband. Initially reticent about Washington's philosophy of industrial education, She finally broke with him in a speech in New York on February 19, 1905, in which she advocated an eclectic approach to the education of blacks. She synthesized the Talented Tenth philosophy of Du Bois and Washington's industrial education theory, but at the same time she vehemently criticized Washington's theory and his character. Opening her speech with praise for Washington's efforts to train the "masses to earn a living," she ended it with a critical assessment of Washington's advocacy of the "total exclusion of academic education." Moreover, she questioned Washington's moral rectitude by claiming that "sometimes he tried to make colored people, who had acquired education, appear as ridiculous as he could, which was unwise and unfair."[47]

Commenting on this New York speech and an earlier one in Charlotte, North Carolina, Washington wrote to Mr. Terrell that while he "liked her conservative speech at Charlotte, I find it quite curious that my friends make radical speeches in the North and conservative speeches in the South."[48]

Mary Church Terrell continued her meddling. In August 1906, in cooperation with the Constitutional League, Mrs. Terrell petitioned President Roosevelt to reinstate black soldiers of Companies B, C, and D of the twenty-fifth Regiment, who received dishonorable discharges for their alleged involvement in the Brownsville, Texas riot. Washington perceived Mrs. Terrell's protest as an attack upon his support of Roosevelt's decision. Reiterating her disapproval, she wrote "A Sketch of Mingo Saunders" in which she described the humiliations suffered by the First Sergeant of Company B, who had served twenty-six years in the service. In spite of her protest, the presidential order prevailed until 1972, when Congress rescinded the dishonorable discharges and restored the black members of the regiment, most of whom were dead, to good standing in the army.[49]

Terrell's affiliation with the NAACP intensified friction between her husband and Washington. In 1909, Mrs. Terrell helped to organize the NAACP and later became a charter member. Her association with the organization led Washington to write Mr. Terrell about how embarrassing it was to him for Mrs. Terrell to be a member of this organization. "Of course," Washington continued, "I am not seeking to control anyone's activities, but I simply want to know where we stand."[50] Despite Mrs. Terrell's membership in the NAACP, Washington thought it advisable to maintain his political ties with Robert Terrell, who, in Washington's words, was a consummate politician. As a gesture of his respect for Judge Terrell, he asked him to give the next commencement address at Tuskegee. For her part, Mary Church Terrell remained active in the NAACP and in 1919 became Vice-President of the Washington, D.C., branch.

She was also involved with other interracial organizations. She joined the Interracial Committee of the District of Columbia in 1930. Continuing her deep concern for the welfare of black youth, she participated in a study that examined the distribution of school appropriations to black and white public institutions in the District. The study, "Color Line in Our Public Schools," not only indicated the inequities of a segregated urban system but foreshadowed the 1954 decision by the United States Supreme Court in the case of *Brown* v. *the Board of Education of Topeka, Kansas*. It concluded:

> Although the subcommittee . . . is confining its attention to the specific questions of the equitable distribution of educational facilities in regard to the two schools in the segment of the school population in the District of Columbia, we cannot refrain from offering a protest against the nefarious segregation engendered by our dual system of education. The impelling tendency of segregation is to fix upon Negroes the much cursed and discussed inferiority complex.[51]

In the same year, she became a member of the Interracial Committee of the Washington Council of Social Agencies. Initially, the committee's objective was to assist social agencies in the creation of summer camp facilities for black children whose parents were unable to pay. Receiving promises from both the Phyllis Wheatley YWCA to enlarge Camp Clarissa Scott for black girls and the YMCA to establish a camp for boys, the committee went further by examining the relation between inadequate recreational facilities and black delinquency. After visiting the local recreation parks and talking with black juvenile delinquents themselves, the committee was convinced that a correlation did exist. It presented its findings and recommendations to the Council of Social Services. It also went further and argued for improved recreational facilities in appearances before each city agency.[52]

In 1931 Terrell joined the Committee on Race Relations of the Washington Federation of Churches (CRRWFC). In that same year the committee initiated two programs to foster better understanding between the races in the nation's capital. In August a subcommittee, composed exclusively of whites, was appointed to persuade managers of several theaters to remove seating restrictions imposed on blacks. Though their efforts were unsuccessful, Terrell viewed their attempt as concrete demonstration of white concern for black problems. In December Mrs. Terrell, as secretary of the CRRWFC, worked assiduously to publish a report that examined the housing conditions of blacks. As a result of the findings of the report, according to Terrell, the city enacted measures that led to the "removal of ninety percent of the black population from the slums to more sanitary and decent quarters."[53]

Terrell was a member of the program committee of the CRRWFC that convened a Conference on the Betterment of Race Relations in Washington, D.C., in February 1932. The conference's purpose was to study the problems of the city and "to create more Christian attitudes and practices in race relations in Washington." The format of the conference included four roundtable sessions on "Housing and Alleys," "Delinquency and Crime," "Employment and Religion," and "Health and Recreation." The sessions were followed by a joint assembly at which a summary of these discussions was given and a statement made of present church attitudes and activities in regard to race relations, together with suggestions for a more effective church program. The conference issued a voluminous report that placed efforts for change in the hands of the church. Such a conclusion was totally unrealistic, since it disregarded the importance of other public institutions, such as the home, the government, the school, and the press in securing better race relations.[54]

Terrell also continued to agitate against racial injustice. In 1910, as a member of the School Board of Education, she had protested several of their decisions. She objected to the transferring of a mulatto girl, who had always attended the public schools for whites, to a school for black children. The mother of the child was white and her father was purported to have a few drops of African blood in his veins. Terrell argued that since the status of a slave had been determined by the mother, this same policy should be employed in this situation. In spite of her protest, the student was transferred to a black school. However, in the same year, Terrell won a battle. The Board adopted a measure introduced by Mrs. Terrell that dropped the entrance test requirement for high school graduates who wanted to attend the normal school. She believed the test discriminated against blacks, especially the oral component, which was one-quarter of the entire test. The black community was pleased by this decision. [55]

In August 1916, Terrell attended the Amenia Conference. It was held at the estate of Joel Spingarn, treasurer of the NAACP, in Troutbeck, New York. The purpose of the meeting was to create a uniform program of action among black leaders. Mrs. Terrell applauded the outcome of the conference, stating, "it was the first time that colored people who differed so widely in their views concerning their problems had arrived at virtual unanimity of opinion in regard to certain principles."[56]

When the United States entered World War I, a large number of women, both black and white, entered the work force. Mary Church Terrell was no exception. She took a position in August 1917 as a federal clerk at the War Risk Insurance Bureau. Her experience in this agency clearly illuminates the problem of federal discrimination during the administration of President Woodrow Wilson. In most federal agencies white and black workers were segregated. However, her employer, unaware that she was black, placed her in a room with white workers. Later informed of his mistake and unwilling to admit segregation existed, the director used "trumped-up charges" to dismiss Mrs. Terrell. On October 16, 1917, she received a letter stating the charges.

> It has been reported that you have taken action on cases contrary to the rules and regulations of the Bureau and contrary to the regulations of the chief medical adviser. It has been found that you have made numerous mistakes, and when these mistakes were called to your attention you caused considerable disturbance and tended to deny responsibility.[57]

Mrs. Terrell was provided an opportunity to prepare a defense against the alleged charges. Surprisingly, she decided not to pursue the issue. She gave as her reason that "she knew that any contest on her part would embarrass and might easily hurt her husband's standing as a judge in the Municipal Court." She added, "I have always believed that a wife has no right to injure her husband's career by what she says or does."[58] Mrs. Terrell had never let this bother her before but, in this case, she may have. Her husband had recently been a victim of a particularly bitter and prolonged attack because he was black and held a high political position.

In 1912 several Southerners had attempted to prevent President Wilson from reappointing Mr. Terrell as judge of the Municipal Court of the District of Columbia. One of the leading critics was Senator James K. Vardaman of Mississippi. He wrote a scurrilous article in his paper *Vardaman's Weekly* that attacked the moral rectitude of Judge Terrell. He referred to him as a "saddle-colored gentleman" and implied that the political appointment of a black man would cause white women to be raped. Mrs. Terrell's papers contain several cartoons of Judge Terrell that had appeared in numerous Southern newspapers in which he is depicted as an ape, monkey, or baboon. When presented as a man, he has large, thick lips, a flat nose, and an animal-like posture.[59] Mrs. Terrell maintained:

> It was harder for me to bear this ordeal because I knew that the very men who were fighting my husband so viciously solely on account of his race owed their political preferment to the fact that their respective states had trampled upon the Colored-American's rights as a citizen and had robbed him of his vote. . . . I literally descended into the very depths of despair every time Judge Terrell was the victim of race prejudice.[60]

In December 1917, she took a position as a clerk in the Census Bureau. This time she was assigned to the work area for blacks. Nevertheless, after several weeks of witnessing the humiliation suffered by many black women who had been mistakenly assigned to white sections and the implementation of a program for segregated bathrooms, Mrs. Terrell protested with her resignation. She spent the remainder of the war working with the War Camp Community Service, an organization which, among other things, assisted in the demobilization of black servicemen.[61]

After World War I, Mary Church Terrell saw the passage of the Nineteenth Amendment as an important accomplishment of interracial understanding and cooperation. Mrs. Terrell's championing of women's suffrage was a result of several factors. First, the establishment of a successful business by Terrell's mother shortly after her divorce had instilled in her the belief that women can excel in areas other than that of a housewife. This idea motivated her to pursue an unorthodox education at Oberlin College, where she enrolled in the classical curriculum, generally taken by men. While a student, her thinking about woman's interests beyond the home was revealed in her essay "Should an Amendment to the Constitution Allow Women the Ballot Be Adopted?" This essay criticized the contemporary argument that women should not be enfranchised.[62]

Second, her association with Frederick Douglass strengthened her involvement in the movement. In her speeches commemorating the Seneca Falls Meeting in 1848, the first large demonstration of the demand for equality by women, she never failed to remind her audiences, composed mostly of women, of the debt women owed to a black man, Frederick

Douglass. She wanted everyone, blacks and whites, to be aware that Douglass seconded Elizabeth Cady Stanton's motion that "women in this country secure to themselves the sacred right of the elective franchise."[63]

Third, her interest in the suffrage issue increased when the Women's Suffrage Committee of Washington, D.C., won a six-year court battle that allowed women to serve on the Board of Education. In 1895, Terrell become the first black and one of the first two women to serve on the board.[64]

Finally, the strong support of Robert Terrell for women's suffrage was another factor in her activism. In two speeches, "Our Women" and "The New Era Woman," he argued that black men should aid women in obtaining suffrage.

> During the Civil War and Reconstruction, women supported men to get the right to vote but afterward forgot about their support. It is now time we aid the woman in getting the suffrage. No race can rise higher than its women. For no woman has done more for its race than the colored women.[65]

Robert Terrell's views on women's suffrage were typical of the majority of black men. On several lecture tours her topics included women's suffrage and she was gratified to find that in the majority of instances black men were ardent supporters of the suffrage issue. The support of black men for the franchise was further revealed in the special edition of the *Crisis* in 1912 devoted to the suffrage issue.[66]

Continuing her goal to sensitize whites to black life, Terrell fostered interracial understanding through speeches and comments at the biennial sessions of the women' s suffrage meetings. In 1898, she addressed the American Suffrage Association in Washington, D.C. Her topic was "The Progress and Problems of Colored Women." In this stirring speech, she vividly described the perils that black women have confronted since slavery. Nevertheless, despite numerous obstacles, black women have progressed.

> Though the slaves were liberated less than forty years ago, penniless and ignorant, with neither shelter nor food, so great was their thirst for knowledge and so herculean were their efforts to secure it, that there are today hundreds of Negroes, many of them women, who are graduates some of them having taken degrees from the best institutions of the land.[67]

Mrs. Isabelle Beecher Stowe, the sister of Harriet Beecher Stowe, the authoress of *Uncle Tom's Cabin*, was so impressed with the speech that she presented Terrell with a bust of her sister.

In 1900, at the Women's Suffrage meeting in Washington, D.C., Mrs. Terrell vehemently opposed the convention's neglect of the injustices suffered by blacks. In her words, "as a colored woman, I hope this Association will include in the resolution the injustices of various kinds of which colored people are victims."[68] At a 1904 meeting Mrs. Terrell (who was described in the conference minutes as "a highly educated woman, showing little trace of Negro blood") emphasized the importance of interracial understanding.

> A resolution asks you to stand up for children and animals; I want you to stand up for children and animals but also for colored people. You will never get suffrage until the sense of justice has been so developed in men that they will give fair play to the colored race. Much has been said about the purchasability of the colored vote. They never sold their votes till they found that it made no difference how they cast them. Then, being poor and ignorant and human, they began to sell them, but soon after the Civil War, I know of many efforts to tempt them to do so which were not successful. My sisters of the dominant race, stand up not only for the oppressed sex but for the oppressed race.[69]

Mrs. Terrell actively campaigned for the ratification of the Nineteenth Amendment. Her most arduous task was persuading black women of the importance of the vote. She ended numerous speeches with these words: "Hold Meetings! Talk to every woman you meet about getting the vote. No matter how much white women need suffrage, colored women need it more."[70]

Though black and white women joined hands in the suffrage movement, Terrell was aware that many suffrage leaders were not genuinely sympathetic to her gospel of interracial understanding. She noticed that many of them spoke in terms of equal suffrage among the races when they were courting black support, but that their public actions and statements often contradicted this position. In a letter to Walter White of the NAACP in 1919, Terrell refers to this duplicity. She points out that Alice Paul, who was the organizer of the suffrage parade in front of the White House in 1913 and who was known as an ardent supporter of black equality, asked Ida B. Wells, who represented the Chicago Suffrage Club of black women, not to march with the white Chicago delegation. Her reason, according to Terrell, was fear of offending white Southern women. Terrell concludes that if white suffragists

Women suffragists in the late 1890s. Mary Church Terrell (center) was active in the campaign for passage of the Nineteenth Amendment and later was an ardent supporter of the Equal Rights Amendment.

could get the amendment passed without enfranchising black women they would.[71]

However, Terrell had high praise for one suffrage leader, Susan B. Anthony. The two leaders met in 1898 at the National American Suffrage Association Convention in Washington, D.C., and formed a friendship that lasted until Anthony's death in 1906. Terrell's papers contain several brochures on the women's movement and a book, *The History of Woman Suffrage*, that were given to her by Anthony. Terrell extolled the suffrage leader as a "genuine advocate of interracial cooperation" in her remarks at the Susan B. Anthony Memorial in 1906 and in her article, "Susan B. Anthony, The Abolitionist."[72]

During the third decade of the twentieth century, Terrell continued to work toward her goal of achieving interracial understanding through another vehicle—politics. On September 23, 1920, because of her active involvement in the suffrage movement, she was appointed Director of the Eastern Division Among Colored Women of the Republican National Committee. She accepted this position for two reasons. First, the history of the Republican Party as a precursor of black equality made it the best instrument to channel further the ideology of black-white understanding. Second, this position would provide an opportunity to keep the black population informed about pending race legislation. In a letter to party members in 1926, Terrell discussed the precarious state of the Dyer Anti-Lynching Bill and asked them to organize writing campaigns to their senators.[73] As an active supporter of the Republican Party, Terrell campaigned for Presidents Harding and Coolidge. In 1929 and 1930, she directed the unsuccessful senatorial efforts of Ruth Hanna McCormick in Illinois.[74]

In addition to her public career, Mary Church Terrell was dedicated to her family. She worried about whether she was a good mother to her two daughters, Phyllis, who had been born in 1898, and Mary, who had been adopted around the turn of the century.[75] She was concerned about their physical well-being, social activities, and intellectual development. In November 1905 Mrs. Terrell postponed a lecture because seven-year-old Phyllis was ill. Her diary, though kept sporadically that year, indicates that on November 15, 1905, she was up all night, trying to relieve the "poor little sufferer" of what the doctor diagnosed as malarial fever. The following diary entry for November 17, 1905 indicates how adeptly Mrs. Terrell combined her role as a mother and as a proponent of racial understanding:

"Took care of Phyllis today—Miss Peters [Terrell's secretary] came and I dictated letters to her while I rocked Phyllis."[76]

Both her diary and her autobiography suggest that Mrs. Terrell was a good mother. She spent numerous summers with her daughters away from Washington. Vacations were spent at Harper's Ferry, Virginia; Oak Bluffs, Massachusetts; New York City; and at Highland Beach, Maryland, where the Terrell summer house was located. On one occasion, Phyllis accompanied her mother to a lecture at the Lancaster, Ohio, Chatauqua.

Mrs. Terrell was greatly concerned about the intellectual development of her daughters. She wanted to provide them with educational opportunities comparable to hers. Both daughters were enrolled in the public schools of Washington, D.C.. However, after Mary, the eldest, graduated from high school and Phyllis completed the first year, Mrs. Terrell decided to enroll them at Oberlin College and Oberlin Academy. In her own words, "I decided to do this because I thought it would be wrong to bring them up having contact with nobody but their own racial group. I felt it was my duty to give them the same chance of measuring arms with white youth that I myself had had."[77] Phyllis and Mary remained at Oberlin for a year. Mary then completed her degree at Howard University and Phyllis at St. Johnsburg Academy in Vermont. Both became teachers in the public school system of Washington, D.C. Later Phyllis married a physician, who taught at Rush Medical School, in Chicago and Mary married a principal of one of the Washington schools.

The first three decades of the twentieth century witnessed the emergence of the ideologies of not only Booker T. Washington and W. E. B. Du Bois but also the ideology of another race spokesman—this time a woman—Mary Eliza Church Terrell. Terrell advocated interracial understanding as her strategy to race relations. The education of blacks about their heritage and whites to the realities of black life were her major emphases. She hoped that through her participation in interracial organizations and politics and her protest against racial injustices an environment of racial understanding could be created. Though her activities as a meddler created friction between her husband, Judge Terrell, and Booker T. Washington, the political benefactor of Mr. Terrell, Mrs. Terrell often refused to compromise. Although she never wavered in her determination to develop better race relations, she nevertheless sometimes felt the need to soften her radicalism to protect the political career of her husband.

As a race spokeswoman, Terrell viewed the passage of the Nineteenth Amendment in 1920 as an important accomplishment of both interracial understanding and cooperation. Hoping that her gospel of interracial understanding would bring about similar results, she vowed to continue her drive to bring about the ultimate result of black-white understanding—racial integration.

Phyllis and Mary Terrell, the daughters of Mary and Robert, ca. 1910. Each of the first three children born to the Terrells died shortly after birth. Phyliss, named in honor of Phillis Wheatley, the black poetess, was born in 1898. Mary was adopted several years later.

FOUR

From Interracial Understanding to Direct Action

The stock market crash in 1929, the depression that followed, the uncertain outlook of the New Deal, and the war policies of the administration of President Franklin D. Roosevelt had a profound effect upon all Americans and especially upon blacks. These conditions engendered a combination of factors—the denial of economic gains previously achieved, discrimination in the armed services, proliferation of lynching, voter disenfranchisement, and general discrimination—that dealt a heavy blow to the already fragile socio-economic and political foundations of blacks.[1] The situation also prompted many leaders of the race, mostly the younger spokesmen, to develop new racial ideologies and strategies. Their approaches led to an ideological schism between the older and younger race leaders. The older people wanted racial integration of blacks and whites, while the younger sought economic integration of social classes. Mary Church Terrell's role in this controversy, though limited, reaffirmed her adherence to the goal of racial integration. However, from 1940 to 1944, because of illness and later the death of her husband, her public activities were minimized. During this hiatus, she assessed her earlier strategy of race relations and shifted toward a more militant one. Her new approach sought a definitive end to racial inequities in America, especially in the District of Columbia, first through the court system and later through such tactics as picketing, boycotting, and sit-ins.

By 1932, Mary Church Terrell, as well as other older race leaders, found herself ideologically and politically out of step with the emerging approaches to race relations by younger black spokesmen. The worsening of the depression caused many leaders, especially the young, to advocate policies that they felt were more consistent with the economic realities of black life.

During the depression, blacks remained on the economic sidelines. To use the common phraseology of the period, they were "the first fired and the last hired." In 1930, blacks constituted 9.7 percent of the total population, and yet they made up 16. 7 percent of the total population on relief. The percentage of the black population on relief was almost twice that of whites—18 percent as opposed to 9.5 percent.[2]

This economic situation encouraged black defections from the Republican Party. This transition, however, had manifested itself in some degree as early as the 1920s. In 1924, a considerable number of black voters left the Republican Party fold to vote for presidential aspirants, Democrat John W. Davis or Progressive Robert La Follette. Both of these candidates promised to treat all citizens equally. When the Republican Party began openly courting Southern white voters in 1928, many black leaders left the party in anger. That year such newspapers as the *Baltimore Afro-American* and the *Boston Guardian* came out for Alfred E. Smith instead of Herbert C. Hoover.[3]

The downward economic spiral in black life during the depression increased discontent with the Republican Party. Many black spokesmen criticized the economic policies of President Hoover. Writing in the NAACP's *Crisis*, Reverdy C. Ransom, Bishop of the African Methodist Episcopal Church, attacked the ineffectual policies of Hoover's Reconstruction Finance Corporation (RFC). "It would take a long time for the funds to trickle down," Ransom maintained, "from the giant and industrial white firms to black firms that were at the bottom." Like Ransom, Lester A. Walton, a journalist, viewed the RFC as "a farce for its implicit objective was to protect white businesses." Citing Hoover's earlier record of support of the lily-white Republican movement in the South and his nomination of Judge Parker for a seat on the Supreme Court, both Ransom and Walton exhorted blacks to repudiate the do-nothing policies of Hoover. Many heeded their plea.[4]

Mary Church Terrell was among those who did not defect from the Republican Party. Adhering tenaciously to Frederick Douglass's dictum—the Republican Party is the ship, all else is open sea—she remained an ardent Republican until 1952. In August 1932, as a campaign worker for the re-election of President Hoover, Terrell refuted criticisms of the RFC by arguing that "if it had not functioned successfully, a great many people would not be able to write checks on banks today and feel sure that those checks would be honored."[5] It seemed paradoxical that a woman who worked so assiduously to eradicate racial injustices would endorse a party in spite of its avowed racist overtures. But Mary Church Terrell maintained that her support was pragmatic since, in her words, "every right that had been bestowed upon blacks was initiated by the Republican Party."[6] It might also be suggested that Terrell's vindication of the Republican Party was motivated by her support of her husband's successful career.

Though firm in her party loyalty, Terrell was nevertheless receptive to new ideas concerning the economic perils of blacks. However, she found some of them disconcerting. In 1932 she read an article by Arthur F. Davis, a young newspaper columnist and literary critic. Davis complained: "Negroes talk too much about the race problem. It has become an obsession with us." He emphasized the need to stop discussions and writings on the race problem for ten years. "This," he believed "would give the present younger generation a chance to grow up without having their minds too warped." Theorizing that the provinciality of the race men was contingent upon their vested interests, he concluded that this idea would probably fail, because "if it was effective every so-called 'Big Negro' in the country would starve to death." He commented sarcastically that it would "probably be a good thing."[7]

In 1933, Terrell attended the Amenia Conference unaware that Davis's pronouncement was to be extended further in a discussion by the younger participants. The conference's objective, as stated by NAACP President Joel Spingarn, was "to gather together a number of representatives of Negro youth, and others, under conditions of intimacy and privacy . . . to encourage informal discussions of the present Status of the Negro, with the hope that a new programme suited to these times may result."[8] Thirty-three young men and women participated. Among them were such future leaders as United Nations Undersecretary Ralph Bunche, sociologist E. Franklin Frazier, literary critic Sterling Brown, and attorney Louis Redding. Ideologically, both the older and younger race leaders agreed on integration but differed on whether it should be done first among the races or among social classes. The conference marked the genesis of a major split in the black leadership between the old and the young. E. Franklin Frazier and Ralph Bunche were the main advocates of economic integration. Mary Church Terrell and Kelly Miller were proponents of racial integration. In order to understand her position on race relations in this stage of her development, it is essential that a brief discussion of these leaders be presented.

Frazier and Bunche had been trained in Northern universities during a time when sociological perspectives began to dominate the study of race relations.

This particular approach to racial problems was influenced by the ideas of Robert Park of the University of Chicago. Park contended that, as far as race relations are concerned "racial minorities are merely social classes . . . race difficulties result from an exaggerated social distance between whites and blacks, which will be bridged inevitably through the process of assimilation."[9] It was these two theorems, the class nature of race relations and the process of assimilation, that influenced Frazier and Bunche.

E. Franklin Frazier, a leading sociologist trained at the University of Chicago, developed Park's theory and wove it into his own work. Frazier believed it was necessary for the black masses to "align themselves with white workers, who shared the same economic problems, to create an economic coalition as a means to struggle against white landlords and capitalists." By 1936, the worsening plight of blacks reinforced the view of the black sociologist that "the status of the Negro in the United States is bound up in the final analysis with the role which the Negro plays in the economic system."[10] In essence Frazier maintained that the problems confronting blacks were more the result of being poor than of being black.

While Frazier espoused the theory of economic integration, Ralph Bunche, a Harvard graduate and head of the Department of Political Science at Howard University, sought to implement it through a labor organization composed of black and white workers. Of the two, Bunche was the stronger critic of the ideology of the older race leaders. He found their belief in racial integration to be "a myth, albeit a dangerous one, for it is a perfect stalking-horse for selfish group politics and a camouflage for brutal economic exploitation." The most important manipulators of the myth "are the ruling classes, who employ it to keep the black and white masses apart, and the older race leaders, who use it to maintain their own position of power."[11]

Like Frazier, Bunche advised that "the hope for improvement in the condition of any American minority group is the hope that can be held out for the betterment of the masses of the dominant group." He argued that "since their basic interests are identical, so must be their programs and tactics."[12] Both Frazier and Bunche theorized that the black population in the United States was a minority group only in a narrow sense. In every other respect it was subject to the same divisive influences impinging upon the life of other groups in the nation.

Bunche hailed the depression as a watershed for it brought out, in bold relief, "the pervasive extent of the sharp class antagonism which the capitalistic system had nurtured."[13] After attending the Howard University conference on the economic status of blacks in 1936, he became convinced that the severity of the crisis demanded a new economic approach that would educate the masses and instruct both black and white workers in the necessity of seeking power through organized labor.[14] He convened a National Negro Congress (NNC) of diverse organizations—labor, religious, civic, racial, and interracial—to forward this end.[15]

The Bunche-Frazier ideology and the NNC were antithetical to the views of the older generation of race proponents such as Mary Church Terrell and Kelly Miller. Kelly Miller was the most outspoken of the two. After graduating from Howard University in 1886, he had spent most of his career as a sociology instructor and administrator at his alma mater and as a nationally-syndicated columnist for Afro-American weeklies. Miller questioned the naivete of young race leaders in their espousal of black-white working class solidarity as the only panacea to racial problems. He found it paradoxical that blacks could advocate such a theory when history had "shown that it was the white workers who formed the mobs which lynched black workers." Miller offered the younger readers some judicious advice: "Do not be too hasty in removing the ancient landmarks which the fathers have set."[16]

Miller, unlike some of the black leaders who attacked the New Deal as ineffectual, emphatically approved of the economic policies of the administration of President Roosevelt. He praised the president for his "conservative liberalism in the times that demanded liberal conservatism."[17]

Like Miller, Mary Church Terrell could not countenance any ideology that de-emphasized racial integration. During the depression she continued to advocate interracial understanding and cooperation and criticized racial discrimination in governmental policies aimed at alleviating the depression. She supported such programs as the Joint Committee on Economic Recovery (JCER) and the Conference on the Participation of Negro Women and Children in Federal Welfare Programs. As a member of the JCER from 1933 to 1934, she participated in drafting a document "Additions to the Policy of the Joint Committee on National Recovery." The report attacked the government's policy of "separate Negro advisory councils in the government, segregated subsistence homestead settlements, different standards in public works or in public relief, and different standards of wages and hours in industry as symptomatic of the limited under-standing of the government to racial patterns in America."[18] The JCER exhorted the government to implement policies of interracial cooperation and understanding instead of racial separatism. The report ended with a plea to "all leaders, both white and black, to face the problem of race relations from this point of view for the new economic order that is being born."[19] The findings of the report further convinced Mary Church Terrell that the separatist ideology of the government was responsible for the National Recovery Act's providing minimal protection for black laborers caught up in the traditional squeeze between the discriminatory practices of trade unions and employer groups.

In 1938, as Chairman of the NAACP Welfare Committee of the District of Columbia, Terrell attended a Conference On the Participation of Negro Women and Children in Federal Welfare Programs. The findings of the conference—that black women and children were recipients of a minuscule portion of the benefits from social welfare legislation when compared to their needs—further vindicated her belief that much New Deal legislation was inequitable. She supported the conference's recommendation that blacks write their political leaders in order "to secure representative black leadership in various administrative posts strategic to full participation of Negro women and children in government programs."[20]

Though Terrell had sharp criticisms of much New Deal legislation, she was willing to help where she could. In her words, "the best way I can help in this economic dilemma is by working for a government agency designed to cure the depression and restore conditions to normalcy."[21] In February 1934, Terrell became a file clerk at the Emergency Relief Division of the Federal Emergency Relief Administration in Washington, D.C. However, by August her director dismissed her because "he had to reduce the work force." He attempted to secure employment for her, recommending her highly for a job, but she was not hired. According to Terrell, she was rejected because of her color.[22] Vexed by her failure to receive further employment, she gave up the attempt and focused her attention on completing her autobiography.

In 1910, Mary Church Terrell had expressed an overwhelming desire to write her life's story, but her constant preoccupation with racial matters prevented her from realizing her aspirations. It was not until 1927, several years after the marriage of her last daughter Phyllis, that she poured herself into her manuscript. Beginning at age sixty-four, this determined woman wrote and rewrote for almost ten years, finally completing the book in 1938. Originally entitled *A Mighty Rocky Road*, it was published as *A Colored Woman In A White World*. The completion of the manuscript was in itself an arduous task but attempting to get it published was even more difficult.

Her manuscript was submitted to and rejected by several publishing companies. Terribly disappointed, Terrell believed that "she could never be comfortable until it was published."[23] On the recommendation of Carrie Chapman Catt, a former suffragist and a friend, she submitted her work to William Barbour, a member of the Fleming Revell publishing firm in Washington, D.C. Barbour thought the work had promise but suggested a thorough rewriting.[24]

Terrell considered both the comments of William Barbour and her earlier rejections and decided to resort to a vanity press—Ransdell Company of Washington, D.C. In 1940, her autobiography was published. Terrell marketed it by lecturing in several metropolitan cities to civic organizations and by writing to family members and friends. *A Colored Woman In A White World* sold for $2.50 a copy. Selling over 1,000 copies by 1942, Terrell sought to interest several publishing companies in printing a second edition. She finally gave up the idea, when Doubleday and Company, in the latest of a series of reject letters from publishers, wrote that "the book would be specialized for our type of operation."[25] Nevertheless periodic requests for her book from both friends and civic organizations were an inspiration to Mrs. Terrell as she grew older.

A Colored Woman In A White World is a voluminous work, running to 421 pages and forty-two chapters. In the preface by H. G. Wells he writes, "apart from discreet flattering to explicitness, this book, in its class and quality, could hardly be better."[26] Without ostentation Terrell vividly and forcefully related the story of a woman who combatted all the forces of discrimination perpetrated against her, her sex, and her race.

> I have recorded what I have been able to accomplish in spite of the obstacles which I have had to surmount. I have done this, not because I want to tell the world how smart I am, but because both a sense of justice and a regard for truth prompt me to show what a colored woman can achieve in spite of the difficulties by which race prejudice blocks her path if she fits herself to do a certain thing, works with all her might and main to do it and is given a chance.[27]

Combining scholarship, interpretive power, and literary style, Mary Church Terrell created a work that highlights the frustrations and injustices with which black women were confronted from the Civil War to the 1930s.

The drafts of her manuscript indicate Terrell's desire to present an objective analysis of her life. In relating the Washington-Terrell controversy, her first draft was quite opinionated, but later drafts are more balanced. This might be attributed to Terrell's reassessment of Booker T. Washington's career during the time when she was writing the book.[28]

The reviews were quite laudatory. Gertrude Martin, a journalist for the *Michigan Chronicle*, found the work "more than an autobiography." She thought that it was "a rich and mellowed record of a Negro woman who ventured and achieved in fields into which no others of her race preceded and hitherto into which few have followed." Charles Wesley, a leading black historian, stated that Terrell had made "a successful step in the right direction by revealing life expectations, so that contemporaries and posterity know of the personal experiences and reactions of Negro life." Robert D. Franklin, director of Shelby County Libraries in Memphis, commented that "she writes well. . . . She reveals herself as a sensitive being caught in a situation which no man has the power to alter very much."[29]

After the publication of her autobiography in 1940, Mary Church Terrell became concerned about whether blacks should participate in World War II. With the coming of the war, the racial-economic battle between the older and younger race leaders waned. The salient issue now was whether blacks should participate in a war that illustrated the discrepancy between the protection of democracy abroad and the failure to practice it at home. From the beginning of the war, many race leaders, both young and old, exhibited ambivalent attitudes about black participation. Adam Clayton Powell, Jr., a young Harlem politician, doubted that blacks, who were "disfranchised, socially ostracized, and educationally-economically deprived would defend the country." John P. Davis, once executive secretary of the Joint Committee on National Recovery, proclaimed that "Negroes had their 'own war' at home against oppression and exploitation from without and against disorganization and lack of confidence within." Ralph Bunche, an avowed critic of both the New Deal and the ideology of the older race leaders, pleaded with blacks "not to cease to agitate their rights." On the other hand, he urged them not to threaten "to remain aloof from the war effort in order to extort concessions from the dominant society. . . . American democracy is bad enough. But in the mad world of crisis today I love it, and I will fight to preserve it." Mary Church Terrell's opinion was that blacks needed to fight both at home and abroad.[30]

Terrell's view was the prevalent attitude of the majority of black leaders in their call for a "Double V," a victory over the enemies abroad on the battlefields and a victory over the enemies at home. In 1941, Terrell's concern about discrimination against blacks in industry and the armed services led to her endorsement of A. Philip Randolph's March on Washington Movement (MOWM). A moral victory was achieved by Randolph when, on June 25, 1941, President Roosevelt issued an executive order establishing a Fair Employment Practices Committee.[31]

During the remaining years of the war, personal problems limited Terrell's public activism. She was hospitalized in 1942 for ailments associated with old age, as she had been in 1938. After the earlier illness she worked diligently as a member of the Advisory Committee on Women's Participation in the New York World's Fair of the District of Columbia. In 1940, she wrote an article that vigorously attacked the unjust ruling of the court in the Scottsboro Case.[32] However, she disengaged herself from all public activities in 1940 after her husband suffered a stroke. Robert Terrell died in September 1944. Her diary, though kept sporadically from 1944 to 1946, suggests that the death of her husband was traumatic for her. She did not resumed her activism until 1946.[33]

But it was a different Mary Church Terrell who returned to the fray. She shifted her tactics from pursuing interracial understanding through attacks on the press and through her writings and speeches to a militant approach that attacked discrimination first through the American court system and later through such direct-action tactics as picketing, boycotting, and sit-ins.

There have been several explanations for the emergence of militancy among blacks immediately after the war. Some writers—James Baldwin, Gunnar Myrdal, and E. Franklin Frazier—attribute this change in the attitudes of blacks to the social upheavals brought about by the war. Other intellectuals—Harold R. Issacs, Martin Kilson, Adelaide Cronwell Hill, Talcott Parsons, and Kenneth B. Clark—describe the increased militancy of blacks in the United States as part of the international struggle for liberation by African and Third World peoples who saw a glaring contradiction between the myth and reality—the idea and the practice—of universal democracy. Still other scholars—Louis Rhodes, Rudolph Martin, Jr., and James Robert Bruce—see the increased civil rights activity among blacks as the product of time and a process of conscious awakening.[34]

In the case of Mary Church Terrell, it seems that the death of her husband, among other things, contributed to her militancy. It sent shock waves through her life. She had known death before, of course, but the death of her husband gave it a new reality—a reality that cast an omnipresent shadow over her own existence. Whatever the cause, Mary

Church Terrell, at age eighty-three, committed herself wholeheartedly to the elimination of racial and sexual discrimination in the District of Columbia and in the United States at large.

In 1946 Mary Church Terrell applied for admission to the American Association of University Women, Washington, D.C., Chapter. Rejected by the board of directors, she immediately appealed to the National AAUW. She resolved to fight stating, "I thought I'd be a coward unless I opened the way for the colored women."[35] A three-year court struggle ensued in which the National AAUW aligned with Terrell against the AAUW-DC. This dilemma split the AAUW-DC. Those opposed to Terrell's admission were led by Juvenile Court Judge Fay Bentley, who persuaded the members to adjudicate the case as a way of resolving whether the National AAUW had absolute power over its local branches.[36] The District Court and the United States Court of Appeals ruled in favor of the AAUW-DC stating that "the National American Association of University Women could not suspend the branch until it changed its by-laws at a national convention to specifically state that members would be accepted regardless of color."[37] In June 1948, in spite of the opposition of the AAUW-DC, the national convention instituted a new by-law which stated:

> The Board of Directors of the American Association of University Women considers it imperative at this time to reaffirm its established membership policy that all women who meet the educational membership requirements are eligible to be members of the Association. Under the national by-laws and under branch by-laws, which can not conflict with those of the national, there can be no authorization for any discrimination on racial, religious, or political grounds.
>
> The Board, therefore, takes for granted that the branches will practice within their own groups those principles which are in line with the association's history, its expressed international policies, its membership in the International Federation of University Women, and its deep concern with all agencies seeking to rebuild a world shattered through discrimination and intolerance.[38]

In 1949, the National AAUW reinstated three black women in the AAUW-DC, among them Mary Church Terrell. Terrell had scored a victory for blacks, especially women, by eradicating one of the vestiges of segregation in the nation's capital.

Beginning in 1946 Mrs. Terrell assiduously campaigned for the passage of the Equal Rights Amendment (ERA). First introduced in 1923 the ERA sought to secure equal rights for women under the law and equal opportunity for them in all fields of American life. Terrell's endorsement of reveals her continual concern to pursue the elevation of women, especially black women.[39]

Another of her efforts to eradicate racial inequities in America was her attack upon the unjust ruling in the Ingram Case. On March 1, 1949, Terrell accepted the position of chairwoman of the National Committee to Free Rosa Ingram and Her Sons (NCFRIS). This case involved the arrest and death sentence of Rosa Ingram, mother of fourteen children, and two of her sons for the alleged murder of a white sharecropper in Leslie, Georgia. The circumstances surrounding the crime as presented in the news releases by the NCFRIS indicated that a neighbor of the Ingrams, a white sharecropper, attacked Mrs. Ingram with a gun for allowing her pigs to trespass on his property. Her two sons witnessed the altercation and her sixteen year old son struck the sharecropper with his gun, resulting in his death. The position of the NCFRIS was that the crime was self-defense and that "it was inconceivable that such an unjust sentence would have been imposed upon a white woman and her two sons."[40]

Prior to Terrell's acceptance of the position of chairwoman, national protest had forced the state of Georgia to commute the death sentence to life imprisonment. As chairwoman, Terrell argued cogently that the state could also be forced to free the Ingrams. Using the leadership skills acquired during her tenure as president of the NACW, she led the fight. Letters were written to prominent American citizens, petitions were presented to President Harry S. Truman and Governor James Tallmadge of Georgia, and a petition containing 100,000 signatures was presented to the Human Rights Committee of the Social and Economic Council of the United Nations and to the General Assembly. It read:

> The signers of this petition wish to lay before the association of the United Nations, a case of injustice done by the United States of America against its own citizens. We are bringing this case to your attention and begging you to give it your earnest thought and discussion, not because we are disloyal to this nation, but especially because we are citizens of this land and loyal to the freedom and democracy which it professes far and wide to observe.[41]

Terrell's tactics eventually led to the release of the Ingrams in 1950.

During the last two decades of her life, Terrell received numerous awards for her unselfish pursuit of human equality. In 1932, her name was placed in the list of Oberlin's most famous 100 Alumna and Alumnae. In 1946,

Wilberforce University awarded her the degree of Doctor of Letters. In 1948, she received a Doctor of Human Letters from her alma mater. In 1949, the Americans for Democratic Action conferred an award upon Terrell for her outstanding work against segregation in the nation's capital.[42]

Terrell's militancy began in the 1940s with her attack on the membership policies of the American Association of University Women, the fight over the Ingram Case, and her support of the Equal Rights Amendment. It culminated in the 1950s when she spearheaded the drive to desegregate public eating places in the nation's capital.

Mary Church Terrell receiving an honorary degree from Howard University. She also recived honorary degrees from Oberlin College and Wilberforce University.

FIVE

From the Podium
to the Streets

The 1950s marked not only the advent of the Cold War, the Atomic Age, and the Red Scare of McCarthyism but an era of reform in race relations. Before the historic *Brown* decision of 1954, mounting pressure from blacks and civil rights groups as well as increased white sympathy gave impetus to a shift in black-white relations. Both the judiciary and the executive branches of the federal government responded to these pressures by using their power to orchestrate major changes that reversed existing patterns of segregation. This period is sometimes characterized as the beginning of the "Second Reconstruction."[1]

The Supreme Court took the initiative in three major decisions that undermined segregation. In *Sweatt* v. *Painter*, the court held that equality involved more than physical facilities. In *G. W. McLaurin* v. *Oklahoma*, the court stated that a black student, once admitted, cannot be segregated. In *Elmer W. Henderson* v. *United States*, the court rendered segregation illegal in railroad dining cars.[2]

It was under the leadership of President Harry Truman that the executive branch became involved in a significant way. On December 5, 1946 Truman created the President's Committee on Civil Rights and charged it with determining where and how governmental authority could be strengthened to safeguard the civil rights of Americans. To redress inequalities, the committee recommended the creation of a permanent Commission on Civil Rights and the expansion of the Civil Rights section in the Justice Department. President Truman implemented these measures. The most significant achievement of Truman' s administration was the desegregation of the armed services in 1946 and 1948. His successor, Dwight D. Eisenhower, chose not to issue executive orders and mandates for civil rights but rather to support such measures indirectly. An important milestone in race relations that occurred during Eisenhower's administration was the desegregation of eating places in the District of Columbia. This effort was led by Mary

Church Terrell in a continuation of her drive to remake the nation's capital into the "Colored Man's Paradise."[3]

On February 28, 1950, Terrell dressed in the hat and gloves that completed a lady's attire, attacked one of the remnants of the nineteenth-century Jim Crow system in Washington, D.C.—segregated public eating places. Confronted with the intransigence of proprietors of restaurants, she realized that the earlier weapons of moral suasion and interracial dialogue were incapable of bringing a definitive end to segregated public facilities. Prodded by the desire to deal discrimination a death blow, at age eighty-seven, she armed herself with such direct-action tactics as picketing, boycotting, and sit-ins.

This organized attack led by Terrell in the 1950s is much less well known than the Montgomery bus boycott of 1955-1956 and the sit-ins that began in Greensboro, North Carolina in 1960, but it played a significant part in the beginning of civil rights movement in this country. These protests marked the advent of the Second Reconstruction in which the judiciary struck down segregation, the executive expressed support, and many whites openly sympathized with black people in their fight against discrimination. It added respectability to such radical tactics as picketing, boycotting, and sit-ins and paved the way for the great popular onslaught against segregation in the sixties. Finally, it represented the last and toughest battle of one of the most vigorous black leaders of the twentieth century—Mary Church Terrell.

For almost half a century Terrell had resided in the nation's capital, then a heavily segregated city except for public transportation. In a 1944 interview published in the *Pittsburgh Courier*, she recalled that "in the 1890s colored people could dine anywhere in the nation's capital, but near the end of the century, these rights were wrested away from us. I remember stopping at the drug store on the corner of 9th and F street for service. The white clerk told me that it was my last service, that the behavior of a loud Negro man there previously had caused them to alter their policy of serving colored people."[4]

The paradox of this historic event was that Terrell and her cohorts, in a three-year court struggle, agitated for rights that had never been denied by law. When Washington was governed by the District Legislative Assembly, laws had been passed, in 1872 and 1873, that required "all eating-place proprietors to serve any respectable well-behaved person regardless of color, or face a $100 fine and forfeiture of their license for one year."[5] Both of these laws disappeared in the 1890s when the District Code was rewritten.

In 1949, the National Committee on Segregation, composed of such notables as Eleanor Roosevelt, Father John LaFarge, and Walter Reuther, head of the AFL-CIO, published a survey on discrimination in Washington, D.C. The report concluded that segregation was ubiquitous and cursorily mentioned the lost laws.[6] Perhaps the most important effect of the report was that lawyers from the Washington Chapter of the National Lawyers' Guild decided to clarify the status of these laws. After a few weeks of legal research, the lawyers found the 1872 and 1873 laws on file in the Library of Congress, the Supreme Court, and in the District Court. These files indicated that the laws had not been repealed. In a legal brief, they recommended to the District Commissioners that the laws "were still in force and it was their duty to begin prosecution of anyone who violated them."[7] For eight months, the District Commissioners considered the legal arguments presented in the brief of the National Lawyers' Guild.

Impatient with the lengthy deliberation of the District Commissioners, a heterogeneous group of citizens formed, in the summer of 1949, the Coordinating Committee for the Enforcement of the D.C. Anti-Discrimination Laws (CCEAD). In later years, Mrs. Terrell was to credit one friend in particular whom she believed sparked the campaign to test the 1872 and 1973 laws—Tomlinson Todd. Todd, who was Terrell's neighbor and a radio personality on the Sunday afternoon program, "Americans All," constantly complained to Terrell that something should be done about the laws. He had discovered their existence while doing research in the Library of Congress. Todd was complaining to the right person. Terrell became the organizer and chairperson of the first demonstration for the enforcement of the 1872 and 1873 laws.[8]

Mary Church Terrell led in the creation of an organization whose structure and program galvanized support from diverse segments of both the black and white community. The amorphous structure of the committee—no constitution, no by-laws, and no membership dues—drew public support from a wide range of labor, religious, women's, and civic organizations. The only requirement for membership was that the applicant "exhibit unrelenting determination and willingness to work for the reinstatement of the laws."[9] The leadership of Mary Church Terrell unified these divergent constituencies to make a successful assault on segregated public eating places.

Under her direction, the CCEAD developed a three-fold course of action: one, to pressure the District Commissioners for a prompt decision to enforce the laws; two, if proprietors refused to abide by the decision (it was assumed to be favorable), to press charges in court; and, three, to implement direct pressure tactics against intransigent proprietors. Direct pressure tactics consisted of a four-point plan—negotiate, boycott, picket, and sit-in. Negotiations consisted of personal interviews with proprietors by selected members of the committee. If these discussions failed, boycotts would begin. The failure of negotiations would be publicized and leaflets requesting that people no longer patronize the store would be distributed. Picketing consisted of a line around a business until demands were met. Sit-ins involved the occupancy of seats at lunch counters to prevent service to acceptable customers. Perceiving picketing and sit-ins as extreme measures, Mary Church Terrell hoped that the committee would not be forced to use them.[10]

During the month of February, the CCEAD began its campaign with frequent conferences in the office of Clark King, the Assistant Corporation Counsel of the District Commissioners. On February 21, 1950, King announced that the Commissioners had decided that the laws were still in force. Nevertheless, he added that the laws must be subjected to a court ruling, and therefore a test case was necessary. As King stated the matter:

> The Acts of Congress and the Regulations of the various Boards of Commissioners since 1874 fail to disclose any express appeal of the Anti-Discrimination Acts of 1872, 1873. The Board of Commissioners is of the opinion that the decision by it as to the present effectiveness of these acts would be inconclusive because it is a matter which ultimately must be settled by the courts.[11]

A group under the leadership of Mary Church Terrell provided a test case. On February 28, 1950 interracial party of four, representing diverse segments of the community requested service at Thompson's Restaurant. Three of the party were black—Reverend Arthur Fletcher Elmes, 65, Pastor of the Peoples Congregational Church; Ms. Essie Thompson, 36, member of the Local 471 United Cafeteria Workers, and Mary Church Terrell. The fourth person was David H. Schull, white, 35, of Annandale, Virginia, a member of the Society of Friends. The four were served at the food counter. Mrs. Terrell was served soup, while the others ordered doughnuts and slices of pie. They were stopped at the cashier's stand where S. W. Becker, Superintendent of Thompson Restaurants of Washington and Baltimore, told Mr. Schull "he could buy food but the other three could not because it is against the rules." Immediately, they went to the office of Clark King to file affidavits. With substantive evidence of the violation of the laws, the District

Commissioners decided to prosecute John Thompson, owner of the restaurant. The Washington Restaurant Association organized a defense fund drive that required each of its affiliates to contribute $25.[12]

Thus began a three-year court battle. During the proceedings in Municipal Court from March 31 to July 10, 1950, the CCEAD was struck with the arguments presented by defense as to the "unreasonableness" of the acts. The defense stated that the laws "interfered with the rights of restaurants and that their enforcement would be resented by the white citizens of the District and would lead to violence and disorder." It became clear to the committee that an empirical study was needed to determine "the extent of discrimination; the degree of hardship imposed on black citizens of Washington; the readiness of white citizens to accept or welcome a change from previous discriminatory practices; and the attitudes of restauranteurs themselves."[13]

Beginning in April of 1950, the CCEAD undertook an extensive survey of discrimination of all public eating places in the District of Columbia. The survey attempted to ascertain which eating places were willing to serve blacks, managements attitude on the issue, and the reaction of white customers to black attempts to secure first-class service. While the survey was in its initial stages, Judge John Meyers of the Municipal Court dismissed the Thompson case on the grounds that the laws had been "repealed by implication." In essence, the court ruling meant that blacks forfeited their rights by their failure to utilize the laws. Shocked and dismayed, Terrell persuaded committee members to continue the survey and demanded that the District Commissioners appeal the case.[14]

The committee continued its surveys and by November, 1850, 145 white and black volunteers had tested 99 downtown restaurants, including all types of lunch counters, soda fountains, and department and dime store food counters. The survey documented both the pervasiveness of segregation in the nation's capital and virtually no support for this policy from white customers.

None of the facilities tested had been known previously to serve blacks. The checkers tested 316 times. They were quiet, orderly, and neat in appearance. Their procedure was to seat themselves in either mixed (black and white) groups or all-black groups of no less than four persons. If served, they ate and left. If refused service, they asked for the manager and called his attention to the 1872 and 1873 laws. At no time did they engage in controversial discussions with the proprietor.[15]

Of the 316 checks made, 188 parties were served and 128 were refused. Of the ninety-nine restaurants surveyed, sixty-three refused to serve blacks on the first and subsequent checks. Of the other restaurants, eight that at first refused to provide service to blacks later changed their policy. However, twenty-eight restaurants that served blacks on the first test refused to serve them on subsequent tests. In no instance did any incident occur to indicate any displeasure whatsoever on the part of patrons of the restaurants. The checkers reported occasional curious glances, but the general attitude of white patrons to the presence of black patrons was one of complete indifference. Nine checkers reported that several whites reacted favorably to their survey. "Isn't it a shame," said one white customer to a refused black patron, "that you can go to one floor of Hecht's department store and buy a television set costing a couple of hundred dollars, but they won't let you sit at the basement lunch counter to spend a nickel for a coke."[16]

It became clear to Terrell and other committee members that Washington would accept a change in the segregated pattern in restaurants and that no disorder would follow. The only negative reaction during the testing period came from restaurant owners and managers and from waitresses instructed by them not to serve black persons. "Have you heard of the 1872 anti-discrimination law?", one checker asked a waitress, who had declined him service. "That law has not been passed yet," was her curt reply.[17]

The Municipal Court ruling in favor of Thompson's Restaurant had no effect on several owners who desegregated as a result of the Committee's sit-ins, but most eating places maintained their segregated facilities. The Committee decided to implement its four-point plan, with the initial target being the variety stores on 7th street, the shopping area with the largest black trade. The first of these stores, Kresge, refused negotiations on any terms. The committee began deliberations on the use of the radical strategies of picketing and boycotts. Like Terrell, the majority of CCEDA members viewed these tactics as anathema to their middle-class ethos. But Terrell asked, "How long can one be respectable and still be effective?"[18] Terrell realized that the unwillingness of Kresge's manager to negotiate made a public demonstration—albeit with dignity—necessary. Once convinced of the necessity of using these weapons, she was never troubled by the possible loss of her respectability in the community.

Confident and resolute, the champion of black equality now aided by a walking cane and hearing aid, led the first detachment of picketers through a snowstorm to protest in front of the Kresge store. After six weeks, the management capitulated. A victory was chalked up for integration.[19]

On February 19, 1951, a full-page ad in support of World Brotherhood Week sponsored by Hecht Company, owner of the largest department store in the District of Columbia, was the catalyst for the committee's second attack on segregation. The ad was striking: a picture of black-white hands clasped in friendship with strong words denouncing the disturbing and undermining racial and religious antagonisms in America. "Brotherhood is . . . an empty vision, until we live as brothers in our states, communities and neighborhoods . . . day by day and year by year."[20] Several weeks after the appearance of the ad, a group including Terrell, addressed the company on the discrepancy between the brotherhood ad and its present policy of segregated lunch counters. An official of the store stated, "You know we don't believe in that ad any more than the people who read it believe in it. . . . How do you think the Hecht Company got as big as it is? Trying to please people, right? The Hecht Company is interested primarily in money. To prove that, we did not do so bad—we made $80 million last year."[21]

Mary Church Terrell was convinced that segregation at Hecht must be ended. On May 24, 1951, in the midst of several attempts at negotiating with the company, the Municipal Court of Appeals announced its decision that since the 1872 and 1873 laws were never legally repealed they were valid. Terrell was convinced that this ruling would alter Hecht's intransigence. However, an unforeseen turn of events shattered her hopes. First, Thompson Restaurant filed an appeal in the Appellate Court, the United States Court of Appeals, and second, the District Commissioners refused to enforce the laws until the higher court rendered a decision.[22] These two events made Hecht even more determined not to negotiate. Immediately, Mary Church Terrell called for the boycotting and picketing of Hecht's department store.

Picketing became not only an effective device for forcing Hecht to negotiate but also an instrument of education. Thousands of blacks and whites were informed of the injustices perpetrated against blacks by the picket banners that read:

NEGROES SPENT 1/2 MILLION DOLLARS
AT HECHT'S LAST YEAR
YET HECHT'S WON'T SERVE NEGROES

AT ITS LUNCH COUNTER

WE ARE PICKETING BECAUSE HECHT'S
SERVES ALL AT THE SALES COUNTER
BUT DISCRIMINATES AGAINST NEGROES
AT THE LUNCH COUNTER

STAY OUT
SEGREGATION PRACTICED HERE

HELP THE NATION
OUT OF DISCRIMINATION
SHOP ONLY AT STORES THAT
TREAT ALL ALIKE

HECHT'S VIOLATES THE LAW
THE MUNICIPAL COURT OF APPEALS
SAYS NO DISCRIMINATION
IN RESTAURANTS

DON'T BUY AT HECHT'S
HECHT'S JIM CROW LUNCH COUNTER
DISGRACES THE NATION'S CAPITAL[23]

Leaflets further educated both races to the facts of racial discrimination in Washington D.C. One stated: "I have visited the capitals of many countries, but only in the capital of my own country have I been subjected to this indignity."[24]

Throughout the long hot summer, public support for the Coordinating Committee for the Enforcement of the D.C. Anti-Discrimination Laws increased. Money and advice was given by whites to sidewalk supervisors:

"Go in and bother them, don't just stand out here, bother them until they give in."

"Why are colored people acting like this, we white people have always treated our colored people right?"

"Here is a dollar, go get yourself some cold beer."[25]

Mary Church Terrell during the picketing protesting segregation at Kresge's. Initially refusing even to talk with Terrell and her group, Kresge's agreed to integrate their eating facilities after six weeks of protests.

These comments suggest a shift in black-white relations in the nation's capital. The following account by a protester sitting-in at Hecht's lunch counter clearly illustrated this phenomenon:

> A high ranking officer sat down next to me. The clerk offered to serve him, but the officer stated that "this other man was here before me, serve him, I am in no hurry." The waitress replied, "he cannot be served because he is colored." The officer ordered a coke. When it was brought, he ordered another and another, until there were six cokes in front of me. The waitress called the manager, who could do nothing about the cokes that had been already served to me. But, he did order the waitress not to take another order from the white officer.[26]

Coupled with white support in Washington, D.C., Mary Church Terrell sought support throughout the world in letters to civic and social organizations and prominent public officials. The response was overwhelming. She not only received words of support but also money. From North Carolina Mutual of Durham came a contribution with the wish that it be used "toward your great undertaking." A business in Alexandria, Virginia, sent a $10 contribution "in support of one of your useful activities." From the United States Ambassador in Monrovia, Liberia, came this expression of concern: "Your letter of June 2 pointing out the increase in the number of public eating places that do not discriminate by color in Washington has reached me. On behalf of my wife and myself, I take the liberty of sending you a check for $28 to cover a week's publishing of your material."[28] The strongest gesture of support for the CCEAD's attack on segregation came from the American Psychological Association. At its sixtieth Annual Convention held in Washington, D.C., the association unanimously voted "not to meet again in Washington because of blatant discrimination perpetrated against its black members and all blacks in the city." Terrell applauded the association's resolution in a letter to the editor of the *New York Times*.[28]

After four months of picketing, the Hecht Company capitulated. The manager informed Terrell that "as of January 16, 1952, all services and departments of the company would be available to Negroes."[29] Continuing her campaign for desegregation, Mary Church Terrell now targeted Murphy's Dime Store. Like Hecht and Kresge, negotiations proved ineffectual. In May 1952 the picket lines appeared. Since Murphy allowed lunch-counter service to blacks only while standing, the committee emphasized this inequity on its banners and leaflets:

MAKE IT RIGHT
IF YOU'RE NOT WHITE
YOU CAN'T SIT DOWN
TO EAT A BITE

HELP TAKE THE NATION
OUT OF DISCRIMINATION
SHOP ONLY AT STORES THAT SERVE ALL ALIKE

MURPHY SAYS "YES"
AT THE SALES COUNTER
NO AT THE LUNCH COUNTER

1/3 OF D.C.'S CITIZENS MUST STAND
UP TO EAT AT MURPHY'S
HELP END DISCRIMINATION

MURPHY'S PUT THE STAND
IN LUNCH STAND.[30]

Many of the picketers sang this song to the tune of "Little Brown Jug":

WE AIM OUR RIGHTS UP VERY FAR
WE HITCH OUR WAGON TO A STAR
IT'S OUR DESIRE
IT'S OUR AMBITION
TO EAT AT MURPHY'S

IT'S VERY DARING WE ADMIT
TO EAT AT MURPHY'S AND EXPECT TO SIT
HORSES LIKE TO EAT AND STAND UP TOO
NO, MR. MURPHY WE WON'T STAND FOR YOU[31]

The tactics of picketing and boycotting along with leaflets and banners proved successful. On September 3, the manager of Murphy's telephoned Mrs. Terrell to request a conference. Mrs. Terrell's press release tells the rest of the story:

> This afternoon at 3 p.m. Mrs. Terrell and Mrs. Stein [the Committee's secretary] met with the District Manager of the store at his request. After an hour of discussion, he agreed to begin serving his customers without discrimination on Thursday morning, September 4.
>
> This great victory climaxes 16 weeks of steadfast picketing 3 days a week. Our first thanks must go to valiant picketers who at great personal sacrifice manned the line of 100 strong each week throughout the hottest summer Washington has known for many years.
>
> This victory brings to a successful close the Dime Store Campaign launched by the Committee just 2 years ago on my 87th Birthday, September 23, 1950.[32]

Along with Terrell's transition from the use of such strategies as moral suasion and interracial dialogue to such direct tactics as picketing, boycotting, and sit-ins, her allegiance to the Republican Party waned. In 1952 Terrell voted for Averell Harriman, a Democrat, in the presidential primary, because he pledged to implement the New Deal of Franklin D. Roosevelt and the Fair Deal of Harry S. Truman. Further evidence of the change in her allegiance to the Republican party was this statement published in several newspapers—"Truman did more for blacks than any other President since Abraham Lincoln." In the election of 1952, Mary Church Terrell voted for the Democratic candidate, Adlai Stevenson.[33]

Terrell's victories at Kresge, Hecht, and Murphy's gave her hope that the United States Court of Appeals, the highest court in the District of Columbia, would render a favorable decision in the Thompson Restaurant case. In support of such a decision the CCEAD asked organizations to file briefs arguing for the validity of the 1872 and 1873 laws. Reverend William Jernigan, vice-president of the committee, received a promise from the newly-elected president of the United States, Dwight Eisenhower, to support all efforts to eliminate segregation in the nation's capital. The President-elect wrote to Reverend Jernigan that "we may not always agree on the means of achieving our ends; but the end is identical and I pledge to do all in my power to end segregation in the District of Columbia."[34]

However, United States Court of Appeals reversed the ruling of the Municipal Court of Appeals on the grounds that the laws "were not valid because of disuse."[35] Under constant pressure from Chairwoman Terrell, the District Commissioners agreed to appeal the case to the Supreme Court. At the same time the Republican National Committee promised blacks three days free of any type of discrimination in hotels and eating places during the upcoming inauguration ceremonies. Viewing this proposal as absurd, Terrell

Mary Church Terrell (center) and other members of the Coordinating Committee for the Enforcement of The District of Columbia Anti-Discrimination Laws picketing in the early 1950s.

had handbills drawn up protesting the idea of lifting segregation for only three days. One handbill read:

> We say: Democracy is a year-round affair. All Americans should
>   be welcome anywhere in our nation's capital regardless
>   of color.
>
> Help us nail down the inaugural committee's promise: Insist on service in any restaurant you wish to enter. If you are refused:
>
> 1. Remind the manager of the inaugural committee' s pledge.
> 2. Report to us at Adams 2-1613.[36]

From April 30 to June 8, 1953, the case of *District of Columbia* v. *John Thompson* became a national symbol of the fight against segregation in the United States. The District of Columbia's case was argued by Vernon E. West and Edward A. Beard, both of the Corporation Council. The District was also represented by Attorney General Herbert Brownell, Jr., and Acting Solicitor General Adam Stein, whose presence attested to President Eisenhower's commitment to ending segregated public accommodations in the nation's capital.[37]

Throughout the two-month-long court proceedings, Mary Church Terrell was harassed by threatening telephone calls and derogatory letters. It became a standard precaution to allow some member of the family other than Terrell to answer all telephone calls and to preview all letters. One letter declared:

> Forcing yourself on white people won't change you any. You will still always be just a negro woman and don't forget that. If you negroes would try to make yourselves welcome instead of forcing yourselves then maybe white people would like you better. Personally, you won't bother me. I have gone to Maryland, where, thank God, we still have segregation. I don't want any part of Negroes, good ones or bad ones, and the only ones I have met are all bad.[38]

Another letter proposed that "Negroes establish their own restaurants; therefore, they won't have to picket all the time," signed by "Thinking Americans." In spite of these verbal attacks, Mary Church Terrell received much praise and numerous awards for her leadership role in the anti-discrimination campaign.[39]

On June 8, 1953, Chief Justice William O. Douglas delivered the court's opinion:

This is a criminal proceeding prosecuted by information against a respondent for refusal to serve certain members of the Negro race in one of its restaurants in the District of Columbia solely on account of the race and color of those persons. . . . The Acts of 1872 and 1873 survived, we think, all subsequent changes in the government of the District of Columbia and remain today a part of the governing body of laws applicable to the District of Columbia.[40]

The first press release of Chairwoman Terrell after the court ruling urged that the fight against discrimination continue. "Insist upon the enforcement of the laws, for these laws can be lost again," she warned. "There is still need to direct our concerns toward ending discrimination in the theaters and hotels that still discriminate."[41]

The public response to the desegregation achievements of Mary Church Terrell was exemplified in a stellar celebration on her ninetieth birthday. The occasion included a reception at the White House, with Mrs. Eisenhower as hostess, a luncheon in the Presidential Ballroom at the Statler Hilton Hotel, a recently desegregated facility, and the dedication of the International Reading Room at Howard University in honor of Mary Church Terrell. Approximately 1,500 guests attended the affair. Numerous speeches and poems praised the accomplishments of this valiant champion of integration. John C. Darry, a friend and a lawyer, eloquently summed up Mary Church Terrell's drive for human equality: "Terrell's defense of her people against unfair and unjust attacks and criticisms was bold and conclusive. She pleaded for time as an element in the solution of our problems—and patience will work it out. But added to time, she appealed for full justice everywhere as a sure harbinger of peace and responsibility."[42]

A poem by Georgia Douglas Johnson, a member of the Coordinating Committee for the Enforcement of the D.C. Anti-Discrimination Laws, provided a fuller appraisal of Terrell's life:

To Mary Church Terrell

From out of the South of tyranny and blight
She came, a potent pilgrim with a dauntless tread
To Oberlin, where wisdom's rays are shed
To gather love of truth and love and light
From granaries supreme and infinite
Then straightway to a hostile world she sped
Unhesitant, unyielding, unafraid

Hope's pinings life a tender ray
Morning is waking flushed with rosy gleam
Night with its shadowy winds to yesterday
And down the wind-way on an inky stream
Seed-time and harvest deftly interplay
And life's fruition is the living dream.[43]

The celebration was highlighted by a stirring address by Terrell. She urged her audience to continue the drive to eradicate remaining vestiges of racial discrimination. She stated that the "accomplishments of the Coordination Committee for the Enforcement of Anti-Discrimination Laws in this small area was difficult but our members know that there is more to be done." Applauding the ruling of the Supreme Court on June 5, 1950, that had outlawed segregation in institutions of higher education—colleges, universities, and particularly professional schools—she remarked that "it shall be the happiest day of my life when our schools [public schools] are integrated."[44] Terrell lived to see the fruition of her dream when, on May 17, 1954, the Supreme Court in the case of *Brown* v. *Board of Education of Topeka, Kansas* declared racial segregation in public schools to be unconstitutional. Two months later, she died.

The assault on segregation orchestrated by Mary Church Terrell in the early 1950s prefigured the goals and tactics of the civil rights movement of the 1960s. She led boycotts and sit-ins when Martin Luther King, Jr., was still in seminary and when the Greensboro students were in grade school.

SIX

Conclusion

On July 24, 1954, Mary Eliza Church Terrell, at age ninety, died at her home in Highland Beach, Maryland.[1] Her body lay in state at the headquarters building of the National Association of Colored Women in Washington. Hundreds of people, from all walks of life, paid their respects to a great leader, who was described by Mrs. Eisenhower as "an example for emulation by all who love their fellowman."[2] *The Washington Evening Star* provided an eloquent editorial tribute:

> Dr. Mary Church Terrell, who died last Sunday at the age of 90, was a gracious lady and a staunch fighter for human freedom. Her most noteworthy service was her constant, patient, and dignified effort to advance the cause of Negro equality; but her interests were far broader than those of a single race. She fought discrimination and bigotry wherever she found it, but always with understanding rather than hatred. She had become a real civic institution in Washington, and the esteem and affection in which she was held was attested by the hundreds of persons from all walks of life who turned out last October to pay her honor on her birthday. She was recently a principal in the Thompson Restaurant Case that brought enforcement of the anti-discrimination laws. . . . Washington is richer because Mary Church Terrell lived here, and her death is a real loss to the nation's capital.[3]

Mary Church Terrell was born into the black elite in Memphis as the Civil War was coming to a close. Her earliest years were spent in a city rocked by violent and bitter racism. She was sheltered as far as was possible by parents who attempted to obliterate any trace of their own slave beginnings. She could not avoid encountering racism, however, when, after her parents' divorce, her mother sent her to school in Ohio. In response to her growing awareness of discrimination, she resolved to excel academically to prove the abilities of black women.

When Mary graduated in 1884 from Oberlin, she was an anomaly—a college-educated woman, a member of the wealthy Terrell family of Memphis, and a mulatto who could have passed for white. After spending a year keeping house for her father, she took a teaching position at Wilberforce University in Ohio, and a year later another at M Street Colored High School in Washington, D.C. It was at M Street (Dunbar) High School that she met her future husband, Robert H. Terrell.

During the years between 1888 and 1896 Mary Church Terrell had to make two major decisions: first, as an intellectual, whether to remain in the United States, a world where she would be a marginal individual, or to seek a world free of prejudice where her abilities would be judged on their own merits. Second, she had to decide whether to live by the rules of the "cult of true womanhood" or to break out of this orthodox Victorian role. After spending two years of travel and study in Europe, she decided not only to remain in the United States but also to dedicate her live to the elevation of her race and sex.

Mary Church Terrell became the apotheosis of the "New Woman." She was self-reliant. She was physically vigorous and energetic. She held independent views. Above all, she made a choice to break the Victorian model for her sex and move out into the world. Many of her contemporaries such as Ida B. Wells, an activist in the anti-lynching movement, Charlotte Hawkins Brown, founder of Palmer Institute, Mary McLeod Bethune, an educator and a member of the black cabinet of Franklin D. Roosevelt, and Anna J. Cooper, a graduate of Oberlin, made similar choices. Terrell saw her role as elevating her race through interracial understanding. To achieve this goal, she was active in racial organizations, wrote prolifically and traveled widely delivering lectures.

In 1896, Terrell became the founder and the first president of the National Association of Colored Women (NACW). Symbolizing unity among black women, this self-help organization fostered sisterly support for its members and created programs that enhanced the moral development of blacks, especially women, through social-welfare institutions. The strategies and objectives of the National Association of Colored Women were at once radical and conservative. It was radically new in that it was a national effort exclusively created and controlled by black women. It established the first formal network of communication among black women throughout the United States. And, last, but certainly not least, it fostered and encouraged the development of leadership skills among middle-class black women.

The NACW was at the same time conservative. It was not feminist in the modern sense of the term. It aimed not to alter the domestic life of its members but to improve it by making them better wives and mothers. It did

Mary Church Terrell receiving the Diamond Cross

not frontally address the issue of segregation. In spite of this failing, many of the local branches in Tennessee and Alabama did implement measures to attack Jim Crow. This avoidance of this issue indicates the unwillingness of the national leadership, including Mary Church Terrell, to deal with political issues.

Terrell's speeches and writings highlighted the living conditions of blacks and their progress in spite of discrimination. In a stirring address delivered in 1904 at the International Congress of Women in Berlin, she vividly described the numerous contributions of her race. Speaking in fluent German she received enthusiastic accolades. Her articles and short stories on lynching, chain gangs, the peonage system, defection of mulattoes, and the disenfranchisement of blacks provide an objective and detailed portrayal of the plight of black people.

Terrell was not a highly original thinker. Her article, "Lynching From a Colored Woman's Point of View (1904)," documented findings similar to those reported by Ida B. Wells in *Southern Horrors* (1892) and *A Red Record* (1895). By comparison to other intellectuals of the 1920s such as W. E. B. Du Bois, Langston Hughes, Alain Locke, and James Weldon Johnson, she was one-dimensional. She failed, for instance, to recognize the importance of economic factors in the creation of racial harmony. Although she worked to enhance the artistic and literary values and racial consciousness of blacks, she did not fully understand the complexity of the black struggle in America as it related to Africa. This lack of focus limited her perspective and blinded her to the depth of race prejudice.

Fighting for her goal of interracial understanding was made difficult at times by her husband's position as Judge of the Municipal Court of the District of Columbia. She sometimes compromised. She continued in her support of the Republican Party (to whom her husband owed his job) in the 1930s when a large number of blacks were defecting from its ranks. And, she softened her radicalism when Jim Crowism was implemented in the federal services during the administration of Woodrow Wilson.

Nevertheless, her approach and techniques of racial understanding were significant. Through her writings and speeches, Terrell became a booster of black morale as she exhorted her people to improve themselves. Her articles educated whites to the realities of black life. She helped to establish interracial organizations; in essence, she was an organization woman. She realized that power for social change, however limited, resided in the organization that physically united blacks and their white supporters in face-to-face contacts at regular meetings.

As conditions in the country changed, Mary Church Terrell was able to adapt. The last two decades of her life marked a transition in her position on race relations and politics. Frustrated by the economic hardships of blacks during the depression and the New Deal, the discrepancy between blacks fighting for democracy abroad during World War II while they were denied it at home, and shocked by the death of her husband, she became a militant working assiduously to bring a definitive end to discrimination in the United States and particularly in the nation's capital. Her battle for justice in the Ingram case, against the membership policy of the American Association of University Women, against the denial of equal rights to women, and against the segregation of public accommodations marked a person who had moved from the use of such strategies as moral suasion and interracial dialogue to more confrontational tactics, culminating in the direct actions of picketing, boycotting, and sitting-ins. The use of these techniques led to a successful assault against segregated public eating places in Washington, D.C. This battle proved that black people could organize and struggle, militantly but nonviolently, against oppression. This anti-segregation drive that Mary Church Terrell led in the early 1950s popularized the strategies that brought black Americans the most profound and far reaching desegregation movement in their history.

In 1914, Mary Church Terrell wrote The Delta Creed of the Delta Sigma Theta Sorority. It is an appropriate epitaph for her:

I will strive to reach the highest educational, moral and spiritual efficiency which I can possibly attain.

I will never lower my aims for any temporary benefit which might be gained.

I will endeavor to preserve my health, for, however great one's mental and moral strength may be, physical weakness prevents the accomplishment of much that might otherwise be done.

I will close my ears and seal my lips to slanderous gossip.

I will labor to ennoble the ideals and purify the atmosphere of the home.

I will always protest against the double standards of morals.

I will take an active interest in the welfare of my country, using my influence toward the enactment of laws for the protection of the unfortunate and weak and for the repeal of those depriving human beings of their privileges and rights.

I will never belittle my race, but encourage all to hold it in honor and esteem.

I will not shrink from undertaking what seems wise and good, because I labor under the double handicap of race and sex! but striving to preserve a calm mind with a courageous, cheerful spirit, barring bitterness from my heart, I will struggle all the more earnestly to reach the goal.[4]

Notes

CHAPTER ONE

1. Mary Church Terrell, "Progress of Colored Women," typescript, January 1890, Mary Church Terrell Papers, Speeches and Writing File, 1890-1904, Container 28, Reel 21, Library of Congress, Washington, D.C., hereinafter cited as MCTP; Mary Church Terrell, *A Colored Woman In A White World* (New York: Ransdell Company, 1940), introduction.
2. Sexism is a form of discrimination based on the belief that sexes have distinctive makeups that determine substantially their respective roles in life. It usually involves the idea that one sex—the male—is superior and has the right to rule the other—the female.
3. Terrell, *Colored Woman In A White World*, p. 2. For biographical sketches of Mary Church Terrell, see Russell L. Adams, *Great Negroes Past and Present* (Illinois: Afro-American Publishing Company, 1963), p. 119; Maxine Block, ed., *Current Biography* (New York: H. W. Wilson Company, 1940), p. 127; Rebecca Chalmers Barton, *Witnesses for Freedom: Negro Americans in Autobiography* (New York: Harper and Row, 1948), pp. 68-69; Sylvia G. Dannett, *Profiles of Negro Womanhood* (New York: Educational Heritage, 1974), p 207. Harry A Poloski, *Negro Almanac* (New York. Bellweather Publishing Company, 1962, p. 755; Wilhelmena S. Robinson, *Historical Negro Biographies* (New York: Publisher Company, 1967), p. 251; Dorothy Sterling, *Lift Every Voice* (New York: Doubleday Company, 1965), p. 55; Edgar A. Toppin, *History of Blacks in America Since 1528* (New York: David McKay, Inc., 1964), p. 420; and Thomas Yenser, ed., *Who's Who in Colored America: A Biographical Dictionary of Notable Living Persons* (Washington, D.C.: Ransdell, Inc., 1938-39), p. 157.
4. James D. Davis, *History of the City of Memphis* (Memphis: Hite, Crumpton and Kelly, 1873), p. 28. For a more complete history of Memphis, see James Roper, *Founding of Memphis, 1818-1820* (Memphis: Memphis Sesquicentennial, Inc., 1970); Gerald Capers, *The Biography of a River Town, Memphis, Its Heroic Age* (Chapel Hill: University of North Carolina Press, 1939), hereinafter cited as *Biography of a River Town*; John M. Keating, *History of the City of Memphis and Shelby County, Tennessee*, 2 volumes (New York: D. Mason and Company, 1888).
5. United States Bureau of the Census, *Eighth Census of United States, Population* (Washington, D.C.,: Government Printing Office, 1863), pp. 456-57.

6. Joseph H Parks, "A Confederate Trade Center Under Federal Occupation," *Journal of Southern History* 7 (August 1941): 289-314, hereinafter cited as *JSH*; Edward Hooper, "Memphis, Tennessee, Federal Occupation and Reconstruction" (Ph.D. dissertation, University of North Carolina, Chapel Hill, 1957), pp. 5-10, 92-95, hereinafter cited as "Memphis Reconstruction"; Joseph H. Parks, "Memphis Under Military Rule, 1862 to 1856," *East Tennessee Historical Society's Publication* 14 (August 1942): 31-58.

7. United States Bureau of the Census, *Ninth Census of United States, Statistics of Population* (Washington, D.C.: Government Printing Office, 1872), p. 268; United States Bureau of the Census, *A Compendium of Ninth Census* (Washington, D.C.: Government Printing Office, 1872), p. 338.

8. Carl Witke, *The Irish in America* (Baton Rouge: Louisiana State University Press, 1956), p. 126; Keating, *History of the City of Memphis and Shelby County*, 1:56; Capers, *Biography of a River Town*, p. 177; Alrutheus A. Taylor, *The Negro in Tennessee, 1865-1880* (Washington, D.C.: The Associated Publishers, Inc., 1941), p. 87.

9. Memphis *Argus*, May 2, 1866; *Nashville Dispatch*, May 3, 4, 5, 6, 9, 1886; *Commercial*, May 3, 1866; *Harper's Weekly*, June 2, 1866; United States Congress, House, *The Report of Memphis Riots and Massacres*, H. Doc. 191, 39th Congress, 1st Session, 1866, p. 6, hereinafter cited as *Memphis Riots*.

10. Hooper, "Memphis Reconstruction," pp 81-84. The stringency of the Disfranchisement Act was prescribed by Military Governor Andrew Johnson.

11. Jack D. Holmes, "The Underlying Cause of the Memphis Riot of 1866," *Tennessee Historical Quarterly* 17 (September 1958): 198-99. According to Holmes, the Irish held 67 percent of the elective and appointive offices in Memphis.

12. United States Congress, House, *Memphis Riots*, pp. 6-7. These troops were stationed in Memphis as a result of an effort by the military authorities to organize an all-Memphis black regiment to be known as the "Corps d'Afrique." For more information, see Parks, "Memphis Under Military Rule," pp. 57-58.

13. Ibid., p. 33; Tennessee General Assembly, 2nd Session, 1865-66. Members of the Congressional Committee included two Radicals—Elihu Z. Washburne of Illinois, Chairman of the Committee, and John M. Broomall of Pennsylvania—and one Conservative—George Shanklin of Kentucky. Shanklin refused to sign the majority report and issued instead his own, "The Views of the Minority." The Radicals were successful in using the Memphis riot to discredit Andrew Johnson. In the Congressional elections of 1866, they captured 143 seats and the Democrats (Conservatives) gained 49 seats.

14. Taylor, *Negro in Tennessee*, pp 74-82, 92-105, 244.

15. Ibid.

16. Ibid.; John Hope Franklin, *Reconstruction: After the Civil War* (Chicago: University of Chicago Press, 1961), pp. 229, 231.

17. Reports of the Chamber of Commerce in Keating, *History of the City of Memphis and Shelby County*, 1:645; II:168. The assessment and tax rate varied from $24,542,315 at $2.00 per $100 in 1871 to $29,971,045 at $2.64 in 1874 to $19,998,166 at $3.00 in 1878.

18. Annette E. Church and Robert Church, *The Robert R. Churches of Memphis: A Father and Son Who Achieved in Spite of Race* (Memphis: A. E. Church, 1974), *passim*; Terrell, *Colored Woman In A White World*, pp. 2-5; M. Sammye Miller, "First Black Millionaire," *Dawn Magazine*, October 3, 1975, p. 4; and *Memphis Evening Scimitar* (Souvenir Edition), October 1891.
19. Terrell, *Colored Woman In A White World*, pp. 8-9.
20. Gladys Bryan Sheppard, *Mary Church Terrell—Respectable Person* (Maryland: Human Relations Press, 1959), p. 20.
21. Terrell, *Colored Woman In A White World*, p. 2.
22. Ibid., p. 10.
23. Ibid., p. 11.
24. Ibid., p. 16
25. Ibid., pp 18-19 The model school at Antioch College was the forerunner of the kindergarten.
26. Ibid., p. 21.
27. Ibid., p. 23.
28. For a complete account of Oberlin and Oberlin College's anti-slavery activity, see Robert S. Fletcher, *A History of Oberlin College From Its Foundation Through the Civil War*, 2 volumes (Oberlin: Oberlin College, 1943); and James H. Fairchild, *Oberlin: The Colony and College*, 1833-1883 (Oberlin: E. J. Goodrich, 1883).
29. Ibid., p. 41. After Terrell's language teacher, Professor Frost, told Matthew Arnold that the young lady who read the passage was "of African descent," Arnold expressed "the greatest surprise imaginable," because he thought "the tongue of the African was so thick he could not be taught to pronounce Greek correctly."
30. Ibid., pp. 39-49.
31. Two other black women graduated with Church in 1884—Anna J. Cooper and Ida Gibbs.
32. Terrell, *Colored Woman In A White World*, p. 62.
33. Ibid., p. 99.
34. Elliott Rudwick *W. E. B. Du Bois: Propagandist of Negro Protest* (New York: Atheneum, 1968), p. 47. For more information on Du Bois's life, see W. E. B. Du Bois, *Dusk of Dawn: An Essay Toward an Autobiography of a Race Concept* (New York: Schocken Books, 1940); Rayford Logan, *W. E. B. Du Bois: A Profile* (New York: Hill and Wang, 1971); Elliott Rudwick, *W. E. B. Du Bois: A Study in Minority Group Leadership* (Philadelphia: University of Pennsylvania Press, 1960); and Francis L. Broderick, *W. E. B. Du Bois, A Negro Leader in Time of Crisis* (Stanford, California: Stanford University Press, 1959).
35. Barbara Walter, "Cult of True Womanhood," in Jean E. Friedman and William G. Shade, eds., *Our American Sisters: Women in American Life and Thought* (Boston: Allyn and Bacon, Inc., 1973), pp. 96-123. Walter provides a succinct analysis of the image of the true woman, a person who devoted all of her energy, time, and creativity to the service of her family.
36. "Advice to New Women," *Review of Reviews* 12 (July 1895):84-85; "New Woman Under Fire," *Review of Reviews* 10 (December 1894):656; Emma

Churcman Hewill, "The New Woman in Relation to the New Man," Westminster 147 (November 1898):576-85; Miles M. Dawson, "The New Woman," Arena 18 (August 1897):43; Boyd Winchester, "The New Woman," Arena 27 (April 1902):367-73

37. Robert Wiebe, *The Search for Order, 1877-1920* (New York: Hill and Wang, 1967), p. 2. For more information on the effects of industrialization upon society, see Samuel P. Hays, *Response to Industrialism, 1885-1914* (Chicago: University of Chicago Press, 1957); Henry Steele Commager, *The American Mind: An Interpretation of American Thought and Character Since the 1880s* (New Haven: Yale University Press, 1950); Richard Hofstadter, *Age of Reform* (New York: Alfred A. Knopf Co., 1955).

38. Lois Banner, who has written several books on women's history, applied the term to women professionals and volunteers. Barbara Welter, an authority on the woman's position in the family, society, and the professions viewed the New Woman as "one who goes outside the home, seeking rewards other than love." Peter Filene, an historian who has analyzed the historic role of the woman, found the "genuine New Woman" not in the home, but "in colleges and professions, and bachelor apartments." He also maintained that the New Woman was the "new girl or spinster." Lois Zanner, *The American Woman from 1900 to the First World War: A Profile of Women in Modern America* (New York: Harcourt Brace and Jovanovich, 1974), p. 413; Barbara Welter, "Cult of True Womanhood," p. 41; and Peter Filene, *Him/Her/Self: Sex Roles in Modern America.* (New York: Harcourt Brace and Jovanovich, 1974), p. 16.

CHAPTER TWO

1. For excellent works on the history of women in America, see Ida Husted Harper, ed., *History of Woman Suffrage, 1883-1900* (New York: Arno Press and the New York Times, 1969); Eleanor Flexner, *Century of Struggle: The Woman's Rights Movement in the United States* (Cambridge, Mass.: Belknap Press, 1959; paperback edition, New York: Atheneum, 1973); Aileen Kraditor, *The Ideas of the Women's Suffrage Movement, 1890-1920* (New York: Anchor Books, Doubleday and Company, 1971); Anne F. Scott, *The American Woman: Who Was She?* (Englewood Cliffs, New Jersey: Prentice-Hall, 1971); Carl Degler, "Revolution without Ideology: The Changing Place of Women in America," in Robert Lifton, ed., *The Woman in America* (Boston: Houghton Mifflin, 1965); William O'Neill, *Everyone Was Brave: The Rise and Fall of Feminism* (Chicago: University of Chicago Press, 1971); Alma Lutz, *Created Equal: A Biography of Elizabeth Cady Stanton* (New York: The John Day Company, 1940); and Robert Smuts, *Women and Work in America* (New York: Columbia University Press, 1959).

2. Self-help organizations of the nineteenth century are discussed in W. E. B. Du Bois's *Efforts for Social Betterment Among Negro Americans* (Atlanta: Atlanta University Publication, no. 14, 1909).

3. Rayford Logan, *The Betrayal of the Negro: From Rutherford B. Hayes to Woodrow Wilson* (New York: Collier Books, 1965), p. 62; C. Vann Woodward, *The Strange Career of Jim Crow* (New York: Oxford University Press, 1955), Chapter 3. For more information on the genesis of segregation in the late nineteenth and early twentieth centuries, see Joel Williamson, *After Slavery: The Negro in South Carolina During Reconstruction, 1865-1890* (Chapel Hill: University of North Carolina Press, 1965); George Brown Tindall, *South Carolina Negroes, 1877-1900* (Baton Rouge: Louisiana State University Press, 1962); Charles H. Wynes, *Race Relations in Virginia, 1870-1902* (Charlottesville: University of Virginia Press, 1961); Vernon Lane Wharton, *The Negro in Mississippi, 1865-1890* (Chapel Hill: University of North Carolina Press, 1947); Richard C. Wade, *Slavery in the Cities: The South, 1820-1860* (New York: Oxford University Press, 1974); Ira Berlin, *Slaves Without Masters: The Free Negro in the Antebellum South* (New York: Pantheon Books, 1975); and Howard N. Rabinowitz, *Race Relations in the Urban South: 1865-1890* (New York: Oxford University Press, 1978).
4. For an analysis of the relative desertion of Northern whites from the black cause after Reconstruction, see Stanley Cohen, "Northeastern Businessmen and Radical Reconstruction," *Mississippi Valley Historical Review* 46 (June 1959): 67-90; William B. Hesseltine, "Economic Factors in the Abandonment of Reconstruction," *Journal of Southern History* 41 (February 1975):39-58.
5. Fannie Barrier Williams, "The Club Movement Among Colored Women," *Voice of the Negro* 1 (March 1904):101.
6. Williams, "Club Movement Among Colored Women," pp. 392-93.
7. Terrell, "Colored Woman's League," MCTP, Box 102-3, Folder 60, MSC.
8. Elizabeth L. Davis, *Lifting As We Climb* (Chicago: Race Relations Press, 1933), p. 18.
9. "Colored Woman's League," MCTP, Box 102-3, Folder 60, Moorland Spingarn Collection, hereinafter cited as MSC, Washington, D.C.; Terrell, "History of the National Association of Colored Women," typewritten, MCTP, Container 38, Reel 27, Library of Congress, hereinafter cited as LC; Terrell, "Club Work Among Women," *New York Age*, January 4, 1900; Williams, "Club Movement Among Colored Women," pp. 386-90; J. Silone Yates, "Report of National Federation of Colored Women's Clubs to the National Council of Women," *Colored American*, January 1905, p. 258.
10. "History of the Club Movement," *Afro-American Journal*, in MCTP, Container 31, Reel 22, LC; Terrell, "Reasons for Using Clubs," MCTP, Box 102-5, Folder 146, MSC.
11. Terrell, *A Colored Woman In A White World* (New York: Ransdell Company, 1940), p. 151.
12. For the history of the General Federation of Women's Clubs, see Jennie June Croly, *The History of the Woman's Club Movement in America* (New York: Henry G. Allen and Company, 1898) and Mary I. Wood, *The History of the General Federation of Women's Clubs* (New York: Norwood Press, 1912).
13. Terrell, "General Federation of Club Women," MCTP, Box 102-5, Folder 69, MSC; John W. Gibson and William H. Crogman, *Progress of a Race, Or the*

Remarkable Advancement of the Colored American (Illinois: J. L. Nichols and
Company, 1902), pp. 216-20.
14. Terrell, "Duty of the National Association of Colored Women to the Race,"
    AME Church Review, January 1900, p. 240
15. Ibid.
16. From the list of women included in the article, "The Ten Living Negro Women
    Who Have Contributed Most to the Advancement of the Race," *Fisk News*,
    May-June 1936, pp. 5-6, at least six, including Mary Church Terrell, had been
    affiliated with the National Association of Colored Women. Mary McLeod
    Bethune, a noted educator and a member of the New Deal Black Cabinet of
    President Roosevelt, was President of the NACW, 1926-1928; Ida B. Wells,
    an activist in the anti-lynching movement, was a member of the NACW,
    1900-1920; Charlotte Hawkins Brown, founder of the Palmer Memorial
    Institute in Sedalia, North Carolina in 1902, was a member; Nannie H.
    Burroughs, founder of a Training School for Girls, was a member; and Hallie
    Queen Brown, an educator, lecturer, and publicist, who brought worldwide
    recognition to Wilberforce University in Ohio as a center of Negro education,
    was a member.
17. Terrell, "First Presidential Address to the National Association of Colored
    Women," Nashville, Tennessee, September 15, 1897, MCTP, Box 102-5,
    Folder 127, MSC also in Container 30, Reel 21, LC. [See the present volume,
    pages 133-138.]
18. *National Notes*, 1896-1899, MCTP, Container 23, Reel 17, LC.
19. United States Bureau of the Census, *Negro Population 1790-1915* (Washington,
    D.C.: Government printing office, 1918), pp. 36-37. These cities were among
    the top twenty cities with the largest percentage of blacks.
20. Terrell, *Colored Woman In A White World*, p. 152; Terrell, "Club Work Among
    Women," *New York Age*, Paris Exposition Edition, no. 19, January 4, 1900,
    in MCTP, Box 102-5, Folder 141, MSC; "Convention A Success," Nashville
    Evening Star, September 2, 1899, p. 12.
21. On Du Bois's philosophy, see Elliott M. Rudwick, *W. E. B. Du Bois,
    Propagandist of the Negro Protest* (New York: Atheneum, 1968).
22. The names below were compiled from the early reports of the National
    Association of Colored Women, 1890-1901, NACW headquarters, Washington,
    D.C. Various articles in the MCTP confirmed that these women were leaders
    either on the national or state level. Biographical information was derived from
    various editions of *Who's Who in America*, *Who's Who in Colored America*,
    obituaries in the *Washington Bee*, 1930-1960, other specialized biographical
    dictionaries, and Fannie E. Williams's article, "Club Movement Among Colored
    Women." Holders of bachelor and graduate degrees: Anna J. Cooper, B.A.,
    1884, M.A., 1887, Oberlin College; Julia C. Jackson Harris, B.A., Atlanta
    University, 1894, M.A. Harvard College, 1904; Elizabeth Ross Haynes, B.A.,
    State Normal School, Montgomery, Alabama, 1900, M.A., Fisk University,
    1903; Mary Jackson McCrorey, B.A., Atlanta University, M.A., Howard
    University; Alice Ruth Nelson, B.A., Straight College, M.A., University of
    Pennsylvania; Minnie McAlphin Pickens, B.A., M.A., Tougaloo College, Ph.D.;

Sadie Tanner Mossell Alexander, B.S., University of Pennsylvania, 1918, M.A., 1919, Ph.D., 1921; Coralie Franklin Cook, B.S., Storer College; Laura Croften Franklin, Scotia Seminary; Evangeline Evelyn Harris, B.A., Indiana State Training School; Georgia Douglas Johnson, B.A., Atlanta University; Kathryn Johnson, B.A., Wilberforce University, 1900; Maria Coles Perkins Lawton, B.A., Howard University; Ethel Hedgeman Lyle, B.A., Howard University; Florida Ruffin Ridley, B.A., Boston Teachers College, 1880; Marion P. Shadd, B.A., Howard University, 1877; Mary E. Vaughn, B.S., Tuskegee Institute; A'Lelia Walker, B.A., Knoxville College; Meta Vaux Warrick, Pennsylvania School of Industrial Arts, 1899; Marguarite J. Murray Washington, B.S., Tuskegee Institute, 1893; Sarah A. Blocker, B.A., Florida State Baptist College; Anna Jones, B.A., University of Michigan; Henrietta M. Archer, B.S., A&M College, Normal, Alabama; Mary C. Jackson, B.S., Tuskegee Institute, 1890; professional degrees: Lucille Bragg Anthony, B.A., Oberlin College, Meharry Medical School, 1902-1907; Alice Woodley McKane, B.A., Hampton Institute, 1886; Medical College of Pennsylvania, 1892; Mabel Whiting, Duff Burenen College; J. Evans, Chicago Burns College, 1899; Violette N. Anderson, LL.B., Chicago Law School; and Lavinia Marian Fleming, LL.B., Howard University.

23. *Colored American*, March 6, 1891
24. *Daily News*, August 16, 1899, in MCTP, Container 46, Reel 31, LC.
25. *Times-Herald*, August 16, 1899, MCTP, Container 23, Reel 16, LC and Box 102-12, Folder 242, 243, MSC.
26. NACW's Constitution, MCTP, Box 102-12, Folder 249, MCS and Container 23, Reel 17, LC.
27. Terrell, "First Presidential Address," MCTP, Box 102-3, Folder 127, MSC; excerpts from the address delivered at the National Council of Women Convention, April 6, 1905, Washington, D.C., MCTP, Container 28, Reel 21, LC. On Brown and Addams, see Christopher Lasch, *The Social Thought of Jane Addams* (Indianapolis: Bobbs Merrill, 1964); Charlotte H. Brown, *The Correct Thing To Do* (Boston: Christopher Publishing House, 1941). Brown was the founder and headmistress of Palmer Memorial Institute in Sedalia, North Carolina, not far from Greensboro. It was an exclusive preparatory school for the wealthiest and best-born black children in the United States. Addams was the founder of a social-settlement house, Hull House, in Chicago. It aimed to improve the lot of the deprived urban dweller.
28. Terrell, "First Presidential Address."
29. United States Bureau of the Census, *Eleventh Census of the United States: 1890* (Washington, D.C.: Government Printing office, 1893), pp. 36-45; United States Bureau of the Census, *Negro Population 1790-1915*, pp. 509, 526.
30. Address delivered at the Biennial Convention of NACW, MCTP, Container 28, Reel 21, LC; Terrell, "Efforts and Aims of Our Noted Women," *The Freeman: An Illustrated Colored Paper*, Indianapolis, Indiana, December 24, 1898 in MCTP, Box 102-12, Folder 243, MSC; Josephine Silone Yates, "Kindergartens and Mother's Clubs As Related to the Work of the National Association of Colored Women," *Colored American*, 1905, pp. 305-7,

31. Progressive Study Club's Yearly Report, 1899, MCTP, Container 23, Reel 17, LC.
32. Yearly Club Reports, NACW Convention, Buffalo, New York, 1901, MCTP, Container 23, Reel 17, LC.
33. Terrell, *Colored Woman In A White World*, p. 153. See Reels 21, 26, 27, LC, for the complete text of the pamphlet. For letters requesting funds for the establishment of kindergartens and day nurseries see, Correspondence File, 1901-1903, MCTP, Container 4, Reels, 3, 4, LC.
34. Terrell, "Duty of the National Association of Colored Women to the Race," p. 345.
35. Quoted in Flexner, *Century of Struggle*, p. 187.
36. Terrell, "Duty of the NACW to the Race," p. 347.
37. Ibid., p. 341; "Report to President, Officers, and Members of the NACW from Tuskegee Women 's Club, " September 15, 1901, MCTP, Container 23, Reel 17, LC.
38. Terrell, "Some Aspects of the Employment Problem As It Concerns Colored People," MCTP, Box 102-3, Folder 114, MSC; "Report of the Phyllis Wheatley Club of New Orleans to the NACW," September 15, 1901, Container 23, Reel 17, LC.
39. Terrell, "Second Presidential Address," MCTP, Container 46, Reel 31, LC.
40. Samuel P. Hays, *Response to Industrialism*, pp. 74-75, 79-82; Robert Wiebe, *Search for Order*, pp. 151, 168, 170, 174-82, 292; George Mowry, *Progressive Era, 1900-1920: The Reform Persuasion* (Washington, D.C.: American Historical Association, 1972).
41. Yearly Reports of Clubs, 1897, 1899, 1901, MCTP, Container 23, Reel 17, LC.
42. Terrell, "Club Work Among Women"; Elizabeth Davis, *The Story of the Illinois Federation* (Chicago: [n.p.], 1922), pp. 95-101.
43. Terrell, "Duty of the NACW to the Race."
44. Yearly Reports of Clubs, 1897, 1899.
45. Ibid., 1901 Yearly Club Report, Container 23, Reel 17, LC.

CHAPTER THREE

1. For more information on the ideology of Booker T. Washington and W. E. B. Du Bois, see August Meier, *Negro Thought in America, 1880-1915: Racial Ideologies in the Age of Booker T. Washington* (Michigan: University of Michigan Press, 1969), pp. 85-100, 207-79; and Elliott M. Rudwick, *W. E. B. Du Bois: Propagandist of the Negro Protest*, second edition (New York: Atheneum, 1968).
2. W. E. B. Du Bois, *Souls of Black Folk* (New York; New American Library, 1903), pp. 53, 126-29.
3. Booker T. Washington, *My Larger Education* (New York: Doubleday, Page and Company, 1911), pp. 23-24; Ernest Davidson Washington, ed., *Selected*

Speeches of Booker T. Washington (New York: Doubleday, Doran and Company, 1932), pp. 75-77.

4. Charles S. Johnson, *Race Relations: Adjustment of Whites and Negroes in the United States* (Massachusetts: D.C. Heath and Company, 1934), pp. 3-5; Peter I. Rose, *The Subject Is Race: Traditional Ideologies and the Teaching of Race Relations* (New York: Oxford University Press, 1968), pp. 39-40; and Gunnar Myrdal, *An American Dilemma: The Negro Problem and Modern Democracy,* 2 vols. (New York: Harper and Row Publishers, 1944), vol. 1:113-17.

5. Mary Church Terrell, *A Colored Woman In A White World* (New York: Ransdell Company, 1940), pp. 33-34.

6. Ibid.

7. Terrell, "What It Means to Be Colored in the Capital of the United States," *Independent,* July 14, 1904, p. 181 [page 283 in the present volume]. "What It Means to Be Colored In The Capital Of The United States," MCTP, Container 38, Reel 28, LC. This article was published without attribution, but Terrell's original handwritten copy is in her papers. For an in-depth analysis of this transition, see Constance McLaughlin Green, *The Secret City: A History of Race Relations in the Nation's Capital* (Princeton, N.J.: Princeton University Press, 1967), p. 182.

8. Terrell, "What It Means to Be Colored," Ibid. Chapter 13 of Terrell's autobiography provides an account of the obstacles she encountered in her attempt to buy a house in Washington, D.C.

9. Terrell, "What it Means to Be Colored," p. 182 [page 285 in the present volume].

10. Ibid., p. 185 [page 290 in the present volume].

11. Terrell, *Colored Woman In A White World*, pp. 157-58.

12. Ibid., p. 159; Diary, February 25, 1905, MCTP, Container 1, Reel 1, LC.

13. Robert H. Terrell to District Superintendent of Pullman Company, June 23, 1910, Robert H. Terrell Papers, hereinafter cited as RHTP, LC and in MCTP, Container 4, Reel 4, LC.

14. Interview with Jacob Harris, December 13, 1979, Durham, North Carolina.

15. Terrell, *Colored Woman In A White World*, pp. 20-21.

16. Terrell, "Paul Laurence Dunbar," *Voice of the Negro*, April 1906, pp. 271-77 [pages 219-230 in the present volume]; also in MCTP, Container 29, Reel 21, LC.

17. Commencement Address at Dunbar High School, typewritten, June 19, 1922, MCTP, Container 29, Reel 21, LC; Annette Frazier to Terrell, June 25, 1922, Walter Anderson to Terrell, August 9, 1922, Evelyn Smith to Terrell, August 15, 1922, MCTP, Container 6, Reel 5, LC.

18. Terrell, "Samuel Coleridge-Taylor, The Great Anglo-African Composer," *Voice of the Negro*, January 1905 [pages 197-203 in this volume]; also in MCTP, Container 29, Reel 21, LC.

19. Terrell, *Colored Woman In A White World*, p. 133. Terrell, "Life of Phyllis Wheatley," *Chicago Defender*, December 27, 1924; Terrell, "Phyllis An African Genius," *The Baha'i Magazine: The Star of the West* (Vol. 19, No. 7) October, 1928 in MCTP, Container 30, Reel 21, LC; Terrell, "Phyllis Wheatley an

African Poetess," typescript, MCTP, Container 30, Reel 22, LC also in MCTP, Box 102-3, Folder 93, MSC; Terrell, "A Son of Howard Scales the Height," MCTP Container 31, Reel 22, LC; Terrell, "Milk From Peanuts, One of Many Discoveries," *Boston Sunday Globe*, March 31, 1927; Terrell, "Man Who Can Make 200 Products From Peanuts, "*Afro*, February 19, 1934; Terrell, "Ernest Just," January 9, 1936, in MCTP, Container 29, Reel 27, LC, also in MCTP, Box 102-3, Folder 65, MSC.

20. Terrell, *Colored Woman In A White World*, pp. 133-34; "Douglass Day," *New York Age*, February 18, 1897.
21. *National Notes*, August 1922, Container 23, Reel 17, LC.
22. United States Congress, Senate, *An Act to Erect a Monument to the Faithful Colored Mammies of the South*, Pub. L. 67-485, 67th Congress, 4th Session, 1923, S.F. 4119; Terrell, "Black Mammy Monument," partial text, n.d., MCTP, Box 102-3, Folder 48, MSC; Terrell to Editor of the *Afro-American*, MCTP, Container 38, Reel 27, LC; "Mammy Monument Would Perpetuate Woman's Shame Says Mrs. Terrell," *Boston Herald*, February 25, 1923.
23. United States Congress, House, Committee on Public Buildings and Grounds, *National Negro Memorial*, Hearings before the Committee on Public Buildings and Grounds, H.R. 1789, 17th Congress, 1st Session, 1928; United States Congress, House, *An Act to Create a Commission to Secure Plans and Designs for and to Erect a Memorial Building*, 17th Congress, 2nd Session.
24. Terrell, "Why I Wrote Phyllis Wheatley Pageant," MCTP, Container 25, Reel 18, LC. Also included is the program of the play presented at Booker T. Washington High School.
25. Terrell to *Washington Post*, May 14, 1927; Terrell to *Washington Evening Star*, January 9, 1927; Terrell to N. K. McGill, *Chicago Defender*, May 24, 1928, MCTP, Container 7, Reel 6, LC.
26. Terrell to *Harper's Magazine*, March 29, 1922; Terrell to Dr. Anson Phelps Stokes, January 23, 1929; MCTP, Container 8, Reel 5,6, LC.
27. In 1888, Tom Moss established a successful grocery store in Memphis, Tennessee. Black Memphisians withdrew their patronage from the white store for Moss's store. White businessmen, according to Terrell, "started a row," and Moss was thrown into jail, and lynched the following day. Outraged, Terrell and Frederick Douglass attempted unsuccessfully to get President Harrison to include in his State of the Union Message a recommendation for a law outlawing lynching. On Moss, see Terrell, *Colored Woman In A White World*, pp. 105, 108. Thomas Nelson Page, "The Lynching of Negroes, Its Cause and Its Prevention," *North American Review*, 178 (January 1904):33-48.
28. Terrell, "Lynching from a Negro's Point of View." *North American Review*, June 1904, p. 854 [page 168 in the present volume]. Terrell mentioned that the editor deleted two words from the original title of the article—Colored Woman—that were replaced with one word—Negro.
29. Ibid.
30. Ibid., p. 855 [169].

31. Terrell to Miss Reapplier, *Chicago Defender*, February 19, 1924; Terrell to Thomas Church, March 26, 1932; MCTP, Container 4, 7, Reel 3, 4, LC; Terrell, *Colored Woman In A White World*, p. 227.

32. Terrell, "A Plea for the White South by a Colored Woman," *Nineteenth Century and After*, 60 (July 1906):84 [page 254 in the present volume]; also in MCTP, Container 38, Reel 28, LC.

33. Terrell, "Peonage in the United States: The Convict Lease System and Chain Gangs," *Nineteenth Century and After*, 62 (August 1907):306 [page 255 in the present volume]; also in MCTP, Container 38, Reel 27, LC. Many were arrested for truancy—standing in one spot for a long time or going to sleep in the depot.

34. Ibid., p. 310 [260].

35. Terrell, *Colored Woman In A White World*, p. 228.

36. Terrell, "Aunt Dinah and Dilsey on Civilizing White Folks," n.d., MCTP, Box 102-3, Folder 51, MSC.

37. Terrell, "Apostasy of Aunt Ann," 1923, MCTP, Container 29, Reel 21, LC.

38. Terrell, "Betsy's Borrowed Baby," n.d., MCTP, Container 29, Reel 21, LC.

39. Terrell, "Not Always What They Seem," n.d., MCTP, Container 29, Reel 21, LC.

40. Terrell, "The Boulder," n.d., MCTP, Container 30, Reel 22, LC.

41. Terrell, "The Progress of Colored Women," Address delivered at the International Congress of Women, Berlin, Germany, 1904, MCTP, Container 29, Reel 21, LC, also quoted in Terrell, *Colored Woman In a White World*, pp. 203-04. For more information on women's conferences, see Terrell, *Colored Woman In a White World*, pp. 197-208, 213, 220, 329, 334, 351, 402, 403; MCTP, Containers 29, 31, Reels 21, 31, LC.

42. Terrell, *Colored Woman In a White World*, pp. 209, 348-49, 353, 405-06.

43. Programs of the Brooklyn Institute of Arts and Science, 1911-1913, MCTP, Container 38, Reel 28, LC.

44. Terrell, "The Mission of Meddlers," *Voice of the Negro*, 2 (August 1905): 567 [page 216 in the present volume].

45. Booker T. Washington to Whitefield McKinlay, November 6, 1901; McKinlay to Washington, November 13, 1901; Robert Terrell to Washington, November 10, 1901, Booker T. Washington Papers, hereinafter cited as BTWP, Correspondence File, 1900-1901, LC, also in Louis Harlan, ed., *Booker T. Washington Papers*, 8 vols. (Urbana: University of Illinois, 1972), vol. 6; 291, 318, 331.

46. Louis C. Gregory to Washington, January 15, 1904; Terrell to Washington, January 25, 1904, BTWP, LC, also in Harlan, *Booker T. Washington Papers*, vol. 7: 391; Robert Terrell, "Theodore Roosevelt," *Voice of the Negro*, August 1904, pp. 542-44.

47. Speech to New York Baptist Missionary Society, February 19, 1905, MCTP, Container 29, Reel 21, LC.

48. Washington to Terrell, February 20, 1906, MCTP, Container 4, Reel 4, LC; RHTP, LC.

49. Terrell, "Appeal to Colored Troops," *Washington Post*, November 18, 1906; Terrell, "The Disbanding of Colored Soldiers," *Voice of the Negro*, December 1906, pp. 554-58; Terrell, *Colored Woman In A White World*, pp. 268-78; Terrell, "A Sketch of Mingo Saunders," *Voice of the Negro*, March 1907, pp. 128-31, also in MCTP, Container 45, Reel 31, LC. For a full treatment of the Brownsville affair, see Ann Lane, *The Brownsville Affair: National Crisis and Black Reaction* (New York: Kennikat Press, 1971).

50. Washington to Robert Terrell, April 27, 1909, June 1909, RHTP, LC; Terrell, *Colored Woman In A White World*, pp. 193-94.

51. Interracial Committee of the District of Columbia, *The Color Line in Our Public Schools* (Washington, D.C., n.p., 1930), p. 12, MCTP, Container 22, Reel 15, LC.

52. Interracial Committee of the Washington Council of Social Agencies, MCTP, Container 22, Reel 15, LC.

53. Committee on Race Relations of the Washington Federation of Churches, MCTP, Container 40, Reel 28, LC.

54. Conference on the Betterment of Race Relations in Washington, D.C., Report of the Committee of Race Relations of the Washington Federation of Churches in *Interracial News*, 1932, MCTP, Container 40, Reel 28, LC.

55. Terrell, *Colored Woman In A White World*, pp. 131-32.

56. Amenia Conference, MCTP, Container 20, Reel 13, LC; Terrell, *Colored Woman in a White World*, p. 195.

57. Colonel Warner, Director of the War Risk Insurance Bureau to Terrell, October 16, 1917, MCTP, Container 5, Reel 4, LC; Terrell, *Colored Woman In A White World*, p. 252.

58. Terrell, *Colored Woman In A White World*, p. 256.

59. *Vardaman's Weekly*, n.d., MCTP, Container 47, Reel 32, LC. For newspaper cartoons, see MCTP, Container 47, Reel 32, LC.

60. Terrell, *Colored Woman In A White World*, p. 262.

61. Ibid., pp. 256-58; War Camp Community Service, MCTP, Container 26, Reel 19, LC.

62. Terrell, "Should An Amendment to the Constitution Allowing Women the Ballot Be Adopted?" handwritten, n.d., MCTP, Container 28, Reel 20, LC.

63. Terrell, "Women's Debt to Frederick Douglass," n.d., MCTP, container 32, Reel 24, LC; Terrell, "The Woman Suffrage Movement and Frederick Douglass," speech delivered at the 60th Anniversary of Seneca Falls Meeting, MCTP, Container 28, Reel 21, LC; "Remarks Made at Memorial Meeting Held in Hudson Theater, New York, March 25, 1904, MCTP, Box 102-3, Folder 71, MSC; and "I Remember Frederick Douglass," Ebony, 1953, pp. 73-80.

64. Harper, *History of Woman Suffrage*, p. 572; Terrell, *Colored Woman In A White World*, pp. 127-29,

65. Robert Terrell, "The New Era Woman" and "Our Women, " n. d., RHTP, LC.

66. Terrell, "The Justice of Woman Suffrage," *Crisis*, September 1912, p. 243; *Crisis*, 1912, *passim*.

67. Terrell, "Progress and Problems of Colored Women."

68. Terrell, *Colored Woman In A White World*, p. 147.
69. Quoted in Harper, *History of Woman Suffrage*, pp. 105-06.
70. Quoted in Terrell, "Justice of Woman Suffrage," speech delivered at Woman's Republican League, January 6, 1918, MCTP, Container 29, Reel 21, LC; Terrell, "What Colored Women Can and Should Do at the Polls," n.d. MCTF Container 21, Reel 14, LC.
71. Terrell to Walter White, March 14, 1919, MCTP, Container 5, Reel 4, LC.
72. Terrell, "Remarks Made at the Memorial for Susan B. Anthony," Hudson Theater, Washington, D.C., March 25, 1906, MCTP, Container 20, Reel 21, LC, Terrell, "Susan B. Anthony," *Voice of the Negro*, June 1906, pp. 411-16 [pages 231-238 in the present volume].
73. Terrell, *Colored Woman In A White World*, pp. 308-315; Terrell, "What Colored Women Can and Should Do at the Polls."
74. Terrell, "Mrs. Ruth McCormick Candidate for United States Senator," campaign speech, 1929, MTCP, Container 22, Reel 15, LC, also in Box 102-3, Folder 109, MSC.
75. Interview with M. Sammye Miller, January 12, 1980, Washington, D.C.
76. Diary, November 15, 17, 1905, MCTP, Container 1, Reel 1, LC.
77. Terrell, *Colored Woman In A White World*, p. 243.

CHAPTER FOUR

1. For information on the plight of blacks during the administration of President Franklin D. Roosevelt, see Richard M. Dalfiume, *Desegregation of United States Armed Forces: Fighting on Two Fronts, 1939-1953* (Columbia: University of Missouri Press, 1969); Herbert Garfinkel, *When Negroes March: The March on Washington Movement in the Organizational Politics for FEPC* (New York:The Free Press, 1959); Louis C. Kesselman, *The Social Politics of FEPC* (Chapel Hill: University of North Carolina Press, 1948); Malcolm Ross, *All Manner of Men* (New York; Reynal and Hitchcock Company, 1948); Louis Ruchames, *Race, Jobs and Politics* (New York: Columbia University Press, 1953); and Raymond Wolters, *Negroes and the Great Depression* (Connecticut; Greenwood Publishing Company, 1970).
2. United States Federal Emergency Relief Administration, "Color or Race of Persons in Relief Families," *Unemployment Relief Census*: October, 1933, United States Summary (Washington, D.C.:1934), pp. 7-9.
3. John Hope Franklin, *From Slavery to Freedom*, 4th edition (New York: Alfred A. Knopf, 1974), pp. 396-98.
4. Reveredy C. Ransom, "Why Vote for Roosevelt," *Crisis*, 39 (1932):343; Lester A. Walton, "Vote for Roosevelt," *Crisis* 29 (1932):394. For the defection of blacks from the Republican Party, see Rita Werner Gordon, "The Change in Political Alignment of Chicago's Negroes During the New Deal," *Journal of American History*, 56 (September 1959):584-603; Harold F. Gosnell, "The Negro Vote in Northern Cities," *National Municipal Review*, 30 (May

1941):264-67, 278; John M. Allswang, "The Chicago Negro Voter and the Democratic Consensus: A Case Study, 1918-1936," *Journal of Illinois State Historical Society*, 60 (Summer 1964):148-75; George Brown Tindall, *The Emergence of the New South, 1913-1945* (Baton Rouge: Louisiana State University Press, 1967).

5. Terrell, "Why Colored People Should Vote Republican," August 1932, MCTP, Container 30, Reel 22, LC.

6. Ibid.

7. *Norfolk Journal and Guide*, April 30, 1932; Terrell to Thomas Church, May 1, 1932, MCTP, Container 9, Reel 7, LC.

8. Joel Spingarn to Terrell, December 22, 1932, MCTP, Container 9, Reel 7, LC.

9. S.P. Fullwinger, *Mind and Mood of Black America: Twentieth Century Thought* (Chicago: Dorsey Press, 1969), p. 92. For more information on Robert Park's theories, see Gunnar Myrdal, *The American Dilemma: The Negro Problem in Modern Democracy* (New York: Harper and Row, 1944), p. 1036; E. Franklin Frazier, "Sociological Theory and Race Relations," *American Sociological Review*, June 1947, pp. 265-71; Oliver C. Cox, "The Racial Theories of Robert E. Park and Ruth Benedict," *Journal of Negro Education*, 13 (Winter 1944):452-63.

10. E. Franklin Frazier, "The Status of the Negro in the American Social Order," *Journal of Negro Education*, 5 (July 1935):307.

11. Ralph Bunche, *A World View of Race* (Washington, D.C.: The Associates in Negro Folk Education, 1936), pp. 84-85.

12. Ralph Bunche, "Critical Analysis of the Tactics and programs Of Minority Groups," *Journal of Negro Education*, 4 (July 1935):320.

13. Ralph Bunche, "Critique of New Deal Social Planning as It Affects Negroes," *Journal of Negro Education*, 5 (January 1936):59.

14. The proceedings of the Howard University Conference are located in the MSC. The conference was sponsored by the Social Science Division of the University and the Joint Committee on National Recovery. Twenty-two major black organizations participated in this short-lived attempt to alleviate discriminatory treatment of blacks during the depression.

15. On February 14, 15, 16, 1936, Bunche convened the National Negro Congress (NNC) in Chicago. Harold Cruse, who has written on black intellectuals, viewed the NNC as a major rival of the NAACP. This probably explains why many of the older race proponents such as Kelly Miller, Mary Church Terrell, and W. E. B. Du Bois were conspicuously absent. The NNC was attended by 800 delegates representing 585 organizations. Their extensive demands included stronger federal guarantees against racial discrimination in every area affecting blacks and economic and social reforms. A. Philip Randolph, President of the National Brotherhood of Sleeping Car Porters, was elected president. Neither Randolph nor Bunche and Davis, the chief architects of the NNC, were successful in creating grassroots black and white working class solidarity. For more information on the NNC, see Eleanor Ryan, "Toward a National Negro Congress," *New Masses*, 4 (June 1935):14-15; Herbert Garfinkel, *When Negroes March*, pp. 107-159; Harold Cruse, *The Crisis of the Negro Intellectual* (New

York: William Morrow and Company, 1967), pp. 171-80; Wolters, *The Negro and the Great Depression*, pp. 353-59; Wilson Record, *The Negro and the Communist Party* (Chapel Hill: University of North Carolina Press, 1951) and *Race and Radicalism: The NAACP and the Communist Party* (New York: Cornell University Press, 1964) and Lewis A. Howe and Irving Coser, *The American Communist Party: A Critical History, 1919-1957* (Boston: Beacon Press, 1957).

16. Kelly Miller, "The Negro Radical Exposed by Kelly Miller," *Crisis*, 15 (September 15, 1934):38.

17. Kelly Miller, "Roosevelt and the Negro in the Present," *Boston Chronicle*, December 9, 1933; Kelly Miller, "Discusses the Election and Lauds the New Deal Program," *Washington Tribune*, November 10, 1934.

18. Joint Committee on Economic Recovery, "Additions to the Policy of the Joint Committee on National Recovery," Washington, D.C., 1933, MCTP, Container 22, Reel 15, LC.

19. Ibid.

20. Conference on the Participation of Negro Women and Children in Federal Welfare Programs, 1938, MCTP, Container 20, Reel 14, LC.

21. Terrell, *A Colored Woman In A White World* (New York: Ransdell Company, 1940), p. 414.

22. Ibid., p. 415.

23. Terrell To Thomas Church, 1933, MCTP, Container 3, Reel 3, LC.

24. William Barbour, Fleming H. Revell Company, to Terrell, March 1, 1939, MCTP, Container 11, Reel 8, LC. For other rejections, see Katherine Key, Secretary to Mr. Latham, Vice-President of MacMillan Company, to Terrell, December 15, 1939; Little, Brown and Company to Terrell, March 26, 1935, April 9, 1935; H. S. Latham, Macmillan Company, to Terrell, January 10, 1940, MCTP, Container 11, Reel 8, LC.

25. Doubleday and Company to Terrell, 1945, MCTP, Container 13, Reel 9, LC.

26. Terrell, *Colored Woman In A White World*, preface.

27. Ibid., introduction.

28. Drafts of Manuscript, MCTP, Containers 36, 37, Reels 13, 14 LC.

29. Gertrude Martin, "Review of Terrell's Autobiography," *Michigan Chronicle*, January 11, 1941, MCTP, Container 47, Reel 32, LC; Charles Wesley, "Negro Auto-biography and History," *Journal of Negro Education*, 10 (April 1945):263; Robert D. Franklin, "Bob Church's Daughter Relates Experiences," *Commercial Appeal*, Memphis, August 31, 1941.

30. Adam Clayton Powell, Jr., "As the Negro Faces War," *Pittsburgh Courier* December 30, 1939; John P. Davis, "Negro in War at Home," *Crisis*, September 9, 1939; Ralph Bunche, "The Role of University in Political Orientation of Negro Youth," *Journal of Negro Education*, 9 (October 1940):579; Diary Entry, September 14, 1939, MCTP, Container 2, Reel 2, LC.

31. Terrell to A. Phillip Randolph, June 20, 1941, MCTP, Container 12, Reel 9, LC. For more information on the March on Washington Movement, see Herbert Garfinkel, *When Negroes March*.

32. District of Columbia Advisory Committee on Woman's Participation in the New York World's Fair, MCTP, Container 27, Reel 20, LC; Terrell, "Scottsboro Case," MCTP, Box 102-3, Folder 110-111, MSC. Terrell was hospitalized at the Battle Creek Sanitarium in Battle Creek, Michigan and on January 11, 1942, she was hospitalized at the Episcopal Ear, Eye and Nose Hospital in Washington, D.C.

33. For obituaries of Robert H. Terrell, see *Washington Post*, *Chicago Defender*, *Pittsburgh Courier*, *Afro-American*, and *Washington Tribune*, September 14, 1944; Diary Entry, 1941-1946, MCTP, Container 2, Reel 2, LC.

34. Richard Dalfiume, "Forgotten Years of Negro Revolution" in Bernard Sternsher, *The Negro in Depression and War, 1930-1945* (Chicago; Quadrangle Books, 1966), p. 299; Adelaide Cronwell Hill, *A Propos of Africa: Sentiments of Negro Americans* (London: Cass, 1969); Kenneth B. Clark and Talcot Parsons, eds., *The Negro American* (Boston: Houghton Mifflin Co., 1965); Louis Rhodes, "Black Symbolism: A Paradigm on the Nature and Development of Black Consciousness" (Ph.D. dissertation, University of Nebraska at Lincoln, 1970); S. Rudolph Martin, Jr., "A New Mind: Changing Black Consciousness, 1950-1970" (Ph.D. dissertation, Washington State University, 1970).

35. Terrell, "No Capital Gains," *Time*, July 14, 1919, p. 39.

36. "University Women Led in Race Bias by D.C.,Judge," Washington *Afro-American*, July 10, 1949.

37. "300 of AAUW Ask Court Ban on Racial Bias," *Chicago Defender*, July 30, 1948; "Action of AAUW," *New York Times*, July 2, 1949; "Courts Ban Mrs. Terrell From University Women Membership," Washington *Afro-American*, June 20, 1948; "Club Race Bias Gets O.K. from U.S. Court," *Chicago Defender*, January 25, 1949,

38. AAUW By-Laws and Resolution adopted, MCTP, Container 20, Reel 13, LC; "AAUW Reaffirms Membership Policy," *Chicago Defender*, December 11, 1949; "Washington Branch Secedes," *Time*, June 24, 1949; "AAUW's Washington Branch Reinstates Three Negro Women," *Ohio Daily Express*, August 1949.

39. Equal Rights Amendment, Container 47, Reel 32, LC.

40. National Committee to Free Rosa Ingram and Her Sons, "Save the Ingrams," pamphlet, n.d., MCTP, Container 49, Reel 33, LC.

41. Petition presented to the Human Rights Committee of the Social and Economic Council of the United Nations and The General Assembly, n.d., MCTP, Container 49, Reel 33, LC.

42. For awards and citations, see MCTP, Container 51, Reel 34, LC.

CHAPTER FIVE

1. For an examination of the Second Reconstruction, see C. Vann Woodward, *The Strange Career of Jim Crow* (New York: Oxford University Press, 1974), pp. 8-10, 122-47, 209-10.
2. John Hope Franklin, *From Slavery to Freedom* (New York: Alfred A. Knopf, 1974), pp. 420-21; Alfred H. Kelly, *The American Constitution* (New York: W. W. Norton, 1948), p. 848. In the Sweatt case, the court maintained that the Law School of the University of Texas must admit blacks in spite of the fact that the state had a separate law school for blacks.
3. On the civil rights record of the Truman administration, see Executive Order 9808, 11 Federal Register 14153 (1947); *Congressional Record*, 80th Congress, 2nd Session (1948), p. 929; United States Commission on Civil Rights, *Freedom to the Free* (Washington, D.C.: Government Printing Office, 1963), pp. 122-55; United States Commission on Civil Rights, "The Negro in the Armed Service," *Civil Rights '63* (Washington, D.C.: Government Printing Office, 1963), pp. 169-224. On civil rights activities during the Eisenhower administration, see Sherman Adams, *Firsthand Report: The Story of the Eisenhower Administration* (New York: Harper and Brothers, 1961), p. 333; Robert Branyan, *The Eisenhower Administration, 1953-61* (New York: Random House, 1971), pp. 103, 216, 496, 611, 619, 1049, 1050, 1051, 1957-72, 1357; Dwight David Eisenhower, *Mandate for Change, 1953-56* (New York: Doubleday and Company, 1967), pp. 234-36, 287, 293, 563.
4. *Pittsburgh Courier*, December 9, 1944.
5. District of Columbia Statutes and Codes, 1890, LC. The 1872 and 1873 laws were enacted soon after the passage of the Thirteenth and Fourteenth Amendments. They assured the newly-freed slave that he stood free and equal before the law. The District Legislative Assembly form of government was created in 1871 and consisted of a Governor, Secretary, Board of Public Works, Board of Health, and a Legislative Council all appointed by the president of the United States, with the concurrence of the United States Senate.
6. Mary Church Terrell, *A Colored Woman In A White World* (New York: Ransdell Company, 1940), pp. 435-36.
7. Committee for the Enforcement of the D.C. Anti-Discrimination Laws, *Here are the Facts*, leaflet, n.d., MCTP, Container 15, Reel 10, LC. The seven lawyers of the National Lawyers' Guild were: Joseph Forer, Chairman of the District Affairs Committee, former Municipal Court Judge James A. Cobb, Daniel Crystal, Margaret A. Haywood, Charles H. Houston, a black, J. H. Krug, and Herbert A. Thatcher. In 1874, Congress replaced the District Legislative Assembly form of government with a Commission of three members appointed by the president with the concurrence of the senate. In 1878, this form of government was made permanent.
8. Terrell, *Colored Woman In A White World*, p. 436. For more information on the genesis of the CCEAD, see Terrell's Radio Broadcast, WOOK, April 6,

1954, MCTP, Container 20, Reel 14, LC and Committee's Memorandums, January 7, 1952, Box 102-12, Folder 230, MSC.

9. Minutes of the first meeting of the CCEAD, September, 1949, MCTP, Container 20, Reel 14, LC; Gladys Sheppard, *Mary Church Terrell—Respectable Person* (Maryland: Human Relations Press, 1959), pp. 41-42.

10. Ibid.; Terrell, *Colored Woman In A White World*, p. 436.

11. Clark King to Terrell, February 21, 1950, MCTP, Container 20, Reel 14, LC.

12. *Washington Star*, February 28, 1950; *Pittsburgh Courier*, March 13, 1950, April, 1950; Terrell, *Colored Woman In A White World*, pp. 455-57.

13. Brief of the Coordinating Committee for the Enforcement of D.C. Anti-Discrimination Laws, Amicus Curiae, MCTP, Container 20, Reel 14, LC.

14. Ibid.; Minutes of the CCEAD, July 10, 1950.

15. Ibid.

16. Brief of the CCEAD.

17. Ibid.

18. Terrell, *Colored Woman In A White World*, pp. 439-40; Terrell's Radio Broadcast, WOOK.

19. Ibid; *Chicago Defender*, *Washington Post*, *Pittsburgh Courier*, January 14, 15, 1951; Terrell, Victory at Kresge, Letter to Friends, typescript, January 15, 1951, MCTP, Container 20, Reel 14, LC, also in Box 102-12, Folder 233, MSC.

20. *Washington Post*, February 19, 1951.

21. Ibid.; Adolph Schalk, "Negroes, Restaurants, and Washington, D.C.," *Catholic World*, 174 (January 1952):279; *Washington Star*, February 22, 1951.

22. *Pittsburgh Courier*, May 24, 25, 26, 1951; Address to Metropolitan Baptist Church, Washington, D.C., June 25, 1951, MCTP, Container 20, Reel 14, LC. It is interesting to note that a split decision of 2-1 upheld the validity of a civil rights statute that barred racial discrimination in the District of Columbia's restaurants. Associate Judges Clagett and Jones took the view that the 1872 act had been repealed by implication by the 1873 act. They went on to rule, however, that the 1873 act was valid. Dissenter Associate Judge Hood held that the Legislative Assembly could not enact police regulations. Since it was his opinion that the civil rights laws in question, both the 1872 and 1873 acts, could be classified as police regulations, he ruled that they were both invalid from the very beginning, and that therefore the dismissal of the prosecution by the trial court should be affirmed.

23. For slogans used on banners, see MCTP, Container 20, Reel 14, LC and Sheppard, *Mary Church Terrell—Respectable Person*, p. 68.

24. Leaflets, n.d., MCTP, Container 20, Reel 14, LC.

25. Terrell, *Colored Woman In A White World*, p. 442; Brief of CCEAD; Sheppard, *Mary Church Terrell—Respectable Person*, p. 71.

26. Ibid.

27. North Carolina Mutual Life Insurance Company of Durham, North Carolina, to Terrell, August 3, 1951; Thomas Company, Alexandria, Virginia, to Terrell, July 8, 1951; United States Ambassador in Monrovia, Liberia, to CCEAD, July 12, 1951, MCTP, Container 16, Reel 11, LC.

28. "Psychologists Vote to Boycott D.C. Until Segregation Is Ended," *Washington Post*, *New York Times*, September 1, 1952; Terrell to Editor of *New York Times*, September 10, 1952.

29. *Washington Post, Chicago Defender*, January 17, 1952.

30. Slogans on banners and leaflets, MCTP, Container 20, Reel 14, LC; Sheppard, *Mary Church Terrell—Respectable Person*, p. 70.

31. Ibid.

32. *Washington Post, Pittsburgh Courier, Washington Star*, September 4, 1952, also in MCTP, Box 102-12, Folder 231, 234, MSC.

33. "Sister of Bob Church Thinks Truman Did More for Negroes than any Other President," *Afro-American*, September 1, 1952.

34. For copies of briefs filed by organizations, see MCTP, Containers 17, 18, Reels 11, 12, LC; *Washington Star*, January 2, 1953, for Eisenhower's comments.

35. *Chicago Defender, Washington Post, Afro-American*, January 22, 1953.

36. Handbill, n.d., MCTP, Container 20, Reel 14, LC. Sheppard, *Mary Church Terrell—Respectable Person*, p. 86.

37. Terrell, *A Colored Woman In A White World*, p. 444; Sheppard, *Mary Church Terrell—Respectable Person*, p. 83.

38. Celebration of Terrell's Life and Works, WOOK Radio Broadcast, n.d., MCTP, Container 20, Reel 14, LC; Former Washingtonian to Terrell, *ca.* May 28, 1953, MCTP, Container 17, Reel 12, LC.

39. Thinking Americans to Terrell, n.d., MCTP, Container 17, Reel 12, LC. Terrell received a citation from the D.C. Branch of the NAACP for her desegregation leadership; Utility Club, Inc., named her Utility Woman of the Year; Barristers Wives of Washington, D.C., selected her woman of achievement; National Council of Negro Women, Inc., named her Woman of the Year; Academy of Political Science made her a life member; National Newspaper Publishers Association awarded her the John B. Russwurm citation; Woman League of Howard University honored her as Woman of the Year; and Omega Psi Phi Fraternity recognized her desegregation efforts.

40. Quoted in "Let's Take It in Stride," *Pittsburgh Courier*, June 13, 1953, July 14, 1953; *Washington Daily News*, June 9, 1953; "Lost Laws," *New Republic*, June 22, 1953, p. 7; *Washington Evening Star*, June 9, 1953; *Washington Afro-American*, June 13, 1953; *Washington Post*, March 15, 1954. The Supreme Court decision was unanimous.

41. *Washington Afro-American*, June 9, 1953, also in MCTP Box 102-12, Folder 236, MSC.

42. *Washington Evening Star*, October 9, 1953; Terrell's Testimonial, MCTP, Container 20, Reel 14, LC.

43. Ibid.

44. Script from "American All" Broadcast, WOOK Radio Station, 90th Birthday of Mrs. Terrell, MCTP, Container 30, Reel 22, LC.

CHAPTER SIX

1. Highland Beach is located on the Chesapeake, near Annapolis. The settlement was founded by the family of Frederick Douglass.
2. "1st Lady in Tribute to Mary Church Terrell," *Washington Post*, July 25, 1954.
3. *Washington Evening Star*, July 29, 1954.
4. Delta Creed, MCTP, Container 21, Reel 14, LC.

Bibliography

I. Primary Sources

Charlotte Hawkins Brown Papers. Arthur and Elizabeth Schlesinger Library. Radcliffe College. Cambridge, Massachusetts.

Interracial Committee for the District of Columbia Papers. Library of Congress. Washington, D.C.

National American Woman Suffrage Association Collection. Library of Congress. Washington D.C.

National Association for the Advancement of Colored People Papers. Library of Congress, Washington, D.C.

National Association of Colored Women Files, 1890-1910. National Association of Colored Women Headquarters. Washington, D.C.

Mary Church Terrell Papers. Library of Congress. Washington, D.C.

Mary Church Terrell Papers. Moorland Spingarn Collection. Howard University. Washington, D.C.

Robert H. Terrell Papers. Library of Congress. Washington, D.C.

Booker T. Washington Papers. Library of Congress. Washington, D.C.

Louis Harlan, ed. *Booker T. Washington Papers*. 8 vols. Urbana: University of Illinois, 1972.

Documents and Reports

Conference on the Betterment of Race Relations in Washington, D.C. *Report of Committee of Race Relations of the Washington Federation of Churches*. Washington, D.C. : n.p., 1932.

Interracial Committee of the District of Columbia. *The Color Line in Our Public Schools*. Washington, D.C.: n.p., 1930.

United States Bureau of the Census. *Eighth Census of the United States: 1860. Population, I*. Washington, D.C.: Government Printing Office, 1863.

United States Bureau of the Census. *Eleventh Census of the United States: 1890. Population, I*. Washington, D.C.: Government Printing Office, 1893.

United States Bureau of the Census. *Negro Population 1790-1915*. Washington, D.C.: Government Printing Office, 1918.

United States Bureau of the Census. *Ninth Census of the United States: 1870. Statistics of Population*. Washington, D.C.: Government Printing Office, 1872.

United States Commission on Civil Rights. *Freedom to the Free*. Washington, D.C.: Government Printing Office, 1963.

United States Commission on Civil Rights. "The Negro in the Armed Forces." *Civil Rights '63*. Washington, D.C.: Government Printing Office, 1963.

United States Congress. House. *An Act to Create a Commission to Secure Plans and Designs for and to Erect a Memorial Building*. 17th Congress, 2nd Session, 1928.

United States Congress. House. *The Report of Memphis Riots and Massacres*. H. Doc. 101, 39th Congress, 1st Session, 1866.

United States Congress. Senate. *An Act to Erect a Monument to the Faithful Colored Mammies of the South*. Pub, L. 67-485. 67th Congress, 4th Session, 1923.

United States Federal Emergency Relief Administration. *Color or Race of Persons in Relief Families. Unemployment Relief Census*. October 1933. Washington, D.C.: Government Printing Company, 1934.

Publications of Mary Church Terrell

Book

A Colored Woman In A White World. New York: Ransdell Company, 1940.

Articles

"Christmas at the White House." *Voice of the Negro*. December 1904, pp. 593-600.

"Club Work of Colored Women." *Southern Workman*. August 8, 1901, pp. 435-38.

"The Disbanding of the Colored Soldiers." *Voice of the Negro*. December 1906, pp. 554-58.

"Duty of the National Association of Colored Women to the Race. " *AME Church Review*. January 1900, pp. 340-54.

"Graduates and Former Students of Washington Colored High School." *Voice of the Negro.* June 1904, pp. 221-27.

"I Remember Frederick Douglass." *Ebony*, 1953, pp. 73-80.

"The International Congress of Women." *Voice of the Negro.* December 1904, pp. 454-61.

"An Interview with W. T. Stead on the Race Problem." *Voice of the Negro.* July 1907, pp. 327-30.

"Lynching from a Negro's Point of View." *North American Review*, 178 (June 1904):853-68.

"The Mission of Meddlers." *Voice of the Negro.* August 1905, pp. 566-68.

"The National Association of Colored Women." *Voice of the Negro.* January 1906, pp. 194-97.

"Needed: Women Lawyers." *Negro Digest.* September 1943, pp. 57-59.

"Paul Laurence Dunbar." *Voice of the Negro.* April 1906, pp. 271-77.

"Peonage in United States: The Convict Lease System and the Chain Gangs." *Nineteenth Century*, 62 (August 1907):306-22.

"Phyllis Wheatley—An African Genius." *The Baha'i Magazine: Star of the West.* (Vol. 19, No. 7) October 1928, pp. 221-223.

"A Plea for the White South by A Coloured Woman." *Nineteenth Century* . July 1906, pp. 70-84.

"The Progress of Colored Women." *Voice of the Negro.* July 1904, pp. 291-94.

"Purity and the Negro." *The Light.* June 1905, pp. 19-25.

"Service Which Should be Rendered the South." *Voice of the Negro.* February 1905, pp. 182-86.

"A Sketch of Mingo Saunders." *Voice of the Negro.* March 1907, pp. 128-31.

"Social Functions During Inauguration Week." *Voice of the Negro.* April 1905, pp. 237-42.

"Society Among the Colored People of Washington." *Voice of the Negro.* April 1904, pp. 150-56.

"Susan B. Anthony, the Abolitionist" *Voice of the Negro.* June 1906, pp. 411-16.

"Samuel Coleridge-Taylor." *Voice of the Negro.* January 1905, pp. 665-69.

"The Washington Conservatory of Music for Colored People." *Voice of the Negro.* November 1904, pp. 525-30.

"What It Means to Be Colored in the Capital of the United States." *Independent.* January 24, 1907, pp. 181-86.

Newspapers

Afro-American, Baltimore, 1934, 1944, 1946, 1948, 1952, 1953.
Afro-American, Washington, D.C., 1936, 1938, 1948-1954.
Argus, Memphis, 1866.
Boston Chronicle, 1933.
Boston Herald, 1923.
Boston Sunday Globe, 1927.
Chicago Defender, 1924, 1927, 1928, 1929, 1946, 1949, 1951-1953.
Commercial, Memphis, 1866.
Daily News, Chicago, 1899.
The Freeman (An Illustrated Colored Paper), 1898.
Leslie Weekly, 1900.
Memphis Evening Scimitar, 1891.
Nashville Dispatch, 1866.
New York Age, 1897, 1900.
New York Times, 1952.
Norfolk Journal and Guide, 1932.
Ohio Daily Express, 1949.
Pittsburgh Courier, 1939, 1944, 1950.
Times-Herald, Chicago, 1899.
Washington Daily News, 1899, 1944, 1950, 1952, 1953.
Washington Evening Star, 1899, 1927, 1950, 1953.
Washington Post, 1906, 1907, 1944, 1951, 1952, 1954.

Interviews

Jacob Harris, Durham, North Carolina, December 13, 1979.
M. Sammye Miller, Washington, D.C., January 15, 1980.

II. SECONDARY SOURCES

Reference Tools

Block, Maxine, ed. *Current Biography*. New York: H. W. Wilson Company, 1940.

Davis, Lenwood G. *The Black Woman in American Society: A Selected Annotated Bibliography*. Massachusetts: G. K. Hall and Company 1975.

Fleming, James G., and Burckel, Christian E., eds. *Who's Who in Colored America, 1950*. Yonkers-on-Hudson, New York: Christian E. Burckel and Associates, 1950.

Poloski, Harry A. *Negro Almanac*. New York: Bellwether Publishing Company, 1967.

Work, Monroe, ed. *Negro Yearbook: An Annual Encyclopedia of the Negro*. Tuskegee, Alabama: Negro Yearbook Publishing Company, 1912.

Yenser, Thomas, ed. *Who's Who in Colored America: A Biographical Dictionary of Notable Living Persons*. Washington, D.C.

Dissertations

Hooper, Edward. "Memphis, Tennessee: Federal Occupation and Reconstruction." Ph.D. Dissertation. University of North Carolina at Chapel Hill, 1957.

Martin, S. Rudolph, Jr. "A New Mind: Changing Black Consciousness, 1950-1970." Ph.D. Dissertation. Washington, State University, 1974.

Rhodes, Louis. "Black Symbolism: a Paradigm on the Nature and Development of Black Consciousness." Ph.D. Dissertation. University of Nebraska at Lincoln, 1970.

Theses

Fields, Emma J. "The Woman's Club Movement, 1877-1900." M.A. Thesis. Howard University. Washington, D.C., 1948.

Price, Margaret Nell. "The Development of Leadership by Southern Women Through Clubs and Organizations." M.A. Thesis. University of North Carolina at Chapel Hill, 1948.

Books

Adams, Russell L. *Great Negroes, Past and Present*. Chicago: Afro-American Publishing Company, 1963.

Adams, Sherman. *Firsthand Report: The Story of Eisenhower Administration*. New York: Harper and Brothers, 1961.

Allen, Robert S., and Pearson, Drew. *Washington Merry-Go- Round*. New York: H. Liveright, Inc., 1931.

Baker, Ray Stannard. *Following the Color Line: American Negro Citizenship in the Progressive Era*. New York: Harper and Row, 1964.

Banner, Lois. *The American Woman from 1900 to the First World War: A Profile of Women in Modern America*. New York: Harper and Row, 1964.

Bardolph, Richard. *The Negro Vanguard*. New York: Vintage Books, 1959.

Barton, Rebecca Chalmers. *Witnesses for Freedom: Negro Americans in Autobiography*. New York: Harper and Row, 1948.

Beauvoir, Simone de. *The Second Sex*. New York: Bantam Books, 1961.

Bennett, Lerone. *Before The Mayflower: A History of the Negro in America, 1619-1964*. Chicago: Johnson Publishing Company, 1969.

Berlin, Ira. *Slaves Without Masters: The Free Negro in the Antebellum South*. New York: Pantheon Books, 1975.

Berman, William C. *The Politics of Civil Rights of Truman Administration*. Columbus, Ohio State University, 1970.

Berstein, Barton, ed. *Politics and Policies of Truman Administration*. Chicago: Quadrangle Books, 1971.

Birmingham, Stephen. *Certain People: America's Black Elite*. Boston: Little, Brown and Company, 1971.

Bontemps, Arna Wendell. *100 Years of Negro Freedom*. New York: Dodd, Mead, 1961.

Branyan, Robert. *The Eisenhower Administration, 1953-61*. New York: Random House, 1971.

Brisbane, Robert H. *The Black Vanguard: Origin of the Negro Social Revolution, 1900-1960*. Valley Forge: Hudron Press, 1970.

Broderick, Francis L. *W. E. B. Du Bois: A Negro Leader in Time of Crisis*. Stanford: Stanford University Press, 1959.

Brown, Charlotte Hawkins. *The Correct Thing to Do, to Say, to Wear*. Boston: The Christopher Publishing House, 1941.

Bunche, Ralph. *A World View of Race*. Washington, D.C.: The Associates in Negro Folk Education, 1936.

_____. *The Political Status of the Negro in the Age of FDR*. Chicago: University of Chicago Press, 1973.

Butterfield, Stephen. *Black Autobiography in America*. Amherst: University of Massachusetts Press, 1974.

Cade, Toni, ed. *The Black Woman: An Anthology*. New York: New American Library, Mentor Books, 1970.

Capers, Gerald. *The Biography of a River Town, Memphis: Its Heroic Age*. Chapel Hill: University of North Carolina Press, 1939.

Chafe, William. *The American Woman: Her Changing Social, Economic, and Political Role, 1920-1970*. New York: Oxford University Press, 1972.

_____. *Women and Equality: Changing Patterns in American Culture*. New York: Oxford University Press, 1977.

Church, Annette E., and Church, Robert. *The Robert R. Churches of Memphis: A Father and Son Who Achieved In Spite of Race*. Memphis: A. E. Church, 1974.

Clark, Kenneth B., and Talcott Parsons, eds., *The Negro American*. Boston: Houghton, Mifflin Company, 1965.

Commager, Henry Steele. *The American Mind: An Interpretation of American Thought and Character Since the 1880s*. New Haven: Yale University Press, 1950.

Conrad, Earl, *Jim Crow America*. New York: Duell, Sloan, and Pearce, 1947.

Crogman, William H., and Gibson, John W. *Progress of a Race, or the Remarkable Advancement of the Colored American*. Illinois: J. Nichols and Company, 1902.

Cruse, Harold. *The Crisis of the Negro Intellectual*. New York: William Morrow and Company, 1967.

Croly, Jennie June. *The History of the Woman's Club Movement in America*. New York: Henry G. Allen and Company, 1898.

Dabney, Lillian Gertrude. *The History of Schools for Negroes in the District of Columbia, 1807-1947*. Washington, D.C.: Catholic University of America, 1949.

Dalfiume, Richard M. *Desegregation of United States Armed Forces: Fighting on Two Fronts, 1939-1953*. Columbia: University of Missouri Press, 1969.

Dannett, Sylvia. *Profiles of Negro Womanhood*. Yonkers, New York: Educational Heritage, 1964.

Davis, Elizabeth. *Lifting As We Climb*. Chicago: Race Relations Press, 1933.

_____. *The Story of the Illinois Federation*. Chicago: n.p., 1922.

Douglas, Ann. *The Feminization of American Culture*. New York: Alfred A. Knopf, 1977.

Du Bois, W. E. B. *Dusk of Dawn: An Essay Toward an Autobiography of a Race Concept*. New York: Schocken Books, 1940.

_____. *Efforts for Social Betterment Among Negroes*. Atlanta: Atlanta University Press, no. 14, 1909.

_____. *Souls of Black Folk: Essays and Sketches*. New York: American Library, 1903.

Eisenhower, Dwight David. *Mandate for Change, 1953-56*. New York: Doubleday and Company, 1963.

Fairchild, James H. *Oberlin: The Colony and College, 1833-1883*. Oberlin: E. J. Goodrich, 1883.

Filene, Peter G. *Him/Her/Self: Sex Roles in Modern America*. New York: Harcourt Brace Jovanovich, 1974.

Fletcher, Robert. *A History of Oberlin College From Its Foundation Through the Civil War*, 2 vols. Oberlin: Oberlin College, 1943.

Flexner, Eleanor. *Century of Struggle, The Woman's Rights Movement in the United States*. Cambridge, Mass.: Harvard University Press, The Belknap Press, 1959.

Franklin, John Hope. *From Slavery to Freedom*. New York: Alfred A. Knopf, 1974.

_____. *Reconstruction: After the Civil War*. Chicago: University of Chicago Press, 1961.

Frazier, Edward Franklin. *Black Bourgeoisie*. New York: The Free Press, 1965.

_____. *The Negro in the United States*. Chicago: University of Chicago Press, 1961.

Fullwinder, S. F. *The Mind and Mood of Black America: Twentieth Century Thought*. Chicago, Illinois: Dorsey Press, 1969.

Garfinkel, Herbert. *When Negroes March: The March on Washington in the Organizational Politics for the FEPC*. New York: The Free Press, 1959.

Gibson, John W., and Crogman, William H. *Progress of Race, or the Remarkable Advancement of the Colored American*. Illinois: J. L. Nichols and Company, 1969.

Giedon, Siegfred. *Mechanization Takes Command*. New York: Norton Press, 1969.

Glasgow, Ellen. *The Woman Within*. New York: Harcourt, Brace, 1954.

Green, Constance. *The Secret City: A History of Race Relations in the Nation's Capital*. Princeton: Princeton University Press, 1969.

Green, Lorenzo. *The Employment of Negroes in District of Columbia*. Washington, D.C.: The Association for the Study of Negro Life and History, 1931.

Harley, Sharon, and Terborg-Penn, Rosalyn, eds. *The Afro-American Woman: Struggles and Images*. New York: National University Publication, 1978.

Harper, Ida Husted, ed. *History of Woman Suffrage, 1883-1900*. New York: Arno Press, New York Times, 1969.

Harris, Abram L., and Sterling D. Spero *The Black Worker: The Negro and the Labor Movement*. New York: Columbia University Press, 1931.

Haynes, George E. *Toward Interracial Cooperation*. New York: Federation Council of Churches, 1926.

Hays, Samuel P. *The Response to Industrialism, 1885-1914*. Chicago: University of Chicago Press, 1957.

Hill, Adelaide Cronwell. *A Propos of Africa: Sentiments of Negro Americans*. London: Cass, 1969.

Hofstadter, Richard. *Age of Reform*. New York: Alfred A. Knopf, 1955.

Howe, Irving, and Coser, Lewis A. *The American Communist Party: A Critical History, 1919-1957*. Boston: Beacon Press, 1957.

Huggins, Nathan, et al. *Key Issues in the Afro-American Experience*. 2 vols. New York: Harcourt, Brace, Jovanovich, 1971.

Ingle, Edward. *The Negro in the District of Columbia*. Baltimore: Johns Hopkins Press, 1893.

Johnson, Charles S. *A Preface to Racial Understanding*. New York: Friendship Press, 1936.

_____. *Patterns of Negro Segregation*. New York: Harper and Brothers Publishers, 1943.

_____. *The Negro College Graduate*. Chapel Hill: University of North Carolina Press, 1938.

_____. *Race Relations: Adjustment of Whites and Negroes in the United States*. Lexington, Mass.: D. C. Heath and Company, 1934.

_____. *To Stem This Tide: A Survey of Racial Tension Areas in the United States*. Boston: The Pilgrim Press, 1943.

Jones, William Henry. *The Housing of Negroes in Washington, D.C.: A Study in Human Ecology*. Washington, D.C.: Howard University Press, 1929.

Jordan, Winthrop. *White Over Black: American Attitudes Toward the Negro, 1550-1812*. Baltimore: Penguin, 1969.

Keating, John M. *History of the City of Memphis and Shelby County, Tennessee*. New York: D. Mason and Company, 1888.

Kellogg, Charles F. *NAACP: A History of the NAACP*. Baltimore: Johns Hopkins University Press, 1967.

Kelly, Alfred H. *The American Constitution*. New York: W. W. Norton and Company, 1948.

Kesselman, Louis C. *The Social Politics of FEPC*. Chapel Hill: University of North Carolina Press, 1948.

Kraditor, Aileen. *The Ideas of the Women's Suffrage Movement, 1890-1920*. New York: Anchor Books, Doubleday and Company, 1971.

Ladner, Joyce A. *A Tomorrow's Tomorrow: The Black Woman*. New York: Doubleday, 1971.

Lamon, Lester C. *Black Tennesseans, 1900-1930*. Knoxville: University of Tennessee Press, 1977.

Lane, Anne. *The Brownsville Affair: National Crisis and Black Reaction*. New York: Kennikat Press, 1971.

Lasch, Christopher. *The Social Thought of Jane Addams*. Indianapolis: Bobbs-Merrill Company, 1965.

Leuchtenburg, William E. *Franklin D. Roosevelt and the New Deal, 1932-1940*. New York: Harper and Row Publishers, 1963.

Lerner, Gerda, ed. *Black Women in White America: A Documentary History*. New York: Pantheon Books, 1972.

Locke, Alain LeRoy. *The New Negro: An Interpretation*. New York: A. and C. Boni, 1925.

Loewenberg, Bert James, and Ruth Bogin, eds. *Black Woman in Nineteenth Century American Life: Their Words, Their Thoughts, Their Feelings*. University Park: Pennsylvania State University, 1976.

Logan, Rayford. *Betrayal of the Negro: From Rutherford B. Hayes to Woodrow Wilson*. New York: Collier Books, 1965.

Lutz, Alma. *Created Equal: A Biography of Elizabeth Cady Stanton*. New York: The John Day Company, 1940.

McCoy, Donald R., and Ruellen, Richard T. *Quest and Response: Minority Rights and the Truman Administration*. Lawrence: University Press of Kansas, 1973.

Meier, August. *Negro Thought in America, 1880-1915: Racial Ideologies in the Age of Booker T. Washington*. Ann Arbor: University of Michigan Press, 1969.

Mowry, George. *The Progressive Era, 1900-1920: The Reform Persuasion*. Washington, D.C.: American Historical Association, 1972.

Myrdal, Gunnar. *An American Dilemma: The Negro Problem and American Democracy*. 2 vols. New York: Harper and Brothers, 1944.

Newby, I. A. *Jim Crow's Defense, Anti-Negro Thought in America*. Baton Rouge: Louisiana State University Press, 1965.

Noble, Jeanne L. *The Negro Woman's College Education*. New York: Teachers College, Columbia University, 1956.

O'Neill, William L. *Everyone Was Brave: The Rise and Fall of Feminism in America*. Chicago: University of Chicago Press, 1971.

Rabinowitz, Howard N. *Race Relations in The Urban South, 1865-1890*. New York: Oxford University Press, 1978.

Redding, Jay Saunders. *The Lonesome Road: The Story of the Negro's Past in America*. New York: Doubleday, 1958.

Robinson, Wilhelmena. *Historical Negro Biographies*. New York: Publishers Company, 1968.

Roper, James. *The Founding of Memphis*. Memphis: The Memphis Sesquicentennial, Inc., 1970.

Rose, Peter I. *The Subject Is Race: Traditional Ideologies and the Teaching of Race Relations*. New York: Oxford University Press, 1968.

Ross, Malcolm. *All Manner of Men*. New York: Reynal and Hitchcock Company, 1948.

Ruchames, Louis. *Race, Jobs and Politics*. New York: Columbia University Press, 1953.

Rudwick, Elliott M. *W. E. B. Du Bois: A Study in Minority Group Leadership*. Philadelphia: University of Pennsylvania Press, 1968.

_____. *W. E. B. Du Bois: Propagandist of Negro Protest*. New York: Atheneum, 1968.

Scott, Anne F. *The American Woman: Who Was She?* Englewood Cliffs, N.J.: Prentice Hall, 1971.

Shannon, Alexander Harvey. *The Negro in Washington: A Study in Race Amalgamation*. New York: W. Neale, 1930.

Sheppard, Gladys Byram. *Mary Church Terrell—Respectable Person*. Maryland: Human Relations Press, 1959.

Silberman, Charles E. *Crisis in Black and White*. New York: Random House, 1964.

Sloan, Irving J. *The Blacks in America, 1492-1977: A Chronology and Fact Book*. New York: Oceana Publications, Inc., 1977.

Smuts, Robert. *Women and Work in America*. New York: Columbia University Press, 1959.

Staples, Robert. *The Black Woman in America: Sex, Marriage and the Family*. Chicago: Nelson-Hall Publishers, 1973.

Sterling, Dorothy. *Lift Every Voice and Sing*. New York: Doubleday, 1965.

Sternsher, Bernard, ed. *The Negro in the Depression and War: Prelude to Revolution, 1930-45*. Chicago: Quadrangle Books, 1969.

Taylor, Alrutheus A. *The Negro in Tennessee, 1865-1880*. Washington, D.C.: The Associated Publishers, Inc., 1941.

Thompson, Daniel C. *The Negro Leadership Class*. Englewood Cliffs, N.J.: Prentice Hall, Inc., 1963.

Tindall, George B. *South Carolina Negroes, 1877-1900*. Baton Rouge: Louisiana State University Press, 1952.

_____. *The Emergence of the New South, 1913-1945*. Baton Rouge: Louisiana State University Press, 1967.

Toppin, Edgar A. *History of Blacks in America Since 1528*. New York: David McKay, Inc., 1964.

Wade, Richard C. *Slavery in the Cities: The South, 1820-1860*. New York: Oxford University Press, 1964.

Washington, Booker T. *My Larger Education*. New York: Doubleday, Page and Company, 1911.

Washington, Ernest Davidson, ed. *Selected Speeches of Booker T. Washington*. New York: Doubleday, Doran and Company, 1932.

Weaver, John Downing. *The Brownsville Raid*. New York: W. W. Norton, 1970.

Wells, Mildred White. *Unity in Diversity: The History of the General Federation of Women's Clubs*. Washington, D.C.: General Federation of Women's Clubs, 1965.

Wharton, Vernon Lane. *The Negro in Mississippi, 1865-1890*. Chapel Hill: University of North Carolina Press, 1947.

Wiebe, Robert. *The Search for Order, 1877-1920*. New York: Hill and Wang, 1967.

Williamson, Joel. *After Slavery: The Negro in South Carolina During Reconstruction, 1865-1890*. Chapel Hill: University of North Carolina Press, 1965.

Wilson, Record. *Race and Radicalism: The NAACP and the Communist Party*. New York: Cornell University Press, 1964.

_____. *The Negro and the Communist Party*. Chapel Hill: University of North Carolina Press, 1951.

Witke, Carl. *The Irish in America*. Baton Rouge: Louisiana State University Press, 1956.

Wolters, Raymond. *Negroes and the Great Depression: The Problem of Economic Recovery*. Connecticut: Greenwood Publishing Company, 1970.

Wood, Mary I. *The History of the General Federation of Women's Clubs*. New York: Norwood Press, 1912.

Woodson, Carter G. *The Negro in Our History*. Washington, D.C.: The Associated Publishers, 1941.

Woodward, C. Vann. *The Strange Career of Jim Crow*. New York: Oxford University Press, 1955.

Wynes, Charles H. *Race Relations in Virginia, 1870-1902.* Charlottesville: University of Virginia Press, 1961.

Young, John. *A Standard History of Memphis.* Knoxville: H. W. Crew and Company, 1912.

Articles

"Advice to New Women." *Review of Reviews,* 12 (July 1895): 84-85.

Allswang, John M. "The Chicago Negro Voter and Democratic Consensus: A Case Study, 1910-1936." *Journal of Illinois State Historical Society,* 60 (Summer 1960): 145-75.

Beal, Francis M. "Slave of a Slave No More: Black Women in Struggle." *Negro History Bulletin* 6 (March 1975):2-10.

Bigglestone, W. E. "Oberlin College and the Negro Student, 1865-1940." *Journal of Negro History,* 56 (July 1971):198-219.

Brewer, William. "Mary Church Terrell." *Negro History Bulletin,* 18 (October 1954):2-6.

Bruce, Josephine B. "What Has Education Done for Colored Women." *Voice of the Negro,* July 1904, pp. 294-98.

Bond, Horace. "Negro Leadership Since Washington." *South Atlantic Quarterly,* 24 (April 1925):115-30.

Bunche, Ralph. "A Critical Analysis of The Tactics and Programs of Minority Groups." *Journal of Negro Education,* 4 (July 1935):308-20.

_____. "Education in Black and White." *Journal of Negro Education,* 4 (July 1936):351-56.

_____. "The Negro in the Political Life of the United States." *Journal of Negro Education,* 10 (July 1941):573-79.

_____. "The Role of Universities in Political Orientation of Negro Youth." *Journal of Negro Education,* 9 (October 1940):571-79.

Catt, Carrie Chapman. "Mary Church Terrell: An Appreciation." *Oberlin Alumni Magazine,* June 1936, p. 6.

Chittendon, Elizabeth F. "As We Climb: Mary Church Terrell." *Negro History Bulletin,* February/March 1975, pp. 351-54.

Cohen, Stanley. "Northeastern Businessmen and Radical Reconstruction." *Mississippi Valley Historical Review,* 46 (June 1959): 67-90.

Cox, Oliver C. "The Racial Theories of Robert E. Park and Ruth Benedict." *Journal of Negro Education,* 13 (Winter 1944):139-49.

Dalfiume, Richard M. "Forgotten Years of Negro Revolution." In *The Negro in the Depression and War: Prelude to Revolution, 1930-1945*, pp. 298-311. Edited by Bernard Sternsher. Chicago: Quadrangle Books, 1966.

Davis, Angela. "Black Woman." *American Scholar*, March 1974, pp. 34-42.

Dawson, Miles M. "The New Woman." *Arena*, 18 (August 1897):43-47.

Du Bois, W. E. B. "A Nation Within A Nation." *Current History*, 42 (June 1935);269-73.

_____. "Postscript." *Crisis*, 41 (June 1939):182-83.

Ellsworth, Clayton S. "Oberlin College." *Negro History Bulletin*, 7 (February 1944):113.

Frazier, E. Franklin. "Sociological Theory and Race Relations." *American Sociological Review*, June 1947, pp. 265-71.

_____. "The Du Bois Program in the Present Crisis." *Race*, 1 (Winter 1935-36):11-14.

_____. "The Status of the Negro in the American Social Order. " *Journal of Negro Education*, 5 (July 1935): 293-307.

"A French View of the Woman's Congress." *Independent*, July 14, 1904, pp. 107-108.

Gordon, Rita Werner. "The Change in Political Alignment of Chicago's Negroes During the New Deal." *Journal of American History*, 56 (December 1969):584-603.

Gosnell, Harold F. "The Negro Vote in Northern Cities." *National Municipal Review*, 30 (May 1941):264-67, 278.

Hawksley, Julia M. "The Influence of Woman's Clubs." *The Westminster Review*, 153 (January-June 1900):455-57.

Hesseltine, William B. "Economic Factors in the Abandonment of Reconstruction." *Journal of Southern History*, 41 (February 1975):39-58.

Hewill, Emma Churchman. "The New Woman in Relation to New Man." *The Westminster Review*, 147 (November 1898):576-87.

"Historical Retrospect of the Celebration." *Negro History Bulletin*, 3 (December 1939):38-40.

Hinton, A. W. "The National Association of Colored Women." *Voice of the Negro*, August 1906, pp. 7-9.

Holmes, Jack D. "The Underlying Cause of the Memphis Riot of 1866." *Tennessee Historical Quarterly*, 17 (September 1958):195-221.

Hunton, Anna H. "A Century's Progress for the American Colored Woman." *Voice of the Negro*, August 1905, pp. 631-33.

_____. "American Colored Woman." *Voice of the Negro*, September 1905, pp. 692-94.

"Lost Laws." *New Republic*, June 22, 1953, p. 7.

"Mary Church Terrell." *Negro History Bulletin*, October 1954, pp. 2, 5.

"Mary Church Terrell, Personal." *Journal of Negro History*, 39 (October 1954):335-71.

Meyer, Annie Nathan. "Woman's Assumption of Sex Superiority." *North American Review*, June 1904, pp. 103-08.

Miller, Kelly. "The Negro Radical Exposed by Kelly Miller." *Crisis*, 15 (September 15, 1934):38-42.

Miller, Sammye M. "First Black Millionaire." *Dawn Magazine*, October 3, 1975, pp. 4-6.

_____."Mary Church Terrell's Letters." *Negro History Bulletin*, September/October 1972, pp. 615-19.

_____. "Portrait of a Black Family." *Negro History Bulletin*, April, May, June 1979, pp. 50-52.

Moody, Helen Walterman. "Unquiet Sex: Woman's Clubs." *Scribner's Magazine*, 22 (July-December 1897):486-91.

Mueller, Ruth Caston. "The National Council of Negro Women, Inc." *Negro History Bulletin*, 18 (November 1954):27-28.

Murray, Margaret P. "Women's Clubs in America." *Nineteenth Century and After*, 47 (January-June 1900):847-54. "New Woman Under Fire." *Review of Reviews*, 10 (December 1894):656-57.

"No Capital Gains." *Time*, July 14, 1949, p. 39.

Nyangoni, Betty. "A Washington Activist: Mary Church Terrell." *AFL-CIO: Washington, D.C. Teachers Local 6*, February 1972, pp. 2, 5.

Page, Thomas Nelson. "The Lynching of Negroes, Its Cause and Its Prevention." *North American Review*, 178 (January 1904):33-48.

Parks, Joseph H. "A Confederate Trade Center Under Federal Occupation." *Journal of Southern History*, 7 (August 1941):289-314.

_____. "Memphis Under Military Rule, 1862-1865." *East Tennessee Historical Society Publication*, 14 (August 1942):31-58.

"A Practical Philosopher." *Negro History Bulletin*, 5 (March 1942):122.

Ransom, Reveredy. "Why Vote for Roosevelt." *Crisis*, 39 (1932):343.

Render, Sylvia. "The Outstanding and the Obscure." *The Quarterly Journal of Library of Congress*, 32, no. 4 (October 1975):307-21.

Rhine, Alice H. "Work of Woman 's Clubs." *Forum*, 12 (September-February 1891-1892):519-25.

Roy, Jesse H. "Colored Judges." *Negro History Bulletin*, 28 (March 1965):158.

Schalk, Adolph. "Negroes, Restaurants and Washington, D.C." *The Catholic World*, 174 (January 1952):279-83.

"Segregation in the District of Columbia." *Negro History Bulletin*, 16 (January 1953):83-84.

Shockley, Ann Allen. "The Negro Woman in Retrospect: Blueprint for the Future." *Negro History Bulletin*, 29 (November 1965):56.

Terrell, Robert H. "Theodore Roosevelt." *Voice of the Negro*, August 1904, pp. 542-44.

"Two Great Women." *Afro Magazine*, February 2, 1954, p. 11.

"University Women Admit Negroes: Washington Branch Secedes." *Time*, January 24, 1949.

Walton, Lester A. "Vote for Roosevelt." *Crisis*, 39 (1932):394.

Washington, Mrs. Booker T. "Club Work A Factor in the Advancement of Colored Women." *Colored American*, 1906, pp. 83-90.

Wells, H. G. "Race Prejudice." *Independent*, 62 (February 14, 1907):381-84.

Welter, Barbara. "Cult of True Womanhood." *In Our American Sisters: Women in American Life and Thought*, pp. 96-123. Edited by Jean E. Friedman and William Shade. Boston: Allyn and Bacon, Inc., 1973.

Wesley, Charles. "International Aspects of the Negro's Status in the United States." *Negro History Bulletin*, February 1948, pp. 113-19.

_____. "Negro Autobiography and History." *Journal of Negro Education*, 10 (April 1945):262-64

Westerfield, Samuel S. "Emancipation Centennial Address." *Negro History Bulletin*, 26 (April 1963):208-09.

Williams, Fannie Barrier. "The Club Movement Among Colored Women." *Voice of the Negro*, 1 (March 1904):99-102, 380-394.

_____. "The Club Movement Among Colored Women of America. " In *A New Negro for a New Century*, pp. 379-428. Edited by J. E. MacBrady. Chicago: American Publishing Company, 1900.

Winchester, Boyd. "The New Woman." *Arena*, 27 (April 1902):367-73.

Woods, Kate. "What Women's Clubs Have Done for Women." *The Chautauquan*, 13 (August 1891):655-56.

Yates, Josephine Silone. "National Association of Colored Women. " *Voice of the Negro*, July 1904, pp.]83-87.

"Yesterday in Negro History." *Jet*, July 28, 1966, p. 23.

"Yesterday in Negro History." *Jet*, July 30, 1970, p. 11.

Mary Church Terrell:

Selected Essays

N.A.C.W. Department Announcement

EDITORS: MRS. B.T. WASHINGTON, DR. REBECCA COLE, IDA WELLS BARNETT, ROSA D. BOWSER, FRANCES JACKSON

We, the Colored Women of America, stand before the country today a united sisterhood, pledged to promote the welfare of our race, along all the lines that tend to its development and advancement. As the National Association of Colored Women we were christened one short month ago, in the nation's capital, where all lovers of progress and peace and true friends of the race stood sponsors. Surely no one conversant with our present status, and concerned about our future, can doubt that there is a crying need of just such a union of forces as our association represents.

As individuals, our women have already accomplished much for the education and cultivation of the race. How much more will they be enabled to effect when, working conscientiously, zealously and intelligently toward the same end, they are one in thought; one in purpose and one in power for good. While as a unit we shall bend our energies to compass the ends for which we have banded together, as diverse and varied will be the plans adopted as are the individualities of the different organizations of which the association is composed. Union of forces is not construed to mean monotony of ways and means, in presenting the work to which we are solemnly and irrevocably pledged. Through the instrumentality of the various members of our sisterhood, we hope to run the whole gamut of human progress and reform.

Originally published in *Woman's Era*, August 1896, pages 3-4.

In leaving each organization to fulfil the mission to which it feels especially called and peculiarly adapted, we feel confident that the greatest amount of good can be accomplished with the smallest expenditure of labor and the least sacrifice of time.

Being neither infallible nor omniscient, if we make an occasional mistake, let us rectify it with all the speed and candor of which honest, earnest women are capable. Having overcome as a race and a sex so many obstacles that to the fainting, faltering heart seemed insurmountable in the past, we shall neither be discouraged at the temporary failures of our friends, nor frightened at the apparent success of our foes.

In accepting the position of honor and trust which my sisters have seen fit to confer upon me, I am keenly, almost painfully alive to the great responsibility assumed. In myself I am nothing, but with the loyal support of conscientious, capable women, all things are possible to us. The duties of my office shall be discharged faithfully, the friends of the association may rest assured, and efficiently, let us trust, for the sake of our common cause. Forgetful of the past, hopeful for the future, let us work in the present with undaunted courage and untiring zeal. With so many heads that are thoughtful and hearts that are true enlisted in our service, how impossible is failure, how inevitable success!

The magnitude of the work to which we seem divinely called and are solemnly pledged, far from affrighting and depressing us, inspires to greater effort, for we feel in undertaking it that

> Humanity with all its fears,
> With all the hopes of future years,
> Is hanging breathless on our fate.

MARY CHURCH TERRELL,

President National Association

First Presidential Address to the National Association of Colored Women

In Union there is strength is a truism that has been acted upon by Jew and Gentile, by Greek and Barbarian, by all classes and conditions alike from the creation of the universe to the present day. It did not take long for men to learn that by combining their strength, a greater amount of work could be accomplished with less effort in a shorter time. Upon this principle of union, governments have been founded and states built. Our own republic teaches the same lesson. Force a single one of the states of the United States to stand alone, and it becomes insignificant, feeble, and a prey to the rapacity of every petty power seeking to enlarge its territory and increase its wealth. But form a republic of United States, and it becomes one of the great nations of the earth, strong in its might.

Acting upon this principle of concentration and union have the colored women of the United States banded themselves together to fulfill a mission to which they feel peculiarly adapted and especially called. We have become *National*, because from the Atlantic to the Pacific, from Maine to the Gulf, we wish to set in motion influences that shall stop the ravages made by practices that sap our strength and preclude the possibility of advancement, which under other circumstances could easily be made. We call ourselves an *Association* to signify that we have joined hands one with the other to work

This unpublished speech is reproduced from the original manuscript in the Library of Congress.

together in a common cause. We proclaim to the world that the women of our race have become partners in the great firm of progress and reform. We denominate ourselves colored, not because we are narrow, and wish to lay special emphasis on the color of the skin, for which no one is responsible, which of itself is no proof of an individual's virtue nor of his vice, which neither is a stamp, neither of one's intelligence nor of ignorance, but we refer to the fact that this is an association of colored women, because our peculiar status in this country at the present time seems to demand that we stand by ourselves in the special work for which we have organized. For this reason it was thought best to invite the attention of the world to the fact that colored women feel their responsibility as a unit, and together have clasped hands to assume it.

Special stress has been laid upon the fact that our association is composed of women, not because we wish to deny rights and privileges to our brothers in imitation of the example they have set for us so many years, but because the work which we hope to accomplish can be done better, we believe, by the mothers, wives, daughters, and sisters of our race than by the fathers, husbands, brothers, and sons. The crying need of our organization of colored women is questioned by no one conversant with our peculiar trials and perplexities, and acquainted with the almost insurmountable obstacles in our path to those attainments and acquisitions to which it is the right and privilege of every member of every race to aspire.

It is not because we are discouraged at the progress made by our people that we have uttered the cry of alarm which has called together this band of earnest women assembled here tonight. In the unprecedented advancement made by the Negro since his emancipation, we take great pride and extract therefore both courage and hope from a condition of dense ignorance. But thirty years ago, we have advanced so far in the realm of knowledge and letters as to have produced scholars and authors of repute. Though penniless as a race a short while ago, we have among us today a few men of wealth and multitudes who own their homes and make comfortable livings. We therefore challenge any other race to present a record more creditable and show a progress more wonderful than that made by the ex-slaves of the United States and that too in the face of prejudice, proscription, and persecution against which no other people has ever had to contend in the history of the world. And yet while rejoicing in our steady march, onward and upward, to the best and highest things of life, we are nevertheless painfully mindful of our weaknesses and defects which we know the Negro is no worse than other races equally poor, equally ignorant, and equally oppressed, we would nevertheless see him lay aside the sins that do so easily beset him, and come forth clothed in all these attributes of mind and grace of character that claims the real man. To accomplish this end through the simplest, swiftest, surest methods, the colored women have organized themselves into this Association, whose power for good, let us hope, will be as enduring as it is unlimited.

Believing that it is only through the home that a people can become really good and truly great, the N.A.C.W. shall enter that sacred domain to inculcate right principles of living and correct false views of life. Homes, more homes, purer homes, better homes, is the text upon which our sermons to the masses must be preached. So long as the majority of people call that place home in which the air is foul, the manners bad and the morals worse, just so long is this so called home a menace to health, a breeder of vice, and the abode of crime. Not alone upon the inmates of these hovels are the awful consequences of their filth and immorality visited, but upon the heads of those who sit calmly by and make no effort to stem the tide of disease and vice will vengeance as surely fall.

The colored youth is vicious we are told, and statistics showing the multitudes of our boys and girls who fill the penitentiaries and crowd the jails appall and discourage us. Side by side with these facts and figures of crime, I would have presented and pictured the miserable hovels from which these youthful criminals come. Crowded into alleys, many of them the haunts of vice, few if any of them in a proper sanitary condition, most of them fatal to mental and moral growth, and destructive of healthful physical development as well, thousands of our children have a wretched heritage indeed. It is, therefore, into the home, sisters of the Association, that we must go, filled with all the zeal and charity which such a mission demands. To the children of the race we owe, as women, a debt which can never be paid, until herculean efforts are made to rescue them from evil and shame for which they are in no way responsible. Listen to the cry of the children, my sisters. Upon you they depend for the light of knowledge, and the blessing of a good example. As an organization of women, surely nothing can be nearer our hearts than the children, many of whose lives so sad and dark we might brighten and bless. It is kindergartens we need. Free kindergartens in every city and hamlet of this broad land we must have, if the children are to receive from us what it is our duty to give.

The more unfavorable the environments of children, the more necessary is it that steps be taken to counteract the hateful influences upon innocent victims. How imperative is it then that we inculcate correct principles, and set good examples for our own youth whose little feet will have so many thorny paths of prejudice, temptation, and injustice to tread.

Make a visit to the settlements of colored people who in many cities are relegated to the most noisome sections permitted by the municipal government, and behold the miles of inhumanity that infest them. Here are our little ones, the future representatives of the race, fairly drinking in the permissible example of their elders, coming in contact with nothing but ignorance and vice, till at the age of six evil habits are formed that no amount of civilizing and christianizing can ever completely break. As long as the evil nature alone is encouraged to develop, while the higher, nobler qualities in little ones are dwarfed and deadened by the very atmosphere which they breathe, the negligent, pitiless public is responsible for the results and is partner of their crimes.

Let the women of the National Association see to it that the little strays of the alleys come in contact with intelligence and virtue, at least a few times a week, that the noble aspirations with which they are born may not be entirely throttled by the evil influences which these poor little ones are powerless to escape. The establishment of free kindergartens! ! you exclaim . . . Where is the money coming from? How can we do it? This charity you advocate though beautiful in theory is nevertheless impossible of attainment. Let the women of the race once be thoroughly aroused to their duty to the children, let them be consumed with desire to save them from lives of degradation and shame, and the establishment of free kindergartens for the poor will become a living, breathing, saving reality at no distant day.

What movement looking toward the reformation and regeneration of mankind was ever proposed that did not instantly assume formidable proportions to the fainthearted. But how soon obstacles that have once appeared insuperable dwindle into nothingness, after the shoulder is put to the wheel, and united effort determines to remove them! In every organization of the Association let committees be appointed whose special mission it will be to do for the little strays of the alleys what is not done by their mothers, who in many instances fall far short of their duty, not because they are vicious and depraved, but because they are ignorant and poor.

Through mother meetings which have been in the past year and will be in the future a special feature of the Association, much useful information in everything pertaining to the home will be disseminated. Object lessons in the best way to sweep, to dust, to cook and to wash should be given by women who have made a special study of the art and science of housekeeping. How to clothe children neatly, how to make, and especially how to mend garments, how to manage their households economically, what food is the most nutritious and best for the money, how to ventilate as thoroughly as possible the dingy stuffy quarters which the majority are forced to inhabit, all these are subjects on which the women of the masses need more knowledge. Let us teach mothers of families how to save wisely. Let us have heart to heart talks with our women that we may strike at the root of evil.

If the women of the dominant race with all the centuries of education, refinement, and culture back of them, with all their wealth of opportunity ever present with them, if these women felt a responsibility to call a Mother's Congress that they might be ever enlightened as to the best methods of rearing children and conducting their homes, how much more do the women of our race from whom the shackles of slavery have just fallen need information on the same subjects? Let us have Mother Congresses in every community in which our women can be counseled. The necessity of increasing the self-respect of our children is important. Let the reckless, ill-advised, and oftentimes brutal methods of punishing children be everywhere condemned. Let us teach our mothers that by punishing children inhumanely, they destroy their pride, crush their spirit and convert them into hardened culprits—whom it will be impossible later on to reach or touch in anyway at all. More than any other race at present in this country, we should strive to implant feelings of self-respect and pride in our children, whose spirits are crushed and whose hearts saddened enough by indignities from which as victims of an unreasonable cruel prejudice it is impossible to shield them. Let it be the duty of every friend of the race to teach children who are humiliated on learning that they are descendants of slaves that the majority of races on the earth have at some time in their history been subjects to another. This knowledge of humiliation will be important when we are victims of racism.

Let us not only preach, but practice race unity, race pride, reverence and respect for those capable of leading and advising us. Let the youth of the race be impressed about the dignity of labor and inspired with a desire to work. Let us do nothing to handicap children in the desperate struggle for existence in which their unfortunate condition in this country forces them to engage. Let us purify the atmosphere of our homes till it becomes so sweet that those who dwell in them carry on a great work of reform. That we have no money to help the needy and poor, I reply, that having hearts, generous natures, willing feet, and helpful hands can without the token of a single penny, work miracles in the name of humanity and right.

Money we need, money we must have to accomplish much which we hope to effect. But it is not by powerful armies and the outlays of vast fortunes that the greatest revolutions are wrought and the most enduring reforms inaugurated. It is by the silent, though powerful force of individual influences thrown on the side of right, it is by arduous persistence and effort to keep those with whom we come in daily contact, to enlighten the heathen at our door, to create wholesome public sentiment in the communities in which we live, that the heaviest blows are struck for virtue and right.

Let us not only preach, but practice race unity, race pride, reverence, and respect for those capable of leading and advising us. Let the youth of the race be impressed about the dignity of labor and inspired with a desire to work. Let us do nothing to handicap children in the desperate struggle for existence in which their unfortunate condition in this country forces them to engage. Let us purify the atmosphere of our homes till it becomes so sweet that those who dwell in them will have a heritage more precious than great, more to be desired than silver or gold.

Nashville, Tennessee
September 15, 1897

The Duty of the National Association of Colored Women to the Race

The National Association of Colored Women had at its second convention every reason to rejoice and be exceeding glad. From its birth in July, 1896, till the present moment its growth has been steady and its march ever onward and upward to the goal of its ambition.

An infant of but three years is this organization, over which I have had the honor to preside, ever since it first saw the light of day in the Capital of the Nation, and yet in those short years it has accomplished a vast amount of good. So tenderly has this child of the organized womanhood of the race been nurtured, and so wisely ministered unto by all who have watched prayerfully and waited patiently for its development, that it comes before you to-day a child hale, hearty and strong, of which its fond mothers have every reason to be proud.

As individuals, colored women have always been ambitious for their race. From the day when shackles first fell from their fettered limbs till now, they have often, single-handed and alone, struggled against the most desperate and discouraging odds, in order to secure for their loved ones and themselves that culture of the head and heart for which they hungered and thirsted so long in vain. But it dawned upon them finally, that individuals working alone, or scattered here and there in small companies, might be ever so honest in

Originally published in the *AME Church Review*, January 1900, pages 340-354.

purpose, so indefatigable in labor, so conscientious about methods, and so wise in projecting plans, yet they would accomplish little, compared with the possible achievement of many individuals, all banded together throughout the entire land, with heads and hearts fixed on the same high purpose and hands joined in united strength. As a result of a general realization of this fact, the National Association of Colored women was born.

Though we are young in years, and have been unable to put into execution some plans on which we had built high hopes, the fruits of organized effort are already apparent to all. If in the short space of three years the National Association had done nothing but give an impressive object lesson in the necessity for, and the efficacy of, organization, it would have proved its reason for existence and its right to live; but, seriously handicapped though we have been, both because of the lack of experience and lack of funds, our efforts have for the most part been crowned with success.

In the kindergartens established by some of our organizations, children have been cultivated and trained. A sanatarium with a training school for nurses has been set on such a firm foundation in a Southern city, and has given such abundant proof of its utility and necessity, that the municipal government has voted it an annual appropriation of several hundred dollars. To our poor benighted sisters in the black belt of Alabama we have gone, and have been both a help and a comfort to these women, through the darkness of whose ignorance of everything that makes life sweet or worth the living, no ray of light would have penetrated but for us. We have taught them the A, B, C, of living, by showing them how to make their huts more habitable and decent with the small means at their command, and how to care for themselves and their families more in accordance with the laws of health. Plans for aiding the indigent, orphaned and aged have been projected and in some instances have been carried to a successful execution. Mother's meetings have been generally held and sewing classes formed. Abuses like lynching, the convict lease system and the Jim Crow car laws have been discussed with a view of doing something to remedy these evils. In Chicago, magnificent work has been done by the Illinois Federation of Colored Women's Clubs through whose instrumentality schools have been visited, truant children looked after, parents and teachers urged to co-operate with each other, public institutions investigated, rescue and reform work engaged in to reclaim unfortunate women and tempted girls, garments cut, made and distributed to the needy poor. In short, what our hands have found to do, that we have cheerfully done. It is not, therefore, because I feel that the National Association of Colored Women has been derelict, or has failed, that I shall discuss its duty to our race, but because I wish to emphasize some special lines of work in which it is already engaging, but to which I would pledge its more hearty support.

The more closely I study the relation of this Association to the race, the more clearly defined becomes its duty to the children.

Believing in the saving grace of the kindergarten for our little ones, at our first convention, as some may remember, I urged with all the earnestness that I could command, that the Association should consider the establishment of kindergartens as the special mission it is called upon to fulfill. The importance of engaging extensively in this effort to uplift the children, particularly those to whom the opportunity of learning by contact what is true and good and beautiful could come through no other source, grows on me more and more everyday. Through the kindergarten alone, which teaches its lessons in the most impressionable years of childhood, shall we be able to save countless thousands of our little ones who are going to destruction before our very eyes. To some the task of establishing kindergartens may seem too herculean for the Association to undertake, because of the great expense involved. Be that as it may, we shall never accomplish the good it is in our power to do, nor shall we discharge our obligation to the race, until we engage in this work in those sections at least where it is most needed.

In many cities and towns the kindergarten has already been incorporated in the public school system. Here it may not be necessary for the Association to work. But wherever the conditions are such that our children are deprived of the training which they can receive from the kindergarten alone, deprived of that training which from the very nature of the case, they so sorely need, there the Association should establish these schools, from which so much benefit to our little ones will accrue.

Side by side in importance with the kindergarten stands the day nursery, a charity of which there is an imperative need among us. Thousands of our wage-earning mothers with large families dependent upon them for support are obliged to leave their infants all day to be cared for either by young brother and sisters, who know nothing about it, or by some good-natured neighbor, who promises much, but who does little. Some of these infants are locked alone in a room from the time the mother leaves in the morning until she returns at night. Their suffering is, of course, unspeakable. Not long ago,

I read in a southern newspaper that an infant thus locked alone in a room all day, while its mother went out to wash, had cried itself to death. Recently I have had under direct observation a day nursery, established for infants of working women, and I have been shocked at some of the miserable little specimens of humanity brought in by mothers, who had been obliged to board them out with either careless or heartless people. In one instance the hands and legs of a poor little mite of only fourteen months had been terribly drawn and twisted with rheumatism contracted by sleeping in a cold room with no fire during the severe winter, while the family with whom it boarded enjoyed comfortable quarters overhead. And so I might go on enumerating cases, showing how terrible is the suffering of infants of working women, who have no one with whom to leave them, while they earn their daily bread. Establishing day nurseries is clearly a practical charity, of the need of which there is abundant proof in every community where our women may be found.

What a vast amount of good would be accomplished, if by every branch of the Association, a home were provided for the infants of working women, who no matter how tender may be their affection for their little ones, are forced by stern necessity to neglect them all day themselves, and at best, can only entrust them to others, from whom, in the majority of cases, they do not receive the proper care. It would not only save the life, and preserve the health of many a poor little one, but it would speak eloquently of our interest in our sisters, whose lot is harder than our own, but to whom we should give unmistakable proof of our regard, our sympathy, and our willingness to render any assistance in our power. When one thinks of the slaughter of the innocents which is occurring with pitiless persistency every day, and reflects upon how many are maimed for life through neglect, how many there are whose intellects are clouded because of the treatment received during their helpless infancy, establishing day nurseries can seem neither unnecessary nor far-fetched; but must appeal directly to us all. No great amount is required to establish a day nursery, and part of the money necessary for its maintenance might be secured by charging each of the mothers who take advantage of it a small sum. In no other way could the investment of the same amount of money bring such large and blessed returns.

To each and every branch of the Association, then, I recommend the establishment of a day nursery, as a means through which it can render one of the greatest services possible to humanity and the race.

For the sake of argument, let us suppose that absolute lack of means prevents an organization from establishing either a kindergarten or a day nursery. Even under such circumstances a part of its obligation to the children may be discharged.

For no organization is so poor both in mental resources and in money that it cannot form a children's club, through which we can do a vast amount of good. Lessons may be taught and rules of conduct impressed, while the children of a neighborhood are gathered together for amusement and play, as in no other way. Both by telling and reading stories, teaching kindness to animals, politeness to elders, pity for the unfortunate and week, seeds may be sown in youthful minds, which in after years will spring up and bear fruit, some an hundred fold. What a revolution we should work, for instance, by the time the next generation stands at the helm, if the children to-day were taught that they are responsible for their thoughts that they can learn to control them, that an impure life is the result of impure thoughts, that crime is conceived in thought before it is executed in deed. No organization of the Association should feel entirely satisfied with its work, unless some of its energy, or some of its brain, or some of its money is used in the name, and for the sake of the children, either by establishing a day nursery, a kindergarten, or forming a children's club, which last is possible to all.

Let us remember that we are banded together to do good, to work most vigorously and conscientiously upon that which will redound most to the welfare and progress of the race. If that be true, I recommend to you, I plead to you, for the children, for those who will soon represent us, for those by whom as a race we shall soon stand or fall in the estimation of the world, for those upon whom the hope of every people must necessarily be built. As an Association, let us devote ourselves enthusiastically, conscientiously, to the children, with their warm little hearts, their susceptible little minds, their malleable, pliable characters. Through the children of to-day, we must build the foundation of the next generation upon such a rock of integrity, morality, and strength, both of body and mind, that the floods of proscription, prejudice, and persecution may descend upon it in torrents, and yet it will not be moved. We hear a great deal about the race problem, and how to solve it. This theory, that and the other, may be advanced, but the real solution of the race problem, both so far as we, who are oppressed and those who oppress us are concerned, lies in the children.

Let no one suppose that I would have a large organization like ours a body of one idea, with no thought, plan or purpose except that which centers about the children. I am an optimist, because I see how we are broadening and deepening out into the various channels of generosity and beneficence, which indicates what a high state of civilization we have already reached. Homes for the orphaned and aged must be established; sanatoriums, hospitals, and training schools for nurses founded; unfortunate women and tempted girls encircled by the loving arms of those who would woo them back to the path of rectitude and virtue; classes formed for cultivating the mind; schools of domestic science opened in every city and village in which our women and girls may be found. All this is our duty, all this is an obligation, which we should discharge as soon as our means will permit. But in connection with such work let us not neglect, let us not forget, the children, remembering that when we love and protect the little ones, we follow the footsteps of Him, who when He wished to paint the most beautiful picture of Beulah land it is possible of the human mind to conceive, pointed to the children and said—"Of such is the kingdom of heaven."

It is frequently charged against the more favored among us who have been blessed with advantages of education and moral training superior to those enjoyed by the majority, that they hold themselves too much aloof from the less fortunate of their people. Without discussing the reasons for such a condition of things, it must be patent to the most careless observer that the more intelligent and influential among us do not exert themselves as much as they should to uplift those beneath them, as it is plainly their duty to do.

It has been suggested, and very appropriately, I think, that this Association should take as its motto—*Lifting as we climb.* In no way could we live up to such a sentiment better than by coming into closer touch with the masses of our women, by whom, whether we will nor not, the world will always judge the womanhood of the race. Even though we wish to shun them, and hold ourselves entirely aloof from them, we cannot escape the consequences of their acts. So, that, if the call of duty were disregarded altogether, policy and self-preservation would demand that we go down among the lowly, the illiterate, and even the vicious to whom we are bound by the ties of race and sex, and put forth every possible effort to uplift and reclaim them.

It is useless to talk about elevating the race if we do not come into close touch with the masses of our women, through whom we may correct many of the evils which militate so seriously against us, and inaugurate the reforms without which, as a race, we cannot hope to succeed. It is often difficult, I know, to persuade people who need help most to avail themselves of the assistance offered by those who wish to lift them to a higher plane. If it were possible for us to send out a national organizer, whose duty it would be to form clubs throughout the length and breadth of the land, it would be no easy matter, I am sure, to persuade some of our women to join them, even though they knew that by so doing they would receive just that kind of instruction and counsel which they so greatly need. This fault is not peculiar to our women alone but is common to the whole human race. Difficult though it be for us to uplift some of our women, many of whose practices in their own homes and in the service of their employers rise like a great barrier to our progress, we should nevertheless work unceasingly to this end until we win their confidence so that they will accept our aid.

Through such clubs as I have just mentioned; the attention to our women might be called to the alarming rapidity with which they are losing ground in the world of labor—a fact patent to all who observe and read the signs of the times. So many families are supported entirely by our women, that if this movement to withhold employment from them continues to grow, we shall soon be confronted by a condition of things serious and disastrous indeed. It is clearly the duty of this, the only organized body of colored women in the country, to study the labor question, not only as it affects the women, but also as it affects the men. When those who formerly employed colored women as domestics, but who refuse to do so now, are asked why they have established what is equivalent to a boycott against us, they invariably tell us that colored women are now neither skilled in the trades nor reliable as working women. While we know that in the majority of cases colored women are not employed because of the cruel, unreasonable prejudice which rages so violently against them, there is just enough truth in the charge of poor workmanship and unreliability to make us wince when it is preferred.

To stem this tide of popular disfavor against us should be the desire and determination of every colored woman in the country who has the interest of her race at heart. It is we, the National Association, who must point out to our women how fatal it will be to their highest, best interests, and to the highest, best interests of their children, if they do not build up a reputation for reliability and proficiency, by establishing schools of domestic science as soon as our means will permit; and it is the duty of this Association to raise funds to start a few of these schools immediately—we should probably do more to solve the labor question, so far as it affects the women than by using any other means we could possibly employ. Let us explain the situation as we may, the fact remains that trades and avocations, which formerly by common consent belonged almost exclusively to our men and women are gradually slipping from their grasp.

Whom does such a condition of things affect more directly and disastrously than the women of the race? As parents, teachers and guardians, we teach our children to be honest and industrious, to cultivate their minds, to become skilled workmen, to be energetic and then to be hopeful. It is easy enough to impress upon them the necessity of cultivating their minds, and of becoming skilled workmen, of being energetic, honest and industrious, but how difficult it is for colored women to inspire their children with hope, or offer them an incentive for their best endeavor under the existing condition of things in this country.

As a mother of the dominant race looks into the sweet innocent face of her babe, her heart thrills not only with happiness in the present, but also with joyful anticipations of the future. For well she knows that honor, wealth, fame and greatness in any vocation he may choose, are all his, if he but possess the ability and determination to secure them. She knows that if it is in him to be great, all the exterior circumstances, which can help him to the goal of his ambition, such as the laws of his country, the public opinion of his countrymen and manifold opportunities, are all his, without the asking. From his birth he is king in his own right, and is no suppliant for justice.

But how bitter is the contrast between the feelings of joy and hope which thrill the heart of the white mother and those which stir the soul of her colored sister. As a mother of the weaker race clasps to her bosom the babe which she loves with an affection as tender and deep as that the white mother bears her child, she cannot thrill with joyful anticipation of the future. For before her babe she sees the thorny path of prejudice and proscription his little feet must tread. She knows that no matter how great his ability, or how lofty his ambition, there are comparatively few trades and avocations in which any one of his race may hope to succeed. She knows that no matter how skillful his hand, how honest his heart, or how great his need, trades unions will close their doors in his face and make his struggle for existence desperate indeed. So rough does the way of her infant appear to many a poor colored mother, as she thinks of the hardships and humiliations to which he will be subjected, when he tries to earn his daily bread, that instead of thrilling with joy and hope, she trembles with apprehension and despair.

This picture, though forbidding to look upon, is not overdrawn, as those who have studied the labor question in its relation to our race can testify. What, then, shall we do? Shall we sit supinely by, with folded hands, drooping heads, and weeping eyes, or shall we be up and doing, determined to smooth out the rough roads of labor over which tiny feet that now patter in play, will soon stumble and fall? To our own youth, to our own tradesmen, we must preach efficiency, reliability, thorough preparation for any work in which they choose to engage. Let us also appeal directly to the large-hearted, broad-minded women of the dominant race, and lay our case clearly before them. In conversing with many of them privately I have discovered that our side of the labor question has never been made a living, breathing, terrible reality to them. In a vague way they know that difficulties do confront colored men and women in their effort to secure employment, but they do not know how almost insurmountable are the obstacles which lie in the path of the rank and file who want to earn an honest living. Let us ask these women both to follow themselves, and teach their children, the lofty principles of humanity, charity and justice which they profess to observe. Let us ask that they train their children to be just and broad enough to judge men and women by their intrinsic merit, rather than by the adventitious circumstances of race or color or creed. Let the Association of colored women ask the white mothers of this country to teach their children that when they grow to be men and women, if they deliberately prevent their fellow creatures from earning their daily bread, by closing the doors of trade against them the Father of all men will hold them responsible for the crimes which are the result of their injustice, and for the human wrecks which the ruthless crushing of hope and ambition always makes. In the name of our children, let us ask, also, that they do all in their power to secure for our youth opportunities of earning a living and of attaining unto the full stature of manhood and womanhood, which they desire for their own. In the name of justice and humanity, in the name of the innocence and helplessness of childhood, black childhood, as well as white childhood, let us appeal to the white mothers of this country to do all in their power to make the future of our boys and girls as bright and promising as should be that of every child, born on this free American soil. It is the women of the country who mould public opinion, and when they say that trades and avocations shall not be closed against men and women on account of race or color, then the day of proscription and prejudice will darken to dawn no more.

As individuals, we have presented our case again and again. Let us now try the efficacy of organized effort; on this, I build great hope. Organization is one of the most potent forces in the world to-day, and the good it is possible for the National Association to accomplish has not yet been approximated by those most sanguine of its success.

And now, I must briefly call your attention to a subject fraught with interest to us all. The health of our race is becoming a matter of deep concern to many who are alarmed by statistics showing how great is the death rate among us as compared with that of the Whites.

There are many reasons why this proportion is so great among us—chief of which are poverty and ignorance of the laws of health. Our children are sent illy clad through inclement weather to school, for instance. Girls just budding into womanhood are allowed to sit all day in wet boots and damp skirts, in both the high and grade schools which they attend. Thus it happens that some of our most promising and gifted young women succumb to diseases, which are the result of carelessness on the part both of parents and teachers. We must call the attention of our mothers to this fact, and urge the school officials to protect the health of our children as far as possible by wise legislation, and thus stop the awful ravages made by diseases which a little care and precaution might prevent.

I must not neglect to mention another duty which the Association owes the race, and which it must not fail to discharge. Creating a healthful, wholesome public opinion in every community in which we are represented, is one of the greatest services we can render. The duty of setting a high moral standard and living up to it devolves upon us as colored women in a peculiar way. Slanders are circulated against us every day, both in the press and by the direct descendants of those who in years past were responsible for the moral degradation of their female slaves. While these calumnies are not founded in fact, they can nevertheless do us a great deal of harm, if those who represent the intelligence and virtue among us do not, both in our public and private life, avoid even the appearance of evil. In spite of the fateful inheritance left us by slavery, in spite of the manifold temptations and pitfalls to which our young girls are subjected all over the country, and though the safeguards usually thrown around maidenly youth and innocence are in some sections entirely withheld from colored girls, statistics compiled by men not inclined to falsify in favor of my race show that immorality among colored women is not so great as among women in countries like Austria, Italy, Germany, Sweden and France.

If I were called upon to state in a word where I thought the Association should do its most effective work, I should say unhesitatingly, "in the home". The purification of the home must be our first consideration and care. It is in the home where woman is really queen, that she wields her influence with the most telling effect. It is through the home, therefore, that the principles which we wish to promulgate can be most widely circulated and most deeply impressed. In the mind and heart of every good and conscientious woman, the first place is occupied by home. We must always remember in connection with this fact, however, that observation has shown and experience has proved that it is not the narrow-minded, selfish women who think of naught save their families and themselves, who have no time to work for neglected children, the helpless sick and the needy poor—it is not such women, I say, who exert in their homes the most powerful influence for good.

And now, finally, let us be up and doing wherever a word may be spoken for principle, or a hand lifted to aid. We must study carefully and conscientiously the questions which affect us most deeply and directly. Against lynching, the convict lease system, the Jim Crow car laws, and all other barbarities and abuses which degrade and dishearten us, we must agitate with such force of logic and intensity of soul that the oppressor will either be converted to principles of justice or be ashamed to openly violate them. Let loyalty to race, as displayed by employing and patronizing our own, in refusing to hold up our own to public ridicule and scorn, let allegiance to those whose ability, character and general fitness qualify them to lead, be two of the cardinal principles by which each and every member of this Association is guided. If we are to judge the future by the emancipation, there is no reason why we should view it with despair. Over almost insurmountable obstacles as a race we have forged ahead until today there is hardly a trade, a profession, or an art in which we have not at least one worthy representative. I challenge any other race to show such wonderful progress along all lines in so short a time, under circumstances so discouraging as that made by the ex-slaves of the United States of America. And though today some of us are cast down by the awful barbarities constantly inflicted upon some of our unfortunate race in the South who have been shot and burned to death by mobs which took no pains to establish the guilt of their victims, some of whom were doubtless innocent, we must remember that the darkest hour is just before the dawn.

As an Association, by discharging our duty to the children, by studying the labor question in its relation to our race, by coming into closer touch with the masses of our women, by urging parents and teachers to protect the health of our boys and girls, by creating a wholesome, healthful public sentiment in every community in which we are represented, by setting a high moral standard and living up to it, and purifying the home, we shall render the race a service, whose magnitude and importance it is not in my power to express.

Let us love and cherish our Association with such loyalty and zeal, that it will wax strong and great, that it may soon become that bulwark of strength and source of inspiration to our women that it is destined to be.

> In spite of rock and tempest's roar,
> In spite of false lights on the shore,
> Sail on, nor fear to breast the sea!
> Our heart, our hopes are all with Thee,
> Our heart, our hopes, our prayers, our tears,
> Our faith, triumphant o'er our fears,
> Are all with Thee, are all with Thee.

What Role Is the Educated Negro Woman to Play in the Uplifting of Her Race?

Should any one ask what special phase of the Negro's development makes me most hopeful of his ultimate triumph over present obstacles, I should answer unhesitatingly, it is the magnificent work the women are doing to regenerate and uplift the race. Judge the future of colored women by the past since their emancipation, and neither they nor their friends have any cause for anxiety.

For years, either banding themselves into small companies or struggling alone, colored women have worked with might and main to improve the condition of their people. The necessity of systematizing their efforts and working on a larger scale became apparent not many years ago and they decided to unite their forces. Thus it happened that in the summer of 1896 the National Association of Colored Women was formed by the union of two large organizations, each of which has done much to show our women the advantage of concerted action. So tenderly has this daughter of the organized womanhood of the race been nurtured and so wisely ministered unto, that it has grown to be a child hale, hearty and strong, of which its fond mothers have every reason to be proud. Handicapped though its members have been, because they lacked both money and experience, their efforts have, for the most part, been crowned with success in the twenty-six States where it has been represented.

Originally published in *Twentieth Century Negro Literature*, edited and arranged by D.W. Culp (Toronto, 1902), pages 172-177.

Kindergartens have been established by some of our organizations, from which encouraging reports have come. A sanitarium with a training school for nurses has been set on such a firm foundation by the Phyllis Wheatley Club of New Orleans, Louisiana, and has proved itself to be such a blessing to the entire community that the municipal government has voted it an annual appropriation of several hundred dollars. By the Tuskegee, Alabama, branch of the association the work of bringing the light of knowledge and the gospel of cleanliness to their poor benighted sisters on the plantations has been conducted with signal success. Their efforts have thus far been confined to four estates, comprising thousands of acres of land, on which live hundreds of colored people, yet in the darkness of ignorance and the grip of sin, miles away from churches and schools.

Plans for aiding the indigent, orphaned and aged have been projected and in some instances have been carried into successful execution. One club in Memphis, Tennessee, has purchased a large tract of land, on which it intends to erect an old folks' home, part of the money for which has already been raised. Splendid service has been rendered by the Illinois Federation of Colored Women's Clubs, through whose instrumentality schools have been visited, truant children looked after, parents and teachers urged to cooperate with each other, rescue and reform work engaged in, so as to reclaim unfortunate women and tempted girls, public institutions investigated, garments cut, made and distributed to the needy poor.

Questions affecting our legal status as a race are sometimes agitated by our women. In Tennessee and Louisiana colored women have several times petitioned the legislature of their respective States to repeal the obnoxious Jim Crow car laws. In every way possible we are calling attention to the barbarity of the convict lease system, of which Negroes and especially the female prisoners are the principal victims, with the hope that the conscience of the country may be touched and this stain on its escutcheon be forever wiped away. Against the one room cabin we have inaugurated a vigorous crusade. When families of eight or ten men, women and children are all huddled promiscuously together in a single apartment, a condition common among our poor all over the land, there is little hope of inculcating morality and modesty. And yet in spite of the fateful heritage of slavery, in spite of the manifold pitfalls and peculiar temptations to which our girls are subjected, and though the safeguards usually thrown around maidenly youth and innocence are in some sections entirely withheld from colored girls, statistics compiled by men not inclined to falsify in favor of my race show that immorality among colored women is not so great as among women in some foreign countries who are equally ignorant, poor and oppressed.

Believing that it is only through the home that a people can become really good and truly great the National Association has entered that sacred domain. Homes, more homes, better homes, purer homes is the text upon which sermons have been and will be preached. There has been a determined effort to have heart to heart talks with our women that we may strike at the root of evils, many of which lie at the fireside. If the women of the dominant race, with all the centuries of education, culture and refinement back of them, with all the wealth and opportunity ever present with them, feel the need of a mother's congress, that they may be enlightened upon the best methods of rearing their children and conducting their homes, how much more do our women, from whom shackles have but yesterday been stricken, need information on the same vital subjects. And so the association is working vigorously to establish mothers' congresses on a small scale, wherever our women can be reached.

From this brief and meager account of the work which has been and is still being accomplished by colored women through the medium of their clubs, it is easy to observe how earnest and effective have been their efforts to elevate the race. No people need ever despair whose women are fully aroused to the duties which rest upon them and are willing to shoulder responsibilities which they alone can successfully assume. The scope of our endeavors is constantly widening. Into the various channels of generosity and beneficence we are entering more and more every day.

Some of our women are now urging their clubs to establish day nurseries, a charity of which there is an imperative need. Thousands of our wage-earning mothers with large families dependent almost entirely upon them for support are obliged to leave their children all day, entrusted to the care of small brothers and sisters, or some good-natured neighbor who promises much, but who does little. Some of these infants are locked alone in the room from the time the mother leaves in the morning, until she returns at night. Not long ago I read in a Southern newspaper that an infant thus locked alone in a room all day, while its mother went out to wash, had cried itself to death. When one reflects upon the slaughter of the innocents which is occurring with pitiless persistency every day and thinks of the multitudes who are maimed for life or are rendered imbecile because of the treatment received during their helpless infancy, it is evident that by establishing day nurseries colored women will render one of the greatest services possible to humanity and to the race.

Nothing lies nearer the heart of colored women than the children. We feel keenly the need of kindergartens and are putting forth earnest efforts to honeycomb this country with them from one extremity to the other. The more unfavorable the environments of children the more necessary it is that steps be taken to counteract baleful influences upon innocent victims. How imperative is it then that as colored women we inculcate correct principles and set good examples for our own youth whose little feet will have so many thorny paths of temptation, injustice and prejudice to tread. So keenly alive is the National Association to the necessity of rescuing our little ones whose evil nature alone is encouraged to develop and whose noble qualities are deadened and dwarfed by the very atmosphere which they breathe, that its officers are trying to raise money with which to send out a kindergarten organizer, whose duty it shall be to arouse the conscience of our women and to establish kindergartens wherever means therefor can be secured.

Through the children of today we believe we can build the foundation of the next generation upon such a rock of morality, intelligence and strength, that the floods of proscription, prejudice and persecution may descend upon it in torrents and yet it will not be moved. We hear a great deal about the race problem and how to solve it. The real solution of the race problem lies in the children, both so far as we who are oppressed and those who oppress us are concerned. Some of our women who have consecrated their lives to the elevation of their race feel that neither individuals nor organizations working toward this end should be entirely satisfied with their efforts unless some of their energy, money or brain is used in the name and for the sake of the children.

The National Association has chosen as its motto: Lifting as We Climb. In order to live strictly up to this sentiment, its members have determined to come into the closest possible touch with the masses of our women, through whom the womanhood of our people is always judged. It is unfortunate, but it is true, that the dominant race in this country insists upon gauging the Negro's worth by his most illiterate and vicious representatives than by the more intelligent and worthy classes. Colored women of education and culture know that they cannot escape altogether the consequences of the acts of their most depraved sisters. They see that even if they were wicked enough to turn a deaf ear to the call of duty, both policy and self-preservation demand that they go down among the lowly, the illiterate and even the vicious, to whom they are bound by the ties of race and sex, and put forth every possible effort to reclaim them. By coming into close touch with the masses of our women it is possible to correct many of the evils which militate so seriously against us and inaugurate the reforms, without which, as a race, we cannot hope to succeed.

Through the clubs we are studying the labor question and are calling the attention of our women to the alarming rapidity with which the Negro is losing ground in the world of labor. If this movement to withhold employment from him continues to grow, the race will soon be confronted by a condition of things disastrous and serious, indeed. We are preaching in season and out that it is the duty of every wage-earning colored woman to become thoroughly proficient in whatever work she engages, so that she may render the best service of which she is capable, and thus do her part toward establishing a reputation for excellent workmanship among colored women.

Our clubs all over the country are being urged to establish schools of domestic science. It is believed that by founding schools in which colored girls could be trained to be skilled domestics, we should do more toward solving the labor question as it affects our women, than by using any other means it is in our power to employ. We intend to lay the Negro's side of the labor question clearly before our large-hearted, broad-minded sisters of the dominant race and appeal to them to throw their influence on the right side. We shall ask that they train their children to be broad and just enough to judge men and women by their intrinsic merit rather than by the adventitious circumstances of race or color or creed. Colored women are asking the white mothers of the land to teach their children that when they grow to be men and women, if they deliberately prevent their fellow creatures from earning an honest living by closing their doors of trade against them, the Father of all men will hold them responsible for the crimes which are the result of their injustice and for the human wrecks which the ruthless crushing of hope and ambition always makes.

Through our clubs colored women hope to improve the social atmosphere by showing the enormity of the double standard of morals, which teaches that we should turn the cold shoulder upon a fallen sister, but greet her destroyer with open arms and a gracious smile. The duty of setting a high moral standard and living up to it devolves upon colored women in a peculiar way. False accusations and malicious slanders are circulated against them constantly, both by the press and by the direct descendants of those who in years past were responsible for the moral degradation of their female slaves.

Carefully and conscientiously we shall study the questions which affect the race most deeply and directly. Against the convict lease system, the Jim Crow car laws, lynchings and all other barbarities which degrade us, we shall protest with such force of logic and intensity of soul that those who oppress us will either cease to disavow the inalienability and equality of human rights, or be ashamed to openly violate the very principles upon which this government was founded. By discharging our obligation to the children, by coming into the closest possible touch with the masses of our people, by studying the labor question as it affects the race, by establishing schools of domestic science, by setting a high moral standard and living up to it, by purifying the home, colored women will render their race a service whose value it is not in my power to estimate or express. The National Association is being cherished with such loyalty and zeal by our women that there is every reason to hope it will soon become the power for good, the tower of strength and the source of inspiration to which it is destined.

And so lifting as we climb, onward and upward we go, struggling and striving and hoping that the buds and blossoms of our desires will burst into glorious fruition ere long. With courage born of success achieved in the past, with a keen sense of the responsibility which we must continue to assume we look forward to the future, large with promise and hope. Seeking no favors because of our color or patronage because of our needs, we knock at the bar of justice and ask for an equal chance.

By Mrs. Mary Church Terrell,
President of the National Association of Colored Women

MRS. MARY CHURCH TERRELL

In all matters affecting the interests of the women of her race, Mrs. Mary Church Terrell, of Washington, D.C., is a leading spirit. Three times in succession she was elected President of the National Association of Colored Women by most flattering majorities. When, according to the provision of the constitution, which limits the term of officers, Mrs. Terrell could not be re-elected president, she was made Honorary President.

She has twice been invited to address the National Woman Suffrage Association at its annual convention in Washington. Her public utterances have always made a profound impression on her hearers and no speakers associated with her have received more applause from audiences or higher praise from the public press than herself. Not many years ago when Congress, by resolution granted power to the Commissioners of the District of Columbia to appoint two women on the Board of Education for the public schools, Mrs. Terrell was one of the women appointed. She served in the board for five years with great success and signal ability.

Mrs. Terrell is the only woman who has ever held the office of President of the Bethel Literary and Historical Association at Washington, the foremost and oldest Lyceum established and controlled by colored people in America. Her splendid work as presiding officer of this organization had much to do with her other subsequent success in attaining similar positions in other bodies of deliberation.

Mrs. Terrell's life has been an interesting one. She was born in Memphis, Tenn., of well-to-do parents.

She graduated at Oberlin College in 1884 with the degree of A.B. In 1888 she received the degree of A.M. from Oberlin. She was for a while a teacher at Wilberforce University at Xenia, Ohio. In 1887 she was appointed teacher of languages in the Colored High School at Washington. She went abroad for further study and travel in 1888 and remained in Europe two years, spending the time in France, Switzerland, Germany and Italy. She resumed her work in Washington in 1890. In 1891 she was offered the registrarship of Oberlin College, being the first woman of her race to whom such a position was ever tendered by an institution so widely known and of such high standard. This place was declined because of her approaching marriage. In 1891 she was married to Mr. Robert H. Terrell, who is a graduate of Howard College and who was recently appointed by President Roosevelt to a Federal Judgeship in the District of Columbia, being one of the two colored men first to receive this high distinction. Mrs. Terrell has a daughter whom she has named Phyllis, in honor of Phyllis Wheatley, the black woman whose verses received the commendation of George Washington and many other distinguished men of her time.

Mrs. Terrell is now engaged by a lecture bureau. She has traveled extensively in the West, speaking before large audiences and everywhere her talks have received the highest praise. The Danville, Ill., "Daily News," speaking of her address before the Chautauqua of that town, says:

"Mrs. Terrell's addresses are the pure gold with less dross of nonsense than any lecturer that has come upon the stage at this Chautauqua. From the first word to the last she has something to say, and says it as a cultured lady in the best of English, which has no tinge of the high falootin or the sensational. Such speakers are rare. She should be paid to travel as a model of good English and good manners."

Mrs. Terrell's eloquent utterances and chaste diction make a deep impression, which must have influence in the final shaping of the vexed problems that confront the Negro race in this country. Her exceptional attainments and general demeanor are a wonderful force in eradicating the prejudice against colored women. She is making an opening for her sisters as no one else is doing or has ever done.

Graduates and Former Students of Washington Colored High School

There is no better High School for colored youths in the United States than the one in Washington, D.C. It would be difficult to name an institution of similar rank, the graduates or former pupils of which have achieved success in such numbers and of such brilliancy as have those who have been trained in the Colored High School of the District of Columbia. In scanning the list of the men and women whose foundation of education and usefulness was laid in the Washington High School for colored youth, one is surprised to see the wide range of vocations they so creditably pursue. In almost every trade and profession open to the colored American, from a judgeship to a janitorship, it is possible to find a man or a woman who has either completed or only partially completed the course of the Washington High School.

When Dewey electrified the world on that eventful day in May a few years ago, one of the seamen who aimed a gun straight and made it bark loud, was a certain colored youth named Jordan, who had studied in the colored High School in Washington. It is even said that he opened the battle of Manila. It is certain, however, that he was placed in charge of a crew of gunners in the forward turret, and that he was afterward promoted to the position of chief gunner's mate. He is now in Annapolis instructing classes in ordnance, the members of which are white, as a rule.

If you had transgressed the law in a certain town in the Philippines during the late unpleasantness there, you would have been brought before a colored

Originally published in *Voice of the Negro*, June 1904, pages 221-227.

man answering to the name of Frank Stewart, also a graduate of the Colored High School of Washington. As captain in the volunteer army in the Philippine campaign, Frank Stewart rendered such effective service and so favorably impressed his superior officers by his superb qualities as a soldier, that he was made president of a town in the Philippines, the civil and criminal jurisdiction of which was placed in his hands by Uncle Sam. Both the Stewart boys, as they were called, while they were studying in the Colored High School here, were graduated from Harvard College with honor. Frank, the ex-president of the Philippine town, is now practicing law in Pittsburgh, while his brother Charles is a dentist in Boston. Speaking of military affairs reminds me that Oliver Davis, another High School boy, now second lieutenant in the United States army, was the first colored man who passed the commission in the army from the ranks. Three of the finest lieutenants in the Spanish-American war, Thomas Clarke, Harry Burgess and William Cardoza, were all high school boys.

If you should visit the training station in Newport to-day, you would probably see Joseph Cook, another representative of the Colored High School, teaching a class in electricity there, whose pupils, from the nature of the case, are white, with rare, if any exceptions. Cook ran a dynamo, an extremely complicated affair, on Admiral Sampson's ship, the New York, while our men of war were making it uncomfortable for Spaniards a few years ago. For some reason, perhaps because Cook was assigned to some other duty on the ship, he was taken from the dynamo and a white man was put in his place, but the latter was unable to master the intricacies of the machine, and was soon given other work to do.

From the examples already given it might be inferred that the Washington High School for colored youth is a sort of West Point or Annapolis on a small scale, but it is a great deal more. The youth who go forth from this school excel not only in military affairs, but in civil pursuits as well. They are distinguishing themselves in the various professions and in as many of the trades as they are permitted to enter.

Dr. West, assistant surgeon-in-chief of Freedman's Hospital, a high school boy, is said to have passed the highest mark in a competitive medical examination held a few years ago. Two of the wealthiest and most skillful colored physicians in Washington, Drs. Francis and Martin, received their scholastic training in the high school. A young physician, Frank Allen by name, now practicing medicine in Allegheny, Pa., had a record both in the public schools of this city and in the medical department of the University of Pennsylvania which it would be difficult to duplicate. For seven consecutive years Dr. Allen stood at the head of his class, and finally refused to allow his classmates in the high school to elect him valedictorian, because he wanted this honor to be conferred upon some one else. In order to matriculate in the medical department of the University of Pennsylvania one must take certain examinations and then enter the third year class. Dr. Allen's papers showed such an unusually deep and comprehensive grasp of the subjects in which he was examined that the Dean of the University made an exception in his favor and permitted him to enter the fourth year class. He had had such little instruction in one of the most difficult subjects in the course that the professor not only held out no hope that he would be able to pass, but was very slow in permitting him to undertake the examination at all. Dr. Allen undertook it, however, and the professor cheerfully admitted that he had made one of the most remarkable records that he had ever known. While Dr. Allen was pursuing his course in the University of Pennsylvania, every day except Sunday was spent at his work. He practiced medicine at night and between times, and was night clerk in a drug store besides.

If you should visit the colored schools of the District of Columbia and ask the majority of the teachers and principals where they acquired their knowledge and secured the mental discipline which enabled them to secure the positions they now hold, they would tell you that they received it in the high school here. To be sure, all have not rested on their oars since they graduated. Many of them have been constantly adding to their store of knowledge by attending the various summer schools or by taking private lessons from well-known teachers in Washington.

The principal of the Manual Training School, Dr. W. B. Evans, the director of the primary grades, Miss Emma Merritt, and two of the supervising principals, Mr. John Nalle and Mr. Ellis Brown, are products of the high school. This is true of the principals of the other colored schools, with but few exceptions. One of the most efficient teachers in the Institute for Colored Youth, founded in Philadelphia by Mrs. Frances Coppin, now conducted by Mr. Hugh M. Brown, is Mr. Alfonso Stafford, a graduate of Washington High School. Mr. Stafford has carefully compiled a history of the men and women of his race who have distinguished themselves in literature, in art and in other fields. This history, which has not yet appeared in print, was used by Mr. Stafford several years ago, while he was teaching in the summer school of Hampton Institute and was highly praised. In the

Manual Training School, Percy Brooks, head of the department of Physics, Stanton Wormley, head of the department of Drawing, and Charles L. Thomas, head of the Biological department in both high schools, are all graduates from the Washington High School. When one thinks of the number and the kind of teachers who have brought the colored schools of Washington up to such a high standard of excellence, and then remembers that the majority have received in the high school the mental discipline which has made such success and such service possible, it is difficult to overestimate the value of this institution to the colored people of the District. It is easy to see what a tremendous power for good it has been.

If you look into the antecedents of the colored youth who have made the most brilliant records at the largest Universities in the country, in nine cases out of ten you will discover that they were trained in the Colored High School of the District of Columbia. The first colored man who ever won the distinction of being commencement orator at Harvard College was Robert Heberton Terrell, who studied in the high school, has taught in that institution, has been Chief of Division of the Treasury Department, and is now presiding in a justice's court in the National Capital. The first colored man who was ever elected class orator at Harvard was Clement G. Morgan, another high school boy, formerly a member of the board of aldermen in Cambridge, Mass., and at present a lawyer of good repute. The young man who won the Pasteur prize at Harvard College, about five years ago, who was twice chosen one of three out of a possible 4,000 to represent Harvard in her debate—first with Princeton and then with Yale—the young man who, in addition to all this honor, was finally elected class orator by young white men representing the wealth, the culture and the brain of the United States, was Roscoe Conkling Bruce, also a former student of the Colored High School here, and at present Dean of the Academic Department at Tuskegee. Napoleon Marshall, who distinguished himself on the athletic field as well as in the recitation room of Harvard, is now Deputy Collector of the City of Boston.

Some years ago, while the Chicago University still had the good taste and the good sense to admit women without imposing conditions from which men are exempt, an examination was held in which a large number of men and women of the dominant race and only one colored girl competed for a scholarship entitling the successful competitor to an entire course through that institution. The only colored girl among the competitors—Cora Jackson—who graduated from the Washington High School, received the highest mark and thus secured this great prize. In Cornell, Yale, Oberlin, Amherst, in the Massachusetts Institute of Technology and in other renown seats of learning, more than one colored youth who has been trained in this *non verbis sed virtute* school, has achieved brilliant success.

Among the expert stenographers in the Brooklyn Naval Yard, is a colored man, Samuel Hudnell, by name, who won this position in a competitive examination. In the Navy Department there is still another product of the Colored High School—Arthur Wells—who is an expert typewriter and stenographer, and who secured this position by his remarkable skill.

One of the late Senator Hanna's secretaries, who had charge of the pensions in which the Ohio constituents were interested, was a young colored man who studied two years in the Washington High School. Albertus Brown entered Senator Hanna's service as a messenger, but he soon proved himself so capable that the Senator promoted him successfully to the position of typewriter, stenographer and under secretary, and he is now serving Gen. Dick, Senator Hanna's successor in the Senate, in the same capacity. In addition to discharging his duties as secretary to Senator Dick, Mr. Brown is taking a course in the law school of Howard University. In the legal profession, the Colored High School has at least two notable representatives not yet mentioned: Mr. William L. Pollard, located in the National Capitol and Mr. Albert B. George, who graduated from the law school of the North Western University and who is now practicing law in Chicago. Those who know Mr. George best, declare that he is one of the most useful citizens in Chicago and that there is no proposition in the legal profession so difficult that he will not attempt to master it.

Among the women who are engaging in educational, philanthropic and missionary work, none is rendering more valiant and effective service than Miss N.H. Burroughs, who is corresponding secretary of the Woman's Convention, one of the most active and progressive organizations in the Baptist church. Miss Burroughs received her training in the Washington High School also.

One of the most successful business ventures attempted by the colored people of the District, is the printing establishment of the Smith Brothers, all of whom studied in the high school. John Smith, the eldest, has been a clerk in the office of the superintendent of public schools for the past eighteen years. In addition to discharging his clerical duties acceptably and well, he has found time to complete a course in the Law School of the Columbian University, and has taken the degree of Doctor of Civil Laws from the Catholic University. Another brother, Francis, who is a teacher in the Manual Training School, has taken the degree of Bachelor of Science, as well as that of mechanical engineering in the Catholic University. Many of the colored letter carriers in the District are high school boys, who have won their positions fairly and squarely in civil service examinations.

But many of the young men and women who have studied in the Colored High School of Washington do not occupy positions so lofty or so lucrative as those to whom reference has already been made. Some are engaging in the so-called menial pursuits. There are comparatively few trades and professions in which colored men and women are permitted to engage. If the struggle for existence is becoming more and more desperate for the white youth on account of the keen competition in the various professions and trades, how much more is this true in the Colored boy's case! Some of the boys who graduate from the Colored High School consider themselves fortunate if they can secure employment as porters on the Pullman cars or get good positions as servants in hotels or private dwellings. How well they do their work is illustrated by the following incident: "I rang the bell for a boy in my hotel this morning and a colored boy answered the call," said one of the best magazine writers in the country, a short time ago. "He gave me all the information I wanted, concisely and accurately, and was a regular Chesterfield in manners, besides. He was evidently well educated. Tell me," said she, "how does it happen that such an intelligent colored boy is satisfied to occupy such a menial position?" The magazine writer need not have propounded this question to me, she might easily have answered it herself if she had only stopped to think.

One hears a great deal about abolishing high schools these days, particularly those largely attended by colored pupils. The arguments presented by those who adhere to this view appear rather plausible and sound at times. But when one considers the wonderful intellectual impetus which the Colored High School has given the youth of Washington, D.C., many of whom, on account of their poverty, would have been unable to get even a sip at the fountain of knowledge, if they could not have quenched their thirst without money and without price, it is difficult to understand how those who are truly interested in elevating a backward and struggling race can stand on such indefensible ground. The Colored High School has been the means of lifting the Negro in the District of Columbia upon a higher intellectual and moral plane, in spite of the fact that there are still many illiterate and vicious specimens, who commit misdemeanors and crimes.

Without the knowledge acquired in the Colored High School, it would have been impossible for the majority of the 400 Colored teachers to occupy the positions of honor and emolument which they now hold. The fact that the successful completion of the high and normal courses may secure for a boy or a girl a position in the public schools is an incentive for the youth of the District to put forth their best efforts. The lack of incentive to effort is one of the main causes of many of the Negro's vices and defects.

The Colored High School of the District of Columbia has been a great blessing, not only to those representatives of the race, who live under the shadow of the Capitol, but to many who dwell in darkness elsewhere. If some who have studied in this institution have fallen short of the mark set for them, the majority have reflected great credit upon their alma mater by doing their work in the world conscientiously and well. And here in Washington, if you scratch a skillful physician, an excellent teacher, an expert type-writer or stenographer, a faithful, efficient letter-carrier, or a good citizen on general principles, you are likely to find a graduate of the Colored High School or somebody who has been trained there.

Lynching from a Negro's Point of View

Before 1904 was three months old, thirty-one negroes had been lynched. Of this number, fifteen were murdered within one week in Arkansas, and one was shot to death in Springfield, Ohio, by a mob composed of men who did not take the trouble to wear masks. Hanging, shooting and burning black men, women and children in the United States have become so common that such occurrences create but little sensation and evoke but slight comment now. Those who are jealous of their country's fair name feel keenly the necessity of extirpating this lawlessness, which is so widespread and has taken such deep root. But means of prevention can never be devised, until the cause of lynching is more generally understood.

The reasons why the whole subject is deeply and seriously involved in error are obvious. Those who live in the section where nine-tenths of the lynchings occur do not dare to tell the truth, even if they perceive it. When men know that the death-knell of their aspirations and hopes will be sounded as soon as they express views to which the majority in their immediate vicinage are opposed, they either suppress their views or trim them to fit the popular mind. Only martyrs are brave and bold enough to defy the public will, and the manufacture of martyrs in the negro's behalf is not very brisk just now. Those who do not live in the section where most of the lynchings occur borrow their views from their brothers who do, and so the errors are continually repeated and inevitably perpetuated.

In the discussion of this subject, four mistakes are commonly made.

In the first place, it is a great mistake to suppose that rape is the real cause of lynching in the South. Beginning with the Ku Klux Klan, the negro has been constantly subjected to some form of organized violence ever since he

Originally published in the *North American Review*, 178 (June 1904), pages 853-868.

became free. It is easy to prove that rape is simply the pretext and not the cause of lynching. Statistics show that, out of every hundred negroes who are lynched, from seventy-five to eighty-five are not even accused of this crime, and many who are accused of it are innocent. And, yet, men who admit the accuracy of these figures gravely tell the country that lynching can never be suppressed, until negroes cease to commit a crime with which less than one-fourth of those murdered by mobs are charged.

The prevailing belief that negroes are not tortured by mobs unless they are charged with the "usual" crime, does not tally with the facts. The savagery which attended the lynching of a man and his wife the first week of March of the present year was probably never exceeded in this country or anywhere else in the civilized world. A white planter was murdered at Doddsville, Miss., and a negro was charged with the crime. The negro fled, and his wife, who was known to be innocent, fled with him to escape the fate which she knew awaited her, if she remained. The two negroes were pursued and captured, and the following account of the tragedy by an eye-witness appeared in the "Evening Post," a Democratic daily of Vicksburg, Miss.

> When the two negroes were captured, they were tied to trees, and while the funeral pyres were being prepared they were forced to suffer the most fiendish tortures. The blacks were forced to hold out their hands while one finger at a time was chopped off. The fingers were distributed as souvenirs. The ears of the murderers were cut off. Holbert was beaten severely, his skull was fractured, and one of his eyes, knocked out with a stick, hung by a shred from the socket. Neither the man nor the woman begged for mercy, nor made a groan or plea. When the executioner came forward to lop off fingers, Holbert extended his hand without being asked. The most excruciating form of punishment consisted in the use of a large corkscrew in the hands of some of the mob. This instrument was bored into the flesh of the man and woman, in the arms, legs and body, and then pulled out, the spirals tearing out big pieces of raw, quivering flesh every time it was withdrawn. Even this devilish torture did not make the poor brutes cry out. When finally they were thrown on the fire and allowed to be burned to death, this came as a relief to the maimed and suffering victims.

The North frequently sympathizes with the Southern mob, because it has been led to believe the negro's diabolical assaults upon white women are the chief cause of lynching. In spite of the facts, distinguished representatives from the South are still insisting, in Congress and elsewhere, that "whenever negroes cease committing the crime of rape, the lynchings and burnings will cease with it." But since three-fourths of the negroes who have met a violent death at the hands of Southern mobs have not been accused of this crime, it is evident that, instead of being the "usual" crime, rape is the most unusual of all the crimes for which negroes are shot, hanged and burned.

Although Southern men of prominence still insist that "this crime is more responsible for mob violence than all other crimes combined," it is gratifying to observe that a few of them, at least, are beginning to feel ashamed to pervert the facts. During the past few years, several Southern gentlemen, of unquestioned ability and integrity, have publicly exposed the falsity of this plea. Two years ago, in a masterful article on the race problem, Professor Andrew Sledd, at that time an instructor in a Southern college, admitted that only a small number of the negroes who are lynched are even accused of assaulting white women. Said he:

> On the contrary, a frank consideration of all the facts, with no other desire than to find the truth, the whole truth and nothing but the truth, however contrary to our wishes and humiliating to our section the truth may be, will show that by far the most of our Southern lynchings are carried through in *sheer, unqualified and increasing brutality*.

But a heavy penalty was paid by this man who dared to make such a frank and fearless statement of facts. He was forced to resign his position as professor, and lost prestige in his section in various ways. In the summer of 1903, Bishop Candler of Georgia made a strong protest against lynching, and called attention to the fact that, out of 128 negroes who had been done to death in 1902, only 16 were even accused of rape.

In the second place, it is a mistake to suppose that the negro's desire for social equality sustains any relation whatsoever to the crime of rape. According to the testimony of eye-witnesses, as well as the reports of Southern newspapers, the negroes who are known to have been guilty of assault have, as a rule, been ignorant, repulsive in appearance and as near the brute creation as it is possible for a human being to be. It is safe to assert that, among the negroes who have been guilty of ravishing white women, not one had been taught that he was the equal of white people or had ever heard of social equality. And if by chance he had heard of it, he had no clearer conception of its meaning than he had of the principle of the binomial theorem. In conversing with a large number of ignorant negroes, the writer has never found one who seemed to have any idea of what social equality means, or who expressed a desire to put this theory into practice when it was explained to him.

Negroes who have been educated in Northern institutions of learning with white men and women, and who for that reason might have learned the meaning of social equality and have acquired a taste for the same, neither assault white women nor commit other crimes, as a rule. A careful review of the facts will show that negroes who have the "convention habit" developed to a high degree, or who are able to earn their living by editing newspapers, do not belong to the criminal class, although such negroes are always held up by Southern gentlemen as objects of ridicule, contempt and scorn. Strange as it may appear, illiterate negroes, who are the only ones contributing largely to the criminal class, are coddled and caressed by the South. To the educated, cultivated members of the race, they are held up as bright and shining examples of what a really good negro should be. The dictionary is searched in vain by Southern gentlemen and gentlewomen for words sufficiently ornate and strong to express their admiration for a dear old "mammy" or a faithful old "uncle" who can neither read nor write, and who assure their white friends they would not, if they could.

On the other hand, no language is sufficiently caustic, bitter and severe, to express the disgust, hatred and scorn which Southern gentlemen feel for what is called the "New Issue," which, being interpreted, means, negroes who aspire to knowledge and culture, and who have acquired a taste for the highest and best things in life. At the door of this "New Issue," the sins and shortcomings of the whole race are laid. This "New Issue" is beyond hope of redemption, we are told, because somebody, nobody knows who, has taught it to believe in social equality, something, nobody knows what. The alleged fear of social equality has always been used by the South to explain its unchristian treatment of the negro and to excuse its many crimes. How many crimes have been committed, and how many falsehoods have been uttered, in the name of social equality by the South! Of all these, the greatest is the determination to lay lynching at its door. In the North, which is the only section that accords the negro the scrap of social equality enjoyed by him in the United States, he is rarely accused of rape. The only form of social equality ever attempted between the two races, and practiced to any considerable extent, is that which was originated by the white masters of slave women, and which has been perpetuated to them and their descendants even unto the present day. Of whatever other crime we may accuse the big, black burly brute, who is so familiar a figure in the reports of rape and lynching-bees sent out by the Southern press, surely we cannot truthfully charge him with an attempt to introduce social equality into this republican form of government, or to foist it upon a democratic land. There is no more connection between social equality and lynching to-day than there was between social equality and slavery before the war, or than there is between social equality and the convict-lease system, or any other form of oppression of which the negro has uniformly bee subjected in the South.

The third error on the subject of lynching consists of the widely circulated statement that the moral sensibilities of the best negroes in the United States are so stunted and dull, and the standard of morality even among the leaders of the race is so low, that they do not appreciate the enormity and heinousness of rape. Those who claim to know the negro best and to be his best friends declare, that he usually sympathizes with the black victim of mob violence rather than with the white victim of the black fiend's lust, even when he does not go so far as to condone the crime of rape. Only those who are densely ignorant of the standards and sentiments of the best negroes, or who wish wilfully to misrepresent and maliciously slander a race already resting under burdens greater than it can bear, would accuse its thousands of reputable men and women of sympathizing with rapists, either black or white, or of condoning their crime. The negro preachers and teachers who have had the advantage of education and moral training, together with others occupying positions of honor and trust, are continually expressing their horror of this one particular crime, and exhorting all whom they can reach by voice or pen to do everything in their power to wash the ugly stain of rape from the race's good name. And whenever the slightest pity for the victim of mob violence is expressed by a negro who represents the intelligence and decency of his race, it is invariably because there is a reasonable doubt of his innocence, rather than because there is condonation of the alleged crime.

Everybody who is well informed on the subject of lynching knows that many a negro who has been accused of assault or murder, or other violation of the law, and has been tortured to death by a mob, has afterward been proved innocent of the crime with which he was charged. So great is the thirst for the negro's blood in the South, that but a single breath of suspicion is sufficient to kindle into an all-consuming flame the embers of hatred ever smouldering in the breasts of the fiends who compose a typical mob. When once such a bloodthirsty company starts on a negro's trail, and the right one cannot be found, the first available specimen is sacrificed to their rage, no matter whether he is guilty or not.

A white man who died near Charleston, South Carolina, in March of the present year, confessed on his death-bed that he had murdered his wife, although three negroes were lynched for this crime at Ravenel, South Carolina, in May, 1902. This murder was one of the most brutal ever committed in the State, and the horrible tortures to which the three innocent negroes were subjected indicated plainly that the mob intended the punishment to fit the crime. In August, 1901, three negroes, a mother, her daughter and her son, were lynched in Carrollton, Miss., because it was rumored that they had heard of a murder before it was committed, and had not reported it. A negro was accused of murdering a woman, and was lynched in Shreveport, Louisiana, in April, 1902, who was afterward proved innocent. The woman who was lynched in Mississippi this year was not even accused of a crime. The charge of murder had not been proved against her husband, and, as the white man who was murdered had engaged in an altercation with him, it is quite likely that, if the negro had been tried in a court of law, it would have been shown to be a case of justifiable homicide. And so other cases might easily be cited to prove that the charge that innocent negroes are sometimes lynched is by no means without foundation. It is not strange, therefore, that even reputable, law-abiding negroes should protest against the tortures and cruelties inflicted by mobs which wreak vengeance upon the guilty and innocent and upon the just and unjust of their race alike. It is to the credit and not to the shame of the negro that he tries to uphold the sacred majesty of the law, which is so often trailed in the dust and trampled under foot by white mobs.

In the fourth place, it is well to remember, in discussing the subject of lynching, that it is not always possible to ascertain the facts from the accounts in the newspapers. The facts are often suppressed, intentionally or unintentionally, or distorted by the press. The case of Sam Hose, to which reference has so often been made, is a good illustration of the unreliability of the press in reporting the lynching of negroes. Sam Hose, a negro, murdered Alfred Cranford, a white man, in a dispute over wages which the white employer refused to pay the colored workman. It was decided to make an example of a negro who dared to kill a white man. A well-known, influential newspaper immediately offered a reward of $500 for the capture of Sam Hose. This same newspaper predicted a lynching, and stated that, though several modes of punishment had been suggested, it was the consensus of opinion that the negro should be burned at the stake and tortured before being burned. A rumor was started, and circulated far and wide by the press, that Sam Hose had assaulted the wife of Alfred Cranford, after the latter had been killed. One of the best detectives in Chicago was sent to Atlanta to investigate the affair. After securing all the information it was possible to obtain from black and white alike, and carefully weighing the evidence, this white detective declared it would have been a physical impossibility for the negro to assault the murdered man's wife, and expressed it as his opinion that the charge of assault was an invention intended to make the burning a certainty.

The Sunday on which Sam Hose was burned was converted into a holiday. Special trains were made up to take the Christian people of Atlanta to the scene of the burning, a short distance from the city. After the first train moved out with every inch of available space inside and out filled to overflowing, a second had to be made up, so as to accommodate those who had just come from church. After Sam Hose had been tortured and burned to death, the great concourse of Christians who had witnessed the tragedy scraped for hours among his ashes in the hope of finding a sufficient number of his bones to take to their friends as souvenirs. The charge has been made that Sam Hose boasted to another negro that he intended to assault Alfred Cranford's wife. It would be difficult for anybody who understands conditions in the South to believe that a sane negro would announce his purpose to violate a white woman there, then deliberately enter her husband's house, while all the family were present, to carry out his threat.

Two years ago a riot occurred in Atlanta, Georgia, in which four white policemen were killed and several wounded by a colored man named Richardson, who was finally himself burned to death. Through the press the public was informed that the negro was a desperado. As a matter of fact, Richardson was a merchant, well to do and law-abiding. The head and front of his offending was that he dared to reprimand an ex-policeman for living in open adultery with a colored woman. When it was learned that this negro had been so impudent to a white man, the sheriff led out a posse, consisting of the city police, to arrest Richardson. Seeing the large number of officers surrounding his house, and knowing what would be his fate, if caught, the negro determined to sell his life dear, and he did. With the exception of the Macon "Telegraph," but few white newspapers ever gave the real cause of the riot, and so Richardson has gone down to history as a black desperado, who shot to death four officers of the law and wounded as many more. Several years ago, near New Orleans, a negro was at work in a corn-field. In working through the corn he made considerable noise, which frightened a young white woman, who happened to be passing by. She ran to the nearest house, and reported that a negro had jumped at her. A large crowd of white men immediately shouldered guns and seized the negro, who had no idea what it meant. When told why he was taken, the negro protested that he had not even seen the girl whom he was accused of frightening, but his protest was of no avail and he was hanged to the nearest tree. The press informed the country that this negro was lynched for attempted rape. Instance after instance might be cited to prove that facts bearing upon lynching, as well as upon other phases of the race problem, are often garbled—without intention, perhaps—by the press.

What, then, is the cause of lynching? At the last analysis, it will be discovered that there are just two causes of lynching. In the first place, it is due to race hatred, the hatred of a stronger people toward a weaker who were once held as slaves. In the second place, it is due to the lawlessness so prevalent in the section where nine-tenths of the lynchings occur. View the question of lynching from any point of view one may, and it is evident that it is just as impossible for the negroes of this country to prevent mob violence by any attitude of mind which they may assume, or any course of conduct which they may pursue, as it is for a straw dam to stop Niagara's flow. Upon the same spirit of intolerance and of hatred the crime of lynching must be fastened as that which called into being the Ku Klux Klan, and which has prompted more recent exhibitions of hostility toward the negro, such as the disfranchisement acts, the Jim Crow Car Laws, and the new slavery called "peonage," together with other acts of oppression which make the negro's lot so hard.

Lynching is the aftermath of slavery. The white men who shoot negroes to death and flay them alive, and the white women who apply flaming torches to their oil-soaked bodies to-day, are the sons and daughters of women who had but little, if any, compassion on the race when it was enslaved. The men who lynch negroes to-day are, as a rule, the children of women who sat by their firesides happy and proud in the possession and affection of their own children, while they looked with unpitying eye and adamantine heart upon the anguish of slave mothers whose children had been sold away, when not overtaken by a sadder fate. If it be contended, as it often is, that negroes are rarely lynched by the descendants of former slaveholders, it will be difficult to prove the point. According to the reports of lynchings sent out by the Southern press itself, mobs are generally composed of the "best citizens" of a place, who quietly disperse to their homes as soon as they are certain that the negro is good and dead. The newspaper who predicted that Sam Hose would be lynched, which offered a reward for his capture and which suggested burning at the stake, was neither owned nor edited by the poor whites. But if it be conceded that the descendants of slaveholders do not shoot and burn negroes, lynching must still be regarded as the legitimate offspring of slavery. If the children of the poor whites of the South are the chief aggressors in the lynching-bees of that section, it is because their ancestors were brutalized by their slaveholding environment. In discussing the lynching of negroes at the present time, the heredity and the environment, past and present, of the white mobs are not taken sufficiently into account. It is as impossible to comprehend the cause of the ferocity and barbarity which attend the average lynching-bee without taking into account the brutalizing effect of slavery upon the people of the section where most of the lynchings occur, as it is to investigate the essence and nature of fire without considering the gases which cause the flame to ignite. It is too much to expect, perhaps, that the children of women who for generations looked upon the hardships and the degradation of their sisters of a darker hue with few if any protests, should have mercy and compassion upon the children of that oppressed race now. But what a tremendous influence for law and order, and what a mighty foe to mob violence Southern white women might be, if they would arise in the purity and power of their womanhood to implore their fathers, husbands and sons no longer to stain their hands with the black man's blood!

While the men of the South were off fighting to keep the negro in bondage, their mothers, wives and daughters were entrusted to the black man's care. How faithfully and loyally he kept his sacred trust the records of history attest! Not a white woman was violated throughout the entire war. Can the white women of the South forget how black men bore themselves throughout that trying time? Surely it is not too much to ask that the daughters of mothers who were shielded from harm by the black man's constancy and care should requite their former protectors, by at least asking that, when the children of the latter are accused of crime, they should be treated like human beings and not like wild animals to be butchered and shot.

If there were one particularly heinous crime for which an infuriated people took vengeance upon the negro, or if there were a genuine fear that a guilty negro might escape the penalty of the law in the South, then it might be possible to explain the cause of lynching on some other hypothesis than that of race hatred. It has already been shown that the first supposition has no foundation in fact. It is easy to prove that the second is false. Even those who condone lynching do not pretend to fear the delay or the uncertainty of the law, when a guilty negro is concerned. With the courts of law entirely in the hands of the white man, with judge and jury belonging to the superior race, a guilty negro could no more extricate himself from the meshes of the law in the South than he could slide from the devil-fish's embrace or slip from the anaconda's coils. Miscarriage of justice in the South is possible only when white men transgress the law.

In addition to lynching, the South is continually furnishing proof of its determination to wreak terrible vengeance upon the negro. The recent shocking revelations of the extent to which the actual enslavement of negroes has been carried under the peonage system of Alabama and Mississippi, and the unspeakable cruelties to which men, women and children are alike subjected, all bear witness to this fact. In January of the present year, a government detective found six negro children ranging in age from six to sixteen years working on a Georgia plantation in bare feet, scantily clad in rags, although the ground was covered with snow. The owner of the plantation is one of the wealthiest men in northeast Georgia, and is said to have made his fortune by holding negroes in slavery. When he was tried it was shown that the white planter had killed the father of the six children a few years before, but was acquitted of the murder, as almost invariably happens, when a white man takes a negro's life. After the death of their father, the children were treated with incredible cruelty. They were often chained in a room without fire and were beaten until the blood streamed from their backs, when they were unable to do their stint of work. The planter was placed under $5,000 bail, but it is doubtful whether he will ever pay the penalty of his crime. Like the children just mentioned hundreds of negroes are to-day groaning under a bondage more crushing and more cruel than that abolished forty years ago.

This same spirit manifests itself in a variety of ways. Efforts are constantly made to curtail the educational opportunities of colored children. Already one State has enacted a law by which colored children in the public schools are prohibited from receiving instruction higher than the sixth grade, and other States will, doubtless, soon follow this lead. It is a well-known fact that a Governor recently elected in one of the Southern States owes his popularity and his votes to his open and avowed opposition to the education of negroes. Instance after instance might be cited to prove that the hostility toward the negro in the South is bitter and pronounced, and that lynching is but a manifestation of this spirit of vengeance and intolerance in its ugliest and most brutal form.

To the widespread lawlessness among the white people of the South lynching is also due. In commenting upon the blood-guiltiness of South Carolina, the Nashville "American" declared some time ago that, if the killings in the other States had been in the same ratio to population as in South Carolina, a larger number of people would have been murdered in the United States during 1902 than fell on the American side in the Spanish and Philippine wars.

Whenever Southern white people discuss lynching, they are prone to slander the whole negro race. Not long ago, a Southern writer of great repute declared without qualification or reservation that "the crime of rape is well-nigh wholly confined to the negro race," and insisted that "negroes furnish most of the ravishers." These assertions are as unjust to the negro as they are unfounded in fact. According to statistics recently published, only one colored male in 100,000 over five years of age was accused of assault upon a white woman in the South in 1902, whereas one male out of every 20,000 over five years of age was charged with rape in Chicago during the same year. If these figures prove anything at all, they show that the men and boys in Chicago are many times more addicted to rape than are the negroes in the South. Already in the present year two white men have been arrested in the national capital for attempted assault upon little children. One was convicted and sentenced to six years in the penitentiary. The crime of which the other was accused was of the most infamous character. A short account of the trial of the convicted man appeared in the Washington dailies, as any other criminal suit would have been reported; but if a colored man had committed the same crime, the newspapers from one end of the United States to the other would have published it broadcast. Editorials upon the total depravity and the hopeless immorality of the negro would have been written, based upon this particular case as a text. With such facts to prove the falsity of the charge that "the crime of rape is well-nigh wholly confined to the negro race," it is amazing that any writer of repute should affix his signature to such a slander.

But even if the negro's morals were as loose and as lax as some claim them to be, and if his belief in the virtue of women were as slight as we are told, the South has nobody to blame but itself. The only object lesson in virtue and morality which the negro received for 250 years came through the medium of slavery, and that peculiar institution was not calculated to set his standards of correct living very high. Men do not gather grapes of thorns nor figs of thistles. Throughout their entire period of bondage colored women were debauched by their masters. From the day they were liberated to the present time, prepossessing young colored girls have been considered the rightful prey of white gentlemen in the South, and they have been protected neither by public sentiment nor by the law. In the South, the negro's home is not considered sacred by the superior race. White men are neither punished for invading it, nor lynched for violating colored women and girls. In discussing this phase of the race problem last year, one of the most godly and eloquent ministers in the Methodist Episcopal Church (white) expressed himself as follows: "The negro's teachers have been white. It is from the white man the negro has learned to lie and steal. If you wish to know who taught the negro licentiousness, you have only to look into the faces of thousands of mulatto people and get your answer." When one thinks how the negro was degraded in slavery, which discouraged, when it did not positively forbid, marriage between slaves, and considers the bad example set them by white masters, upon whom the negroes looked as scarcely lower than the angels, the freedman's self-control seems almost like a miracle of modern times. In demanding so much of the negro, the South places itself in the anomalous position of insisting that the conduct of the inferior race shall be better, and its standards higher, than those of the people who claim to be superior.

The recent lynching in Springfield, Ohio, and in other cities of the North, show how rapidly this lawlessness is spreading throughout the United States. If the number of Americans who participate in this wild and diabolical carnival of blood does not diminish, nothing can prevent this country from becoming a byword and a reproach throughout the civilized world. When Secretary Hay appealed to Roumania in behalf of the Jews, there were many sarcastic comments made to the press of that country and of other foreign lands about the inhuman treatment of the negro in the United States. In November, 1903, a manifesto signed by delegates from all over the world was issued at Brussels, Belgium, by the International Socialist Bureau, protesting against the lynching of negroes in the United States.

It is a source of deep regret and sorrow to many good Christians in this country that the church puts forth so few and such feeble protests against lynching. As the attitude of many ministers on the question of slavery greatly discouraged the abolitionists before the war, so silence in the pulpit concerning the lynching of negroes to-day plunges many of the persecuted race into deep gloom and dark despair. Thousands of dollars are raised by our churches every year to send missionaries to Christianize the heathen in foreign lands, and this is proper and right. But in addition to this foreign missionary work, would it not be well for our churches to inaugurate a crusade against the barbarism at home, which converts hundreds of white women and children into savages every year, while it crushes the spirit, blights the hearth and breaks the heart of hundreds of defenseless blacks? Not only do ministers fail, as a rule, to protest strongly against the hanging and burning of negroes, but some actually condone the crime without incurring the displeasure of their congregations or invoking the censure of the church. Although the church court which tried the preacher in Wilmington, Delaware, accused of inciting his community to riot and lynching by means of an incendiary sermon, found him guilty of "unministerial and unchristian conduct," of advocating mob murder and of thereby breaking down the public respect for the law, yet it simply admonished him to be "more careful in the future" and inflicted no punishment at all. Such indifference to lynching on the part of the church recalls the experience of Abraham Lincoln, who refused to join church in Springfield, Illinois, because only three out of twenty-two ministers in the whole city stood with him in his effort to free the slave. But, however unfortunate may have been the attitude of some of the churches on the question of slavery before the war, from the moment the shackles fell from the black man's limbs to the present day, the American Church has been most kind and generous in its treatment of the backward and struggling race. Nothing but ignorance or malice could prompt one to disparage the efforts put forth by the churches in the negro's behalf. But, in the face of so much lawlessness to-day, surely there is a role for the Church Militant to play. When one reflects upon the large number of negroes who are yearly hurled into eternity, unshriven by priest and untried by law, one cannot help realizing that as a nation we have fallen upon grave times, indeed. Surely, it is time for the ministers in their pulpits and the Christians in their pews to fall upon their knees and pray for deliverance from this rising tide of barbarism which threatens to deluge the whole land.

How can lynching be extirpated in the United States? There are just two ways in which this can be accomplished. In the first place, lynching can never be suppressed in the South, until the masses of ignorant white people in that section are educated and lifted to a higher moral plane. It is difficult for one who has not seen these people to comprehend the density of their ignorance and the depth of their degradation. A well-known white author who lives in the South describes them as follows:

> Wholly ignorant, absolutely without culture, apparently without even the capacity to appreciate the nicer feelings or higher sense, yet conceited on account of their white skin which they constantly dishonour, they make, when aroused, as wild and brutal a mob as ever disgraced the face of the earth.

In lamenting the mental backwardness of the white people of the South, the Atlanta "Constitution" expressed itself as follows two years ago: "We have as many illiterate white men over the age of twenty-one years in the South to-day as there were fifty-two years ago, when the census of 1850 was taken." Over against these statistics stands the record of the negro, who has reduced his illiteracy 44.5 per cent in forty years. The hostility which has always existed between the poor whites and the negroes of the South has been greatly intensified in these latter days, by the material and intellectual advancement of the negro. The wrath of a Spanish bull, before whose maddened eyes a red flag is flaunted, is but a feeble attempt at temper compared with the seething, boiling rage of the average white man in the South who beholds a well-educated negro dressed in fine or becoming clothes. In the second place, lynching cannot be suppressed in the South until all classes of white people who dwell there, those of high as well as middle and low degree, respect the rights of other human beings, no matter what may be the color of their skin, become merciful and just enough to cease their persecution of a weaker race and learn a holy reverence for the law.

It is not because the American people are cruel, as a whole, or indifferent on general principles to the suffering of the wronged or oppressed, that outrages against the negro are permitted to occur and go unpunished, but because many are ignorant of the extent to which they are carried, while others despair of eradicating them. The South has so industriously, persistently and eloquently preached the inferiority of the negro, that the North has apparently been converted to this view—the thousands of negroes of sterling qualities, moral worth and lofty patriotism to the contrary notwithstanding. The South has insisted so continuously and belligerently that it is the negro's best friend, that it understands him better than other people on the face of the earth and that it will brook interference from nobody in its method of dealing with him, that the North has been persuaded or intimidated into bowing to this decree.

Then, too, there seems to be a decline of the great convictions in which this government was conceived and into which it was born. Until there is a renaissance of popular belief in the principles of liberty and equality upon which this government was founded, lynching, the Convict Lease System, the Disfranchisement Acts, the Jim Crow Car Laws, unjust discriminations in the professions and trades and similar atrocities will continue to dishearten and degrade the negro, and stain the fair name of the United States. For there can be no doubt that the greatest obstacle in the way of extirpating lynching is the general attitude of the public mind toward this unspeakable crime. The whole country seems tired of hearing about the black man's woes. The wrongs of the Irish, of the Armenians, of the Roumanian and Russian Jews, of the exiles of Russia and of every other oppressed people upon the face of the globe, can arouse the sympathy and fire the indignation of the American public, while they seem to be all but indifferent to the murderous assaults upon the negroes in the South.

The Progress of Colored Women

"I expected to see a dozen clever colored women, but instead of twelve I saw two hundred. It was simply an eye opener." This is the way one white woman expressed herself, after she had attended a convention of colored women held in Chicago about four years ago. This sentiment was echoed by many other white women who assisted at the deliberations of the colored women on that occasion. These Chicagoans were no more surprised at the intelligence, culture and taste in dress which the colored women displayed than white people of other cities. When the National Association of Colored Women held its biennial two years ago in Buffalo, New York, the logic, earnestness and common sense of the delegates were quite as much a nine days' wonder as it was in Chicago. "I hold myself above the pettiness of race prejudice, of course," said one of the best women journalists in the country, "but for all my liberal mindedness the four days session of this federation of colored women's clubs has been a revelation. It has been my lot, first and last to attend a good many conventions of women—'Mothers, Daughters,' and what not, and of them all, the sanest, the liveliest, the most practical was that of the colored women." And so quotation after quotation might be cited to prove that even the white people who think they know all about colored people and are perfectly just in their estimate of them are surprised when they have an ocular demonstration of the rapidity with which a large number of colored women has advanced. When one considers the obstacles encountered by colored women in their effort to educate and cultivate themselves, since they became free, the work they have accomplished and the progress they have made will bear favorable comparison, at least with that of their more fortunate sisters, from whom the opportunity of acquiring

Originally published in *Voice of the Negro*, July 1904, pages 291-294.

knowledge and the means of self culture have never been entirely withheld. Not only are colored women with ambition and aspiration handicapped on account of their sex, but they are almost everywhere baffled and mocked because of their race. Not only because they are women, but because they are colored women are discouragement and disappointment meeting them at every turn. But in spite of the obstacles encountered, the progress made by colored women along many lines appears like a veritable miracle of modern times. Forty years ago for the great masses of colored women there was no such thing as home. To-day in each and every section of the country there are hundreds of homes among colored people, the mental and moral tone of which is as high and pure as can be found among the best people of any land. To the women of the race may be attributed in large measure the refinement and purity of the colored home. The immorality of colored women is a theme upon which those who know little about them or those who maliciously misrepresent them love to descant. Foul aspersions upon the character of colored women are assiduously circulated by the press of certain sections and especially by the direct descendants of those who in years past were responsible for the moral degradation of their female slaves. And yet, in spite of the fateful heritage of slavery, even though the safe guards usually thrown around maidenly youth and innocence are in some sections entirely withheld from colored girls, statistics compiled by men not inclined to falsify in favor of my race show that immorality among the colored women of the United States is not so great as among women with similar environment and temptations in Italy, Germany, Sweden and France.

Scandals in the best colored society are exceedingly rare, while the progressive game of divorce and remarriage is practically unknown.

The intellectual progress of colored women has been marvelous. So great has been their thirst for knowledge and so herculean their efforts to acquire it that there are few colleges, universities, high and normal schools in the North, East and West from which colored girls have not graduated with honor. In Wellesely, Vassar, Ann Arbor, Cornell and in Oberlin, my dear alma mater, whose name will always be loved and whose praise will always be sung as the first college in the country broad, just and generous enough to extend a cordial welcome to the Negro and to open its doors to women on an equal footing with the men, colored girls by their splendid records have forever settled the question of their capacity and worth. The instructors in these and other institutions cheerfully bear testimony to their intelligence, their diligence and their success. As the brains of colored women expanded, their hearts began to grow. No sooner had the heads of a favored few been filled with knowledge than their hearts yearned to dispense blessings to the less fortunate of their race. With tireless energy and eager zeal colored women have worked in every conceivable way to elevate their race. Of the colored teachers engaged in instructing our youth it is probably no exaggeration to say that fully eighty per cent, are women. In the backwoods, remote from the civilization and comforts of the city and town colored women may be found courageously battling with those evils which such conditions always entail. Many a heroine of whom the world will never hear has thus sacrificed her life to her race amid surroundings and in the face of privations which only martyrs can bear.

Through the medium of their societies in the church, beneficial organizations out of it and clubs of various kinds colored women are doing a vast amount of good. It is almost impossible to ascertain exactly what the Negro is doing in any field, for the records are so poorly kept. This is particularly true in the case of the women of the race. During the past forty years there is no doubt that colored women in their poverty have contributed large sums of money to charitable and educational institutions as well as to the foreign and home missionary work. Within the twenty five years in which the educational work of the African Methodist Episcopal church has been systematized, the women of that organization have contributed at least five hundred thousand dollars to the cause of education. Dotted all over the country are charitable institutions for the aged, orphaned and poor which have been established by colored women, just how many it is difficult to state, owing to the lack of statistics bearing on the progress, possessions and prowess of colored women. Among the charitable institutions either founded, conducted or supported by colored women, may be mentioned the Hale Infirmary of Montgomery, Alabama, the Carrie Steel Orphanage of Atlanta, the Reed Orphan Home of Covington, and the Hains Industrial School of Augusta, all three in the state of Georgia; a home for the aged of both races in New Bedford and St. Monica's home of Boston, in Massachusetts, Old Folks Home in Memphis, Tennessee, and the Colored Orphan's Home of Lexington, Ky., together with others which lack of space forbids me to mention. Mt. Meigs Institute is an excellent example of a work originated and carried into successful execution by a colored woman. The school was established for the benefit of colored people on the plantations in the black belt of Alabama. In the township of Mt. Meigs the population is practically all colored. Instruction given in this school is of the kind best suited to the needs of the people for whom it was established. Along with some scholastic training girls are taught everything pertaining to the management of the home, while boys are taught practical farming, wheelwrighting, blacksmithing and have some military training. Having started with almost nothing, at the end of eight years the trustees of the school owned nine acres of land and five buildings in which several thousand pupils had received instructions, all through the energy, the courage and the sacrifice of one little woman.

Up to date, politics have been religiously eschewed by colored women, although questions affecting our legal status as a race is sometimes agitated by the most progressive class. In Louisiana and Tennessee colored women have several times petitioned the legislatures of their respective states to repel the obnoxious Jim Crow Car Laws. Against the Convict Lease System, whose atrocities have been so frequently exposed as of late, colored women here and there in the South are waging a ceaseless war. So long as hundreds of their brothers and sisters, many of whom have committed no crime or misdemeanor whatever, are thrown into cells, whose cubic contents are less than those of a good size grave, to be overworked, underfed and only partially covered with vermin-infested rags, and so long as children are born to the women in these camps who breathe the polluted atmosphere of these dens of horror and vice from the time they utter their first cry in the world till they are released from their suffering by death, colored women who are working for the emancipation and elevation of their race know where their duty lies. By constant agitation of this painful and hideous subject they hope to touch the conscience of the country, so that this stain upon its escutcheon shall be forever wiped away.

Alarmed at the rapidity with which the Negro is losing ground in the world of trade some of the far sighted women are trying to solve the labor question, so far as it concerns the women at least, by urging the establishment of Schools of Domestic Science wherever means therefor can be secured. Those who are interested in this particular work hope and believe that if colored women and girls are thoroughly trained in domestic service, the boycott which has undoubtedly been placed upon them in many sections of the country will be removed. With so few vocations open to the Negro and with the labor organizations increasingly hostile to him, the future of the boys and girls of the race appears to some of our women very foreboding and dark.

The cause of temperance has been eloquently espoused by two women, each of whom has been appointed National Superintendent of work among colored people by the Woman's Christian Temperance Union. In business colored women have had signal success. There is in Alabama a large milling and cotton business belonging to and controlled by a colored woman who has sometimes as many as seventy-five men in her employ. Until a few years ago the principal ice plant of Nova Scotia was owned and managed by a colored woman, who sold it for a large amount. In the professions there are dentists and doctors, whose practice is lucrative and large. Ever since a book was published in 1773 entitled "Poems on Various Subjects, Religious and Moral by Phyllis Wheatley, Negro Servant of Mr. John Wheatley," of Boston, colored women have given abundant evidence of literary ability. In sculpture we are represented by a woman upon whose chisel Italy has set her seal of approval; in painting by one of Bougoureau's pupils and in music by young women holding diplomas from the best conservatories in the land.

In short, to use a thought of the illustrious Frederick Douglass, if judged by the depths from which they have come, rather than by the heights to which those blessed with centuries of opportunities have attained, colored women need not hang their heads in shame. They are slowly but surely making their way up to the heights, wherever they can be scaled. In spite of handicaps and discouragements they are not losing heart. In a variety of ways they are rendering valiant service to their race. Lifting as they climb, onward and upward they go struggling and striving and hoping that the buds and blossoms of their desires may burst into glorious fruition ere long. Seeking no favors because of their color nor charity because of their needs they knock at the door of Justice and ask for an equal chance.

The International Congress of Women

Recently held in Berlin, Germany

It is doubtful whether it is in the power of any human being to do full justice to the International Congress of Women which recently met in Berlin, Germany, through the medium of words. Women from all over the civilized world were there—from Greenland's rocky mountains, and from India's coral strands, so to speak—and they came there in crowds. The Germans are noted for the thoroughness and precision with which they plan and conduct their affairs. This trait in their character was never more in evidence than at this congress which the German women planned. I doubt whether it would be possible for the women of any other country in the world to arrange a meeting which could surpass, if, indeed, it could ever equal, that wonderful meeting in Berlin. This opinion is not confined to myself alone, but I have heard many others give utterance to the same thought. In articles recently written by Mrs. May Wright Sewall, the ex-president of the International Council of Women, and Mrs. Adelaide Johnson, a sculptor, practically the same view is expressed. A well known woman, who occupies a very conspicuous position in one of the largest organizations of women in the United States, confessed to me in Berlin that if she ever heard the International Congress intended to hold a meeting in this country, she would pack up bag and baggage, before it was time for it to convene, and skip for parts unknown.

Nothing which could contribute to the success of the meeting was left undone. Everything which could add to the pleasure or to the comfort of

Originally published in *Voice of the Negro*, December 1904, pages 454-461.

the guests was carefully arranged. The wealthiest and best people in Berlin were deeply interested in the Congress and they proved the extent of their interest in a most substantial way. In some of the elegant homes generously placed at the service of the committee on arrangements, delegates or speakers were entertained. In others magnificent receptions were held. The writer was entertained by one of the wealthiest and most prominent families in Berlin. Not a single room but a suite was placed at my disposal, while my well-bred and amiable hostess assigned me a maid who stood ready to answer my every beck and call.

Count von Bulow, who lives in the residence formerly occupied by the great Bismarck, and Count von Posadonsky, one the chancellor and the other secretary of state, gave an elegant garden party to the delegates and speakers of the congress. We were thus afforded an opportunity of meeting these distinguished German statesmen and their wives as well as seeing the spacious grounds surrounding these historic mansions in the very heart of Berlin. In a short article it would be impossible to name all the receptions and social functions given in honor of the International Congress, to each of which I was invited and everywhere most cordially received. The Hon. Charlemagne Tower, United States Ambassador to Germany, was especially courteous and gracious to me at the reception which he gave.

In arranging to entertain the guests of the congress, money seemed to be no object at all, for the plans were made on a most lavish scale. For instance, every delegate or speaker who came to that meeting was invited to attend a performance at any theatre to which she cared to go, free of charge. This one form of entertainment alone must have cost an enormous sum. At some of the receptions given in private houses renowned singers and other artists had been secured for the entertainment of the guests. At the opening banquet at least 2,000 people sat down to tables which groaned under the delicacies of the season. At the close of the session the city of Berlin gave a banquet which seemed less like a reality than a dream, when one beheld the room of almost barbaric splendor, in which the feast was spread, looked at the artistic decorations, listened to the heavenly music and drank in the scene as a whole.

It has never been my privilege to listen to addresses more learned, more earnest and more eloquent than those which were delivered in Berlin. In order to enjoy the meetings, however, it was absolutely necessary to understand both German and French. For this reason some well known American delegates were unable to comprehend the meaning of the very addresses which they would have enjoyed the most. Although I was prepared to meet progressive, intelligent women at the International Congress, I did not expect to see them in such numbers, I must confess. I had no idea of the rapidity with which the woman movement had spread abroad. It was a constant surprise to me, too, to see how many women among the aristocracy are deeply, genuinely and actively interested in the education and elevation of their sex.

Although I shall not attempt to give a detailed account of my sojourn in Paris or London, after I left Berlin, still I cannot resist the temptation briefly to refer to my visit to the countess of Warwick, one of the best known, one of the most beautiful as well as one of the most useful women in England. The countess and I were booked to address the International Congress the same day and in the same section, because she had been asked to discuss subjects which were closely akin. A sudden illness, however, prevented the countess from fulfilling her engagement, to the bitter disappointment of everybody concerned. When she learned that I was coming to London, she wrote me a letter, while I was still in Paris, inviting me most cordially to call. She had already gone to her country seat, she said, but she would be glad to return to her city residence to see me. And so she did. And a more democratic, a more intelligent, a more gracious and a more ideally beautiful woman than the countess of Warwick it would be hard to find.

While referring to the titled women I met abroad I must not fail to mention the name of Princess Maria Rohan, whose head is as full of excellent ideas as her heart is filled with the desire to do good deeds. The picture which this distinguished lady sent me, since I came home, will serve to remind me of many a pleasant conversation we had together in Berlin.

While I was in London it was my good fortune and privilege to meet Mr. W. T. Stead, the editor of the *Review of the Reviews*, and the author of many good books, one of which, the "Americanization of the World," he was gracious enough to give me. I prize the book very highly, not only because of its literary value, but because it contains an inscription written by this noted author's own hand. Mr. Stead is one of the most democratic men, one of the most brilliant conversationalists, one of the most whole-souled, genial gentlemen in the world. The advice he gave, the encouragement and inspiration received from him during the two visits we had together will abide with me like a precious treasure so long as I live. When I met him for the first time, he had already commented upon my article on lynching, which appeared in the June number of the *North American Review*, in the kindest and most complimentary way. The colored people of the United States have very few friends who champion their cause so loyally, so fearlessly and so eloquently as Mr. W. T. Stead.

One of the pleasantest afternoons passed in England was spent in the home of an American gentleman, who lives in London with his wife and three handsome, interesting children. I have met many Americans whose views on the race problem are just and as broad as it is right for them to be. But I have never met any living human creature—black, white, grizzle or gray—who is more bitterly and violently opposed to the injustice and barbarities perpetrated upon the colored people of this country, who is more willing and eager to do everything in his power to suppress the lawlessness of which they are the victims, and who is more determined to use every means at his command to secure for them their inalienable rights than is Mr. John Milholland, who formerly lived in New York. After talking several times with this splendid representative of the best American manhood, I felt that I had discovered the William Lloyd Garrison of the present day.

There was one man whom I met abroad who made a very deep impression upon me, I must confess. Samuel Coleridge Taylor is his name. I shall always look back upon the afternoon and evening spent with this great composer and his charming wife as a veritable red letter day in my life. Samuel Coleridge Taylor is a great musician, to be sure. He knows all about harmony, sharps and flats, but he knows many other things besides. He is a cultured gentleman, who converses well on any subject. He is the worthy son of his African father, who was a noted physician in one of the largest hospitals in England, when he died. Mr. Coleridge Taylor's intelligent and amiable English wife has a voice, which is sonorous, rich and sweet. As her gifted husband accompanied her, while she sang several of his dainty little lyrics with so much feeling and art, I thought it would be a long time before I should behold a more beautiful picture of domestic harmony and bliss. Mr. Coleridge Taylor is looking forward to his visit in Washington next fall with great anticipations of pleasure, with genuine enthusiasm, in fact. Unless providence interferes most seriously with his plans he will surely come to the United States in the autumn.

At the dinner table the conversation turned naturally and imperceptibly upon the manifestations of race prejudice in England and in the United States. After dinner Mr. and Mrs. Coleridge Taylor and I attended a concert, at which the youthful famous composer conducted an orchestra, composed of some of the fairest, prettiest English girls I have ever seen. As I saw this great musician's face light up with fire and enthusiasm for his art, I raised my heart to God in gratitude and praise that this gifted son of the muses dwells in a land in which his transcendent genius is neither crippled nor crushed by a blighting prejudice and a cruel oppression based on the color of his skin.

In Paris I had a very striking and a very pleasant illustration of the proverbial affability and politeness of the French. Ever since I learned that a colored man, Mr. H. O. Tanner by name, had painted a picture in Paris, which was awarded the first prize over innumerable others, executed by picked artists from all over the world, and that this picture had been purchased by the government of France, I have had a great yearning to see it. When I was a young woman, in company with my father, I beheld the wonderful works of art in the Louvre and in the Luxembourg gallery of Paris for the first time. If anyone had prophesied then that a picture painted by a colored man would ever occupy a position of honor among these masterpieces of ancient and modern times, I should have expressed very grave doubts indeed. Since that time this miracle has been performed, for Mr. Tanner's painting was placed in the Luxembourg a few years ago. As soon as I decided to go to Paris, therefore, after I left Berlin, I made up my mind that in this French city, which contains such a bewildering profusion of masterpieces, I should see Mr. Tanner's "Raising of Lazarus," if I saw nothing else. Imagine, therefore, how bitter and keen was my disappointment, when on reaching the Luxembourg with a heart full of joyous expectancy I learned that Mr. Tanner's picture was no longer there. Although the Luxembourg is by no means small, it is not large enough to hold all the pictures which are painted and accepted by the government from year to year. In order to do justice to everybody concerned, therefore, the pictures of artists from one country are exhibited one year, those painted by artists from another the next year and so on down the line. As ill luck would have it, the pictures of the American artists were not on exhibition this year, so that Mr. Tanner's had been removed. In my disappointment and despair I approached one of the guards and almost tearfully told him my tale of woe. I besought him on bended knee to secure permission for me to see Mr. Tanner's picture, if such a thing could possibly be done. I admitted that I was not acquainted with the artist, but I declared that I knew his father, his mother, his sisters, and his brothers, and when I finished I am sure the guard thought I belonged to the family myself. I told him I could not return to my country with my head erect and I knew I could never die happy, if I did not see the picture painted by this great American artist, of whom every

Negro in the United States is so very proud. When I finished, this kind hearted guard gave a delightful shrug of his French shoulders, which was a cross between encouragement and doubt, and promised to do everything he could to obtain my heart's desire. He then gave me the name of M. Benedit, the superintendent of the Luxembourg, and advised me to write to him. I rushed home as fast as I could and wrote M. Benedit a letter, each and every word of which was a prayer or a tear. Almost by return mail I received a reply from this most obliging and courteous French official, stating that he would be very happy to comply with my request. He told me that the permission he was about to give me was very rarely granted, but that if I presented his letter to one of the guards of the Luxembourg, Mr. Tanner's painting would be immediately unfolded to my view. Armed with this precious letter, I betook myself again to the Luxembourg and gave it to one of the guards. After consulting for a short time with those in authority, he returned and told me that Mr. Tanner's picture was no longer in the Luxembourg, but that it was in one of the rooms in the Louvre. I was spared any anxiety which I might otherwise have had by being informed that one of the guards would be sent with me immediately to the Louvre to show me the picture which I so much desired to see. Thus it was that I had the rare privilege and the exquisite pleasure of feasting my eyes upon the masterpiece of a colored man, which will bear witness for many years to come to the artistic talent of the race to which this artist belongs.

In one short article it would be impossible for me to relate all the delightful experiences I had abroad. A word or two must be added with reference to the status of colored people across the sea. In France there is absolutely no prejudice against a man on account of the color of his skin, so far as I was able to ascertain or to see. There are innumerable cases of inter-marriage between black and white, which causes no commotion nor comment at all. In Germany there seems to be no prejudice based on the color of a man's skin. It is conceivable that a colored man of ability might become an officer in the German army, whereas such distinction, at present certainly could not possibly be attained by a Jew. In England there is a slight antipathy toward all dark races. England's career in South Africa has not been good for her morals, I fear. The feeling is general in England, so far as I could glean from conversations with representative English people, that the Lord God of Hosts has ordained that the pale-faced Caucasian should rule over all the peoples on the face of the earth and possess the fullness thereof, and many of their cousins on this side of the water have been deluded into believing the same thing. In spite, however, of this deep seated conviction, no obstacle is placed by the English people in the path of those representatives of the dark races, who possess extraordinary gifts. It is impossible for the average foreigner to comprehend the race problem, as it presents itself in the United States. The people across the sea cannot understand why educated, cultivated ladies and gentlemen of color are handicapped or socially ostracized at all. Even the most intelligent foreigner finds it difficult to believe that colored men, women and children are still being lynched in the United States. And if they are aware of this fact, it is almost impossible to convince them that colored men are ever hanged, shot or burned to death except for what is so falsely and maliciously called the usual crime. I have made up my mind, therefore, that for the rest of my natural life, I shall devote as much of my time and strength as I can to enlightening my friends across the sea upon the condition of the race problem in the United States, as it really is.

And now as I review my trip abroad, I feel that if it was possible for me to interest even a few people in foreign lands in the struggle which the women as well as the men of my race are making to rise from the degradation and ignorance forced upon them for nearly 300 years, my mission was gloriously fulfilled. If it was possible to present even a few facts about the progress of our women as well as about that of the race as a whole which were not generally known before, the object of my voyage was fully attained.

Thanks to the pernicious activity of our enemies, the vices and defects of the Afro-American are far better known abroad than are his virtues, his achievements and his good deeds. The evil we do as a race is paraded from the Cape of Good Hope to the North Pole, while the good is borne on the wings of dame rumor and is carried on the columns of the press but a few short roods. If, therefore, it were possible to convince even a few Europeans that the Afro-American is not so black as he is frequently painted, and that he is waging a desperate and courageous warfare to secure the highest and best things in life; if it were possible to convince even a few people across the sea that as a race we are striving with all our heart, soul, mind and strength to quit us like women and men, my voyage of more than 6,000 miles was not made in vain. In private conversations with Germans, French, Norwegians, Danes, Finlanders, Spaniards, Italians, Austrians and Swedes, in the speeches made in England, and in the two addresses delivered before the International Congress of Women in Berlin, I insisted that in spite of opposition relentless and obstacles almost insurmountable the Afro-American can present today such a record of progress in education, industry, finance and art as has never been made under such discouraging circumstances, in such a short time by any race since the world began. I insisted also that the one phase of the Afro-American's development which makes me most hopeful of his ultimate triumph over present obstacles is the magnificent work which the women are doing to regenerate and elevate the race. And no people ever need despair, whose women are fully aroused to the duties which rest upon them and are willing to shoulder responsibilities, which they alone can successfully assume.

Samuel Coleridge-Taylor

The Great Anglo-African Composer. The two Concerts Conducted by Him in Washington, D.C.

An event unique in the history of the world, so far as the records show, and certainly unprecedented in the annals of this country occurred in Washington, D.C., a few days ago. In Convention Hall, the largest auditorium of the National Capital, two concerts were given which attracted the attention of musicians, not only in the United States, but wherever music is sung and enjoyed. The reason why these concerts were of international rather than national interest is not difficult to understand.

In the first place the cantata which was sung and which is considered by the highest musical authorities in England and this country a genuine classic of modern times, was written by a young Englishman, who would be classified as a Negro in the United States. The chorus of two hundred and the three soloists who sang were all colored. Samuel Coleridge-Taylor, the composer, had come from his English home expressly to conduct his work, which he was to hear sung for the first time by people belonging to the race with which he himself is identified. The orchestra of the Marine Band, whose fifty-two members are all white, accompanied the chorus, and was directed, of course, by the colored composer. It is safe to assert that never before in the history of this country was the orchestra of the Marine Band guided by a colored man's baton.

Among the distinguished people who attended the concert the first night were the Secretary to the President of the United States and his wife, representatives of the Diplomatic Corps, members of the Cabinet, musicians and authors of national repute and many others well-known in the official and social life of the country. An audience of 3,000 packed the hall to the doors. As the hour drew near for the concert to begin, the eyes of all were

Originally published in *Voice of the Negro*, January 1905, pages 665-669.

turned toward that portion of the hall in which the famous composer would first appear. Finally somebody spied him and began to cheer. Then the vast audience caught sight of him and broke forth into such rapturous applause that the large building fairly shook. A greater ovation than the one given to Samuel Coleridge-Taylor by all colors, classes and conditions of men, when he made his first bow to an American audience, it would be impossible for any artist to receive. And the recipient of so much homage richly deserves it, too. Staid and conservative Englishmen who would not be accused by their bitterest enemy of indulging in fulsome flattery of anybody are declaring that Samuel Coleridge-Taylor is one of the greatest, if not the greatest composer whom Great Britain has ever produced. In originality and orchestration some say he is the equal, if not the superior, of Wagner. Be that as it may, it is a fact that this young man, who is not yet thirty years old, already stands on a pinnacle of fame which few can ever hope to reach.

The son of a full-blooded African, who was an eminent surgeon, and an English woman, this genius was born in London in the month of August, 1875. Like all other prodigies he gave unmistakable proof of his great gift, when he was a small child. As he himself says, he could read notes and play on the violin, before he knew the alphabet. Having won a scholarship in the Royal College of Music in London he pursued his course there and after a most brilliant career of four years graduated with high honor. He had not been studying long, before he wrote a composition for stringed instruments which was awarded a prize and which Dr. Standford, himself a noted composer and instructor in the Royal College of Music, considered of sufficient merit to render in public under his own direction. Before he was twenty-three, Coleridge-Taylor had written Hiawatha's Wedding Feast, the first part of the trilogy founded on Longfellow's poem which won him fame and which was produced with such brilliant effect in Washington a few days ago. In 1899 Minnehaha's Death, the second part of the trilogy, was rendered at the North Staffordshire Festival. The next year, Hiawatha's Departure, the last canto, was sung in London in Albert Hall by the Royal Choral Society, the premier musical organization of England and one of the most noted in the world. About one year ago this same society rendered Hiawatha for the fifth time under the most brilliant circumstances imaginable. Heading the list of persons was the king. Then the cantata was sung by 1,000 voices accompanied by an orchestra in which there were 150 instruments, at least. Next January the Royal Choral Society will sing Hiawatha for the sixth time, which establishes a record in this regard.

Certainly the work of no other living composer has ever been rendered consecutively by this great musical organization so many times. Although the canto of Hiawatha is only four years old, it has already been sung in England more than two thousand times. It has also been rendered by some of the best choral societies in the United States, notably in St. Louis, Des Moines, Cleveland, Boston, Hartford, and elsewhere.

No one who heard Hiawatha in Washington a few nights ago could be surprised at the popularity which it has acquired in England. The chorus and the soloists seemed inspired. The effect was thrilling from the beginning to the end. Such a volume of sound as poured forth from the chorus in the fortissimo passages has rarely been heard. The peculiarly plaintive quality of tone usually heard in the singing voice of colored people was never used more effectively than in the rendition of the passages describing the suffering of the Indians by famine and Hiawatha's anguish at Minnehaha's death. It was admitted without the slightest hesitation by the leading white musicians of Washington that such excellent chorus singing had never been heard in the National Capital before. One high authority declared that the tone, shading, phrasing, precision and response to every movement of the composer's baton displayed by the colored chorus was a lesson in choral singing which it would not be easy for the majority of musical organizations to learn.

Although the solos throughout the canto are extremely difficult, they were all rendered by the artists who sang them. Mr. Arthur Freeman, the tenor, is a teacher of music in the St. Louis public schools for colored children. As a concert singer Mr. Harry Burleigh, the baritone, has won an enviable reputation throughout the East and West. For several years he has been engaged as a soloist in St. George's Church in New York of which the eminent Dr. Rainsford is rector. The baritone solos in Hiawatha were sung by Mr. Burleigh with such accuracy, fervour and charm of voice that the vast audience was transported with delight and expressed their pleasure in loud and prolonged applause.

Mme. Estelle Clough, whose home is in Worcester, Mass., sang the soprano solos with graphic power and thrilling effect. When the last note of the chorus describing Hiawatha's farewell had died away, the feeling was general among those who had attended the concert that it was an epoch-making occasion in the history of the colored people of the United States.

Concerning the orchestration of Hiawatha which is as rich in variety as it is in harmony, musicians speak in the greatest admiration and unreserved praise. Although the music of this cantata lacks neither science nor scholarship, it is so simple, natural and unaffected that everybody whose souls can be moved by the concourse of sweet sounds can appreciate and enjoy it thoroughly. It would be difficult to find a better illustration of the musician's power to fit the music to the words than that afforded by Mr. Coleridge-Taylor in Hiawatha. In the Wedding Feast the bars describing Iagoo, the marvelous story teller, are as perfect a portrait of a human being as music can possibly paint. When the chorus sings—

> "None could run as fast as he could,
> None could dive as deep as he could,"

the humor and fun are so irresistible that one cannot repress a smile. We can almost see the handsome Pau Puk Keewis, as he begins his mystic dance, first "very slow in step and gesture," and then "more swiftly and still swifter, whirling, spinning round in circles." The tenor solo, "Onaway, Awake, Beloved," is one of the daintiest, dreamiest little love songs imaginable. Although Mr. Coleridge-Taylor can write music full of mirth and spirit and swing, he is strongest, when he describes the tragedies and passions of the human heart. In the prelude to the canto on Minnehaha's death the three chords in particular, which stir the soul to its very depths, Hiawatha's prayer for food, Minnehaha's dying song and Nokomis' lament are so thrilling and heart-breaking that few can listen to them with dry eyes. The burial of Minnehaha is as mournful a dirge as ever wailed forth the anguish of a broken heart. One would be obliged to search a long time before he could find music which describes more accurately and pathetically than this the utter desolation and poignant grief that are felt, when a loved one is laid in the cold ground and left there alone.

But even if there has been any doubt about the place in the musical world to which the composer of Hiawatha should be assigned at the end of the first concert, such doubts would have been quickly dispelled by the second. After hearing Coleridge-Taylor's compositions for the chorus, violin and piano, which were rendered on the occasion, even the most captious and difficult critic would have proclaimed him a musician and composer of the first rank. At this second concert this Anglo-African's racial affiliations were strongly revealed by three choral ballads which had never been sung before and which were dedicated to the Coleridge-Taylor Society of Washington for which they were written. At the festival which will be held in Norwich next

October, they will be sung in England for the first time. In one of these ballads the dream of the slave who lay beside the ungathered rice, as he rode triumphantly in his sleep along the Niger's bank and heard the lion's roar, is graphically and brilliantly told. The pathos of the measures which disclose his lifeless body as it "lay, a worn out fetter that the soul thrown away" has rarely been surpassed.

> "Loud he sang the Psalm of David,
> He a Negro and enslaved,"

is a chorus of tremendous richness, harmony and power, in which the development and growth of the musician's faculties, since his first composition were written are clearly seen.

One of the most interesting as well as enjoyable features about this second concert in Washington was the rendition of three African dances heard in public for the first time and played by Clarence Cameron White, a young violinist which gives promise of making his mark. When Mr. Coleridge-Taylor seated himself at the piano to accompany Mr. White, it was observed that the composer plays this instrument with perfect skill and greatest ease.

Although Mr. Coleridge-Taylor has composed fifty works, the greatest of which in his own opinion is his Atonement. In talking with him about his compositions one day, he said, "If you wish to know which work of mine I consider the most original and best, it is the Atonement. I think the people who heard it at the Albert Hall, when it was sung by the Royal Choral Society on Ash Wednesday last, were touched more deeply by it than they were by Hiawatha, in spite of many stupid newspaper critics. And I have had more kind things said about it than about most things. Of course it will never be so popular as Hiawatha, but popularity is far from being everything."

The Atonement was sung for the first time in the United States last February in St. Thomas's Church, one of the oldest and wealthiest churches in New York. On a list of the sustaining members of the society which rendered it were enrolled the names of such men as Andrew Carnegie, J. Pierpont Morgan, Bishop Potter and others of equal prominence.

When Coleridge-Taylor visited the White House and President Roosevelt saw him for the first time, he is said to have exclaimed in surprise, "Why, you are only a boy." That is precisely the impression the great composer makes upon everybody who meets him. Although he is twenty-nine, he looks like a boy in his teens. One cannot talk with him long, however, without discovering that his mental faculties are mature and his fund of information great. A more modest and unassuming man than Coleridge-Taylor it would be exceedingly hard to find. And he is as affable and kindly of manner as he is modest. One thing he will not do, however; he says he will not, because he cannot. He absolutely refuses to make a speech on any occasion for anybody about anything. In reply to a speech made by a young girl in the colored high school of Washington, who presented him with a beautiful, silver-tipped baton made from the wood of a tree which grew upon the illustrious Frederick Douglass estate, he said: "I tried to make a speech in England once at eight o'clock in the evening. When I was half way through with it, I broke down. And so, it would be utterly impossible for me to make a speech at ten o'clock in the morning." Then he sat down. Something occurred a short while after that, which made him burst forth into speech, in spite of himself. The 500 pupils in the colored high school sang half a dozen choruses, which pleased him so much that he could not refrain from complimenting them and their director, Miss Harriette Gibbs. "I am delighted with your singing," he said. "I am sure one could not hear such singing from pupils of your age in all England."

In appearance Mr. Coleridge-Taylor resembles his African father rather than his English mother, for his complexion is brown and there is a decided curl to his hair. His features are fine, however, and his countenance is very pleasing indeed. In stature he is medium and is a bit thin.

Mrs. Coleridge-Taylor is an intelligent, amiable English woman with an unusually fine voice. Young Hiawatha is just four years old, as perfect and handsome a specimen of boyhood as one would care to see, and his little sister, who is a blonde by the way, is just two.

If the Coleridge-Taylor concerts proved one thing more than another, it is that there is no musical Parnassus too lofty or too steep for colored people to scale. By some it has been established as an axiom that the colored man's musical ability is limited to his skill in rattling bones, picking the banjo and twanging the guitar. But Coleridge-Taylor's marvelous achievements prove beyond a doubt that the colored man's ability has been greatly underestimated.

In decreeing that this genius should be born in England, the fates that spun the threads of Coleridge-Taylor's life were very kind indeed. In Great Britain his color constitutes no barrier to success. Since his genius first revealed itself to the musicians of his native land, he has had the same encouragement and incentive to develop his talents and press toward the highest possible mark that a white man under similar circumstances would have had. Since his first great composition was produced at the North Staffordshire Festival five years ago, he has been invited to contribute something to every succeeding event of the kind. And he has accepted the invitation.

Just before Coleridge-Taylor left England for America he was elected by an overwhelming majority conductor of the Handel Society, which next to the Royal Chorus Society, is the oldest, wealthiest, and most important musical organization in England. Naturally there were many musicians with years of service to their credit and of pure, unadulterated English extraction who aspired to this great honor. The fact that this coveted and important position was given to a man who is hardly more than a youth and who is half African, at that, speaks volumes for his genius and the confidence in his ability which the English musicians repose.

Coleridge-Taylor is not thirty years old, as has been said, and yet he has undoubtedly written works which will be immortal. His future, therefore, is very bright indeed. What may we not expect him to contribute to his art in years that are to come?

Service Which Should
be Rendered the South

When the two words "Service and the South" are mentioned in the same breath, one involuntarily thinks of the needs of the freedman and the variety of the ways in which assistance may be rendered the race to which he belongs. The trials and tribulations, the poverty and degradation of large numbers of colored people in the South loom so large before us, when we speak of the service which should be rendered in that section of the United States that our eyes are closed to every other view. When one attempts to name the services it is possible to render colored people in the South, he finds the number so large that he gives up the effort to enumerate them in despair. There are few people pleased with average intelligence and possessed of a modicum of knowledge about conditions generally obtaining in the South, who could not mention a variety of ways in which colored people living there might be profitably served.

Among the many subjects discussed on the platform, in the pulpit and by the press it would be impossible to name one, on which it is more difficult to express new thoughts than the need of lifting colored people to a higher plane. In this country of many men, each and every one of whom is likely to have from one to a dozen minds on the subject in a dozen minutes, there is nothing on which there is greater unanimity of opinion than that the colored man's mental and moral condition is deplorable and low. If, therefore, one should consume any time in expatiating on the opportunities of service to colored people, which are either opening or should be opened in the South, it would afford as fine an example of what very learned folks call a work of supererogation as anything which I could possibly cite.

There is one kind of service which might and should be rendered the

Originally published in *Voice of the Negro*, February 1905, pages 182-186.

South, however, that is rarely discussed. Generally speaking, the country is blind to the unfortunate mental and spiritual condition of a large number of its citizens, who need civilizing and Christianizing even more, perhaps than the freedman, with whose voices and defects we are so frequently regaled. It is impossible to imagine a service more difficult or more dangerous in some cases to the individual who undertakes it than the one to which I refer. It is as much like bearding the lion in his den as anything with which it can be compared. The number of those who are willing to enter this special department of missionary work is by no means large.

Briefly stated, this service consists in freeing the white South from the thralldom of its prejudices, emancipating it from the slavery of its petty, narrow views which choke the good impulses and throttle the better nature of even its worthiest citizens, teaching them the difference between the highest, purest patriotism and a harmful sectional pride, instilling into the people as a whole a sense of justice which will prevent them from either inflicting or withholding penalties for wrongdoing and crime according to the color of a man's skin, finally, breathing into the hearts of all a compassion and a Christian charity which shall extend even to the despised and oppressed.

It is a dangerous thing to thrust a torch before the face of him who loves darkness and who has dwelt so long in the murky, inky shades of night that he has become wedded to its gloom. No one who has studied conditions in the South as they exist today can doubt that the average white man dwells in a state of mental and moral darkness, so far at least as his relation to his colored brother is concerned, which it will be difficult to dispel. It is equally certain that it will be impossible to elevate the masses of a backward, struggling race, until the scales of prejudice and injustice fall from the eyes of the stronger people, by whom the progress of the weaker may be so easily retarded and without whose consent and support it will require almost superhuman strength for the latter to rise. If the enactments recently made in almost every state of the South are an index of the mind and heart of the white people of that section, the hostility toward the colored man was never more pronounced than it is today and the determination to keep him as near the level of the brute never stronger than it is at the present time. No service could be more patriotic, therefore, in the highest, best sense of that word than that of broadening the mind, arousing the conscience and touching the heart of the dominant race in the South in the colored man's behalf. And yet the need of enlightening, and civilizing the thousands of ignorant, slothful, unaspiring and vicious white people of the South is rarely urged and discussed.

He who makes two blades of grass grow where only one sprung up before does a meritorious work for which he deserved credit and thanks. But as life is more than meat and the body more than raiment, he who helps to plant in the human heart a spirit of charity and mercy toward a weak and struggling people, where bitterness and cruelty reigned before, is truly a benefactor of mankind. At the present time there is nothing of which the United States stands in greater need than broad-minded, Christian men and women who have the moral courage to show the white South how rash, short-sighted and wicked is its course toward the colored man and what an irreparable injury it is doing him by the misrepresentations and falsehoods which it is constantly circulating against the whole race.

Even by Southerners who are supposed to be intelligent, just and broad-minded, the colored man's vices are exaggerated beyond a semblance of truth, in spite of the facts that his accusers are responsible for many of them themselves his defects are emphasized in every possible way, his moral nature flouted and his menial ability underestimated and scoffed. In some instances this misrepresentation may not be the result of deliberate malice. I try to believe that some Southerners do not realize how unjust and untruthful they are in their tirades against the slandered race. By looking continually and exclusively on one side of the race problem and a misguided loyalty to the sophistries and the traditions of the past, their intellect is stunted, so far as their ability to grasp any subject touching their colored brother is concerned, and their reasoning faculties are dwarfed, so that they are easily seduced from the truth. By a little exaggeration of the colored man's vices, by a little suppression of proofs of his unparalleled advancement, by a judicious use of epithets, such as social equality and others which mislead and poison the public mind, by a watchful and searching skepticism with respect to evidence in favor of the Negro and a convenient credulity with respect to every report of tradition which can be used to prove the latter's depravity, the white South has almost succeeded in convincing the world that it is a martyr and the freedman is a brute.

In answering the question, "Why is the prejudice against the colored man in the North greater now than at any time since the war?" the *American Missionary Magazine* for November made the following reply: "*The constant iteration on the part of the dominant South that the Negro is a failure,* that the education of the Negro only makes him more indolent and dangerous

207

though absolutely false, secures attention by virtue of its repetition, and comes to be accepted as true by those who have not the evidence to the contrary." No truer or more forcible utterance on the race problem has been made for a long time. By this same constant repetition of foul slanders against colored women and charges of bestiality preferred against colored men not only are many white people in the South who try to be fair and just persuaded to believe them, but multitudes in the North are converted to this view. The rapidity with which the South has poisoned the mind of the North against the colored man by printing and uttering falsehoods about him is a splendid tribute to the persuasiveness, plausibility, persistency and power of the South, while it proves what an effective weapon systematic misrepresentation of a race in the hands of the skillful and unscrupulous may be. The more one studies the situation, the more convinced he must become that the so-called problem can never be solved, until the minds of the white people in the South are broadened, their hearts softened and their consciences touched. Concerning the crying need of missionary work among the white people of the South, it may truly be said that the harvest is white, but the laborers are few. The Southern Education Board is to be commended for the efforts it is putting forth to civilize and educate the Southern whites. Surely none should rejoice more heartily in the Christian enterprise than the victims of the ignorance and depravity which this board will endeavor to enlighten and reform. It will require men and women who are strong in intellect, lofty of purpose and stout of heart to undertake this work among the white people of the South, and these evangels of light must also be filled with the spirit of Christ. The task of proving to the white South its fallacies in dealing with the colored man and the cruelty of that attitude toward him which it has pledged itself to maintain and defend will not be easy to perform.

When one thinks of the lawlessness which so generally prevails in the South today, among the educated and rich as well as among the ignorant and poor, he can have no doubt of the crying need of men and women who are willing to devote their lives to the work of creating a holy respect for law and order among all classes of white people of that section.

Not long ago a distinguished white clergyman in Louisville, Kentucky, arose in his pulpit one Sabbath morning and startled his congregation by declaring that "home life is safer in the dominions of the Ameer of Afghanistan than in the United States of America. There are more murders," said he, "in the city of Louisville with a population of 200,000 than there are in the great city of London with a population of nearly 7,000,000. There are more murders in the State of Kentucky with a population of 2,000,000 than there are in Great Britain with a population of 40,000,000. Finally there are more murders in the United States than in the whole of Europe with Italy and Turkey left out and Russia included. No other civilized nation," said he, "approaches this in the matter of murders, and those which come nearest to it are such countries as Italy and Turkey, where the assassin's knife is freely used and where men allow their anger and hate and disgraceful passions to rule their conduct." These statistics so shocked several distinguished gentlemen in the South that they determined to investigate the matter for themselves. But after a thorough study of the subject they admitted that the figures given by the Louisville clergyman could not be truthfully denied.

In commenting upon the blood-guiltiness of South Carolina a short while ago the *Nashville American*, one of the largest and most reliable papers in Tennessee declared that if the killings in other States had been in the same ratio to population as in South Carolina, a larger number of people would have been murdered in the United States during 1902 than fell on the American side in the Spanish and Phillipine wars. At the annual dinner of the Author's Club given in honor of the Lord Chief Justice of England in December, 1904, Sir Arthur Conan Doyle, who presided, devoted a part of his speech to the laxity with which law against murder is administered in the United States. During the Boer war, he said, England lost 22,000 lives. But during the same three years this country lost 10,000 more lives, that is, 32,000 by murder and homicide. Ex-Ambassador White declared a few weeks ago that with the single exception of Sicily more murders are committed in the United States than in any other civilized country in the world.

There is little doubt that the red record of this country may be accounted for in large measure by the impunity with which colored people are lynched in the South almost every day in the year, while their murderers not only go unpunished in many cases, but are frequently not even called to account. So rapidly has the crime of lynching spread that it is no one particular section of the country, as it was a few years ago, but it is constantly breaking out here and there in places where one would least expect to find it. Lynching is an appetite which grows by what it feeds upon and it is also a contagious disease which the whole country has caught.

In the South, as elsewhere, one form of lawlessness begets another. The brain of the Southern white man is never quite so active and fertile as when it is bent upon devising ways and means for humiliating or degrading colored people. And so in addition to Disfranchisement Acts, of Jim Crow Car Laws we have the Convict Lease System, that new form of slavery which in some respects is more cruel and more hopeless than the old. Under this iniquitous institution sanctioned by the law of the Southern States, thousands of colored people are yearly thrown into damp, dark, disease-breeding cells, whose cubic contents are less than those of a good-sized grave. They are overworked, underfed and only partially covered with vermin-infested rags. Although children are born to the colored women in these camps by the score, one reads of no indignant protest made by the enlightened, Christian white women of the South, nor do we hear that the lessees of the criminals are for this reason called to account by the State. There is no doubt that many colored men are beaten to death in these camps, and yet no crusade against this brutality is started by the white church. Almost every child knows that hundreds of hard-working, willing colored people are systematically defrauded of their earnings and are virtually held in a condition of slavery by the Contract Labor System with no hope of redress or justice in the Southern courts. But the average Southern white man is never quite so eloquent as when he is discoursing upon the idleness, unreliability or dishonesty of his colored help. And so one might go down the list of crimes perpetrated upon colored people by the South. The amazing thing is the unconsciousness and blindness of the most enlightened white people of that section to their own shortcomings and sins. Having for so many years magnified their own virtues and minimized those of the race they have systematically persecuted and oppressed they are unable either to appraise themselves at their true value or place a proper estimate upon their brother in black. It is well-known that those who are given to falsifying after repeating their fabrications a certain number of times come to believe in them themselves. The blindness with which the South is afflicted, and which prevents her from either seeing herself as others see her or beholding her colored brother in his true light is gradually spreading to the North. When she herself is not only sinning against the creature made in the image of God, but she is leading, even forcing others to sin against him, too.

Study the race problem from whatever view one may, he cannot help reaching the conclusion that the dominant race in the South must be regenerated and lifted to a higher spiritual plane, before this problem can be solved. The white South insists that the colored man shall be honest, virtuous and law-abiding, while many of her so-called best citizens pursue the opposite course. It is somebody's duty therefore to open the eyes of the white South to the inconsistency as well as the injustice of demanding that a weak and handicapped race just forty years out of bondage should be more correct in conduct, stronger in character and more consistent in its practice of Christianity than one which has enjoyed the blessings of freedom for centuries, and possesses innumerable opportunities for attainments and improvements at the present time.

There is great need of missionary work among colored people in the South, of course. Justice and humanity demand that the masses of this backward and struggling race should be lifted from the degradation into which it was shoved and held for nearly 300 years. But the need of earnest, consecrated, Christian missionaries among the masses as well as the upper classes of the white South is just as urgent, more urgent perhaps, than work among colored people in that section. Only those who are made of the sterner stuff out of which heroes are carved and who have the courage to fly in the face of the traditions and convictions of the people among whom they live should enlist in the work of regenerating the white South. There is great, there is imperative need of such workers today. And nowhere could they render more patriotic, more valiant and more Christ-like service than among those representatives of the dominant race in the United States who live in the South.

The Mission of Meddlers

The world is indebted more to the square inch to meddlers than any other species of the genus homo. Instead of being an oasis in a desert of uninhabitable planets, the earth would be a howling wilderness today if the desire to meddle had not been strongly implanted in man. Man is used here in the generic sense, of course, though it is a fact not generally known, that the bump of meddlesomeness is more highly developed on the male side of the human family than upon the female.

As much as meddlers have contributed to the progress, comfort and happiness of mankind, they have never been appreciated at their true worth. They have been despised and rejected by a set of ingrates, who have greedily devoured the gifts, while they have denounced and kicked the giver. It would be possible to break the whole of the ten commandments, seriatim or otherwise, and have no more odium attaching to your wicked person than if you were known to be a meddler. Call the average high-minded citizen a meddler, and he will fight as quickly as if you called him a thief.

And yet, all the laws governing the realm of science were discovered by meddlers. If Newton had not meddled with an apple which fell quite naturally and innocently from an apple tree, we should all know as little about the law of gravitation as the average bachelor of arts knows about art. If Benjamin Franklin had not meddled with electricity by means of a kite, the millionaires who made fortunes out of lightning rods, would probably have died paupers, or have ended an uneventful existence as ordinary citizens of the middle class, in a country whose aristocracy is based on wealth.

But scientific investigation and meddling are two entirely different things,

Originally published in *Voice of the Negro*, August 1905, pages 566-568.

it is claimed. Reduced to their lowest terms, however, it is easy to see that the only difference which exists between them is the name. The same difference exists between vulgar gambling, which all decent people denounce, and polite dealing in futures, of which they generally approve.

Meddling is the mother of discovery and invention. It is the desire to handle or get close to something with which one is not familiar, so as to learn something which he does not yet know. For inventions and labor-saving machinery of all kinds are directly and solely indebted to the meddler.

There are also other fields of usefulness, in which this much abused individual has made himself indispensable. He is a friend worth having. Those who wish to rise rapidly in the world can do no better thing than find the biggest meddler in town and bind him to their hearts with hoops of steel. Their success in life will then be assured. They will scarcely achieve it, however, on flowery beds of ease. No rose is without its thorn and no meddler without his fault. He is apt to be exciting now and then, particularly, when he is in the throes of prophecy, or feels called upon to give advice. The meddler is nothing, if not solicitous, and, therefore, unduly apprehensive at times. If he is especially interested in a merchant, in nine cases out of ten, he will rush into his establishment some fine day, tell the proprietor that business is going to rack and ruin, and that he is heading straight for the poorhouse. This sort of prophecy is never enjoyed by the victim. For this reason the meddler often gets himself disliked. In spite of the shock to his nerves, however, the merchant in question is the gainer by the experience, whether he is willing to acknowledge it or not. If his business methods are good, the jar he has received will do him no serious harm. After he regains his equilibrium, he will be more confirmed than ever in the way he has already gone. It will certainly set him to thinking, which is the greatest service that can be rendered by any man's best friend. If the jolt which the meddler gives leads the merchant to see that his methods are bad, he has no one but his majesty, the meddler, to thank, when he is rich enough to be at the head of a trust. It would be interesting to know how many men have been saved from bankruptcy and how many brilliant business careers have been saved by the timely words of a meddler.

In counting the benefits without number which the meddler confers upon an ungrateful world, one cannot help wondering why this great benefactor of mankind is held in such repute. There is, no doubt, that the fault lies entire at the door of Webster's Unabridged. This bulky volume is responsible for the outrageous injustice perpetrated upon one of humanity's best friends.

"To meddle," says Webster, "is to interpose officiously," and a meddler is described as a person "who interferes, or busies himself with things in which he has no concern."

This definition tickles the selfish old crustaceans to death, for they consider that it absolves them completely from all responsibility for their neighbor's welfare. Caring for nobody but themselves, they gloat in ghoulish glee over a definition which permits them to interpret any human interest in one's neighbor as an "officious interference in things in which they have no concern." They also roll the definition like a sweet morsel under their tongues, while they label as meddlers those who obey the scriptural injunction to love one's neighbor as himself. When they see an unfortunate brother going to rack and ruin, they simply let him slide down the incline without a word of warning. Then they thank the Lord loudly that they are not as other men are, meddlers and officious interferers. Inhuman indifference to a brother's fate is called "attending strictly to one's own business." If an unusually courageous person insists that help should be given to the victim either of his own mistakes or of a perverse fate, the man who boasts that he never meddles will ask as did a certain other person whom we all know by reputation but whom very few admire, "Am I my brother's keeper?"

Thus it happens that wrongs are left unrighted, crimes unpunished, mistakes unrectified and grief unassuaged, because the world is so dreadfully afraid of meddling. There is no doubt that some people who are eager to render assistance withhold it, because they have a genuine aversion to anything which even looks like officious interposition. It is certain also that succor is denied the needy and distressed more often by those whose stony hearts and sordid spirits make them impervious to the woes of the world than by those who are honestly afraid of meddling.

All meddlers are not helpful, of course. Some preachers and humanitarians bungle their work and do more harm than good. Any virtue under certain circumstances may become a vice. In spite, however, of the mistakes which some meddlers make, in spite of the fact that some are actuated by base and unworthy motives, if statistics could be gathered on the subject, the figures would show, I am sure, that more hearts have ached and more people have failed of success from the little rather than too much meddling.

Everybody who has tried to advance the interests of the human race by redressing wrongs or by inaugurating reforms has first been called a meddler. An acknowledged philanthropist or public benefactor may be defined as a meddler, whose labors have been crowned with success.

William Lloyd Garrison was warned not to meddle with things which did not concern him, when he began his crusade against slavery. He and the other abolitionists were threatened with ruin and destruction, if they did not attend to their own affairs. But if Garrison, Phillips and Sumner had not interfered with this peculiar institution and had not persuaded others to do likewise, how long slavery would have continued to torture its victims and disgrace the civilization of the United States it is difficult to tell.

In the United States there is an imperative need of meddlers today—active, insistent and fearless meddlers who will spend their time investigating institutions, customs and laws whose effect upon the citizens of any color or class is depressing or bad. The crying need of the whole wide world is meddlers. In Great Britain, Ireland is waiting for a large number of the aggressive, humane kind to appear. In Russia the dumb, driven cattle made in the image of God, but reduced to the level of brutes are in sore need of the meddler who has here a great and glorious work to perform. The Russian meddler should inquire and ask questions and interrogate those who are responsible for the outrages perpetrated upon helpless human beings, until the oft repeated questions about "other people's business" so arouse the conscience and touch the hearts of the thoughtless, the indifferent and the wicked that the answer will be given in a general and complete redress of wrongs. In Russia and Germany and elsewhere as well the Jew needs the service of the meddler, who shall ask why the narrow and vicious of all races and creeds are permitted to pursue and persecute a people whose ability and whose virtues are so conspicuous and whose hand is raised against none.

In the United States the field which the conscientious meddler alone can work is surely white, but the laborers are few. Here the meddler should take it upon himself to ask disagreeable questions about the political corruption which makes a single white man in one section equal to seven in another, the fundamental law of the land to the contrary notwithstanding. The meddler in the United States should inquire why intelligent, worthy and well-to-do citizens are denied the rights guaranteed them by the constitution, because their complexion happens not to be fashionable in the particular section which treats them as peons and slaves, while men who are inferior to them both in intelligence and respectability are cheerfully granted all their rights, privileges and immunities, simply because their faces are white, although it is through no effort, or merit or prowess on their part that this desirable complexion has been secured. In the United States there is an imperative need of a host of meddlers who will carry out Webster's definition of themselves to the letter and go so far as "to interfere officiously," if need be, where corruption of any kind is apparent and the transgression of the law is clear.

The path of meddlers with a benevolent purpose has never been strewn with roses and will never be, until human nature is radically changed. The lot of the meddler will never be a happy one, when he feels called upon to investigate systems and institutions designed by the evil and cruel to injure and degrade their fellowman. Martin Luther lead a very strenuous existence, after he meddled with the Catholic Church. Martin Luther's experience has been duplicated by reformers of all ages and climes. But meddlers who are earnest and determined do not fear to give offence to those whose affairs they investigate and mayhap disturb and they are not afraid to work. Neither cowardice nor laziness can be truthfully laid at the successful meddler's door. And a meddler has a right to lay claim to success, if his inquiries and interference with "other people's affairs" cause others to propound questions and interpose objections, until the transgressor finds his way uncomfortably hard, even though the meddlesome individual who threw the first rock into the path does not live to see it abandoned altogether.

Among the people of no country or race is there urgent need of meddlers—the benevolent and earnest kind, than among the dark-skinned citizens of the United States. Those who have had advantages of education and culture do not, as a rule, make sufficient inquiries about the habits and the condition of the unwashed, the unlettered and the unkempt. The literate do not interfere sufficiently with the illiterate, whose conduct and whose crimes bring shame to the race and disgrace to themselves, while the lot of all, the just as well as the unjust, is made increasingly hard thereby. Meddlers, more meddlers let us have. Those who have the courage to interfere with the customs and laws which condemn little children to deformity, disease and death. Those who dare ask prejudiced, caste-ridden bigots by what right they humiliate and harass their fellowmen simply on account of a difference in color, class or races; deprive them of the right to earn a living and so block their path with obstacles and frustrate their desperate efforts to advance that the existence of the persecuted and oppressed is rendered a Gehenna on earth.

There are meddlers and meddlers, of course. There are those who are malicious and those who are not; those who pry into "other people's affairs" for the sake of the rare bits they can find and hawk about, those who are moved to pursue certain investigations, because their motives are lofty and pure. One has no more right to infer that a meddler must necessarily be inspired by malice, because some meddlers have been vicious, than he has to take it for granted that all who complete a medical course must be ignorant and incompetent, because some doctors have been quacks.

But people are very much like geese. Long years ago somebody gave the meddler a bad reputation and said all meddlers are alike. His neighbor said the same thing and so did his, and so on down the line. We are all saying the same thing today. Nothing the poor meddler can ever do will save him from contempt and abuse. He will always be a martyr to the unreasonable prejudice and the shameful ingratitude of his beneficiaries. We are determined that no good thing shall come out of Nazareth. The meddler will be misrepresented and abused to the end of time.

Paul Laurence Dunbar

In the death of Paul Laurence Dunbar the nation as a whole as well as the race to which he belonged have sustained an irreparable loss. He was undoubtedly the greatest poet his own race has ever produced and it is certain Nature has bestowed the gift of poetry upon few, if any, Americans, with more lavish hand than she did upon Paul Dunbar. "Conquerors are a race with whom the world could well dispense," said a great writer, "but a true poet, a man in whose heart resides some effluence of wisdom, some tone of the eternal melodies, is the most precious gift that can be bestowed upon a generation."

The story of Paul Dunbar's life is familiar to all. He was born in poverty in 1872 and spent his youth in Dayton, Ohio in unceasing, grinding toil. Both his parents were slaves, his father having escaped from Kentucky into Canada. Fortunately for the son, however, his parents determined that he should enjoy the educational advantages of which they themselves had been deprived, as he was sent to the public schools of Dayton, Ohio, and from which he graduated, when still in his teens. As soon as he knew how to write, his mother says, he began to scribble rhymes and gave evidence of his genius, when he was only seven years old. Obliged to support himself and his mother he secured employment as an elevator boy, after he graduated from the public schools, and it was while engaged in this most prosaic occupation that many of his first poems were written. At that time his life must have been a constant insurrection between the spirit that would soar and the wretched circumstances in which he was placed and which bound him fast to the earth. But while he was chained like a galley slave to the ropes of the elevator earning only $4 a week, the wings of his aspiration refused to be clipped and bore him ever higher and higher.

Originally published in *Voice of the Negro*, April 1906, pages 271-277.

Paul Dunbar's first appearance as a poet occurred in Dayton, Ohio in 1891, when he was 19 years old, when he was presented to the members of the Western Association of Writers and read a poem. This scene was described by Dr. James Newton of Mason, Ill., as follows: "About half way down the programme the presiding officer announced the reading of a poem by Paul Dunbar. Just the name for a poet, I thought. Great was the surprise of the audience to see stepping lightly down the aisle, between the rows of fluttering fans and assembled beauty and wit of Dayton, a slender Negro lad, as black as the core of Cheop's pyramid. He ascended the rostrum with the coolness and dignity of a cultured entertainer, and delivered a poem in a tone as musical as Apollo's lute. He was applauded to the echo between the stanzas and heartily encored at the conclusion. He then disappeared from the hall as suddenly as he entered it, and many were the whispered conjectures as to the personality of the man and the originality of his verses, *none believing it possible that one of his age and color could produce a thing of such evident merit.* Show me a white boy of nineteen who can excel or even equal this black boy's 'Drowsy Day.' "

After repeated inquiries this man of the dominant race who had been so surprised at the ability of Paul Dunbar possessed and so transported by his reading succeeded in finding the rising laureate of the Colored race in the store in which he worked. He was seated in a chair in the lower landing of the elevator, Dr. Newton says, hastily glancing at the July *Century* and jotting down notes on a handy pencil tablet. Not having time to converse with Dr. Newton, Paul invited him into the elevator and during a few excursions from floor to floor the black poet told his newly found friend the story of his life. In writing to Dr. Newton soon after their first meeting, Mr. Dunbar, whose spirit at that time seemed almost broken, expressed himself as follows: "My hopes are no brighter than when you saw me. I am getting on no better, and what would be impossible, no worse. I am nearer discouraged than I have ever been."

Shortly after this, however, the clouds which had hung so heavy and menacing in the young poet's sky began to clear away and a brighter day dawned. When the illustrious Frederick Douglass, who had become deeply interested in the young poet, was Haitien Commissioner to the World's Fair in 1893, he made Mr. Dunbar his secretary. From that time forth it was no longer necessary for the poet to engage in menial labor to support himself and mother. His first volume of poems *Oak and Ivy* which was published by his Dayton employer in 1893 brought him instant recognition and his second volume entitled *Majors and Minors*, published two years later greatly increased his fame. Mr. Howells, the dean of American literature, paid the young poet a glowing tribute which undoubtedly enabled him to secure recognition in certain quarters which would otherwise have been withheld perhaps. James Whitcomb Riley, the Hoosier poet, compared Dunbar's "Drowsy Day" with Longfellow's "Rainy Day" and did not hesitate to declare that the black man's poem was superior to his white brother's both in lyrical power and in harmony of expression. So far back as in 1892, when the name of Paul Dunbar had just begun to be heard James Whitcomb Riley sent him the following characteristic letter:

Denver, Col., Nov. 27, 1892.

Paul Dunbar Esq.—See how your name is traveling, my chirping friend. And it's a good, sound name, too, that seems to imply the brave fine spirit of a singer who should command wide and serious attention. Certainly your gift as evidenced by this "Drowsy Day" poem alone, is a superior one, and therefore, its fortunate possessor should bear it with a becoming sense of gratitude and meekness, always feeling that for any resultant good, God's is the glory, the singer but His very humble instrument. Already you have many friends and can have thousands more by being simply honest, unaffected and just to yourself and the high source of your endowment. Very earnestly I wish you every good thing.

Your friend,
James Whitcomb Riley.

In the best magazines of the country like *Scribner's*, the *Century* and others there appeared a series of Negro songs and ballads which impressed themselves upon the reader as being among the best of the kind yet produced.

The name of Paul Dunbar was signed to them, but probably not one of every hundred who read and enjoyed these characteristic little verses, so finished in form and instinct with the true race spirit dreamed that their author was really a Negro. The versification was that of an accomplished writer, whose excellent method was noticeable in spite of the rude dialect used. It was evident to the student that he had mastered more fully than most writers of Negro verse the real genius of the race whose characteristics his verses portrayed. For a long time the editors of the magazine themselves did not know he was a Negro. They accepted his productions on their merits, which in itself was a high compliment, since only the best of lighter verse appears in magazines to which Mr. Dunbar contributed. When Mr. Dunbar tried to sell his serious verses in the classic style of English composition, they were refused, although a high estimate was placed upon them by some of the best literary critics of the day, because his characteristic Negro poems were considered so superior and were in such demand.

Mr. Dunbar's reputation as a writer was not enhanced by his prose, although he wrote many short stories and several novels. Among the latter his first "The Uncalled," which was published in *Lippincott's* magazine, was probably the best. Altogether Mr. Dunbar published 17 volumes, the last of which *Howdy Honey, Howdy* came from the press just a short time before he died, February 9th. The list of his works is as follows:

> Oak and Ivy, published in 1893.
> Majors and Minors, published in 1895.
> Lyrics of Lowly Life, containing an introduction by Wm. Dean Howells.
> Folks from Dixie, 1898.
> The Uncalled, 1898.
> Strength of Gideon and Other Stories, 1900.
> Love of Landry, 1900.
> Candle Lightin' Time, 1901.
> Fanatics, 1901.
> Sport of the Gods, 1902.
> The Heart of Happy Hollow.
> Lyrics of Love and Laughter, 1903.
> In Old Plantation Days, 1903.
> Lil Gal, 1904.
> When Malindy Sings, 1904.
> Lyrics of Sunshine and Shadow, 1905.
> Howdy Honey, Howdy, 1906.

After Mr. Dunbar's marriage to Miss Alice Ruth Moore in 1898, he came to Washington to live and was employed for a time in the Congressional Library. Like James Whitcomb Riley no one could read Mr. Dunbar's productions so well as he could himself, so that he was in great demand as a reciter and gave entertainments all over the country, until he was physically unable to stand the strain.

In a short sketch like this it is impossible to give either a satisfactory review of Mr. Dunbar's poems or a comprehensive sketch of his life.

Only a cursory glance at each must suffice.

In Paul Dunbar's poems there is neither affectation nor fustian. He is always true to himself and to his subject. His ideals were not in foreign climes and distant lands, but in the scenes he himself beheld every day and in the people with whom he himself had walked and talked. He had an eye to see, an intellect to understand, a heart to feel and the heart to portray what had passed before him. His hope and despair, the joys and sorrows of his own heart as well as those of his own race he gives articulate voice and every word rings true. Is his muse a bit disheartened and sad? Every line the poet pens is steeped pathos and every cadence a sigh. His own sensibilities are so tremblingly alive that one can feel them pulsate and throb under their mask of words.

Nature appeals to him strongly. The rising of the storm, the woods in summer and winter, the patter of the rain are his delight and charm him into song. The thoughts of love which inflame his heart kindle him to melody. His love of children was genuine and great, and inspired some of his tenderest lines. The sight of a little brown baby and the tragic death of Ella May move him to pity and eloquence. His songs are born of genuine emotion and are the very pulse beats of his heart. Now buoyant, now pathetic, sometimes satirical and then ingenuous, now stern and then tender, Paul Dunbar has words for every mood of man's heart. His own heart was indeed "an aeolian harp swept by an ever varying breeze." His convictions were invariably expressed with undiluted earnestness and unflinching honestly, no matter what he discussed. It seemed possible for him to transcribe feelings diametrically opposite to each other with equal skill. The desire to cite poems which would best illustrate his versatility is a temptation which I must resist. Everybody who has read Mr. Dunbar's poems will bear testimony to this fact.

His deep and ardent loyalty to his race bursts forth occasionally into white heat. His "Ode to Ethiopia" quickens the pulse and stirs to its depths the heart of the strongest and most phlegmatic member of the race. With what a fine outburst of enthusiasm he recounts the reasons for his pride in his race whose

Name is writ on Glory's scroll
In characters of fire.

What a magnificent tribute he has paid his people for the long suffering, uncomplaining manner in which they bore the trials and tribulations heaped upon them during slavery and the Christ-like manner in which after emancipation they forgave those who had despitefully used them, in the following lines:

No other race, or white or black,

When bound as thou wert to the rack,
So seldom stooped to grieving.
No other race, when free again,
Forgot the past and proved them men
So noble in forgiving.

Again when Frederick Douglass dies:

And Ethiopia with bosom torn
Laments the passing of her noblest son,

Paul Dunbar, inspired by reverence and affection for his illustrious benefactor and friend pays him one of the rarest and finest tributes ever offered by poet to mortal man.

Oh Douglass, thou has passed beyond the shore,
But still thy voice's ringing o'er the gale.
Thou's taught thy race how high her hopes may
  soar
And bade her seek the heights, nor faint nor fail
She will not fail, she heeds thy stirring cry,
She knows thy guardian spirit will be nigh
And rising from beneath the chastening rod,
She stretches out her bleeding hand to God.

It is difficult to speak of his ode to "The Colored Soldiers" in terms of quiet moderation and use language which may not smack of exaggeration to some. How Paul Dunbar glories in their dauntless courage and delights to recount the great service they rendered their country during the Civil War:

So when war in savage triumph,
Spread abroad his funeral pall—
Then you called the colored soldiers,
And they answered to your call.

And like hounds unleashed and eager
For the life blood of the prey,
Sprung they forth and bore them bravely
In the thickest of the fray.

And where'er the fight was hottest—
Where the bullets fastest fell,
There they pressed unblanched and fearless
At the very mouth of hell.

He takes a pardonably fierce delight in reminding this country that his race is not indebted entirely to others for its emancipation from the awful bondage it endured.

> Yes the blacks enjoy their freedom
> And they won it dearly too;
> For the life blood of their thousands
> Did the southern fields bedew:
>
> In the darkness of their bondage,
> In their depths of slavery's night:
> Their muskets flashed the dawning
> And they fought their way to light.
>
> They were comrades then and brothers,
> Are they more or less to-day?
> They were good to stop a bullet,
> And to front the fearful fray.
>
> They were citizens and soldiers,
> When rebellion raised its head;
> And the traits that made them worthy—
> Ah! these virtues are not dead.
>
> And their deeds shall find a record
> In the registry of Fame;
> For their blood has cleansed completely
> Every blot of slavery's shame.
>
> So all honor and all the glory
> To those noble sons of Ham—
> To those gallant colored soldiers,
> Who fought for Uncle Sam.

So long as there remains in this country a man even remotely connected with the race, whose soldiers have been so immortalized by the eloquence and the music of the verses just quoted, and so long as the blood courses warm in the heart of such a man, so long will it thrill under this heroic ode, one of the best that was ever written and which can be compared only with Burn's "Scots, who hae wi' Wallace bled."

It can be asserted without fear of successful contradiction that in range of genius as well as in power and aptness of expression Mr. Dunbar has not been excelled by any poet in the United States. If he infrequently rose into the region of great ideas, the peculiar conditions surrounding him and not his mental limitations are responsible for this failure to soar aloft. To some of his more serious poems reference has already been made. In the same class his "Life," "Comparison," "A Creed and Not a Creed," together with others equally as good, are as elevated in sentiment, as profound in philosophy, as musical in tone, as perfect in form and as complete in treatment as some of the best poems written by the most inspired singers of the past.

Attention has already been directed to the attitude of the editors who published Mr. Dunbar's poems and who insisted upon his confining himself to dialect. So far as I know, with but a single exception, this advice was given him by all his literary advisers and friends.

In two little stanzas entitled "The Poet," which Mr. Dunbar wrote to explain his position with reference to the more serious efforts which he wished to make but from which he was withheld by the public one cannot help feeling the bitter regret which disturbed his peace of mind and the resentment which rankled in his heart.

THE POET

He sang of life serenely sweet,
With now and then a deeper note,
On some high peak, nigh yet remote,
He voiced the world's absorbing beat.

He sang of love, when earth was young,
And love itself was in his lays,
But ah! the world, it turned to praise,
A jingle in a broken tongue.

It is always pleasant for me to recall that the first time I ever heard of Paul Dunbar was when the illustrious Frederick Douglass told me about him, while we were in his library at Cedar Hill one afternoon and read me one of the young poet's early productions entitled the "Drowsy Day". Previous to the reading, however, Mr. Douglass had spoken with deep feeling about the young man's poverty and had expressed regret that he had been so seriously handicapped in his career. And so as he afterward read the poem, the great man was so deeply affected by it, that he could not restrain his tears. When Mr. Dunbar first took up his residence in Washington, he lived in a house at 1934 4th street N.W., next door to the one in which we were living at that time. Near neighbors as we were, it was quite natural that we should see a great deal of each other and we did. Being a hero worshiper by nature and inclination as well as by cultivation, particularly where members of my own race are concerned, I did not try to conceal from Mr. Dunbar how great and genuine was my admiration of his gifts and how brilliant were the hopes I entertained of his future success. It happened, therefore, that many a time he honored me by coming to my home to read me his poems or his short stories, telling me in what magazine they had appeared or would appear. He would also tell me how much he had received for his articles, when I was impertinent enough to inquire, which I frequently did, just for the pleasure of hearing how well he was compensated for the product of his genius and his brain. On one occasion he invited me to his home, so that he might read a play which he had just written and which I hope may some day be produced.

Mr. Dunbar was a man of charming personality with a bold, warm, buoyant humor of character which manifested itself delightfully to his friends. Mingled with his affability of manner were a dignity and poise of bearing which prevented the overbold from coming too near. While there was nothing intrusive or forward about Paul Dunbar, when he found himself among eminent scholars or distinguished people in the highest social circles, he showed both by his manner and his conversation that he felt he was just exactly where he was entitled to be. There was nothing that smacked of truckling, and nobody in the wildest flight of his imagination could dream that Paul Dunbar felt particularly flattered at the attention he received. The maturity of intellectual power was manifested in his conversation as well as in his writing and his fund of information was remarkable, considering both his youth and his meager opportunities for culture.

His wit was decidedly pungent at times and then nobody in his presence was immune therefrom. His sense of the ludicrous was highly developed and nothing ridiculous or funny escaped him. I can never hear certain styles of music rendered without being convulsed, when I remember the comments made by Dunbar at a musical we attended once.

Last July Mr. Dunbar extended me a cordial invitation to be the guest of himself and his mother, while I was attending the convention of the Ohio Federation of Colored Women's clubs which was held at Dayton, Ohio, and which I had been asked to address. I accepted and spent several days at his home. I am glad I did, for I am sure I learned more about the character of the man and the genius of the poet during the short visit with him in

Dayton than it would have been possible for me to ascertain in any other way. I account it a privilege to have had such an excellent opportunity of becoming thoroughly acquainted with the greatest poet the race has ever produced. During the few days spent with Mr. Dunbar last summer I discovered there were depths in his character that I had never sounded and qualities of heart of which I had never dreamed, although I saw him frequently while he lived in Washington.

Owen Meredith says that

The heart of a man is like that delicate weed
Which required to be trampled on, boldly indeed
Ere it gives forth the fragrance you wish to extract.
Tis a simile, trust me, if not new, exact.

Whether affliction and sorrow always bring out the best there is in a man, I cannot say. I do know however, that the physical and mental pain which Paul Dunbar endured for at least a year before he passed away, developed the highest and noblest qualities in him. When I saw Paul Dunbar last summer, he was shut in, wasted and worn by disease, coughing his young and precious life away, yet full of cheer, when not actually racked with pain, and perfectly resigned to his fate. I shall always think of his patience under his severe affliction as a veritable miracle of modern times. In the flush of early manhood, full of promise and still greater literary achievement in the future than he had been able to attain in the past, fond of life as the young should be and usually are, there he sat, rapidly losing his physical strength every hour, and yet, miracle of miracles, no bitter complaint of his cruel fate did I hear escape his lips a single time. The weakness and inertia of his worn and wasted body contrasted sadly and strangely with the strength and activity of his vigorous mind. As I looked at him, pity for the afflicted man himself and pity for the race to which he belonged and which I knew would soon sustain such an irreparable loss in his death almost overcame me more than once. As incredible as it may appear, his moods were often sunny and then it was delightful to hear the flood of merriment roll cheerily from his lips.

It was gratifying to see the homage paid Mr. Dunbar by some of the most cultured and some of the wealthiest people of the dominant race in Dayton. As soon as I reached his house, I saw a chair most elaborately decorated in royal purple and was informed that a company of distinguished people of the dominant race had improvised a birthday party for the young poet a few days before I arrived and had thus festooned this chair in his honor. One of

Mr. Dunbar's white friends did all his stenography for him for nothing, refusing to take a cent of pay. What an invaluable service was thus rendered is easily seen and appreciated, when it is known that Mr. Dunbar's last two volumes of poems, *Lyrics of Sunshine and Shadow*, and *Howdy, Honey, Howdy*, were prepared for publication by this same generous and unselfish friend. Mr. Dunbar's mother told me that the white people of Dayton had helped her care for her son in every conceivable way.

On one occasion after some beautiful girls had called to pay their respects to Mr. Dunbar and had gone, in a nervous effort to relieve the tension of my own feelings, I turned to him and said, "Sometimes I am tempted to believe you are not half so ill as you pretend to be. I believe you are just playing the roll of interesting invalid, so as to receive the sympathy and the homage of these beautiful girls." "Sometimes I think I am just loafing myself," he laughingly replied. How well he remembered this was shown a short while after I returned home. He sent me a copy of his *Lyrics of Sunshine and Shadow* which at that time was his latest book. On the fly leaf he had written with his own hand, a feat which during the 1st year of his illness he was often unable to perform, the following lines.

Look hyeah, Molly
Aint it jolly
jes a loafin 'roun'?
Tell the judge
Not to hedge
For I am still in town.

Whether Paul Dunbar will be rated a great poet or not, no human being can tell. It is impossible for his contemporaries either to get a proper perspective of his achievement or to accurately gauge his genius. Personally I believe he will occupy as high a place in American literature as Burns does in the British, if not higher.

But whether Paul Dunbar will be rated great or not, it is certain that he has rendered an invaluable service to his race. Because he has lived and wrought, the race to which he belonged has been lifted to a higher plane. Each and every person in the United States remotely identified with his race is held in higher esteem because of the ability which Paul Dunbar possessed and the success he undoubtedly attained.

Indeed the whole civilized world has greater respect for that race which some have the ignorance to underestimate and others the hardihood to despise, because this black man, through whose veins not a drop of Caucasian blood was known to flow, has given such a splendid and striking proof of its capacity for high intellectual achievement.

The more one thinks of the obstacles Paul Dunbar was obliged to surmount, the more remarkable appear both the quality and quantity of the literary labor which he performed. Other poets have been poor before and were cruelly handicapped for years by hard and grinding toil. In the history of men who have enlightened the world through the medium of their pens or lightened its sorrows by their wit and mirth, poverty is no new thing. Milton was poor and so was Burns, between whom and Paul Dunbar there is a striking similarity in several respects. But Milton and Burns were forced to fight poverty alone. Prejudice against their race did not rear its huge and hideous proportions athwart their path to literary achievement and success. Heine's position, so far as concerns prejudice against his race, more closely resembles Paul Dunbar's than that of any poet with whom he may be compared perhaps. But Heine's burden was far lighter than the one which the black American poet was forced to carry.

Heine was a Jew to be sure, and he was born and reared in Germany where Jews are hated and ostracized. But in the very beginning of Heine's career he was blessed with a comfort and an inspiration which Paul Dunbar was denied. Heine's race from time immemorial had produced authors and poets and great men galore. Therefore, no taunt of racial inferiority flaunted itself in Heine's face and filled his soul with tormenting doubts concerning his ability to succeed in a literary career. More than a hundred years before Paul Dunbar was born Phyllis Wheatley, a little African girl who had been brought to this country packed like a sardine in a slave ship had poured forth her soul in song, to be sure. But in spite of the fact that she was a slave, she was loved and encouraged and protected by her devoted master and mistress so that the atmosphere which she herself breathed was more conducive to the development of her talent than that in which Paul Dunbar lived. And so to a certain extent, at least Paul Dunbar had to blaze his path.

Though the empyrean soul of Paul Laurence Dunbar has winged its way to another world, the light of its celestial nature, which often groaned under the weight of a weary life, will never be dimmed. In the flower and fruit of his genius he has bestowed upon his country and his race an imperishable gift. In grateful appreciation of his services and in genuine affection Paul Dunbar lies to-day enshrined in our hearts, a far nobler mausoleum, after all, than one built of marble could possibly be.

Susan B. Anthony, The Abolitionist

Among the men and women who have paid tributes to Susan B. Anthony since she closed her eyes in death March 13th, not one owes her such a debt of gratitude as I myself. My obligation to her is twofold, for I am a woman as well as a representative of that race for whose freedom Miss Anthony worked so indefatigably, so conscientiously and so well. The debt of gratitude which women, not only in this country, but all over the civilized world owe Miss Anthony is great enough to be sure. But the representatives of that race which but fifty years ago bowed under a yoke of cruel bondage in this country in addition to bearing the burdens of a handicapped sex, owe her a debt of gratitude which cannot be expressed in words.

Though Miss Anthony rendered signal and conspicuous service during those dark days, when there was neither light nor shadow of turning for the slave, the work she subsequently performed for the amelioration of the condition of women was so prodigious that her anti-slavery record during the last decade or two has become partially obscured. Nevertheless, among the abolitionists who strove so earnestly to break the fetters of the slave, not one worked with such sublime heroism and more ardent zeal than did that noble woman, whose loss is so sincerely mourned all over the civilized world. It is difficult to speak of such valiant and valuable service as that rendered by Miss Anthony to my race in language which some may not consider extravagant and fulsome. There are so many recorded, indisputable facts, however, which show the incredible amount of work she performed in behalf of my oppressed race as well as her own handicapped sex, so many facts which prove her clear title to our gratitude and love that it is unnecessary for me or anybody else to resort to fiction to add one jot or one tittle to her fame.

Originally published in *Voice of the Negro*, June 1906, pages 411-416.

From the moment Susan B. Anthony accepted the invitation of the American Anti-Slavery Society to assist it in breaking the fetters of the oppressed, till the shackles had fallen from the last slave, she consecrated herself to this cause with all her heart and soul and labored for it with unflagging zeal. Routes for herself and others were planned and meetings arranged with the greatest skill and care. Into towns great and small, some of them off the railroad and reached only by stage, Miss Anthony went, preaching the gospel of freedom, portraying the horrors of slavery and imploring the people to extirpate it root and branch. With the mercury many degrees below zero, we see her emerging from one snow drift, only to plunge into another, or shivering with cold in a sleigh nearly buried in a snow bank, while the bewildered driver goes to the nearest farm house, only to discover that he has missed the road and driven over a fence into a field, but urged, nevertheless by the dauntless, determined Miss Anthony to do his level best to reach the town for which they are bound, so that she may touch the hearts and arouse the conscience of the people in behalf of the imbruted, wretched slave.

During a winter of unusual severity, when the men who were her co-laborers in the cause of abolition broke down physically, one after another, cancelled their engagements and converted their letters to their family and friends into veritable Jeremiads, full of the most pathetic complaints about their heads, their backs, their throats, their lungs, and their eyes, Miss Anthony trudged bravely, heroically on. Though she herself doubtless ached many a time from her head to her feet, was sick for the comforts to which she had been accustomed in her comfortable home but which she often lacked on the road, and was sad and heavy of heart because of the awful persecution which as a woman supporting two unpopular causes she was forced to endure, so literally did she crucify the flesh in behalf of that cause for whose triumph she worked with such desperate, effective earnestness, she neither missed a single engagement nor lost a day from her work. In every fibre of her being she loathed an institution which robbed an unfortunate race of every right that men hold dear, tore mother from child and separated husband from wife. Having devoted this unnatural, brutal system to destruction, so far as in her lay, she allowed neither height nor depth nor any other creature to turn her aside from this work.

So great was the confidence reposed in Miss Anthony's ability by the men who represented the brain and the conscience of the abolition movement that the whole State of New York was at one time placed under her control. "We want your name to all letters and your hand in all arrangements," Mr. May, the secretary of the Anti-Slavery Society wrote her once. "I think," said he, "that the efficiency and the success of our operations in New York this winter will depend more upon your personal attendance and direction than upon that of any other worker. We need your earnestness, your practical talent, your energy and your perseverance to make the conventions a success. We want your cheerfulness and your spirit, in short, we want yourself."

Considering how many giants there were in those days among the dominant sex, this was high praise indeed for a representative of that half of humanity, whose mental inferiority and dearth of intellectual prospects were accepted as foregone conclusions both by wise men in the new and progressive West and by their brothers in the ancient and stagnant East.

In addition to being violently hated by the advocates of slavery in the North as well as in the South, Miss Anthony had no sooner proclaimed the Garrisonian doctrine "No Union With Slaveholders," than she incurred the bitter hostility of that party destined to crush the rebellion and break the fetters of the slave, but which at one time did not stand for the abolition of slavery and simply opposed its extension. It happened, therefore, in a series of meetings planned one season for the Anti-Slavery Society by Miss Anthony, she was mobbed in every city and town she entered from Albany to Buffalo. But neither the winter's cold nor the white heat of wicked men's wrath could force or frighten her from the work in behalf of freedom and justice to which she had devoted her life and consecrated her powers. When at Syracuse, New York, eggs were promiscuously thrown around and about her and benches were broken, when pistols and knives gleamed in every direction, Susan B. Anthony, the only woman in the midst of that hissing, howling, murderous mob stood determined, fearless and serene. Hideous effigies of herself were dragged through the streets and burned, but such exhibitions of hatred only nerved her all the more for the holy warfare in which she was engaged.

But Miss Anthony's service to the anti-slavery movement did not consist entirely either in the speeches which she herself delivered or in the meetings she arranged for others. The emancipation proclamation had no sooner been issued by Abraham Lincoln than this far-sighted woman and close student of human nature saw clearly that the resourceful, infuriated masters who had lost their human chattels would do everything in their power to render this document null and void. The fact that the jails of loyal Kentucky were filled with slaves from Alabama, Georgia and Mississippi who were advertised to be sold for their jail fees according to law, just as they were before their emancipation was proclaimed, filled Miss Anthony with the gravest apprehension and inspired her to work in their behalf with renewed energy and redoubled zeal. Firmly convinced that the only way of securing freedom for the slave was by and through an act of Congress, Miss Anthony and Mrs. Elizabeth Cady Stanton called upon the women of the free States to do their duty to their government as well as to the slave by signing petitions urging Congress to pass a law forever abolishing slavery in the United States. As a result of this call the Woman's National Loyal League was formed. With her headquarters in Cooper Union in New York City and without the guarantee of a single cent for expenses Miss Anthony worked throughout the long hot summer of 1863 with might and main, scattering letters far and wide, arousing men and women to a sense of their duty and directing the affairs of this organization with the sagacity and the skill of a general. Not until the Senate had passed a bill prohibiting slavery and there was no doubt about the intention of the House to concur did Miss Anthony cease to secure and send petitions to Congress and close her headquarters in Cooper Union. The untiring, persistent, consecrated chief of this Woman's National Loyal League, the head, the heart, the feet and the hands of that magnificent movement was the noble, justice-loving woman whose memory is so dear to us today.

Not only in her public work and by her platform utterances did Miss Anthony help to create sentiment in behalf of an oppressed and persecuted race, but by her daily example and by her private conversation as well. Shortly after she had left home for the first time to teach, she wrote her family that she had had the pleasure of visiting four colored people and taking tea with them. With great emphasis she asserted that "it affords me unspeakable satisfaction to show this kind of people respect in this heathen land." Again she writes a scathing denunciation of some "meek followers of Christ" as she sarcastically calls them, who refused to allow a colored man to sit in their Church in Tarrytown, New York, and who could not worship the God who is no respecter of persons with their sable companion sitting by their side.

If at any time Miss Anthony's zeal in behalf of the race for whose freedom she had labored so faithfully and so hard seemed to abate, it was not because she desired justice for them less, but because she yearned for justice toward all God's creatures more. Having worked with such genuine, devoted loyalty and such unflagging zeal to help free an oppressed race, it is no wonder that Miss Anthony was wounded to the heart's core, when the men whom she had rendered such invaluable assistance in this cause, coolly advised her to wait for a more convenient season or refused absolutely to assist her, when she implored them to help her secure justice and equality before the law for her own disfranchised sex. Although Miss Anthony was accustomed to the hisses of the mob and the persecution of her enemies, this attitude of her former co-laborers and friends, which literally seemed ingratitude more strong than traitors arms, almost vanquished her.

Though Susan B. Anthony was an ardent advocate and an eloquent champion of an oppressed race, she will be known to future generations principally for the prodigious amount of work she accomplished for the amelioration of the condition of her sex. When she was born near Adams, Mass., in 1820, not a single college or university in the United States admitted women. Miss Anthony was 13 years old before the initiative was taken by Oberlin, which was the first college in this country just, broad and benevolent enough to extend a cordial initiation to the Colored-American and to open its doors to women on an equal footing with men. When Susan B. Anthony was young, if a woman by some fortunate chance had acquired a thorough education, it was considered extremely indelicate and decidedly impolitic for her to let the public know she possessed such intellectual attainments. If she did, her chances of getting a husband were exceedingly slim.

Sixty years ago, when the agitation for equal rights began, only one occupation, not menial, was open to women, and the pay received by the woman teacher was very small as compared with the salary paid men. The woman who was strong physically, who enjoyed excellent health, who did not faint at the sight of a mouse or some man who precipitated himself unexpectedly in her presence was considered coarse and unrefined.

Even in so enlightened a state as Massachusetts before 1855 a woman could not hold her own property, either earned or acquired by inheritance. If unmarried, she was obliged to place it in the hands of a trustee, to whose will she was subject. If she contemplated marriage, and desired to call her property her own, she was forced by law to make a contract with her intended husband, by which she gave up all title or claim to it. The common law of Massachusetts held man and wife to be one person, but that person was the husband. By will he could not only deprive her of all his property, but even of the property she herself had owned before her marriage. The husband had the income of his wife's real estate till she died, and if they had a living child, his ownership of the real estate continued to his death. A husband could forbid a wife in Massachusetts to buy a loaf of bread or a pound of sugar or contract for a load of wood to keep the family warm. A wife did not own a rag of her own clothing. Her husband could steal her children, rob her of her clothing and her earnings, neglect to support the family, while she had no legal redress. Not until 1879 was an act passed in Massachusetts which provided that a married woman might own her own clothing to the value of $2,000.

Today much of this injustice to women is recalled only as any other relic of the dark ages is mentioned. Not only in Massachusetts, but in nearly all our states, a married woman can hold her own property, if it is held or bought in her own name and can make a will disposing of it. A married woman can make contracts, carry on business, invest her own earnings for her own use—and she is also responsible for her debts.

Today, thanks to the herculean labor and the heroic sacrifices of Susan B. Anthony and the other noble women who aided her, the best schools, colleges and universities in the country open their doors to women, while in a goodly number of countries across the sea a similar opportunity of cultivating their minds is afforded them. In four States of the Union the elective franchise has been granted to women. In Wyoming, Utah, Colorado and Idaho women go to the polls with their husbands and sons. In addition to the profession of teaching, women preach, practice medicine, plead before the courts as lawyers and engage in nearly as many vocations as do men. In many states the presence of women as members of School Boards, Boards of Visitors to the Penal and Correctional Institutions and other organizations of a similar nature attracts no attention at all and is considered a matter of course. In certain States women still have no legal authority over their children, but there has been a great gain on this point during the last twenty years.

That such a revolution in sentiment concerning the sphere and capacity of women has been wrought, that such golden opportunities for self-culture and usefulness in the world are offered women today is due in large measure to Susan B. Anthony, who for nearly sixty years devoted her life to this work.

It has always been gratifying to me to know that Frederick Douglass was among the first men in this country to advocate equal rights and equal opportunities for women. It was Frederick Douglass who saved from defeat the resolution urging women to secure for themselves the elective franchise which was offered in Seneca Falls, July 1848, where the first woman's rights convention ever called in the United States or in the world, for that matter, was held. Eleven resolutions were presented and all had been unanimously carried except this one to which reference had been made. Frederick Douglass and Mrs. Elizabeth Cady Stanton, realizing that the power to choose rulers and make laws was the right by which all others could be secured, advocated this resolution with such eloquence and logic that it was finally carried by a small majority. When Frederick Douglass himself was disfranchised on account of his race, it was gratifying to reflect that he was not so inconsistent and selfish as to wish to deny to woman the rights and privileges withheld from her simply on account of her sex. For the same arguments advanced against the right of women to participate in the affairs of their government and their respective States are used by those enemies of the Colored American who have robbed him of his right of citizenship in 11 States.

It was my privilege and pleasure to be entertained by Miss Anthony and her sister Mary in their comfortable and interesting home in Rochester, New York, a year ago last December. The time spent under the roof of those great-souled, progressive, hospitable women will always be recalled as red letter days in my life. The two volumes of her own life written by Ida Husted Harper which Miss Anthony presented to my little daughter as a Christmas gift in 1904, and the four volumes of the *History of Woman Suffrage* which she gave me, each and every one of which contains an inscription written by her own dear hand, together with numerous pamphlets which she sent me from time to time are and will ever remain among the most cherished treasure which I possess.

From the moment Susan B. Anthony was capable of thinking for herself till she entered upon her well-earned rest, her life was one long protest against injustice in all its forms toward any of God's creatures, whether man or woman, black or white. So permeated was she herself with a glowing, all-consuming desire for justice that it is no wonder she was able to kindle the sacred flame in the breast of so many with whom she walked and talked. So long as there lives in the United States a single human being through whose veins flows one drop of African blood, so long will Susan B. Anthony be held in grateful remembrance, so long will her name be loved and revered. Although Miss Anthony worked continually and faithfully to secure justice for every American and actually accomplished much to compass this end, a vast amount of work along this line yet remains to be done. May Miss Anthony's prayer for justice, for which she hungered and thirsted 86 years, but for which, to a certain extent at least, she hungered and thirsted in vain soon be answered all over the world. May Justice, absolute, impartial Justice, without regard to race, color, sex or class soon extend her dominions to the uttermost part of the earth. May the spirit of Susan B. Anthony, who was the incarnation of justice, enter the breast of a mighty host of American women and impel them to battle against injustice as fearlessly and valiantly as did our peerless leader who did not know the meaning of compromise or surrender and scorned the suggestion of defeat. But Susan B. Anthony is gone, that friend of the oppressed, that champion of right. To the thorny, tear-wet path her weary feet have trod I would not call her back. To her memory has been erected a monument more precious than marble, more enduring than brass or stone. In the heart of a grateful race, in the heart of the manhood of the world she lives and Susan B. Anthony will never die.

A Plea for the White South by a Coloured Woman

The indifference manifested by the whole American nation to the obstacles to progress which now confront the best white people in the South is as amazing as it is painful. Occasionally one hears about the cruel yoke of bondage under which coloured people in the South groan at the present time. It is safe to assert that few if any words either spoken or written on this subject are untrue, since it is well nigh impossible to exaggerate the facts. But the coloured American is not the only slave in the South to-day. There are hundreds of white men who have been blessed with splendid intellects, who are kind and tender of heart and who yearn to be true to their higher, better natures, who dare not follow the dictates of their conscience and be just, because they languish in the chains forged by a tyrannical public opinion and a cruel, vindictive intolerance of those who dare dissent from prevailing views.

If the South were a Sodom and Gomorrah in which no justice-loving, law-abiding white men could be found, as one is tempted to describe it when he thinks how frequently crime is committed in that section and how seldom the criminal, if he be white, gets his just deserts, the prospects for the white man's future would be far gloomier than are those of the race which he so cruelly wrongs. It cannot be denied that the majority of white people in the South acquiesce in the crimes committed by the lynchers, the white caps, and the Constitution-smashers, who have violently snatched the right of citizenship from more than a million men, for if they did not, these particular

Originally published in *Nineteenth Century*, July 1906, pages 70-84.

varieties of lawlessness would disappear in a very short time. But the tacit consent given to lawlessness by the just and upright white men in the South is the result of intimidation, rather than a deliberate purpose on their part to sanction wrong.

For this reason it is plainly the duty of the North, East and West to protect the South from itself. It matters not that the South spurns the advice and declines the assistance of other sections in the United States. If a good citizen or a consistent Christian should see a man committing suicide by plunging a dagger into his heart or jumping into a river, would he stand still and let him take his life, because his desperate brother did not want him to interfere? When one section of this country is reverting to barbarism by adopting methods common to the dark ages, such as excluding the children of a certain race or class from the public schools, first on one pretext and then another, and thereby forcing future American citizens to grow up in ignorance as dense and as dark as that with which the Russian peasants are cursed to-day; when one section of this country is resorting to such antediluvian, anti-Christian measures as the Ameer of Afghanistan would be ashamed to approve, shall the wiser, saner members of the national family stand still and see their rash and wicked brother toboggan to his ruin?

There are at least three reasons why the nation as a whole should give prevailing conditions in the South their careful and conscientious consideration. The weightiest argument which could be advanced in behalf of this proposition is that it is the country's duty to the South itself. A great deal is written and spoken about the New South to-day. Orators from all sections wax eloquent about the phenomenal change of heart toward the North and the great breadth of view toward the freedmen manifested by the 'New South.' One need only study conditions which obtain in the South to-day, however, to be convinced that the people of that section were never more deeply rooted and grounded in the opinions which they have always held, were never more determined to be governed by them in everything affecting both public and private affairs, and were never more bent upon enacting these views into law, so far as in them lies, than they are to-day. By deeds as well as by words the South is daily proving how resolute and unshaken it is in its purpose to defy even the Constitution of the United States, whenever it runs counter to its opinions and offends its prejudices.

So frequently and persistently does the South display the Confederate flag, for instance, that the Department of the Potomac G.A.R. has recently passed resolutions expressing 'the regret and sorrow with which it views the public display of an emblem which tends to keep alive the bitterness and animosity engendered by the war.' It was also resolved that 'such a course tends to instill into the minds of coming generations aversion, if not hostility, to our national emblem, and is not in accord with the oft-repeated professions made by the Southern people of their love for the national emblem and their devotion to the Union.'

It cannot be too strongly emphasized, nor too often repeated, that there is a class of white people in the South who are as irrevocably opposed to injustice and lawlessness as human beings can possibly be. It would be as unjust to charge the whole white South with wilful, malicious violation of the Constitution, because the citizens generally countenance its infraction by their silence, as it would be to accuse the whole North of approving disfranchisement of coloured men because northerners do not protest. It would be as absurd to say that all white people in the South sanction the injustice and barbarity of which coloured men, women, and children are so often the unfortunate victims in that section, as it would be to claim that everybody in the North disapproves of these crimes against the coloured man and is willing to accord him his rights.

Before the term 'White South,' as used in this article, is defined, it is cheerfully admitted that there are exceptional white men in the South, whose ideals and standards are as high as are those of the purest, best citizens anywhere in the United States. But when the 'South' or the 'White South' is referred to in this article, those people are designated who mould the public opinion which manifests itself through the laws enacted by the legislatures of the respective southern states, and through the customs which are generally observed and which amount to an unwritten law.

If the laws recently enacted in nearly every State in the South are an index of the mind and the heart of the people of that section, and if actions speak louder than words, the South was never more hostile to the coloured man, as well as to his friends, and was never more determined to keep him as near the level of the brute as possible than it is to-day. Reduced to the lowest terms, the test put to every question which arises for discussion in the South, no matter to what it may directly pertain, is its possible bearing upon the race problem. To the South's inability to forget the results of the Civil War, and to its attitude toward the emancipated race, may be attributed its inability to make the mental, spiritual, and material progress which it might otherwise easily attain. The mind cannot (certainly the mind does not) flourish in an atmosphere which is close and impure, and which is neither recharged nor purified by fresh currents and revivifying draughts of new thoughts. That there have been comparatively few contributions made by southern writers to the best literature of the country is an indisputable fact. Nothing but the enforced narrowness of view and the imperious bigotry which hang like a pall over the mind can explain this dearth of literary talent in the South.

Not long ago, in discussing the place occupied by the South in American letters, Professor George Edward Woodberry, Professor of Comparative Literature in Columbia University, New York City, expressed himself as follows:

> The South is uncritical. The power of criticism, which is one of the prime forces of modern thought in the last century, never penetrated the South. There was never a place there, nor is there now, for *minorities of opinion* and still less for individual protest, for germinating reforms, for frank expression of a view differing from that of a community. In this respect the South has been as much cut off from the modern world, and still is, as Ireland from England in other ways. It lies outside the current of the age, and this is one reason why there has been such an absence of ideas in its life. It is curious to observe that what the South has afforded to general literature, in the main was given into the hands of strangers. The Virginian record was written by Thackeray's imagination. The theme of slavery was written in *Uncle Tom's Cabin*, the one book by which the South survives in literature, for better or for worse.

With scarcely a single exception the inventors of labour-saving machines and appliances, for which this country has become so famous, hail from the North. The report of the Civil Service Commission recently issued shows that Louisiana, Alabama, Mississippi, Arkansas, Texas, Georgia, South Carolina, and Tennessee have not their share of Federal appointments, because the applicants for positions from those States are not qualified to receive them. The failure of the southern States to furnish eligibles for registers from which appointments are chiefly made is shown by the fact that of the 383 appointments from technical registers, only 35 went to the South. On the 5th of October, when these figures were compiled for the report, there remained on all the registers of a technical character only fifty southern eligibles, many with such low ratings as to preclude the likelihood of their being reached for certification. The report of the Civil Service Commission proves conclusively that the South is greatly in arrears in securing the plums to which it is entitled by an equitable distribution of government jobs on the basis of one in every 10,000 citizens, because there are so few applicants for positions living in that section who have the proper technical qualifications. Most every southern applicant wants to be a clerk, and as a matter of fact the South has furnished 58.21 per cent of all clerk appointments; but the demand is for men with technical qualifications, scarcely any for clerks. When, therefore, the Commission desires to give the South the preference, it finds itself without eligibles and must fall back on those States which have already received their full share. This tangible proof of the intellectual inertia of the South, as revealed by the report of the Civil Service Commission, tallies with a statement made in the *Atlanta Constitution* just three years ago. In lamenting the mental inertia and backwardness of the South, this newspaper, which is one of the largest and most reliable journals in this section, expressed itself as follows: 'We have as many illiterate white men in the South to-day over twenty-one years as there were fifty-two years ago, when the census of 1850 was taken.'

This barrenness of brain and this dearth of intellectual activity, in a section inhabited by men and women in whose innate mental inferiority nobody believes, can be accounted for on one hypothesis alone. It is due to the brain blight, superinduced by the ban placed upon the freedom of thought. And this freedom of thought will always be a mental impossibility in the South, until the white people of that section cease to make their coloured brother the subject of paramount importance, cease to insist that there shall be but a single, solitary opinion, both concerning his rights and privileges as a citizen and the treatment which must be accorded him by all members of the dominant race, whether they concur in the opinion of the majority or not.

As the intellectual faculties of the southern white people have been dwarfed, because they have placed consideration of the coloured man and his status among them above everything else, because they have allowed nobody, no matter whence he hailed nor how competent he was to judge, to dissent from the generally accepted view without paying a heavy penalty for defying public sentiment, so progress along financial and commercial lines has been impeded, because the white people of the South have been busier raising huge barriers in the coloured man's path to knowledge and achievements, along various lines which he might have otherwise attained, than they have been developing the wonderful natural resources of their rich and fertile land. The South has greatly prospered since the war. It is tilling its fields, working its mines of coal and ore, and filling its coffers with gold. But there is no doubt that much greater commercial prosperity would have been attained by the South if the same attention had been bestowed upon improving its agricultural facilities as has been given to devising ways and means of handicapping a struggling, backward race. Southern States like South Carolina and Georgia, for instance, which formed a part of the original thirteen, are poor and backward indeed compared with some of their younger sisters in the West, like Iowa and Illinois. Some of the eastern and western states that were admitted into the Union long after the Revolutionary War are not so rich in natural resources as are some of the southern States among the original thirteen. And yet these younger children in the national family have progressed far more rapidly along intellectual and financial lines than their elders in the South, because the inhabitants of the former have expended all their powers of body and mind building up a strong, substantial commonwealth and developing their resources to the fullest extent. None of their precious energy has been dissipated in frantic, hysterical efforts to hold in perpetual subjection a heavily handicapped race and to coerce others into adopting their standard of conduct and accepting their views. Gratifying, therefore, as has been the development of the South's agricultural and mineral resources, there is no doubt that the progress along these lines might have been greater if so much strength of the best white people in the South had not been expended manufacturing expedients for keeping their coloured brother in what they call 'his place.' The fear manifested by the southern white people that their coloured brother might, if not prevented, soar to heights which they are determined he shall never scale appears all the more groundless and inconsistent when it is recalled how strenuously they insist that he belongs to a naturally inferior race. But this is only one of the many illogical, irrational positions into which the South is trapped, and is only one of the many points on which it is obliged to stultify itself, because of its misguided, fanatical loyalty to the fetish of race prejudice, before which every knee must bow. Thus many a southern white man, possessing those qualities of intellect and those graces of heart which would have admirably fitted him to be a leader in affairs of high and noble emprise, has contented himself with being a mere policeman, whose only ambition in life was to keep a close watch upon the coloured man's aspirations, strike him upon the head with a bludgeon and arrest him, either when he aspired too high or tried to escape from the narrow intellectual, political, and social inclosure into which each and every member of his race, without regard to individual merit or capacity, had been forcibly corralled. In being deprived of the service of men who have thus prostituted their talents, not only the South but the whole nation has sustained an irreparable loss.

244

If there were any signs of improvement among southern white people as a whole, so far as concerns their attitude toward every subject which bears, even remotely, upon the race problem, their prospects, as well as those of the people who are oppressed, would be far brighter than they are. But no microscope now on the market is sufficiently powerful to enable even the lynx-eyed to detect the slightest change for the better. Legislatures in the southern States are never more enthusiastic and industrious than when they are bent upon enacting measures for the purpose of repressing the coloured man's aspirations by law. To-day one State legislature will exhaust Webster's Unabridged trying to find language sufficiently strong and lurid to express the necessity of dividing the taxes so that coloured children shall have no more schools than taxes paid by their parents will support. To-morrow another State will actually pass a law, as Louisiana has done, prohibiting the public schools for coloured children from instructing them beyond the fourth or fifth grades, with the understanding that what they get in the five grades shall be none too good. All the southern States, with the exception of Florida, Georgia, Tennessee, and Arkansas, have robbed coloured men of their right of citizenship, and have thus reduced more than 1,000,000 Americans to the level of serfs and slaves. So pernicious has been the influence of the far South that a border State like Virginia, only a stone's throw from the district in which the national capital is located, has disfranchised coloured men. Maryland, encouraged by Virginia's success in violating the amendments to the Constitution, tried with all her might and main just a few months ago to emulate her neighbour's unworthy example. Jim Crow cars enter and leave the National Capital filled with indignant, humiliated coloured citizens every hour in the day. Under such circumstances neither the most sanguine citizen in the North nor the most optimistic members of the oppressed race in the United States can lay the flattering unction to his soul that the South has accepted the result of the Civil War and is willing to grant coloured men the rights, privileges, and immunities of citizenship guaranteed them by the Constitution. No truer statement of the South's position to-day could possibly be made than that expressed by General Lee in his address to the Confederate Veterans at their reunion in Louisville last summer. Without mincing matters, or making unnecessary apologies, he declared that the South had accomplished, by peaceful revolution, what it had been unable to effect by means of war.

One might go on indefinitely supplying evidence to prove that, as a whole, the South is as implacable and unreconstructed, so far as concerns its attitude toward that part of the Constitution which guarantees the freedman his rights as well as towards those who insist that these rights be respected, as it was at the close of the war. There is a law—call it human, divine, retributive justice or what you will, but there is an inexorable law which decrees that those who persistently and cold-bloodedly oppress the weak shall not for ever escape the consequences of their guilt. Therefore, those who love the South and who have its interests at heart should never cease to labour and remonstrate with it, till it has been turned from its evil way. It is plainly the nation's duty, therefore, to do everything in its power to emancipate the South from the thraldom of its own prejudices; release it from the slavery of the brain-blighting, soul-crushing intolerance of other people's views; teach it the difference between the highest, purest patriotism and a narrow, sectional pride; instill into it a sense of justice which will prevent it either from inflicting or withholding penalties for wrong-doing and crime on account of the colour of a man's skin; and finally breathe into the hearts of the people as a whole a broad, Christian charity which will extend even to their former slaves.

Secondly, the South should be rescued from its follies and sins, not only because it will work its own destruction if it continues to pursue its present course, but because the spiritual and moral welfare of the American people as a whole is greatly imperilled thereby. What with its shameful record on lynching, what with its crimes committed by desperadoes belonging to various bands of organized violence, what with its Convict Lease system, that new form of slavery which obtains in nearly every State in the South and is in some respects more cruel and more crushing than the old; what with its Contract Labour system, designed and practiced for the purpose of deceiving and defrauding ignorant, defenseless coloured labourers; what with the shocking number of murders and homicides committed in so many instances with impunity, the South is in an unfortunate and alarming condition indeed. In Governor Hayward's message to the General Assembly of South Carolina in January of the current year he admits with sorrow and regret the reign of lawlessness in the State, and deplores the fact that although an appropriation to apprehend lynchers has been set aside at his request, no convictions had been made. With great intensity of feeling he declared that such outrages as those which so frequently occur in his State lead to all disregard of law, the cheapening of human life, and undermines our very civilization. In discussing the blood-guiltiness in Governor Hayward's State a short time ago, the *Nashville American*, one of the fairest and most reliable newspapers in the

South, stated that if the killing in other States had been in the same ratio to population as in South Carolina, a larger number of people would have been murdered in the United States during 1902 than fell on the American side in the Spanish and Philippine wars.

Although coloured men are usually the victims of the lawlessness and cruelty committed with the knowledge and consent of some of the Southern Commonwealths, white men from the North have occasionally suffered too. Only last December a sickening story of this cruel suffering was related by two white boys from Seymour, Ind., who had escaped from a Convict Lease camp in Mississippi, whose Governor, by the way, recently kicked a coloured convict nearly to death, because while blacking this high State official's shoes, the unfortunate convict said something to which the Governor took exception. These boys declared they found white men in the convict camps of Mississippi who had been held as slaves for ten years. The experience of the Indiana boys tallies with that of two New York boys who together with 200 others were lured to Florida last fall by promises of work at good pay. When they reached their service place, however, they were partly starved, flogged, shot, and finally placed in a chain gang and compelled to work until they fainted, when they were whipped for the weakness. According to official statistics a coloured man was lynched in Mississippi every eighteen days in 1905, and of this number only two were even charged with what is so falsely and maliciously called the 'usual crime.' One was shot because he was accused of writing an insulting letter, and one because he was charged with making threats. Crimes heinous enough occur in the North, it is true, but it is inconceivable that an institution so diabolical as the Convict Lease system could flourish anywhere in the North, East, or West with the knowledge and consent of either the citizens or the officials of the respective States. A short time ago the Grand Jury of Ware Co., Georgia, declared that at least twenty citizens of that county were held as slaves in a camp owned by one of the leading members of the Georgia legislature. The witnesses who were called testified that brutalities practiced in this camp were too revolting to be described.

Thus the white youth of the South are being hardened and brutalized by the shocking spectacles they are forced to witness on every hand. Truly the South is sowing seeds of lawlessness and cruelty which in the very nature of the case will spring up armed men in the years to come. Accounts of deeds of violence recently perpetrated by white students upon coloured people amply prove this fact. Last December the cadets of Virginia Military Institute of Lexington, Va., made a revengeful raid on the house of a coloured man, beat him unmercifully and marched him, half dead, to jail, simply because it was rumoured that he either fired a shot at a cadet himself, or knew the man who did. Not only by examples of cruelty and lawlessness, but also by social and political demarcations based exclusively upon race and class, the white youth of this country are being tainted in every conceivable way. 'Resolved, That a Jim Crow Car Law should be Adopted and Enforced in the District of Columbia' was the subject of a discussion engaged in in January of the present year by the Columbian Debating Society of the George Washington University, which is situated in the National Capital, and the decision was rendered in favour of the Jim Crow car.

In discussing questions bearing upon national, State, or municipal affairs, or touching matters of private concern, the South never fails to interject its views on the race problem and render a decision accordingly, no matter how remotely connected with the subject these views may be nor how great may be the advantages accruing to the South if it will temporarily sink these extraneous opinions out of sight. For instance, there is no doubt that southern white women would be greatly benefited by joining the General Federation of Women's Clubs and thereby coming into contact with some of the brightest minds in the United States. But only a few months ago the Alabama Federation of Women's Clubs voted down a resolution favouring such a union, because a coloured woman was admitted as a delegate in Milwaukee a long time ago, and that, too, in spite of the fact that the General Federation has since then adopted rules, so as to atone for thus offending their southern sisters, which practically exclude coloured women from the Federation altogether. And so one fact after another might be cited to prove that the South's present attitude of mind and state of heart preclude the possibility of progress. Stagnation of an individual or a collection of individuals invariably means retrogression in the end. That one section of this union cannot retrograde without dragging down all the others is an axiom.

If, therefore, the North, East, and West feel they are not their brother's keeper, and are not moved by the missionary spirit to lift the South out of the slough of stagnation in which it now lies, surely the second point urged as a reason for making a plea in its behalf will appeal to every patriot in the land. To all who give the subject careful consideration it must be clear that self-preservation and an intelligent concern for the nation as a whole command all true patriots to act, and act at once. If one section of this country is permitted to trample with impunity upon any provision of the

Constitution with which it takes issue, another will surely resort to the same expedient to render null and void any section or clause to which it is opposed. It does not require a great amount of profundity or perspicacity to see that the violation of one fundamental law invariably leads to the infraction of another.

If general observance of the law by the citizens of a country is a test of a nation's civilization, and if statistics on this subject count for anything, then the United States of America belongs at the very foot of the civilized nations' class. Quite recently ex-Ambassador Andrew White declared that with the single exception of Sicily more murders are committed in the United States than in any other civilized country in the world. Not long ago a well-known white clergyman in Louisville, Ky., startled his congregation one Sunday morning by declaring that home life is safer in the dominions of the Ameer of Afghanistan than it is in Kentucky.

There are more murders [said he] in Louisville, Ky., with 200,000 people than there are in London with nearly 7,000,000. There are more murders in Kentucky with its 2,000,000 people than in Great Britain with a population of 40,000,000. Finally there are more murders in the United States than in the whole of Europe, with Italy and Turkey left out and Russia included.

This statement was made, of course, before the wholesale slaughter of the Russian Jews.

No other civilized nation [said this Louisville clergyman] approaches this in the matter of murders, and those which come nearest to it are Italy and Turkey, where the assassin's knife is freely used and where men allow their anger and hatred and disgraceful passions to rule their conduct.

Several distinguished men in the congregation were so shocked at these statistics that they determined to study the subject themselves, but after a careful investigation had been instituted, they admitted these figures could not be truthfully denied.

At the annual dinner of the Authors' Club, given in honour of the Lord Chief Justice of England in December 1904, Sir Arthur Conan Doyle devoted a part of his remarks to the laxity with which the law against murder is administered in the United States. During the Boer War, he said, Great Britain had lost 22,000 lives. But during the same three years the United States had lost 10,000 more, that is 32,000 lives, by murder and homicide *in a time of peace*. Many of these crimes, he said, had gone unpunished.

The Lord Chief Justice took occasion to corroborate what Sir Arthur had said.

It is painful to every true American, of course, to know that lawlessness prevails to such an extent in the country he loves. It is the duty of true patriots, however, to stare disagreeable facts in the face, for in no other way will it be possible to remedy some of the evils which exist. And no matter how seriously the coloured American may be handicapped to-day, nor how grievously he was oppressed in the past, there are no truer patriots in the United States to-day than are the 10,000,000 coloured people who know and love no fatherland but this. In every war which this country has waged in the past, coloured men have fought and died with a courage and a patriotism surpassed by none.

Is it not true that this country's red record, which can neither be concealed nor denied, may be accounted for in large measure by the impunity with which crimes are committed against coloured people in the South? Coloured men, women, and children are being shot to death, flayed alive, and burned at the stake, while the murderers not only escape punishment as a rule, but are rarely, if ever, called to account. So rapidly has the crime of lynching spread that now it is confined to no one particular section, but we see it breaking out here and there in places where we would least expect to find it. During the riot which occurred in New York City a few years ago, an eye-witness declared that poor old coloured men who were returning peacefully and unsuspectingly home from their work, were cruelly set upon and brutally beaten by ruffians for no reason whatsoever, except that they were coloured. If, therefore, the North, East, and West are not moved by a sense of duty to save the South from itself and protect coloured men in their rights, the sooner those sections realize that self-preservation demands immediate and vigorous action on their part, the more surely will they be able to avert national tragedies which sanctioned lawlessness invariably precipitates.

If the events which transpired before the Civil War teach one lesson more than another, it is that tolerating wrong, temporizing with injustice, and long forbearance with evildoers are sure to bring shame, disgrace, and sorrow upon the nation that makes the fatal mistake. Putting off till to-morrow the correction of national evils which should be made to-day simply delays for a little the hour of wrath which is sure to strike. And when the day of retribution finally dawns, then the difficulty of throttling evils, grown great and strong by time, is increased a thousandfold. Delay is wicked; delay is dangerous; delay means death, are the words of warning written upon every page of the United States history from the day the Declaration of Independence was signed till Fort Sumter was fired upon by rebel guns. The French Revolution taught France the danger of delay in redressing the wrongs of the oppressed. Russia is learning the same lesson, to her sorrow and cost, to-day. God grant that our own beloved land may not be forced to atone a second time in a nation's blood and tears for tacitly consenting to cruel wrongs heaped upon the oppressed.

But if the first two reasons for making a plea in behalf of the South are not sufficient to arouse those who love their country, surely the third will appeal to all who love their fellow men. It is useless to talk about elevating the masses of a backward, struggling race until the scales of prejudice fall from the eyes of the stronger people, by whom the progress of the weaker is retarded, and without whose consent and support it will be impossible for the weaker to rise. In the South to-day an intelligent coloured man or woman suffers a veritable martyrdom. From the books they have read, and from the speeches of the Revolutionary fathers, which breathe forth hatred of oppression in every line, the intelligent coloured people in this country have learned to love liberty more than they love life. The love of freedom with which the very thin air in this country is heavily charged is inhaled by coloured Americans at every breath, and yet they know they are not free. They see they are not free to develop their God-given faculties and engage in any pursuit to which both their capacity and inclination lead them, and on account of which they might brilliantly succeed, although this is the privilege enjoyed by the representatives of every other race who land on American shores. Although it cannot be truthfully asserted that coloured people are free anywhere in the United States in the same sense as are all other Americans, whether indigenous or adopted, their yoke of bondage is heaviest in the South. In that section there are nearly 8,000,000 human beings, some of whom have very little, others a larger proportion of African blood coursing through their veins, who virtually occupy the position of serfs, when they are not actually held as slaves, in this Government founded upon liberty and equality before the law of all. The tortures endured by Tantalus, famished with hunger and parched with thirst, as he gazed upon food and water placed within his sight but out of reach, were not more terrible than are those suffered by coloured people in the United States who see all other races and nationalities enjoying opportunities of various kinds which they, too, long to possess, but of which they are systematically and continually deprived. The pity of it is that the just and generous hearted sons and daughters of the South who would gladly rescue, so far as in them lies, the deserving members of the downtrodden and handicapped race from their cruel fate are deterred from following the dictates of humanity, because they know what a heavy penalty for their deeds of kindness they will be obliged to pay.

One of the discouraging phases of the coloured man's status in the South is the persistency with which his strong and powerful brothers criticize and condemn the whole race for the mistakes made and the crimes committed by the few. For this reason no greater service could be rendered the coloured people of this country by those who have their interests at heart than to show the white South how rash and wicked is its course toward the freedmen in its midst, and what an irreparable injury it is doing them by the misrepresentations which it constantly circulates against the whole race. Even by southerners who are supposed to be broad-minded and just, the coloured man's vices are constantly exaggerated beyond a semblance of truth, in spite of the fact that his accusers are themselves responsible for most of them, his defects are emphasized in every possible way, and his mental ability either underestimated or scoffed at. In many instances these misrepresentations are not the result of deliberate malice. There is no doubt that many southerners do not realize how unjust and untruthful they are in their tirades against the oppressed race.

By looking continually and exclusively at one side of the race problem, and by a misguided loyalty to the sophistries and traditions of the past, their intellect is stunted, so far as concerns their ability to grasp any subject touching the coloured American, their reasoning faculties are dwarfed, and they are literally seduced from the truth. By a continual exaggeration of the coloured man's vices, by a studied suppression of the proofs of his marvelous advancement, by a judicious though malicious use of epithets, such as social equality, negro domination, and others which poison and mislead the public mind; by a watchful, searching skepticism with respect to evidence in the coloured man's favour, and a convenient credulity with respect to every report or tradition which can be used to prove the coloured man's depravity, the South has almost succeeded in persuading the whole world that it is a martyr and the coloured American is a brute. When a race or class is marked in any community, when its vices and defects are upon everybody's tongue and its depravity is conceded by all, it requires an amount of courage, goodness, and grit such as few human beings possess, for a single individual in that underestimated or slandered class to live down the opprobrium of which he is a vicarious victim. It is an axiom that whatever the hardships and misfortunes of a race may be, they fall with greatest severity upon women. The treatment accorded coloured women in the United States is but another proof of this well-established rule. A minister of the Gospel hailing from the South stood in the pulpit of New York Church, and declared, not long ago, that virtue in coloured women is so rare that any consideration of it is futile. There are very few men of any race, no matter how low in the social scale they may be, who can be induced to give damaging evidence against the character of a woman, no matter how frail or friendless she may be nor how urgent the necessity that her unsavoury record be exposed. But this rule of chivalry usually observed by all men toward all women, and to which the South insists it is pledged, has not always protected coloured women in the United States.

In 1895 the President of the Missouri Press Association sent an open letter to Miss Belgarnie of England, well known for her interest in the coloured people of the United States, which, with the exception of the slander recently uttered by the minister to whom reference has just been made, is probably the most unjustifiable and venomous attack ever made upon the womanhood of any race by a man. After painting in the most lurid colours possible the depth of the coloured American's degradation, he cites an example to prove his case against coloured women, which for coarse vulgarity and malicious mendacity cannot be surpassed in the bewildering confusion of false charges preferred against the victims of oppression and degradation by those who are responsible for their ruin. More than that, Southern white women who shine brilliantly in the galaxy of letters are not ashamed to prostitute their talent by publicly proclaiming their coloured sister's immorality to the world in both the newspapers and leading periodicals of the North, while they gloat in ghoulish glee over her shame. It is difficult to understand how the women of any race, under any circumstances and for any reason whatever, could bring themselves to slander in so wanton, so wholesale, and so cold-blooded a manner the womanhood of another race, particularly if those who wield the withering, blighting, character-assassinating pens are the daughters of parents responsible in the sight of God and men for the heredity and environment of the very women whose moral delinquencies they expose and assail. And so it happens that the very air which a coloured girl breathes in that section where the majority live is heavy with traditions and accusations of the frailty of both her race and her sex. Statistics, however, which have been compiled by white men themselves, show that in spite of the fateful heritage of slavery, in spite of the numerous pitfalls laid to entrap coloured girls, and though the safeguards usually thrown around maidenly youth and innocence are, in at least one section of this country, withheld from coloured girls, immorality among coloured women in the United States is not so great as among women similarly situated in at least five foreign lands.

As a preparation for the war of the Rebellion, Mr. Lincoln declared that the ringleaders in the conspiracy against this government had been assiduously debauching the public mind for thirty years. Ingenious sophisms were invented, he said, by which the right-thinking people of that section were deceived and misled. In the war which the professional negro-haters (not the whole South) have made upon the liberty of coloured people ever since their emancipation was proclaimed, precisely the same base methods have been pursued. The rapidity with which the South has poisoned the mind of the North against coloured people, and has succeeded in withdrawing from them the sympathy and assistance of those who were once known to be their best friends, is a splendid tribute to the persuasiveness, the persistency, the plausibility and the power of the South, while it resembles nothing so much as a skillful trick of legerdemain.

View the conditions which now obtain in the South from any standpoint one may, he must inevitably reach the conclusion that for the sake of the South itself, for the sake of the nation as a whole, and for the sake of 8,000,000 human beings crying for justice and a fair chance, strenuous efforts should be made by the North, East, and West to instill into the Southern people a wholesome reverence for the law. Failure to inflict upon an individual, or a collection of individuals, the penalty for wrongdoing and crime is simply to encourage still further defiance of the law. Therefore the men in the North, East, and West who are aiding and abetting political corruption and crime wherever it may exist, by allowing those who commit it to go unpunished and unrebuked are equal in guilt with those who flagrantly violate the law.

Washington, D.C.

Peonage in the United States

The Convict Lease System and the Chain Gangs

In the chain gangs and convict lease camps of the South to-day are thousands of coloured people, men, women, and children, who are enduring a bondage, in some respects more cruel and more crushing than that from which their parents were emancipated forty years ago. Under this modern *regime* of slavery thousands of coloured people, frequently upon trumped-up charges or for offenses which in a civilized community would hardly land them in gaol, are thrown into dark, damp, disease-breeding cells, whose cubic contents are less than those of a good-sized grave, are overworked, underfed, and only partially covered with vermin-infested rags. As the chain gangs and the convict lease system are operated in the South to-day they violate the law against peonage, the constitutionality of which was affirmed by the Supreme Court two years ago. In the famous case of Clyatt *versus* the United States, Attorney-General Moody, recently placed upon the bench of the Supreme Court, represented the Government, while Senator Bacon and others appeared for Clyatt, a resident of Georgia, who had been convicted in the Federal Courts of that State and sentenced to four years' hard labour on the charge of having held two coloured men in peonage on account of debt, in violation of the law. In his brief, Attorney Moody declared that the executive arm of the law, so far as the enforcement of the statute against peonage was concerned, has been practically paralysed.

'Notwithstanding the fact that several United States Courts have held this law to be constitutional' (said Judge Moody), 'the Government is powerless to

Originally published in *Nineteenth Century*, August 1907, pages 306-322.

compel its enforcement or observance, even in the most typical and flagrant cases. We think we may truthfully say' (continues Judge Moody) 'that upon the decision of this case (Clyatt *v.* the United States) hangs the liberty of thousands of persons, mostly coloured, it is true, who are now being held in a condition of involuntary servitude, in many cases worse than slavery itself, by the unlawful acts of individuals, not only in violation of the thirteenth amendment to the constitution, but in violation of the law which we have under consideration.'

With one or two exceptions, perhaps, no case decided by the Supreme Court within recent years involved graver considerations than were presented by the questions raised in the Clyatt case, for the constitutionality of the law against peonage was thereby affirmed.

If anybody is inclined to attach little importance to Judge Moody's description of the conditions under which thousands of peons are living in the South to-day, on the ground that they may be simply the exaggerated statement of a Northerner who, at best, has received his information second hand, let him listen to the words of a man, born and reared in the South, who was commissioned a few years ago to investigate the convict camps in his own State. After Colonel Byrd, of Rome, Ga., had inspected every county camp in the State which it was possible for him to discover, he addressed himself to Governor Atkinson, who for years had been trying to improve existing conditions, as follows:

'Your Excellency never did a more noble deed nor one that has been more far reaching in good or beneficial results to a helpless and friendless class of unfortunates than when you sent Special Inspector Wright into the misdemeanour camps of Georgia two years ago. His one visit did valiant service for human beings that were serving a bondage worse than slavery. True they were law-breakers and deserved punishment at the hands of the State, but surely the State has no right to make helpless by law and then to forsake the helpless to the mercies of men who have no mercy. Surely there can be no genuine civilization when man's inhumanity to man is so possible, so plainly in evidence.'

Immediately after the constitutionality of the law against peonage was affirmed by the Supreme Court in March 1904, Judge Emory Speer, of Savannah, Georgia, one of the most eminent jurists in the country, began to attack the chain gangs of the South on the ground that they violate both the thirteenth amendment and the law against peonage. Since the thirteenth amendment declares that 'involuntary servitude except as punishment for crime, whereof the party shall have been duly convicted, shall not exist in the

United States,' Judge Speer attacked the chain gangs, because men, women, and children by the hundreds are forced into involuntary servitude by being sentenced to work upon them, who are not even charged with crime, but are accused of some petty offence, such as walking on the grass, expectorating upon the side walk, going to sleep in a depot, loitering on the streets, or some similar misdemeanors which could not by any stretch of the imagination be called a crime. Judge Speer also declared it to be his opinion that even those who sentence these helpless and friendless people to the chain gangs, and thus force them into involuntary servitude, are guilty of violating the law and are liable to punishment therefore; since it was explicitly stated in the decision rendered by the Supreme Court that even though 'there might be in the language of the court either a municipal ordinance or State law sanctioning the holding of persons in involuntary servitude, Congress has power to punish those who thus violate the thirteenth amendment and the law against peonage at one and the same time.

In spite, however, of the overwhelming weight of evidence showing that atrocities are daily being perpetrated upon American citizens in almost every State of the South, with the connivance of those who administer the law, which are as shocking and unprintable as those endured by the Russian Jew, in spite of the power which the Supreme Court asserts is possessed by Congress, but feeble efforts are being put forth to suppress the chain gangs and the convict lease camps of the South. It is surprising how few there are among even intelligent people in this country who seem to have anything but a hazy idea of what the convict lease system means.

The plan of hiring out short term convicts to an individual or a company of individuals who needed labourers was adopted by the southern States shortly after the war, not from choice, it is claimed, but because there was neither a sufficient number of gaols nor money enough to build them. Those who need labourers for their farms, saw mills, brick yards, turpentine distilleries, coal or phosphate mines, or who have large contracts of various kinds, lease the misdemeanants from the county or State, which sells them to the highest bidder with merciless disregard of the fact that they are human beings, and practically gives the lessee the power of life and death over the unfortunate man or woman thus raffled off. The more work the lessee gets out of the convict, the more money goes into his gaping purse. Doctors cannot be employed without the expenditure of money, while fresh victims may be secured by the outlay of little cash when convicts succumb to disease and neglect. From a purely business standpoint, therefore, it is much more profitable to get as much work out of a convict as can be wrung from him at the smallest possible expense, and then lay in a fresh supply, when necessary, than it is to clothe, and shelter, and feed him properly, and spend money trying to preserve his health. It is perfectly clear, therefore, that it is no exaggeration to say that in some respects the convict lease system, as it is operated in certain southern States, is less humane than was the bondage endured by slaves fifty years ago. For, under the old *regime*, it was to the master's interest to clothe and shelter and feed his slaves properly, even if he were not moved to do so by considerations of mercy and humanity, because the death of a slave meant an actual loss in dollars and cents, whereas the death of a convict to-day involves no loss whatsoever either to the lessee or to the State.

Speaking of this system a few years ago, a governor of Kentucky said:

'I cannot but regard the present system under which the State penitentiary is leased and managed as a reproach to the commonwealth. It is the *system* itself and not the officer acting under it with which I find fault. Possession of the convict's person is an opportunity for the State to make money—the amount to be made is whatever can be wrung from him without regard to moral or mortal consequences. The penitentiary which shows the largest cash balance paid into the State treasury is the best penitentiary. In the main the notion is clearly set forth and followed that a convict, whether pilferer or murderer, man, woman, or child, has almost no human right that the State is bound to be at any expense to protect.'

Again, at a meeting of the National Prison Association which was held in New Orleans a few years ago, a speaker who had carefully studied the convict lease system declared that the convicts in the South, most of whom are negroes, are in many cases worse off than they were in the days of slavery. 'They are bought as truly,' said he, 'are more completely separated from their families, are irretrievably demoralized by constant evil association and are invariably worse off when they leave the camps than when they entered.' 'Over certain places where the convicts of Alabama are employed,' said an authority on penology, 'should be written the words "All hope abandon ye who enter here," so utterly demoralizing is the entire management.' And so it would be possible to quote indefinitely from men all over the country in every station of life, from judges, governors of States, prison experts, and private citizens, whose testimony without a single exception proves conclusively that the convict lease system in particular, and the chain gang on general principles, are an insult to the intelligence and humanity of an enlightened community.

It is frequently asserted that the convict lease camps and other forms of peonage are dying out in the south. First one State and then another passes laws against leasing convicts to private individuals or attempts to pass such a law, or, if it still adheres to the convict lease system, it tries to provide for the inspection of the camps by men appointed to do this work by the State. But facts which have been brought to light during the last year or two show that those who extract comfort from the reports which announce the disappearance of the convict camps and the chain gangs build their hope upon a foundation of sand. During the year 1906 allegations of the existence of slavery in Florida were made to the department of justice, and evidence was produced to show that hundreds of men, the majority of whom were coloured, but a few among the number white, were virtually reduced to the condition of slaves.

Facts were produced which showed that the officers of the law, the sheriffs themselves, were parties to reducing to a condition of slavery the coloured people who work in the phosphate and coal mines, in the lumber mills or on the turpentine farms of Florida, for instance. These camps were inspected by a woman who was commissioned, it is said, by those high in authority to secure the facts. Only last September a government detective disguised as a man anxious to purchase timber lands, visited the railroad camps of Blount Co., Tenn., and secured evidence against some of the most prominent contractors in that section, which showed that hundreds of coloured men have systematically been deprived of their liberty, while it is impossible to state how many of them lost their lives.

Before the grand jury the victims of this barbarous system of peonage, many of whom had been brought to Tennessee from North and South Carolina, told pitiable tales of their suffering and maltreatment and related stories of seeing men killed, dragged to the river in blankets, weighted, and then sunk into the water, which are too horrible to believe. As a result of this trial one of the largest railroad contractors of Knoxville, Tenn., was indicted by the grand jury on the charge of peonage, the indictment containing twenty-five counts.

Upon the evidence of a coloured soldier who was with President Roosevelt in Cuba, and who sawed his way to freedom through the floor of the shack in which he was confined at night, together with a large number of peons, the man who thus held him in bondage in Missouri was sentenced to three and a half years in the penitentiary of Fort Leavenworth, Kansas, in addition to paying a fine of five thousand dollars and costs. Several others who were engaged in conducting this particular camp, among them the son of the chief offender, were also sentenced to the penitentiary, fined, and obliged to pay the costs. Last spring six coloured people filed suits against a family by whom they had been held in a state of peonage in Ashley Co., Ark. Their complaint set forth inhuman treatment, imprisonment in gaols in various places, that they were bound like beasts, paraded through public streets, and then imprisoned on plantations, where they were compelled to do the hardest kind of labour without receiving a single cent.

While coloured people were originally the only ones affected to any great extent by the practice of peonage in the southern States, in recent years white people in increasingly large numbers have been doomed to the same fate. For instance, only last July the chairman of the Board of Commissioners of Bradford Co., Florida, was arrested for holding in a state of peonage an orphan white girl sixteen years old. The girl declares that she was so brutally treated, she started to walk to Jacksonville, Fla. When she had gone six miles, she was overtaken, she says, by her hard task-master and forced to walk back by a road covered with water in places, so that she was obliged to wade knee deep. When she returned, she declared her master beat her with a hickory stick and showed bruises to substantiate the charge. Last October a wealthy family, living in Arkansas, was convicted of holding two white girls from St. Louis, Mo., in peonage, and was forced to pay one of the white slaves one thousand dollars damages, and the other 625 dollars. The farmer had induced the girls to come from Missouri to Arkansas, and then promptly reduced them to the condition of slaves. In the same month of October came the startling announcement that one thousand white girls, who are rightful heiresses to valuable timber lands in the wilds of the Florida pine woods, wear men's clothing and work side by side with coloured men who are held in slavery as well as the girls. Stories of the treatment accorded these white slave girls of Florida, which reached the ears of the Washington officials, equal in cruelty some of the tales repeated in *Uncle Tom's Cabin* by Harriet Beecher Stowe. In the black depths of pine woods, living in huts never seen by civilized white men other than the bosses of the turpentine camps, girls are said to have grown old in servitude. These girls are said to be the daughters of crackers who, like fathers in pre-historic times, little value the birth of a girl, and sell the best years of their daughters' lives to the turpentine or sulphur miners and to the lumber men for a mere song. To be discharged from one of these camps means death to an *employe*. Since they receive nothing for their services, their dismissal is no revenge for an angered foreman or boss. The slaves are too numerous to be beaten, and it is said to be a part of the system never to whip an *employe*, but invariably to shoot the doomed man or woman upon the slightest provocation, so that the others might be kept in constant subjection.

Two white men of Seymour, Indiana, went to Vance, Mississippi, not very long ago, to work for a large stave company, as they supposed; but when they reached Vance, they were told they must go to the swamp and cut timber. When they demurred, the foreman had them arrested for securing their transportation money 'on false pretenses.' The squire before whom they were taken fined each of them 45 dollars and costs. They were then obliged to ride twenty-three miles on horseback to Belen, the county seat, where they were kept three days and given one meal. Then they were taken to Essex, Mississippi, turned over to the owner of a plantation, placed in a stockade at night and forced to work under an armed guard. They were ordered to work out their fine at *fifteen cents a day*, such a contract being made by the *court officers themselves*. These Indiana men learned during the nine days they were in this Mississippi stockade that there were men on the plantation who had been there for ten years trying to work out their fines. Before one fine could be worked out a new charge would be trumped up to hold them. Only last August a young white man who had lived in New York returned to his home, half starved, his body covered with bruises, resulting from unmerciful beatings he had received in a State camp in North Carolina, and related a story which was horrifying in its revelations of the atrocities perpetrated upon the men confined in it. This young white man claimed that at the time he escaped there were no less than twenty other youths from New York unable to return to their homes, and enduring the torture to which he was subjected by inhuman bosses every day. According to this young New Yorker's story, there were about one thousand men at work in this camp, each of whom was obliged to contribute 50 cents a week toward the support of a physician.

'On one occasion' [said he] 'the foreman threw heavy stones at me, one of which struck me on the head, knocking me senseless, because I sat down to rest. For hours I lay on the cot in my shack without medical aid, and I bear the mark of that stone to-day. For refusing to work because of lack of nourishment, for our meals consisted only of a slice of bread and a glass of water, I saw the foreman take a revolver, shoot a young negro through the leg and walk away, leaving him for dead. This fellow lay for days without medical aid and was finally taken away, nobody knows where. Three Italians were killed and two others were severely injured in a fight between the foreman and labourers, and yet not one of these men was arrested. Since the post office was under the control of the men running the camp, the letters written by the New York boys to their friends and relatives never reached their destination.'

The cases just cited prove conclusively that not only does peonage still rage violently in the southern States and in a variety of forms, but that while it formerly affected only coloured people, it now attacks white men and women as well.

From renting or buying coloured men, women, and children, who had really fallen under the ban of the law, to actually trapping and stealing them was a very short step indeed, when labour was scarce and the need of additional hands pressed sore. Very recently, incredible as it may appear to many, coloured men have been captured by white men, torn from their homes and forced to work on plantations or in camps of various kinds, just as truly as their fathers before them were snatched violently by slave catchers from their native African shores. Only last February (1906) two cotton planters of Houston Co., Texas, were arrested for a kind of peonage which is by no means uncommon in the South to-day. The planters needed extra help, so they captured two strong, able-bodied negroes, whom they charged with being indebted to them, and with having violated their contracts. Without resort to law they manacled the negroes and removed them to their plantations, where they forced them to work from twelve to sixteen hours a day without paying them a cent. The sheriff who arrested the planters admitted that this practice of capturing negroes when labour is needed on the plantations has prevailed for a long time in Madison Co., Texas, where the population is mainly negro. The captured men are worked during the cotton-planting season, are then released with empty pockets and allowed to return to their homes as best they can, where they remain until they are needed again, when they are recaptured.

But the methods generally used by the men who run the convict camps of the South or who own large plantations, when they need coloured labourers, are much more skilled and less likely to involve them in trouble than those which the Texans just mentioned employ. Coloured men are convicted in magistrates' courts of trivial offenses, such as alleged violation of contract or something of the kind, and are given purposefully heavy sentences with alternate fines. Plantation owners and others in search of labour, who have already given their orders to the officers of the law, are promptly notified that some available labourers are theirs to command and immediately appear to pay the fine and release the convict from gaol only to make him a slave. If the negro dares to leave the premises of his employer, the same magistrate who convicted him originally is ready to pounce down upon him and send him back to gaol. Invariably poor and ignorant, he is unable to employ counsel or to assert his rights (it is treason to presume he has any) and he finds all the machinery of the law, so far as he can understand, against him. There is no doubt whatever that there are scores, hundreds perhaps, of coloured men in the South to-day who are vainly trying to repay fines and sentences imposed upon them five, six, or even ten years ago. The horror of ball and chain is ever before them, and their future is bright with no hope.

In the annual report of the 'Georgia State Prison Commission,' which appeared only last June, the secretary shows that during the year 1905-06, there was a decrease of fully 10 per cent in the number of misdemeanour convicts on the county chain gangs in Georgia, notwithstanding the fact that there has been an increase among the felony convicts. This decrease in the number of misdemeanants is explained as follows: 'Owing to the scarcity of labour, farmers who are able to do so pay the fines of able-bodied prisoners and put them on their plantation to work them out.' 'Had it not been for the fact that many farmers have paid the fines of the men convicted,' explains the prison commission, 'in order to get their labour, there is no doubt that there would be an increase instead of a decrease in the number on the misdemeanour gangs.' This very frank admission of the open manner in which the law against peonage is deliberately broken by the farmers of Georgia is refreshing, to say the least. Surely they cannot be accused by prudish and unreasonable persons of violating the thirteenth amendment by mysterious methods hard to detect and transgressing the peonage law in secret, when the decrease in the number of misdemeanants of a sovereign State is attributed in a printed report to the fact that the farmers are buying up able-bodied negroes a bit more briskly than usual.

While the convict lease camps of no State in the South have presented conditions more shocking and cruel than have those in Georgia, it is also true that in no State have more determined and conscientious efforts to improve conditions been put forth by a portion of its citizens than in that State. In spite of this fact it is well known that some of the wealthiest men in the State have accumulated their fortunes by literally buying coloured men, women, and children, and working them nearly, if not quite, to death. Reference has already been made to the report submitted to the Georgia legislature a few years ago by Colonel Byrd, who was appointed special commissioner to investigate the convict lease camps of his State. In reviewing this report the *Atlanta Constitution* summed up the charges against the convict lease system as follows: 'Colonel Byrd's report was not written by a Northerner, who does not understand conditions in the South, or the people living in that section' (as is so frequently asserted, when one who does not live in the sunny south dares to comment on anything which takes place below Mason's and Dixon's line); 'but it is written by one of the South's most distinguished citizens who did not deal in glittering generalities, but in facts.' Colonel Byrd gave a truthful account of his trips to the camps, of his visits in the day time and at night, when none knew of his coming. He made it a rule, he said, to arrive at each camp unannounced, and he has told us exactly what he saw with his eyes and heard with his ears. Of the fifty-one chain gangs visited, Colonel Byrd discovered that at least half were operated exclusively by private individuals who had practically the power of life and death over the convicts. Seldom was provision made for the separation of the sexes, either during work by day or sleep by night. Little or no attention was given to the comfort or sanitary conditions of the sleeping quarters, and women were forced to do men's work in men's attire. The murder of the men and the outrage of the women in these camps, the political pulls by which men occupying lofty positions in the State were shielded and saved from indictment by grand juries, formed the subjects of many indignant editorials in the *Atlanta Constitution*.

Briefly summed up, the specific charges preferred by one of the South's most distinguished sons who had made a most painstaking and exhaustive investigation of the convict lease camps of Georgia are as follows:

(1) Robbing convicts of their time allowances for good behaviour. According to Colonel Byrd, there were not five camps in the State that had complied with the law requiring them to keep a book in which the good or bad conduct of each convict shall be entered daily. In the event of good conduct the law provides that a prisoner's term of confinement shall be shortened four days during each month of service. In fifteen out of twenty-four private camps the contractors did not give the convicts a single day off for good service, nor did they even make pretence of doing so.

(2) Forcing convicts to work from fourteen to twenty hours a day.

(3) Providing them no clothes, no shoes, no beds, no heat in winter, and no ventilation whatever in single rooms in summer in which sixty convicts slept in chains.

(4) Giving them rotten food.

(5) Allowing them to die, when sick, for lack of medical attention.

(6) Outraging the women.

(7) Beating to death old men too feeble to work.

(8) Killing young men for the mere sake of killing.

(9) Suborning jurors and county officers, whose sworn duty it is to avenge the wrongdoing of guards.

It is when he struck the convicts leased to private individuals that Colonel Byrd took off his gloves, as the *Atlanta Constitution* well said, and dipped his pen in red ink. In these private camps Colonel Byrd found the convicts, men committed at the most for some trivial offence or perhaps none at all, had no clothes except greasy, grimy garments, which in many cases were worn to threads and were worthless as protection. These men, women, and children, for there were children only eight years old in the camps inspected by Colonel Byrd a few years ago, were badly shod and in the majority of cases went barefoot the year round. In many of the pine belt gangs, where the convicts were buried in the fastness of mighty pine forests, they went from year's end to year's end without a taste of vegetables. Usually after the convicts returned from their fourteen hours' work they were given raw chunks of meat to prepare for their own dinner. In the matter of buildings the report was no less severe. In a camp owned by a well-known Georgian, Colonel Byrd found eleven men sleeping in a room ten feet square and but seven feet from floor to ceiling, with no windows at all, but one door which opened into another room. In another camp the convicts slept in tents which had no bunks, no mattresses, and not even a floor. Fully thirteen of the camps out of twenty-four contained neither bunks nor mattresses, and the convicts were compelled to sleep in filthy, vermin-ridden blankets on the ground. And the men were obliged to sleep chained together.

Many of the camps had no arrangements and scarcely miserable excuses for means of warming the barn-like buildings in which the convicts were confined during stormy days and wintry nights. The suffering the helpless inmates were forced to endure in winter, according to Colonel Byrd's description, must have been terrible, while in the summer they were locked into the sweat boxes without ventilation, in order that the lessee might save the expense of employing night guards.

'In two instances,' said Colonel Byrd, 'I found by the bedside of sick convicts tubs that had been used for days without having been emptied and in a condition that would kill anything but a misdemeanour convict.' But Colonel Byrd's description of the insanitary condition of some of the camps and the horrors of convict life are unprintable. He calls attention to the fact that the death rate in the private camps is double that of the county camps. In one of the camps one out of every four convicts died during their incarceration. In another camp one out of every six unfortunates who had committed some slight infraction of the law, if he were guilty at all, was thrust into a camp which he never left alive. In twenty-one out of twenty-four private camps there were neither hospital buildings nor arrangements of any kind for the sick. After describing the lack of bathing facilities, which Colonel Byrd says gave the convicts a mangy appearance, he refers to the inhuman beatings inflicted upon the convicts. A leather strop was the instrument of punishment found by the commissioner in all the camps, 'and my observation has been,' said he, 'that where the strap has been used the least the best camps exist and the best work is turned out by the convicts.'

In the camp in which the negroes looked worst the commissioner found very few reported dead. On the very date of inspection, however, there were three men, all new arrivals, locked in the filthy building, sick. They said they had been there a week, and two of them looked as though they could not recover. In another camp there was not even a stove, and the negroes had to cook on skillets over log fires in the open air. There were no beds at all and the few blankets were reeking with filth, as they were scattered about over a dirty floor.

In his report Colonel Byrd called particular attention to a few of the many cases of brutality, inhumanity, and even murder which came under his own personal observation. In the banner camp for heavy mortality the commissioner found two men with broken legs, so terribly surrounded as practically to make it impossible for them to recover. Both in this camp and in others there were numerous instances of sudden deaths among convicts, which were attributed to brain trouble and other diseases. On reliable authority Colonel Byrd learned that the guards in one of the camps visited had just a short while before his arrival literally beaten one of the convicts to death and then burned his remains in his convict suit with his shackles on. 'A reputable citizen,' said Colonel Byrd, 'told me that he had seen the guards beating this convict, and that in their anger they had caught him by the shackles and run through the woods, dragging him along feet foremost.' He stated he had gone before the grand jury of Pulaski Co., where the camp was situated, and had sworn to these facts, but that Mr. Allison, who ran this camp, had friends on the jury and that other citizens had thought it would be best to hush the whole deplorable affair up, so as to keep it out of the newspapers and courts. The superintendent of the camp simply claimed that the murderous negro had died of dropsy and was buried in his stripes and shackles to save time.

The camp of W. H. and J. H. Griffin in Wilkes Co. was described as being 'very tough.' It was in that camp that Bob Cannon, a camp guard, beat to death an aged negro named Frank McRay. The condition in this camp was too horrible to describe. The prison was an abandoned kitchen or outhouse in the yard of a large *ante bellum* residence. Every window in it had been removed and the openings closely boarded up and sealed. It was a small square box with not even an augur hole for air or light.

'When the door was opened' [said Colonel Byrd], 'and I had recovered from the shock caused by the rush of foul air, I noticed a sick negro sitting in the room. How human beings could consign a fellow being to such an existence I cannot understand any more than I can understand how a human being could survive a night of confinement in such a den. There was an open can in the centre of the room and it looked as if it had not been emptied in a fortnight. A small bit of cornbread lay on a blanket near the negro, and that poor victim, guilty of a misdemeanour only, while sick, confined in this sweat-box dungeon, humbly asked to be furnished with a drink of water.

It was in this gang that I found Lizzie Boatwright, a nineteen-year-old negress sent up from Thomas, Ga., for larceny. She was clad in men's clothing, was working side by side with male convicts under a guard, cutting a ditch through a meadow. The girl was small of stature and pleasant of address, and her life in this camp must have been one of long drawn out agony, horror, and suffering. She told me she had been whipped twice, each time by the brutal white guard who had beaten McRay to death, and who prostituted his legal right to whip into a most revolting and disgusting outrage. This girl and another woman were stripped and beaten unmercifully in plain view of the men convicts, because they stopped on the side of the road to bind a rag about their sore feet.'

Be as sanguine as one may, he cannot extract much comfort from the hope that conditions at present are much better, if any, than they were when Col. Byrd made this startling, shocking revelation, as the result of a careful investigation of these camps several years ago, since camps for misdemeanour convicts are being conducted by private individuals to-day just as they were then. The eighth annual report of the Prison Commission, issued May 1905, shows that thirteen of the misdemeanour convict camps in the State of Georgia are worked for and in some cases by private individuals, contrary to law, who hire them directly from the authorities having them in charge after conviction with no legal warrant from the county authorities in those counties where they are worked. These convicts, according the last year's report from Georgia, are entirely in the custody and control of private individuals. The officials hire them in remote counties, never seeing them after delivery, and the county authorities where they are worked never exercise supervision over or control of them.

The law explicitly states that the Prison Commission of Georgia shall have general supervision of the misdemeanour convicts of the State.

> 'It shall be the duty of one of the Commissioners, or, in case of emergency, an officer designated by them, to visit from time to time, at least quarterly, the various camps where misdemeanour convicts are at work, and shall advise with the county of municipal authorities working them, in making and altering the rules for the government control and management of said convicts. . . . And if the county or municipal authorities fail to comply with such rules, or the law governing misdemeanour chain gangs [reads the statute], then the Governor with the Commission shall take such convicts from said county or municipal authorities. Or the Governor and Commission in their discretion may impose a fine upon each of the said county or municipal authorities failing to comply with such rules or the law.'

But this law is easily evaded, because the county authorities where the convict is sentenced have established no chain gang, and the county authorities where the convict is worked none, so that neither can be proceeded against by the Commission. 'The Prison Commission of Georgia has repeatedly called the attention of the General Assembly to this condition,' says the report, and cannot refrain from again doing so, hoping that some means may be devised by which this violation of the law may be prevented.

Again and again efforts put forth by humane people, both in Georgia and in other southern States, to correct abuses in the camps have been frustrated by men high in authority, who belong to the State legislatures and who make large fortunes out of the wretches they abuse. Colonel Byrd called attention to the fact that the whole political machinery of the State and county stood in with the lessees, because the first money earned by the poor victims paid the cost of trial and conviction. Not a dollar of the rental for the convicts reached the county treasurer, he declared, till sheriff, deputy sheriff, county solicitor, bailiffs, court clerks, justice of the peace, constables and other officials who aided to put the convict in the chain gang were paid their fees in full. 'It is not to be supposed,' said Colonel Byrd, 'that these people would be in favour of destroying a system profitable to themselves.' The following incident throws some light on this point. A coloured man was convicted of larceny and sentenced to twelve months on the chain gang. The county solicitor personally took charge of him, carried him to a private camp, where the contractor gave him 100 dollars in cash for this prisoner. A few months later it was discovered that the man was innocent of the crime. Both the judge and the jury before whom he was convicted signed a petition to the Governor praying for the prisoner's release. The county solicitor refused to sign it, however, because he had received his 100 dollars in advance and distributed it among the other court officials and did not want to pay it back.

There are in Georgia at the present time 1,500 men who were sold to the highest bidder the 1st of April, 1904, for a period of five years. The Durham Coal and Coke Co. leased 150 convicts, paying for them from 228 dollars to 252 dollars apiece per annum. The Flower Brothers Lumber Co. leased one hundred and paid 240 dollars a piece for them for a year. Hamby and Toomer leased five hundred, paying 221 dollars a head. The Lookout Mountain Coal and Coke Co. took 100 at 223.75 dollars a head.

The Chattahoochee Brick Co. secured 175 men at 223.75 dollars apiece per annum. E. J. McRee took one hundred men and paid 220.75 dollars for each. In its report the Prison Commission points with great pride to the fact that for five years, from the 1st of April, 1904, to the 1st of April, 1909, this batch of prisoners alone will pour annually into the State coffers the gross sum of 340,000 dollars with a net of 225,000 dollars, which will be distributed proportionately among the various counties for school purposes.

In 1903 a man whose barbarous treatment of convicts leased to him by Tallapoosa and Coosa Counties, Alabama, had been thoroughly exposed, and who had been indicted a number of times in the State courts, succeeded in leasing more convicts for a term of three years without the slightest difficulty, in spite of his record. The grand jury for the May term, 1903, of the District Court of the middle of Alabama returned ninety-nine indictments for peonage and conspiring to hold parties in a condition of peonage. In these ninety-nine true bills only eighteen persons were involved. Under the convict lease system of Alabama the State Board of Convicts then had no control whatever over the County convicts, and if they were leased to an inhuman man there was absolutely nothing to prevent him from doing with them what he wished. During the trial of the cases in Alabama to which reference has been made, a well-known journalist declared over his signature that when the chief of the State Convict Inspecting Bureau, who had been sent to Tallapoosa Co. to investigate conditions obtaining in the penal camps there, reported that some of the largest landowners and planters in the State were engaged in the traffic of selling negroes into involuntary servitude, the Governor took no further steps to bring about the conviction of the guilty parties.

In Alabama a justice of the peace in criminal cases has power to sentence a convicted prisoner to hard labour for a term not exceeding twelve months. He is required under law to make a report of such cases to the Judge of Probate of his respective county, and to file a mittimus with the gaoler of each man who is tried before him who has been convicted and fails to give bond. As soon as a man was convicted in Tallapoosa and Coosa counties by a Justice of the Peace, who was in collusion with the party or parties who had a contract with the county for leasing the county convicts, he would turn each of them over to the lessee without committing them to the county gaol, and without filing a certificate of these convictions with the Judge of Probate. Since there was no public examiner to go over the books of the Justice of the Peace, it was easy, when they were examined by order of the grand jury, to explain away as a mistake any discrepancies upon the docket. Since there was nothing on the docket of the Justice of the Peace to show the length of time the man was to serve, he was held by the lessee, until he broke down or managed to escape. Moreover, the prosecution of the cases mentioned showed that trumped-up charges would be frequently made against negroes in the two counties mentioned for the most trivial offenses, such as happened in the case of one convict who was arrested for letting one man's mule bite another man's corn. It also came out in the trial that when the sentence of two convicts expired at the same time they were often provoked into a difficulty with each other and then each man would be taken down before a Justice of the Peace without the knowledge of the other, and persuaded to make an affidavit against the other man for an affray. Both would then be tried before a Justice, convicted and sentenced to imprisonment at hard labour for six months, and this would go on indefinitely. It was also developed at this Alabama trial that there was often no trial at all. An affidavit would be sworn out, but never entered upon the docket, and after a mock trial the man would be sentenced for three months or six and the judgment never entered up.

If there was an examination by the grand jury of the county, there would be no way for it to secure the facts, and no one in the community seemed to think it was his duty to make any charges. Between A and B, both of whom were convicted of peonage in Alabama in 1903, it is said that there was an understanding that the men arrested in A's neighborhood were to be tried before C, one of B's brothers-in-law, while those whom B wanted would be tried before one of A's, who was Justice of the Peace. If material ran short, the men held by the A's were taken down and tried before B's brother-in-law and turned over to B and *vice versa*. It can easily be seen that negroes—friendless, illiterate, and penniless—had no salvation at all except when the strong arm of the United States Government took them under its protection. Although the grand jury at the May term of 1903 declared that Tallapoosa and Coosa counties were the only localities in the State where peonage existed, subsequent arrests of persons who were bound over by a United States Commissioner to await the action of the United States grand jury at the December term of 1903 proved conclusively that there were many cases of peonage in Covington, Crenshaw, Pike, Coffee, Houston, and other counties in the State of Alabama.

Describing the convict lease system, as it is operated in Mississippi, one of the best attorneys in that State said:

'This institution is operated for no other purpose than to make money, and I can compare it with nothing but Dante's Inferno. Hades is a paradise compared with the convict camps of Mississippi. If an able-bodied young man sent to one of these camps for sixty or ninety days lives to return home, he is fit for nothing the rest of his natural life, for he is a physical wreck at the expiration of his term.'

As in other States, the convict camps of Mississippi are operated by planters or others who have secured a contract from the County Board to work all prisoners sent up by the magistrates or other courts. A stipulated sum per capita is paid for the prisoners, who have to work out their fines, costs, and living expenses, receiving practically nothing for their labour. As spring comes, officers of the law become exceedingly busy looking up cases of vagrancy or misdemeanour, so as to supply their regular patrons.

It is interesting and illuminating to see what class of men have been indicted for holding their fellows in bondage in the stockades of the South. A few years ago a leading member of the Georgia legislature, together with his brothers, operated an extensive camp in Lowndes Co. Witnesses testified before the grand jury that in this camp, owned by a member of the legislature, the brutalities practiced were too revolting to describe. It is also interesting to know that a member of that same family was awarded 100 convicts on the 1st of April 1904, and this lease is good for five years. Witnesses testified that this member of the Georgia legislature operated a camp in which prisoners were stripped and unmercifully lashed by the whipping bosses for the slightest offence. It was also alleged that this lawmaker for a sovereign State and his brothers were accustomed to go into counties adjoining Lowndes, pay the fines of the misdemeanour convicts, carry them into their Ware county camp and there keep them indefinitely.

The grand jury claimed that at least twenty citizens of Ware Co. were held as slaves in the camp owned by the brothers to whom reference has been made, long after their terms had expired. An ex-sheriff of Ware Co. and a well-known attorney of Georgia pleaded guilty not very long ago to the charge of holding citizens in a condition of peonage, and were each fined 1,000 dollars (500 dollars of which was remitted) by Judge Emory Speer. A sheriff in Alabama was recently indicted for peonage. Manufacturers of Georgia and railroad contractors in Tennessee have recently been indicted for holding men and women in involuntary servitude. The chairman of the Board of Commissioners of Bradford Co., Fla., was indicted not long ago for the same offence. In March 1905 the Federal Grand Jury indicted the city of Louisville and the superintendent of the workhouse for violating the federal statute against peonage.

There is no doubt whatever that every misdemeanour convict in the chain gangs and convict lease camps in the South operated by private individuals could appeal to the courts and secure release. Incarceration of misdemeanour convicts in these camps is as much disobedience of the laws as the original offence which led to conviction. There is no doubt that every misdemeanour camp in the southern States which is controlled by private individuals is a nest of illegality. Every man employing misdemeanour convicts for private gain is a law-breaker. Every county official who leases or permits to be leased a misdemeanour convict for other than public work transgresses one of the plainest statutes on the law books of some of the States in which the offence is committed, and violates an amendment to the constitution of the United States besides. There is no lack of law by which to punish the guilty, but they are permitted to perpetrate fearful atrocities upon the unfortunate and helpless, because there are thousands of just and humane people in this country who know little or nothing about the methods pursued in the chain gangs, the convict lease system and the contract labour system, which are all children of one wicked and hideous mother, peonage.

The negro was armed with the suffrage by just and humane men, because soon after the War of the Rebellion the legislatures of the southern States began to enact vagrant or peonage laws, the intent of which was to reduce the newly emancipated slaves to a bondage almost as cruel, if not quite as cruel, as that from which they had just been delivered. After the vote had been given the negro, so that he might use it in self-defence, the peonage laws became a dead letter for a time and lay dormant, so to speak, until disfranchisement laws were enacted in nearly every State of the South. The connection between disfranchisement and peonage is intimate and close. The planter sees the negro robbed of his suffrage with impunity, with the silent consent of the whole country, and he knows that political preferment and great power are the fruits of this outrage upon a handicapped and persecuted race. He is encouraged, therefore, to apply the same principle for profit's sake to his business affairs. The politician declared that the negro is unfit for citizenship and violently snatches from him his rights. The planter declares the negro is lazy and forces him into involuntary servitude contrary to the law. Each tyrant employs the same process of reasoning to justify his course.

The Disbanding of the Colored Soldiers

Three companies of Colored soldiers have been disbanded, it is true. The order has actually been executed and the men who have valiantly fought the country's battles in both the Spanish-American and the Philippine wars and had many a hard fight with the Indians besides are scattered to the four winds of the earth, dismissed from the army of the United States in disgrace—discharged without honor, which deprives them of the right of retirement after thirty years of service on three quarters pay, and deprives them of the privilege of ending their days in the Soldiers Home, to the support of which at least one has been contributing for twenty-six years and many of them for more than twenty years. Not only are the dismissed soldiers deprived of these privileges which mean so much to all who have served in the army, in their later years, but they are forever debarred from any civil or military employment under the government. It is said to be the first time in the history of the United States that the president has personally or officially ordered the discharge of an enlisted man in either the army or the navy.

The reason for disbanding companies B, C and D, which formed the battalion just dismissed in disgrace, are so well known as to need no repetition in this article. On August 13, when the colored soldiers had been stationed at Fort Brown near Brownsville, Texas, only two weeks, people were suddenly aroused about midnight by the firing of guns, which is said to have proceeded from each barrack of the three colored companies. In the general confusion which followed, one man was killed and the arm of the chief of police was so badly wounded that it had to be amputated.

Immediately after the first shots were heard, it is said, a number of men

Originally published in *Voice of the Negro*, December 1906, pages 554-558.

variously estimated from nine to twenty, climbed over the wall between the fort and the town. Since these men were dressed in khaki uniform and wore blue shirts, it is claimed that they must have been colored soldiers, although a man who was sent by the Constitution League to investigate the affair, declares that it is a common thing for civilians to wear khaki uniforms in Brownsville. In Major Penrose's report of the melee, however, he declares that within five minutes after the shooting occurred, the entire command paraded and all men were found present or accounted for and rifles in racks closed. That is to say, if the nine or fifteen men who climbed over the wall which separates the fort from the town were soldiers belonging to the Twenty Fifty Infantry, they performed the remarkable feat of shooting up the town, returning to their barracks, cleaning their rifles and locking them in the racks in the short space of five minutes and at the most, eight minutes. In the annual report made by the Secretary of War, the following comment upon this phase of the matter occurs: "The evidence makes it clear that the firing had not ceased when the men began to form in line and therefore that all the guns with which the firing was done could not have been in the racks when the sergeants in charge of quarters went to unlock the racks, although they testified that they were there. It is also certain that during the formation of the companies, or immediately after, the men who had done the shooting must have returned to their places so as to respond to the roll call or that some one answered for them."

In order to remove the affair from the realm of the fantastical and mythical, it is necessary to believe that the sergeants told a deliberate falsehood, when they declared that all the guns were in the racks and that the men who did the shooting were able to slip in unseen by the guards and take their places without detection. In his report to Secretary Taft, Brigadier Gen. McCaskey called the attention of the War Department to the men for whom warrants were issued and who were then in confinement at Fort Sam Houston in the following manner: "It is noted that most of these men were on duty as members of the guard or in charge of barracks at Fort Brown during the hours of the disturbance. The reason for selecting these men, or the manner in which their names were procured is a mystery. As far as known," he writes, "there is no evidence that the majority of them were in any way directly connected with the affair. It seems to have been a dragnet proceeding."

The men who were victims of this "dragnet proceeding," as Gen. McCaskey calls it, were the non-commissioned officers holding the keys of the arm racks of the respective companies, the sergeant of the guard and the sentinel on post in rear of the company barracks on the night of the melee; an enlisted man, whose cap is said to have been found in the city, though the charge was not substantiated, and two men who had been assaulted by white men in Brownsville, together with the men who were with them at the time. Speaking of the soldiers who were imprisoned reminds me of a very interesting little bit of Major Blockson's report which shows how the officers of the law do things down in Texas. Although there was absolutely no reason why the men who were arrested should have been so humiliated and degraded, according to the opinion of Gen. McCaskey, nevertheless Captain McDonald of the Texas State Rangers, to whom the committee of Brownsville citizens invited by Major Penrose to investigate the affair, delegated their authority, demanded that these suspected men be turned over to himself. Major Penrose, however, declined to give them to him, knowing, of course, what would probably be the result of surrendering to the tender mercies of Texas justice, colored men who had been accused of murdering one white man and wounding another. But McDonald of Texas insisted upon having them and had to be threatened with arrest for contempt before he desisted from his attempt to take them, the orders from the war department and a Texas judge to the contrary notwithstanding. Major Blockson who reported this circumstance to his superiors could not refrain from paying the gallant captain of the Texas Rangers a glowing compliment for the impetuous and imperious manner in which he behaved, when the colored soldiers were not surrendered to him by Major Penrose. "It is possible," says Major Blockson, "that McDonald might have fought the entire battalion (referring to the three colored companies) with his four or five rangers, were their obedience as blind as his obstinacy. It is said here he is so brave he would not hesitate to charge hell with one bucket of water." Surely the South cannot complain that its many virtues are not fully appreciated and magnanimously recognized by their countrymen in other sections, for they seem to have sort of an idolatrous worship for the dare devil spirit which the gallant southerner delights so to exhibit in season and out. One shudders to think what might have been the fate of the colored men whom McDonald insisted upon taking, if he had succeeded in forcing the military authorities to accede to his demand.

Leaving the charges against the soldiers and the alleged evidence against them, let us glance for a moment at the causes which led to the disturbance, August 13. Secretary Taft says that in June, objection was made to the stationing of this battalion at Fort Brown, by a resident of Brownsville, in a letter transmitted through Senator Culbertson, to which the secretary sent the following reply. "My Dear Senator: I have the honor to acknowledge receipt of your letter from Mr. Sam P. Wrenford, of Brownsville, Texas, stating certain objections to the stationing of Negro troops at Fort Brown, and in reply to say that the matter of possible objections of this character was very carefully considered, before the order was made. I regret that I cannot see my way clear to rescind it. The fact is that a certain amount of race prejudice between white and black seems to have become almost universal throughout the country, and no matter where colored troops are sent there are always some who make objection to their coming. It is a fact, however, as shown by our records, that colored troops are quite as well disciplined and behaved as the average of other troops, and it does not seem logical to anticipate any greater trouble from them than from the rest. Friction occasionally arises with intemperate soldiers, wherever they are stationed, but *the records of the Army also tend to show that white soldiers average a greater degree of intemperance than colored ones*. It has sometimes happened that communities which objected to the coming of colored soldiers, have, on account of their good conduct, entirely changed their view and commended their good behavior to the War Department. A change of station was necessary for these colored troops and one third of the regiment (a battalion) had already been sent to Fort Bliss, Tex., more than six months ago. Since that time no complaint concerning their conduct has reached the War Department, so far as I know. It was also necessary to send the entire regiment to the same locality, and to have sent it anywhere else would have involved two moves for the battalion now at Fort Bliss within about six months. This would have been an injustice to the troops concerned, and would, in addition, have entailed considerable extra expense upon the Government. Trusting this explanation may be satisfactory to your constituents, I remain, Very truly yours,"

Wm. H. Taft, Sec. of War.

This letter shows that the white citizens of Texas began to protest against having the colored soldiers stationed at Fort Brown as soon as they learned it was the government's plans to quarter them in that state. It was to be expected, therefore, that the soldiers would meet with a very chilly reception—and they did. In the report which Major Penrose made two days after the Brownsville affair, he admits that the enlisted men were subjected to all sorts of indignities as soon as they reached Fort Brown. Major

Blockson also wrote to Secretary Taft that many white people in Brownsville "think the colored soldier should be treated like the Negro laborer of the South." And then Major Blockson took occasion to remark that it "had to be confessed that the colored soldier is much more aggressive in his attitude on the social equality question than he used to be." All of which goes to prove that this everlasting social equality question must be injected into everything which affects the colored people, no matter whether it bears directly upon the point at issue or not.

In less than a week after the colored soldiers reached the inhospitable atmosphere of Fort Brown, one of them was knocked down by a white man who was talking on the street with some women, because the colored soldiers dared to pass on the sidewalk where the white women were standing, instead of going into the street. In the affidavit which the assaulted soldier made, he claimed he did not touch one of the women in passing, but walked between them and the fence. When the two soldiers were opposite the white man, (Tate by name, who is still employed in the customs service, by the way), the latter drew a revolver from his hip pocket, struck the colored soldier on the side of the head and knocked him down, saying as he did so with an oath, "I'll learn you to get off the sidewalk when there is a party of ladies on the walk." Another colored soldier was pushed off a ferry, landing into mud and water, because the white man who told him to move on thought he did not go as fast as he should. As was to be expected under the circumstances, the charge which the South so delights to prefer against colored men was not long deferred. On the afternoon of the night that Brownsville was "shot up" a certain Mr. Evans came to Major Penrose and complained that his wife had been seized from behind by a colored man, who she was positive was a soldier, because he was in khaki uniform, but whom she could not identify. In commenting upon this particular charge, Major Penrose declares in his report to the Secretary of War: "His (Evans) statement that his wife was seized by a soldier I was inclined to doubt, as prostitutes are too common in the town." Major Penrose also called attention to the fact that the aforesaid Mr. Evans was "unfortunate in living very near the Tenderloin." Considering the well known attitude of the white people of the town toward the colored soldiers, it is not at all surprising that something happened to disgrace them in the public eye nor can we doubt the truth of Major Blockson's statement that "the differences between the soldiers and citizens are irreconcilable." We can readily understand also how this same officer was forced to reach the conclusion that while "the suspected men might get a fair trial here at hands of civil authorities, they could not properly be protected from mob violence."

But now that the soldiers have been disgraced and dismissed, what can be done about it?

So long as the public is deeply interested and genuinely sympathetic and so long as men of powerful influence in national affairs are determined to sift the matter to the bottom and if possible, to bring relief to the disgraced soldiers, there is reason to hope for the best. One of the strongest and surest foundations upon which to build our hopes is the attitude of the president himself. The day after the Foraker and Penrose resolutions which called for information regarding the discharge of the three companies of the Twenty-fifth Infantry, were introduced into the Senate, President Roosevelt is said to have stated at a Cabinet meeting, that he wished none of his friends to oppose them. In his reply to the cable sent by the Constitution League, the president also intimated that if new facts in the soldiers' favor were presented to him, he would certainly give them respectful consideration. Through its representatives who went to Fort Reno to hear from the lips of the soldiers themselves, the whole story of the Brownsville disturbance, the Constitution League believes it has secured evidence sufficient to induce the president to reopen the case. One of the most encouraging phases of the question as it now stands is the position taken by two of the strongest men in the United States Senate. Senator Foraker of Ohio is determined to know just why the order to dismiss the colored soldiers without honor was given and executed. In the resolution introduced by him the first day the Senate met, he asked for all the information on the subject which it is possible to secure. It also calls for precedents for the president's course. "Resolved by the Senate," reads the resolution presented by Senator Foraker, "That the Secretary of War be and hereby is directed to furnish the Senate copies of all official letters, telegrams, reports, orders, etc., filed in the War Department in connection with the recent discharge of the enlisted men of Companies B, C and D, Twenty-fifth United States Infantry, together with a complete list of the men discharged, showing the record of each, the amount of retained pay (under section 1281 et seq., Revised Statutes), if any, to the credit of each man at the time of his discharge, the ruling of the War Department, if any has been made in this or any similar case, as to the effect upon his right to such retained pay, and also the ruling of the War Department, if any has been made in this or any similar case, as to the effect of such discharge upon the right of an enlisted man to retire on three quarters pay, with an allowance for subsistence and clothing (under Section 1260 et seq. of the Revised Statutes), and his right to enter a national soldiers' home (under Section 4821 et seq. of the Revised Statutes): his right to be buried in a national cemetery (under Section 4878 et seq. of the Revised Statutes) and his right to receive transportation and subsistence from the place of discharge to his home, as provided for in section 1290 et seq. of the Revised Statutes: also a complete official record of the Twenty-fifth Regiment, United States Infantry, from the time of its muster in to the date of the discharge of Companies B, C, and D."

Before Senator Foraker presented his resolution, however, Senator Penrose of Pennsylvania had offered one, simply providing that the president be requested to communicate to the Senate, "if not incompatible with the public interests, full information bearing upon the recent order dismissing from the military service of the United States three companies of the Twenty-fifth Infantry, United States troops (colored)."

But Senator Spooner objected most strenuously to Senator Penrose's resolution on the ground that the clause "if not incompatible with the public interests" is entirely unnecessary. According to Senator Spooner, Senator Penrose's resolution leaves it to the discretion of the president to send as much or as little information as he sees fit, whereas the Senator from Wisconsin insists that the Senate has a perfect right to know the whole story from A to Izzard. In his speech on the Penrose resolution he told his brother Senators that he would be very much disappointed indeed, if it passed instead of the one offered by Senator Foraker. The fact that both the Penrose and the Foraker resolution passed without a single dissenting voice, speaks volumes for the Senate of the United States. With such tremendous forces at work in their behalf, there is every reason for the soldiers and their friends to take on fresh courage and new hopes. In concluding his report on the discharge of the Colored soldiers, Secretary Taft himself holds out a ray of hope. "It is possible," says he, "that evidence may be adduced in future which will tend to exculpate some of the men now discharged, both from participation in the crime and assistance in the conspiracy of silence to prevent the detection of the offenders: and whenever such facts are shown in respect to anyone affected by the order, they will be brought to your (the president's) attention, and I understand, will render such persons eligible to re-enlistment."

After my interview with Secretary Taft, when he promised me he would suspend the president's order till he returned, I felt that whatever he might say or do in the future, he sympathized deeply with the soldiers who had been disgraced. It is certainly the first time in the history of the country that a cabinet officer has ever consented to suspend an order issued by the president of the United States, and Secretary Taft would never have flung defiance at precedent, if he had not believed there was good and sufficient reason for taking such an unusual, if not dangerous step.

As disheartening as is the fate of nearly 200 colored soldiers who were dismissed from the army in disgrace, although the record of the majority was brilliant and clean, still the tragedy is not without its blessings to the race. In spite of General Garlington's charge that we hold together in crime, we who know conditions exactly as they exist, realize that this lack of unity in everything which affects us as a race has been the greatest stumbling block in our path. We have been able to hang together in nothing. When I poured forth my woe into the ear of Col. Thomas Wentworth Higginson, immediately after the order to disband the colored battalion had been issued, he could not think or talk about the terrible disgrace of the soldiers for rejoicing that at last colored people could stand together on some one thing. Today the hearts of the 10,000,000 colored people of this country, beat as one. The catastrophe has united us for a time at least. Union even for a short time and one issue will do a bit of good at least. It will surely establish a precedent and set a good example at one and the same time. Moreover the fearful fate which has overtaken the colored battalion has opened the lips of former friends who have been silent in spite of the awful atrocities perpetrated upon the race for many years. And so for the time being, at least, let us regard the terrible catastrophe which has filled the whole race with grief as an evil out of which good will eventually come.

What It Means to Be Colored in the Capital of the United States

[The special interest in the present article rests in the fact that it describes conditions in Washington, a city governed solely by the United States Congress. It is our only city which represents the whole country. It lies between the two sections, North and South, and it has a very large negro population. The article is timely now that Senator Foraker has brought before the Senate the dismissal without honor of the negro battalion. The writer is a colored women of much culture and recognized standing—EDITOR.]

Washington, D.C., has been called "The Colored Man's Paradise." Whether this sobriquet was given to the national capital in bitter irony by a member of the handicapped race, as he reviewed some of his own persecutions and rebuffs, or whether it was given immediately after the war by an ex-slave-holder who for the first time in his life saw colored people walking about like freemen, minus the overseer and his whip, history saith not. It is certain that it would be difficult to find a worse misnomer for Washington than "The Colored Man's Paradise" if so prosaic a consideration as veracity is to determine the appropriateness of a name.

For fifteen years I have resided in Washington, and while it was far from being a paradise for colored people, when I first touched these shores it has been doing its level best ever since to make conditions for us intolerable. As a colored woman I might enter Washington any night, a stranger in a strange land, and walk miles without finding a place to lay my head. Unless

Originally published in the *Independent*, January 24, 1907, pages 181-186. Terrell is not credited. The original handwritten version is in her papers.

I happened to know colored people who live here or ran across a chance acquaintance who could recommend a colored boarding-house to me, I should be obliged to spend the entire night wandering about. Indians, Chinamen, Filipinos, Japanese and representatives of any other dark race can find hotel accommodations, if they can pay for them. The colored man alone is thrust out of the hotels of the national capital like a leper.

As a colored woman I may walk from the Capital to the White House, ravenously hungry and abundantly supplied with money with which to purchase a meal, without finding a single restaurant in which I would be permitted to take a morsel of food, if it was patronized by white people, unless I were willing to sit behind a screen. As a colored woman I cannot visit the tomb of the Father of this country, which owes its very existence to the love of freedom in the human heart and which stands for equal opportunity to all, without being forced to sit in the Jim Crow section of an electric car which starts from the very heart of the city—midway between the Capitol and the White House. If I refuse thus to be humiliated, I am cast into jail and forced to pay a fine for violating the Virginia laws. Every hour in the day Jim Crow cars filled with colored people, many of whom are intelligent and well to do, enter and leave the national capital.

As a colored woman I may enter more than one white church in Washington without receiving that welcome which as a human being I have a right to expect in the sanctuary of God. Sometimes the color blindness of the usher takes on that peculiar form which prevents a dark face from making any impression whatsoever upon his retina, so that it is impossible for him to see colored people at all. If he is not so afflicted, after keeping a colored man or woman waiting a long time, he will ungraciously show these dusky Christians who have had the temerity to thrust themselves into a temple where only the fair of face are expected to worship God to a seat in the rear, which is named in honor of a certain personage, well known in this country, and commonly called Jim Crow.

Unless I am willing to engage in a few menial occupations, in which the pay for my services would be very poor, there is no way for me to earn an honest living, if I am not a trained nurse or a dressmaker or can secure a position as a teacher in the public schools, which is exceedingly difficult to do. It matters not what my intellectual attainments may be or how great is the need of the services of a competent person, if I try to enter many of the numerous vocations in which my white sisters are allowed to engage, the door is shut in my face.

From one Washington theatre I am excluded altogether. In the remainder certain seats are set aside for colored people, and it is almost impossible to secure others. I once telephoned to the ticket seller just before a matinee and asked if a neat-appearing colored nurse would be allowed to sit in the parquet with her little white charge, and the answer rushed quickly and positively thru the receiver—NO. When I remonstrated a bit and told him that in some of the theatres colored nurses were allowed to sit with the white children for whom they cared, the ticket seller told me that in Washington it was very poor policy to employ colored nurses, for they were excluded from many places where white girls would be allowed to take children for pleasure.

If I possess artistic talent, there is not a single art school of repute which will admit me. A few years ago a colored woman who possessed great talent submitted some drawings to the Corcoran Art School, of Washington, which were accepted by the committee of awards, who sent her a ticket entitling her to a course in this school. But when the committee discovered that the young woman was colored they declined to admit her, and told her that if they had suspected that her drawings had been made by a colored woman they would not have examined them at all. The efforts of Frederick Douglass and a lawyer of great repute who took a keen interest in the affair were unavailing. In order to cultivate her talent this young woman was forced to leave her comfortable home in Washington and incur the expense of going to New York. Having entered the Woman's Art School of Cooper Union, she graduated with honor, and then went to Paris to continue her studies, where she achieved signal success and was complimented by some of the greatest living artists in France.

With the exception of the Catholic University, there is not a single white college in the national capital to which colored people are admitted, no matter how great their ability, how lofty their ambition, how unexceptionable their character or how great their thirst for knowledge may be.

A few years ago the Columbian Law School admitted colored students, but in deference to the Southern white students the authorities have decided to exclude them altogether.

Some time ago a young woman who had already attracted some attention in the literary world by her volume of short stories answered an advertisement which appeared in a Washington newspaper, which called for the services of a skilled stenographer and expert typewriter. It is unnecessary to state the reasons why a young woman whose literary ability was so great as that possessed by the one referred to should decide to earn money in this way. The applicants were requested to spend specimens of their work and answer certain questions concerning their experience and their speed before they called in person. In reply to her application the young colored woman, who, by the way, is very fair and attractive indeed, received a letter from the firm stating that her references and experience were the most satisfactory that had been sent and requesting her to call. When she presented herself there was some doubt in the mind of the man to whom she was directed concerning her racial pedigree, so he asked her point-blank whether she was colored or white. When she confessed the truth the merchant expressed great sorrow and deep regret that he could not avail himself of the services of so competent a person, but frankly admitted that employing a colored woman in his establishment in any except a menial position was simply out of the question.

Another young friend had an experience which, for some reasons, was still more disheartening and bitter than the one just mentioned. In order to secure lucrative employment she left Washington and went to New York. There she worked her way up in one of the largest dry goods stores till she was placed as saleswoman in the cloak department. Tired of being separated from her family she decided to return to Washington, feeling sure that, with her experience and her fine recommendation from the New York firm, she could easily secure employment. Nor was she overconfident, for the proprietor of one of the largest dry goods stores in her native city was glad to secure the services of a young woman who brought such hearty credentials form New York. She had not been in this store very long, however, before she called upon me one day and asked me to intercede with the proprietor in her behalf, saying that she had been discharged that afternoon because it had been discovered that she was colored. When I called upon my young friend's employer he made no effort to avoid the issue, as I feared he would. He did not say he had discharged the young saleswoman because she had not given satisfaction, as he might easily have done. On the contrary, he admitted without the slightest hesitation that the young woman he had just discharged was one of the best clerks he had ever had. In the cloak department, where she had been assigned, she had been a brilliant success, he said. "But I cannot keep Miss Smith in my employ," he concluded. "Are you not master of your own store?" I ventured to inquire. The proprietor of this store was a Jew, and I felt that it was particularly cruel, unnatural and cold-blooded for the representative of one oppressed and persecuted race to deal so harshly and unjustly with a member of another. I had intended to intercede for my young friend, but when I thought how a reference to the persecution of his own race would wound his feelings, the words froze on my lips. "When I first heard your friend was colored." he explained, "I did not believe it and said so to the clerks who made the statement. Finally, the girls who had been most pronounced in their opposition to working in a store with a colored girl came to me in a body and threatened to strike. 'Strike away,' said I, 'your places will be easily filled.' Then they started on another tack. Delegation after delegation began to file down to my office, some of the women my very best customers, to protest against my employing a colored girl. Moreover, they threatened to boycott my store if I did not discharge her at once. Then it became a question of bread and butter and I yielded to the inevitable—that's all. Now," said he, concluding, "if I lived in a great, cosmopolitan city like New York, I should do as I pleased, and refuse to discharge a girl simply because she was colored." But I thought of a new similar incident that happened in New York. I remembered that a colored woman, as fair as a lily and as beautiful as a Madonna, who was the head saleswoman in a large department store in New York, had been discharged, after she had held this position for years, when the proprietor accidentally discovered that a fatal drop of African blood was percolating somewhere thru her veins.

Not only can colored women secure no employment in the Washington stores, department and otherwise, except as menials, and such positions, of course, are few, but even as customers they are not infrequently treated with discourtesy both by the clerks and the proprietor himself. Following the trend of the times, the senior partner of the largest and best department store in Washington, who originally hailed from Boston, once the home of Wm. Lloyd Garrison, Wendell Phillips and Charles Sumner, if my memory serves me right, decided to open a restaurant in his store. Tired and hungry after her morning's shopping a colored school teacher, whose relation to her African progenitors is so remote as scarcely to be discernible to the naked eye, took a seat at one of the tables in the restaurant of this Boston store. After sitting unnoticed a long time the colored teacher asked a waiter who passed her by if she would not take her order. She was quickly informed that colored people could not be served in that restaurant and was obliged to leave in confusion and shame, much to the amusement of the waiters and the guests who had noticed the incident. Shortly after that a teacher in Howard

University, one of the best schools for colored youth in the country, was similarly insulted in the restaurant of the same store.

In one of the Washington theaters from which colored people are excluded altogether, members of the race have been viciously assaulted several times, for the proprietor well knows that colored people have no redress for such discriminations against them in the District courts. Not long ago a colored clerk in one of the departments who looks more like his paternal ancestors who fought for the lost cause than his grandmothers who were victims of the peculiar institution, bought a ticket for the parquet of this theater in which colored people are nowhere welcome, for himself and mother, whose complexion is a bit swarthy. The usher refused to allow the young man to take the seats for which his tickets called and tried to snatch from him the coupons. A scuffle ensued and both mother and son were ejected by force. A suit was brought against the proprietor and the damages awarded the injured man and his mother amounted to the munificent sum of one cent. One of the teachers in the Colored High School received similar treatment in the same theater.

Not long ago one of my little daughter's bosom friends figured in one of the most pathetic instances of which I have ever heard. A gentleman who is very fond of children promised to take six little girls in his neighborhood to a matinee. It happened that he himself and five of his little friends were so fair that they easily passed muster, as they stood in judgment before the ticket-seller and the ticket taker. Three of the little girls were sisters, two of whom were very fair and the other a bit brown. Just as the little girl, who happened to be last in the procession, went by the ticket taker, that argus-eyed sophisticated gentleman detected something which caused a deep, dark frown to mantle his brow and he did not allow her to pass. "I guess you have made a mistake," he called to the host of this theatre party. "Those little girls," pointing to the fair ones, "may be admitted, but his one," designating the brown one, "can't." But the colored man was quite equal to the emergency. Fairly frothing at the mouth with anger he asked the ticket taker what he meant, what he was trying to insinuate about that particular little girl. "Do you mean to tell me," he shouted in rage, "that I must go clear to the Philippine Islands to bring this child to the United States and then I can't take her to the theatre in the National Capital?" The little ruse succeeded brilliantly, as he knew it would. "Beg your pardon," and the ticket taker, "don't know what I was thinking about. Of course she can go in."

"What was the matter with me this afternoon? mother," asked the little brown girl innocently, when she mentioned the affair at home. "Why did the man at the theatre let my two sisters and the other girls in and try to keep me out?" In relating this incident, the child's mother told me her little girl's question, which showed such blissful ignorance of the depressing, cruel conditions which confronted her, completely unnerved her for a time.

Altho white and colored teachers are under the same Board of Education and the system for the children of both races is said to be uniform, prejudice against the colored teachers in the public schools is manifested in a variety of ways. From 1870 to 1900 there was a colored superintendent at the head of the colored schools. During all that time the directors of the cooking, sewing, physical culture, manual training, music and art departments were colored people. Six years ago a change was inaugurated. The colored superintendent was legislated out of office and the directorships, without a single exception, were taken from colored teachers and given to the whites. There was no complaint about the work done by the colored directors no more than is heard about every officer in every school. The directors of the art and physical culture departments were particularly fine. Now, no matter how competent or superior the colored teachers in our public schools may be, they know that they can never rise to the height of a directorship, can never hope to be more than an assistant and receive the meager salary therefore, unless the present regime is radically changed.

Not long ago one of the most distinguished kindergartners in the country came to deliver a course of lectures in Washington. The colored teachers were eager to attend, but they could not buy the coveted privilege for love or money. When they appealed to the director of kindergartens, they were told that the expert kindergartner had come to Washington under the auspices of private individuals, so that she could not possibly have them admitted. Realizing what a loss colored teachers had sustained in being deprived of the information and inspiration which these lecturers afforded, one of the white teachers volunteered to repeat them as best she could for the benefit of her colored co-laborers for half the price she herself had paid, and the proposition was eagerly accepted by some.

Strenuous efforts are being made to run Jim Crow street cars in the national capital. "Resolved, that a Jim Crow law should be adopted and enforced in the District of Columbia," was the subject of a discussion engaged in last January by the Columbian Debating Society of the George Washington University in our national capital, and the decision was rendered in favor of the affirmative. Representative Heflin, of Alabama, who introduced a bill providing for Jim Crow street cars in the District of Columbia last winter, has just received a letter from the president of the East Brookland Citizens' Association "indorsing the movement for separate street cars and sincerely hoping that you will be successful in getting this enacted into a law as soon as possible." Brookland is a suburb of Washington.

The colored laborer's path to a decent livelihood is by no means smooth. Into some of the trades unions here he is admitted, while from others he is excluded altogether. By the union men this is denied, altho I am personally acquainted with skilled workmen who tell me they are not admitted into the unions because they are colored. But even when they are allowed to join the unions they frequently derive little benefit, owing to certain tricks of the trade. When the word passes round that help is needed and colored laborers apply, they are often told by the union officials that they have secured all the men they needed, because they places are reserved for white men, until they have been provided with jobs, and colored men must remain idle, unless the supply of white men is too small.

I am personally acquainted with one of the most skilful laborers in the hardware business in Washington. For thirty years he has been working for the same firm. He told me he could not join the union, and that his employer had been almost forced to discharge him, because the union men threatened to boycott his store if he did not. If another man could have been found at the time to take his place he would have lost his job, he said. When no other human being can bring a refractory chimney or stove to its senses, this colored man is called upon as the court of last appeal. If he fails to subdue it, it is pronounced a hopeless case at once. And yet this expert workman received much less for his services than do white men who cannot compare with him in skill.

And so I might go on citing instance after instance to show the variety of ways in which our people are sacrificed on the altar of prejudice in the Capital of the United States and how almost insurmountable are the obstacles which block his path to success. Early in life many a colored youth is so appalled by the helplessness and the hopelessness of his situation in this country that in a sort of stoical despair he resigns himself to his fate. "What is the good of our trying to acquire an education?" We can't all be preachers, teachers, doctors and lawyers. Besides those professions there is almost nothing for colored people to do but engage in the most menial occupations, and we do not need an education for that." More than once such remarks, uttered by young men and women in our public schools who possess brilliant intellects, have wrung my heart.

It is impossible for any white person in the United States, no matter how sympathetic and broad, to realize what life would mean to him if his incentive to effort were suddenly snatched away. To the lack of incentive to effort, which is the awful shadow under which we live, may be traced the wreck and ruin of scores of colored youth. And surely nowhere in the world do oppression and persecution based solely on the color of the skin appear more hateful and hideous than in the capital of the United States, because the chasm between the principles upon which the Government was founded, in which it still professes to believe, and those which are daily practiced under the protection of the flag, yawns so wide and deep.

A Sketch of Mingo Saunders

**Late First Sergeant Company B. Twenty-Fifth Infantry, United States Army.
Dismissed Without Honor After Serving Twenty-Six Years.**

To look at Mingo Saunders, late 1st Sergeant Co. B of the Twenty-fifth Infantry, nobody would believe that he had just been dismissed from the Army without honor, after serving continuously and faithfully for twenty-six years. His countenance is as unruffled and as free from any trace of melancholy as is one of Raphael's angels, and in general demeanor he is as cool as the proverbial cucumber. To be sure I had 'phoned Sergeant Saunders to come to see me just as soon as I learned his Washington address through the courtesy of the War Department. But when I realized all at once that this man, who, I fancied, must be the picture of despair from the very nature of the case must even then be on his way to my residence, I was suddenly seized with a dread of meeting him and wondered why on earth I had asked him to call. But when I actually saw Sergeant Saunders in the flesh, as serene and mild as a May morning, at evident peace with himself and all the world, I was provoked that he could be so calm.

If the consciousness of innocence lends to the countenance contentment and peace, then there is no doubt whatsoever that Mingo Saunders is free from guilt. Almost any jury would acquit him of the charge of participating in the Brownsville disturbance on his face. Even in a man who has enjoyed superior educational advantages and training, the philosophical manner with which Sergeant Saunders bears his dismissal without honor from the Army, in spite of his long and faithful service would be rare, but in a man who has had almost no education at all, it is very remarkable indeed. And his

Originally published in *Voice of the Negro*, March 1907, pages 129-130.

sweetness of spirit is by no means the result of indifference to his fate or the inability to realize the terrible misfortune that has overtaken him, but it is because he feels he has done his very best to discharge all the obligations resting upon a soldier from the day he enlisted till he became the victim of circumstances over which he had absolutely no control and is manly enough to accept what a cruel fate has sent him without a whine. When the man, who but a few weeks ago was 1st Sergeant in Co. B of the Twenty-fifth Infantry was a boy, schools for the youth of his race in Marion Co., S.C., where he was born, were very rare indeed. Even where there were schools and the desire to learn, the poverty of a child's parents frequently made it impossible for him to avail himself of the educational advantages offered and to gratify his thirst for knowledge. This was the case with Mingo Saunders. After attending school just long enough to learn to read and write a bit, his parents were obliged to put him to work. From his earliest recollection, he says, he wanted to be a soldier. "Once I saw a military company parading in Charleston, S.C.," he said, "and I thought it was the prettiest sight I had ever seen. I made up my mind right then and there that I would be a soldier some day, if I lived. Picking up a newspaper one day I read that there was a call for soldiers and that there was a recruiting station in Charleston. Just as soon as I could get there, I went and enlisted in the Army on the 16th day of May, 1881."

It is amusing to hear Sergeant Saunders describe the sensation of disappointment—an experience through which probably nine out of ten recruits pass, when he discovered that the life of a soldier was by no means one of idleness and ease. "Before I entered the Army," said he, "I thought that all a soldier had to do was put on a pretty uniform and parade every now and then," with a hearty laugh at his own ignorance, "but I soon learned better than that." "Please tell me about the battles in which you have actually engaged," I said. "I want to know something about the service you have seen." In complying with this request Sergeant Saunders displayed the most remarkable memory possessed by any human being with whom I am personally acquainted. Place after place in this country and abroad and date after date on which engagements occurred in which he participated are reeled off apparently without the slightest effort. Fortunately for me, however, he had in his pocket an official record of his service in the Army which had been give him by the War Department. From these official documents I learned that Mingo Saunders was with the 5th Army Corps in the campaign against Santiago, Cuba, June, July and August, 1898. On July 15 he was at

El Caney and in front of Santiago July 2nd, 3rd, and again on the 10th and 11th. With his pliers together with the other soldiers in his company he helped cut the wires in sight of El Caney, while the bullets were cutting the rest. It is thrilling to hear Saunders tell the story of the battle of El Caney. "The bullets rained down on us," said he, "like hail out of the sky, but we kept on moving forward, advancing alternate by rushes. One of the men killed in this battle stood right by my side."

While Saunders' company was held in reserve, so that it might re-enforce the 10th Cavalry, another Colored Regiment at San Juan, and they were all peacefully sleeping one night, they were suddenly awakened by a shower of bullets in their camp. The soldiers were completely demoralized for a time, of course. But as soon as Saunders awoke and realized what had happened he formed Company B and reported to his Captain. It was during the campaign in Cuba that Sergeant Saunders had the opportunity and the pleasure of giving Lieut. Col. Roosevelt and his Rough Riders some food, after they had lost all their rations in an engagement with the enemy. "Boys," called Col. Roosevelt coming into our camp one day, "can you give us some rations? And I can see Col. Roosevelt now," remarked Saunders in relating this story, "just as plain as I saw him that day in Cuba. Our men had just received a fresh supply, so we all gladly divided our hard tack and bacon with the lieutenant-colonel of the Rough Riders, now president of the United States."

With the Eighth Army Corps Saunders also served in the Philippine War during the insurrection from 1899-1901. He was at La Loma, October 9th, 1899, and at O'Donnell, November 18, the same year. In 1900 he was at Commizi, January 5; at Subig, January 29, February 9-10, and September 21 and 23.

The most thrilling experience which Saunders had during his service in the army, perhaps, was when he, as leader, with two other men, carried a telegram through the enemy's country from Bam Bam to O'Donnell, November 28, 1899. The message had to be taken by Sergeant Saunders at night over a road which he had traveled but once before and which was alive with hostile Filipinos, each one carrying a rifle. The message contained important orders from General Burt to Major Johnson of the 9th Infantry, who was also in command of the 25th. "We men traveled fifty yards apart," said Saunders, "so that if one were captured, the others might have a chance to escape. Being in the lead I crossed the streams first and examined the ground thoroughly to see if there were any insurgents around. As soon as

I crossed, I whistled, the man behind me did the same and the third man whistled twice as a signal that we had landed safe on the other side. As we slipped along, dodging first one danger and then another, we often came so near outposts of Filipinos that we could hear them talk. At four o'clock in the morning we reached O'Donnell and went into the midst of our own camp without being known. I was certain it was best to conduct the men through our own outposts without giving a signal or being seen, and I did so."

Returning the next day, Saunders had proceeded two-thirds of the distance to his own camp, when he came upon Company C of the 9th Infantry, which was engaged in a battle with the insurgents. The captain of this company was so sure Saunders and his two companions would be murdered, if they went further without protection that he detained them till he could send the 22nd Infantry to guard the brave, black soldiers to their own camp. Saunders was also with the first party of Americans who ever ascended Mt. Ararat, and under Lieut. Martin (who has since become a captain) helped to locate a camp containing 2,000 insurgents. Among the many deeds of valor which may be placed to the colored soldier's credit is the rescue of four white men who belonged to the 9th and 12th Infantry, and who had been held as prisoners by the Filipinos for six weeks. "The faces and heads of the men were terribly gashed with bolos," said Sergeant Saunders, in relating the story. "Two of the men had been shot, one of whom survived the wound and the other was killed instantly." Among the services rendered by this brave black soldier which contributed no little to the victory of his country's arms may be mentioned the capture of insurgents on several occasions, with their rifles, bolos, sabres and the destruction of a certain distillery with all the enemy's supplies.

Sergeant Saunders also knows a bit about Indians, since he was in the Dakotas for a considerable time. As a sharpshooter he has medals which show the accuracy of his aim. Ever since February 3, 1900, Saunders has been first sergeant of his company and there is no doubt that if he had been an educated man, he would be very little, if any, below the rank of captain. Although Saunders has enlisted nine times, he has been injured but once in all those twenty-six years, having been struck in the eye by a soda bottle which exploded and which made him one-quarter blind, as his enlistment paper states.

Although Sergeant Saunders is by no means an old man (he is not much more than fifty years old), he has been a veritable father to the young men of his race, who have enlisted in the army. Just as soon as he had the opportunity, he would take them aside and advise them as to the best course to pursue, if they wished to succeed and be promoted.

Nothing illustrates Sergeant Saunders' breadth and generosity more than the following incident:

A certain young colored man who had graduated from one of the best schools in the East, enlisted in the Army and was in Company B in the Philippines. He was detailed to act as Sergeant Saunders' clerk. Feeling that he was superior to the First Sergeant from an educational point of view the clerk was rather slow about performing the duties assigned him. But Saunders bore with him patiently and made no complaint. Finally, however, the clerk entered a protest of some kind to the commanding officer, who asked Saunders for an explanation. Disgusted at the young clerk's behavior Captain Martin read him a lecture which he will probably never forget. But—and this is the point—Sergeant Saunders was asked shortly after this occurrence to recommend one of his men for the position of clerk at headquarters. Saunders knew that if the man appointed to that place gave satisfaction, he would probably be promoted in a few months to the position of Color-Sergeant, a rank higher than his own, for which the fortunate man would receive more pay than himself. Feeling that his young refractory clerk was the man best qualified from an educational point of view to fill the position he immediately recommended him to General Burt, who appointed him. When I expressed surprise that he could so far forget the misbehavior of his former clerk as to use his influence to advance him in the service, Sergeant Saunders declared that he could never understand how anybody who called himself a man could stand in the way of a fellow's promotion simply because he himself did not like him, or because the two had had a scrap, when there was no other reason to oppose him.

By nature Mingo Saunders is a philosopher, which accounts, of course, for his remarkable poise and peace. When I asked him how he could bear his terrible misfortune so calmly, he replied that everybody in this world must have a certain amount of trouble. "If it is not one thing, it is sure to be another. I have always been very lucky," said he. "I have had plenty to eat and enough to wear. I have been in the army twenty-six years, as you know, without receiving so much as a scratch. That little wound in the eye isn't worth talking about. I am a heap sight better off than those fellows who have come home from their service in the Philippines and Cuba crazy or in poor health. And I am better off than the fellows who got killed, some of them shot right by my side. And so, to tell the truth, I sometimes think this discharge was due me. Besides I know I am innocent and I am sure the other fellows are just as innocent as I am, and I tell you, that helps me a heap." Nothing illustrates the high estimate placed upon the character of Saunders by his officers more than the statement made by Sergeant Penrose: "When I asked Saunders if he knew anything about the Brownsville trouble and he told me he didn't, I knew he was telling the truth."

"Mingo Saunders is the best non-commissioned officer I have ever known," said Brigadier-General A. S. Burt, during a conversation I had with him not long ago. "And I have been in the army forty years," he continued.

The 25th Infantry has always been the joy and pride of General Burt's heart. It is delightful to hear him discourse upon their many virtues. "They are the best soldiers in the world," he says with emphasis and fire in his eyes, which is a challenge for anybody to dispute him. Unless my memory has played me a trick, General Burt told me that the 25th Infantry was the first body of soldiers out both in the Spanish-American and the Philippine wars. While General Burt was taking his Colored soldiers to Cuba, he was frequently asked during their stops at southern stations whether he thought the Negroes would fight. ' "Will your Colored men fight, General?' I was asked over and over again," said General Burt, firing with indignation at the very idea that anybody could even ask such a question. "Will they fight?" I replied, "Why, they would charge into hell, fight their way out and drag the devil out by the tail."

An Interview with
W. T. Stead on
the Race Problem

"I do not believe in putting a protective tariff upon a race which has had a good long start and lays claim to superiority over another, so as to insure this supremacy forever and let the race which has had hard luck and few chances get along the best it can and take what happens to be left." Mr. Stead, who is nothing, if not original and emphatic, never said anything with heartier enthusiasm than when he expressed this opinion to me in Washington a few days ago. It would be hard to find a man broader and more generous in his attitude toward the dark races of the earth than the editor of the English *Review of Reviews*. Since he has the courage of his convictions and strong, fearless language at his tongue's end with which to express them, it is decidedly entertaining and refreshing to hear him talk on the subject. I was deeply impressed with Mr. Stead's interest in the dark races, when I met him in London two years ago. As soon, therefore, as he wrote me he intended to visit the United States, I determined to interview him on the race problem. But interviewing Mr. Stead on the race problem in London and performing the same feat in the United States are two different propositions entirely, I was destined to learn, when in response to an invitation I called upon the distinguished gentleman and his wife at their hotel. We had hardly exchanged greetings, before a tall, thin, nervous gentleman appeared, to whom I was introduced by Mr. Stead who informed me that he is the editor of an American magazine. Evidently divining my intentions the American editor dealt my hopes a crushing blow on sight as

Originally published in *Voice of the Negro*, July 1907, pages 327-330.

follows. "Mr. Stead and I have divided the world between us. He has the eastern hemisphere and I have the western. Mr. Stead can say anything he pleases about affairs in the eastern, can express himself about problems affecting colored people over there or talk about anything else, but he must absolutely refrain from discussing that subject here." "Why, I wouldn't discuss the race problem as it manifests itself in the United States for worlds," quickly interposed Mr. Stead. "That would be exceedingly indelicate and improper. I couldn't think of outraging the proprieties to such an extent. But surely you will have no objection, if I talk a few minutes with Mrs. Terrell about Africans way off in South Africa." My gratitude to Mr. Stead for finding a way out of the difficulty was boundless. And having secured from his American friend a half reluctant consent to this arrangement, Mr. and Mrs. Stead and I retired to their apartment to discuss Africans in South Africa, still vowing not to touch the race problem in the United States with a ten foot pole.

"In the first place," said Mr. Stead, plunging into the subject with the directness and vim so characteristic of him, "I believe that Africans in South Africa and England and everywhere else in the world,"—"except in the United States, of course" I injected by way of reminder, "should have every possible advantage and chance, so as to enable them to catch up with their fellows belonging to other races more fortunate and advanced. I do not believe that a protective tariff should be placed upon white people, so as to enable them always to keep in the ascendancy. If they cannot hold their own without extra aids and props, they should occupy the place they can hold in a fair and free competition with others. If anybody should be shown special consideration and given extra aid, it is the representative of an oppressed and heavily handicapped race, which receive many kicks, but gets few boosts. What impressed me most, while I was in the Transvaal" said Mr. Stead, "was that the Boers worried terribly about what would become of themselves, if Africans were educated and caught up with them. They did not express the fear that Africans might be inferior to them, but they were greatly agitated over the thought that the natives might possibly be equal or superior to them, if they had a fighting chance. If you give these Africans the same educational facilities which we enjoy and open the doors of trade to them and admit them to the various professions," the Boers would ask me, "what will become of us?" "If you can't hold your own with your superior heredity and environment and your splendid opportunities, when you are obliged to compete with these Africans," I would tell them, "you deserve to fail."

"But you would not think of applying this doctrine of equal opportunity and equal educational facilities to the race problem in the United States, would you, Mr. Stead," I inquired. "Perish the thought," said that distinguished gentleman, "I am simply talking about the Africans in South Africa." "How are colored people treated in England?" I inquired. "Let us talk about that for a bit, for England is so much nearer home." "Well, they are usually treated like other human beings," was the quick reply. "Those who attend the universities are treated well both by the students and the instructors. Several of them have won prizes, you know. A number of black men have studied at the Inns of Court and have been successful barristers, in England." "A few years ago did not some colored people from America have trouble in one of your hotels?" I asked. "I have never heard of colored people having a disagreeable experience at a London hotel but once in my life," said Mr. Stead. "That happened, when some Americans insisted that the proprietor of a London hotel should eject some of their colored countrymen who had already registered, had been assigned rooms and were in the dining room taking a meal. But even in that case, the Englishman refused to accede to the demands of his American guests, who left the hotel in consequence. By the way, one of the members of the common council of London is a jet black man, who hails from the Trinidad Islands, I believe. When I told some of my Boer friends about the black barristers we have had in England and the black councilman from the Marylebone district in London, they grew red in the face with excitement and rage and one of them exclaimed hotly, "Conditions like those are enough to start a revolution."

"What do you think of 'Social Equality?'" I asked. "'Social Equality' indeed," repeated Mr. Stead in a tone which was half fun and half scorn. "There has never been a day in my life, when I felt like arrogating to myself superiority over any human being. I believe that social equality should be divorced from race and color just as much as I believe that political equality should be separated from sex. Whenever I advocated a square deal for the natives, the question of social equality was invariably sprung by my friends in South Africa to confound me and cover me with confusion and shame. How would you like to have your daughter marry a black man, somebody would be sure to ask with a confidence of tone and a defiance which indicated plainly they thought they had caught me in the meshes of my own heresy and folly, at last. Well, I would not want my daughter to marry a costermonger for that matter, so long as he remained a costermonger and nothing more. But if that same costermonger should educate himself and become a cultured gentleman, I should not have the slightest objection to receiving him as my son-in-law. So far as my daughter's marrying a black man is concerned, I doubt very much that I should urge her to seek such a mate. All other things being equal I believe people are happier, when they marry in their own social circle and race. But I know a jolly lot of black men, I should a jolly sight rather have my daughter marry than some white men I know." Let no one forget at this juncture that Mr. Stead was not discussing the race problems in America. He was still talking about the Africans he had met in England and South Africa.

"We have entertained dark people in our own home again and again and have been entertained by them, haven't we?" This question was addressed to Mrs. Stead who had been intensely interested in what her distinguished husband had said and had approved every sentiment he expressed. "Yes indeed we have," came the prompt reply. "Do you remember that East Indian of whom we were all so fond?" (You see, Mrs. Terrell we have race problems in England. I have always felt very keenly the terrible injustice perpetrated upon dark races by the white.")

"Let me tell you about a meeting which was held in my office at Mowbray House, London, not long ago," said Mr. Stead. "It will interest you, I am sure. Certain representatives of the various dark races, among them Japanese, East Indians, Africans and others gathered in my office to discuss the superiority of the dark races over the white, if you please. And my word for it," said Mr. Stead half rising from his chair with enthusiasm engendered by the vivid recollection with which the events of that meeting were recalled, "my word for it, they made out a good case against us."

"Have you not observed how much greater is the friction to day between the white and dark races all over the world, wherever they come in close contact, than it ever was before?" "Certainly I have," replied Mr. Stead with a smile. "That is the most hopeful sign of all, I think. The truth of it is, the dark races all over the world are progressing so rapidly that their white brothers are becoming genuinely alarmed. Japan's victory over Russia has done more to prove that a dark skin is no more a badge of inferiority and weakness than a white face is a sign of superiority and strength than anything which has happened in a long time—than anything which has ever happened, perhaps. No man cares whether a cat is in his room or not. But people who are perfectly willing to have a cat remain, would protest strongly against his presence, if that same cat were suddenly metamorphosed into a man. On the same principle, white men who but a few years could tolerate colored people nicely and actually liked some of them, as human beings without capacity, without either ambition or hope to achieve, can see no good thing in their race today, now that they seem to be throwing off their lethargy and demonstrating beyond a peradventure of doubt that they possess intellectual capacity of a high order and can achieve brilliantly, when given half a chance. I want to repeat what I have already said. I believe the friction between the white and dark faces today is caused more by the fear which white people entertain that the dark races of the earth may eventually overtake and outstrip them than by what some people call "the natural antipathy" which exists between a fair skin and a black one." "Of course," I reminded Mr. Stead again, for fear he might forget it, "You are not discussing the race problem in this country at all. You are still expatiating upon the African in South Africa or the Ethiopians in England or Madagascar or anywhere else they happen to be in evidence except in the United States." "That is correct," replied Mr. Stead, while his steel blue eyes fairly danced with the humor of the situation. Then Mr. and Mrs. Stead and I laughed outright.

"You have travelled in Africa extensively," I said. "Please tell me something about the morality of African men." "That I will," was the hearty response. "Assaults upon white women by native men practically never occur in Africa. This is all the more striking, because the African men do much of the housework for Englishmen and Europeans. They nurse the children, play the role of chambermaid and thus come into the closest possible contact with white women, and yet one almost never hears of assaults upon them by the natives." I did not have the courage to interrogate Mr. Stead on the attitude of the white foreigners who go to Africa toward the native women. "In Africa," continued Mr. Stead, "the natives do nearly all the menial work, while the whites shun it. The white man's attitude toward manual labor in Africa is the white man's curse. I once told a native that there are few, very few Africans in England. 'Who in the world does the work in England then,' he inquired in great surprise. When the men of a subject race do all the manual labor, it nearly always happens that the dominant race looks down upon work and scorns those who perform it. The same condition exists, when one sex does all the drudgery. Among races and tribes in which women do all the hard work, while the men hunt and fish, women are regarded but little more than beasts of burden. The white male has only one point of superiority over his colored brother, but he has two points over the colored women, because of the position which all women occupy. His face is white and he is a man with all the power and privilege possessed by him because of his sex. For this reason, it is all the more difficult for colored women to secure the respect and consideration from white men which they deserve and should receive." "Remember now, you are still talking about Africans in South Africa. You are not referring to conditions in the United States." "To be sure," he replied, "I would not have you apply anything I have said to the status of colored women in the United States for a farm."

"It is sometimes claimed that Africans are innately inferior to the white races, because they have contributed so little to the civilization of the world," I said. "There isn't much in that," replied Mr. Stead. "Egypt was the cradle of civilization, was it not? To be sure it is claimed that Egyptians are not classed as Africans, as that word is generally used. But nobody knows how close was the connection between the Ethiopians and Egyptians. Besides, you must remember that Africa is Africa. There are many things which affect the progress of a people. The climate for instance. If Africans had lived in Europe and Europeans had been indigenous to African soil, I doubt very much indeed that the white men would have done any more in Africa than have the Africans themselves. As it is, Europeans have not done so well in Africa. Have you read General Butler's book? He claims that Africa will always be the black man's continent. He says the existence of a certain kind of mosquito alone will make it impossible for the white man to thrive, if he can live at all, in Africa. According to General Butler, this particular mosquito first bites a black child which is not at all injured by the kiss and then bites a white man who dies." Mr. and Mrs. Stead were very much amused at General Butler's discovery and deduction,—"Who knows," queried Mr. Stead, "but there may be something in it. Even a mosquito may have a great deal to do with the civilization of the country." Just then a knock was heard, the door opened and in walked the editor, who took upon himself the delightful task of escorting Mr. Stead around and advising him what not to discuss. My doom was sealed, I knew, and I accepted my fate with philosophical resignation. "You did not mind my telling Mr. Stead he must not discuss the race problem, did you Mrs. Terrell?" coolly inquired the Editor. "Certainly I did," I replied, following the example set by the Father of His Country. Then the editor launched forth upon such a tirade about malicious newspaper people, who violate all the properties and outrage good taste and lack everything which resembles prudence and common sense that the pain of bidding Mr. Stead good bye was considerably lessened, so overcome was I with confusion and shame at the terrible arraignment which the editor made and crushed with the knowledge of my sins. I did not regret my temerity, however, and was glad I succeeded in securing the great and brilliant and generous-hearted Stead's opinion of Africans in South Africa, if he was not permitted by his literary mentor to discuss the race problem in the United States.

The Justice of Woman Suffrage

It is difficult to believe that any individual in the United States with one drop of African blood in his veins can oppose woman suffrage. It is queer and curious enough to hear an intelligent colored woman argue against granting suffrage to her sex, but for an intelligent colored man to oppose woman suffrage is the most preposterous and ridiculous thing in the world. What could be more absurd than to see one group of human beings who are denied rights which they are trying to secure for themselves working to prevent another group from obtaining the same rights? For the very arguments which are advanced against granting the right of suffrage to women are offered by those who have disfranchised colored men. If I were a colored man, and were unfortunate enough not to grasp the absurdity of opposing suffrage because of the sex of a human being, I should at least be consistent enough never to raise my voice against those who have disfranchised my brothers and myself on account of race. However, the intelligent colored man who opposes woman suffrage is very rare, indeed. While on a lecture tour recently I frequently discussed woman suffrage with the leading citizens in the communities in which I spoke. It was very gratifying, indeed, to see that in the majority of instances these men stood right on the question of woman suffrage.

Frederick Douglass did many things of which I am proud, but there is nothing he ever did in his long and brilliant career in which I take keener pleasure and greater pride than I do in his ardent advocacy of equal political rights for women, and the effective service he rendered the cause of woman suffrage sixty years ago. When the resolution demanding equal political rights for women was introduced in the meeting held at Seneca Falls, N.Y., in

Originally published in *The Crisis*, 4 (September 1912), pages 243-245.

1848, Frederick Douglass was the only man in the convention courageous and broad minded enough to second the motion. It was largely due to Douglass's masterful arguments and matchless eloquence that the motion was carried, in spite of the opposition of its very distinguished and powerful foes. In his autobiography Douglass says: "Observing woman's agency, devotion and efficiency, gratitude for this high service early moved me to give favorable attention to the subject of what is called 'woman's rights' and caused me to be denominated a woman's rights man. I am glad to say," he adds, "that I have never been ashamed to be thus designated. I have been convinced of the wisdom of woman suffrage and I have never denied the faith."

To assign reasons in this day and time to prove that it is unjust to withhold from one-half of the human race rights and privileges freely accorded the other half, which is neither more deserving nor more capable of exercising them, seems almost like a reflection upon the intelligence of those to whom they are presented. To argue the inalienability and the equality of human rights in the twentieth century in a country whose government was founded upon the eternal principles that all men are created free and equal, that governments get their just powers from the consent of the governed, seems like laying one's self open to the charge of anachronism. For 2,000 years mankind has been breaking down the various barriers which interposed themselves between human beings and their perfect freedom to exercise all the faculties with which they have been divinely endowed. Even in monarchies old fetters, which formerly restricted freedom, dwarfed the intellect and doomed certain individuals to narrow, circumscribed spheres because of the mere accident of birth, are being loosed and broken one by one.

What a reproach it is to a government which owes its very existence to the loved freedom in the human heart that it should deprive any of its citizens of their sacred and cherished rights. The founders of this republic called heaven and earth to witness that it should be called a government of the people, for the people and by the people; and yet the elective franchise is withheld from one-half of its citizens, many of whom are intelligent, virtuous and cultured, and unstintingly bestowed upon the other half, many of whom are illiterate, degraded and vicious, because by an unparalleled exhibition of lexicographical acrobatics the word "people" has been turned and twisted to mean all who were shrewd and wise enough to have themselves born boys instead of girls, and white instead of black.

But why grant women the suffrage when the majority do not want it, the remonstrants sometimes ask with innocent engaging seriousness. Simply because there are many people, men as well as women, who are so constructed as to be unable to ascertain by any process of reason what is the best thing for them to have or to do. Until the path is blazed by the pioneer, even some people who have superior intellects and moral courage dare not forge ahead. On the same principle and for just exactly the same reason that American women would reject suffrage, Chinese women, if they dared to express any opinion at all, would object to having the feet of their baby girls removed from the bandages which stunt their growth. East Indian women would scorn the preferred freedom of their American sisters as unnatural and vulgar and would die rather than have their harems abolished. Slaves sometimes prefer to bear the ills of bondage rather than accept the blessings of freedom, because their poor beclouded brains have been stunted and dwarfed by oppression so long that they cannot comprehend what liberty means and have no desire to enjoy it.

Phyllis Wheatley—
An African Genius

When you call George Washington "First in Peace," please remember that a young slave girl was the first person in the world, publicly, to refer to him in that way. It was Phyllis Wheatley, a young African poetess, who wrote a poem in his honor and in one of the lines addressed him as "First in peace and honours," several years before the Declaration of Independence was signed.

If you had been walking down the streets of Boston, Mass., one day in 1761 you might have seen a poor little black girl, wrapped only in a piece of carpet, shivering with the cold. If you had asked "What is your name, little girl?" She would not have understood you, and even if she had understood and answered your questions, her name would have sounded very queer to you. For she was a little foreigner. She had been born in Africa, had been stolen from her native land, packed like a sardine in a slave ship with many others of her countrymen, and suffered the horrors and tortures of what was called "the middle passage" and had been brought by white men into this country to be sold as a slave.

A lady who wanted to train a young woman servant to take the place of an old one who was growing too old to work, went to the slave market in Boston to see what she could find in that line. The pathetic face of the shivering child appealed to this woman so strongly that she bought her in spite of the fact that her little body appeared so frail.

Sixteen months from that time she was reading the most difficult passages in the Bible. Six years from the day she was sold she had become so proficient in speaking and writing the English language she had written a

Originally published in *The Baha'i Magazine: Star of the West*, Vol. 19, No. 7 (October 1928), pages 221-223.

poem to the University of Cambridge, nine years from the day she had been bought as a slave she had published a poem on the death of a distinguished clergyman, and twelve years after entering Mrs. Wheatley's service her volume of poems was published in London.

Phyllis was very fortunate in having Mrs. Wheatley as her mistress. Let us pause long enough to give a rousing, rising vote of thanks to that lady. The law did not force her to be merciful to the little slave and nobody expected her to give the girl a change.

In her new home Phyllis became the special servant of Mrs. Wheatley's twins, Nathaniel and Mary, who were ten years older than their slave. One day Mary saw the little African trying to form letters on the wall with a piece of chalk. She doubtless thought it would be great fun to teach her. She tried and the progress made by her black pupil was the sensation of that time. What a debt of gratitude her race and the whole world owe to Mary Wheatley! Very soon Phyllis began to write poems "for her own amusement," as the preface of her book states. "As to her writings," says her master, "her own curiosity led her to it."

Phyllis did not know when or where she was born. She only knew she came from somewhere in Africa. She must have been born either in 1753 or 1754—not later than 1754, it is thought. She was probably between seven and eight years of age when she was dragged more dead than alive from the slave ship in Boston.

When she was twenty years old her health began to fail and her friends thought a sea voyage would do her good. Mr. Wheatley happened to be going abroad on business and he took Phyllis with him to England where she had the time of her young life. She was the guest of the Countess of Huntingdon, was received by the Lord Mayor of London and by Lord Dartmouth, was feted, petted and honored by the culture and aristocracy of Great Britain. Her book entitled "Poems on Various Subjects, Religious and Moral, by Phyllis Wheatley Negro Servant of John Wheatley of Boston in New England," was published during this visit in 1773. It was dedicated to her English hostess and patroness as follows: "To the Right Honourable the Countess of Huntingdon, the following pages are most respectfully inscribed, by her much obliged, very humble and devoted servant, Phyllis Wheatley." Thus it was that the Wheatley family became immortalized, for it would long have been forgotten, if it had not been for the genius of a slave.

In order to prove to those who would doubt that the African girl really wrote the poems Mr. Wheatley had some of the most distinguished citizens in New England vouch for this fact. In one of the preliminary pages of the book, his excellency, Thomas Hutchinson, governor, and the lieutenant-governor, together with sixteen other representative citizens signed their names to the following statement: "Phyllis, a young Negro girl, who was but a few years since brought an uncultivated barbarian from Africa, has ever since been and is now under the disadvantage of serving as a slave in a family in this town, has been examined by some of the best judges and is thought qualified to write them."

On the day Phyllis received a letter from George Washington, then commander-in-chief of the army and the future president of the United States, in which he complimented her upon the poem written in his honor, she must have been very happy indeed. He addressed her as "Miss Phyllis,"and declared she exhibited "striking proof of poetical talent." "If ever you come to Cambridge or near headquarters," he wrote her, "I shall be happy to see a person so favored by the muses and to whom nature has been so liberal and beneficent in her dispensation. I am with great respect, your obedient, humble servant, George Washington."

When she was about twenty-five Phyllis married John Peters, a man of her own race, and seems to have been unhappy. She lived only five years after her marriage and was working in an ordinary boarding house when she died, Dec. 5th, 1784, in her thirty-first year. This poetess was a full-blooded African, so that her talent and attainments cannot be attributed to the mixture of Caucasian or any other blood in her veins.

If any other human being, black, white, yellow, red, or brown, has ever made such marvelous intellectual progress and achieved such great literary success in such a short time under similar circumstances as Phyllis Wheatley, the records of history do not show it.

The History
of the
Club Women's
Movement

Writing the history of the club movement among our women is a very large order for the necessarily limited space of a magazine article. But I shall present as many facts as I can, and make no statement about any phase of the subject which can not be verified by documentary evidence in my possession. The first and real reason that our women began to use clubs as a means of improving their own condition and that of their race is that they are progressive. The effort made by colored women to educate and elevate themselves would read like a fairy tale if it were written. But, unfortunately for the race, it has not been written. Ignorance for which the group was not responsible, made it impossible for newly emancipated slaves to keep a record. And after there was a general diffusion of education in the group, the necessity of keeping a record was not generally felt.

But in spite of absence of records, from rare pamphlets, occasional newspaper clippings, bits of chapters in books and conversations and those familiar with the early efforts to rise above ignorance and degradation, it is clear that the progress made by colored women in seventy-five years is little short of a miracle. From the day the colored woman's fetters were broken, her mind released from the darkness of ignorance in which it had been held

Originally published in the *Aframerican Woman's Journal*, Summer-Fall, 1940, pages 34-38.

for nearly three hundred years and she could stand erect in the dignity of womanhood, no longer bound but free, till this minute, generally speaking, she has been forging steadily ahead, acquiring knowledge and exerting herself strenuously to promote the welfare of the race.

For a long time colored women who had enjoyed educational advantages worked as individuals to improve their condition. In their respective communities many have often struggled single-handed and alone against the most discouraging and desperate odds to secure for themselves and their loved ones the opportunities which they so sadly needed and so ardently desired. But it dawned upon them finally that individuals working alone or in small companies might be ever so honest in purpose, so indefatigable in labor, so conscientious about methods and so wise in making plans, nevertheless, they could accomplish little compared with the possible achievement of many individuals all banded together throughout the whole land with heads and hearts fixed on the same high purpose and hands joined in united strength. The realization of this self-evident fact gave birth to the club movement among our women.

And so, in Washington, D.C., the Colored Woman's League, of which Mrs. Helen Cook was president, was organized in June, 1892. Its Preamble reads as follows:

> WHEREAS, in Union there is Strength, and
> WHEREAS, we, as a people, have been and are the subject of prejudice, proscription and injustice, the more successful, because the lack of unity and organization,
> Resolved, That we, the colored women of Washington, associate ourselves together to collect all facts obtainable, showing the moral, intellectual, and social growth and attainments of our people; to foster unity of purpose; to consider and determine methods which will promote the best interests of the colored people in any direction that suggests itself.
> Resolved, That we appeal to the colored women of the United States, interested in the objects set forth, to form similar organizations, which shall cooperate with the Washington League, thus forming a National League in which each society shall be represented.

On January 11, 1894, the Colored Women's League was incorporated. The Act of Incorporation reads as follows:

THE COLORED WOMAN'S LEAGUE

To whom it may concern:

We, the undersigned, being of full age, citizens of the United States, and a majority of us being citizens of the District of Columbia, do hereby certify that we have united and formed ourselves into an association for industrial and educational purposes under the laws in force in the said District of Columbia, including the act approved May 5, 1870, and the act amendatory thereof, approved April 23, 1884, and all other laws in force in said District of Columbia relating thereto.

Act 1. The name of the Association shall be the Colored Women's League.

Act 2. The term of said League shall be perpetual.

Act 3. The object of the League is the education and Improvement of Colored Women and the promotion of their interests. Also to provide a suitable building in which it may carry on its educational and industrial work.

Act 4. The number of trustees for the first year shall be nine.

Act 5. The capital stock shall not be less than $5,000, not more than $50,000 divided into shares of $5 each.

In testimony whereof we have hereunto set our hands and seals this 11th day of January, 1894.

> Helen A. Cook, (seal)
> Charlotte F. Grimke, (seal)
> Josephine B. Bruse, (seal)
> Anna J. Cooper, (seal)
> Mary Church Terrell, (seal)
> Mary J. Patterson, (seal)
> Evelyn Shaw, (seal)
> Ida D. Bailey, (seal)

Acknowledged and subscribed to before
James H. Meriwether,
Notary Public

With the exception of Mrs. Anna J. Cooper and myself, nobody whose name appears above is living. It is interesting to note in passing that Mary J. Patterson received the degree of A.B. from Oberlin College in 1862, and was the first colored woman in the world, so far as the records show, to receive that degree.

So far as I have been able to ascertain by careful and diligent research, the Colored Woman's League was the first club organized by our women for the definite purpose of becoming national. In the 1893 May and June issue of

Ringwood's *Afro-American Journal of Fashion*, a magazine published in Cleveland, Ohio, my article entitled "What the Colored Woman's League Will Do," appeared. The following excerpts from it emphasize the League's effort to become national.

"A national organization of colored women could accomplish so much good in such a variety of ways that thoughtful, provident women are strenuously urging their sisters all over the country to co-operate with them in this important matter. In unity there is strength and in unity of purpose there is much inspiration.

The Colored Woman's League, recently organized in Washington, has cordially invited women in all parts of the country to unite with it, so that we may have a national organization similar to the federated clubs of the women of the dominant race. The local societies are subject in no way whatsoever to the League." The Preamble is then quoted to show the purpose of the League.

"There is every reason for all who have the interests of the race at heart," continues the article, "to associate themselves with the League, so that there may be a vast chain of organizations extending the length and breadth of the land devising ways and means to advance our cause. We have always been equal to the highest emergencies in the past, and it remains for us now to prove to the world that we are a unit in all matters pertaining to the education and elevation of our race."

The League's desire to encourage and assist young people possessing talent is cited and the duty of gathering statistics showing what has been done in literature science and art is emphasized. The establishing of trade schools is urged.

"If, through the Colored Woman's League organizations should spring up all over the country, whose chief aim would be to gather under their wing as many young women as possible," says the article, "whose minds should be enlightened, whose fingers trained and whose sentiments elevated by personal contact with cultured, refined women, the race problem would be on the high road to solution. . . . Beside the practical good it will do, the League will foster the spirit of unity among us, a virtue which we so unfortunately lack and so sadly need. . . . Several organizations have already declared themselves willing to work hand in hand with it. With Mrs. J. Silone Yates as president, and Miss Anna Jones as secretary, Kansas City already boasts of a society numbering 150 members. Others will soon emulate their worthy example and the League will be an established fact, enabling us to work out our own salvation in that effective and successful manner possible only to earnest, zealous women." So far as available records show, this is the first article appearing in any publication announcing that a national organization of colored women had been formed.

No history of the Club movement of the women of our group, who had organized to become national, would be complete without relating those activities in which they were engaged. The activities of the Colored Woman's League were varied and wide in scope!

There was a night school in which classes in literature, language and other subjects were taught by teachers who volunteered their services gratuitously. A class in German and one in English Literature were taught by the writer. A member of one of these classes afterwards graduated from one of the eastern colleges for women and is now at the head of one of the important departments in our public schools.

A model kindergarten was opened with fifteen young women in the training class under a woman of national reputation. The school had two sessions daily and a total enrollment of 40 children. A free kindergarten was opened in the morning and in the afternoon one for children who could afford to pay fifty cents per month. The League started the training class and opened the kindergarten before these were incorporated in the Washington public school system. The Industrial Committee conducted a sewing class, and a course in kitchen gardening for girls under eighteen was offered. Children were taught actually to perform ordinary duties in the home. The League defrayed the expenses of a girl in the Manassas Industrial School. A day nursery for children, whose mothers were obliged to leave home to work, was also maintained.

The Woman's Protective Union was formed. It was composed of societies in Washington, each of which had its own separate and specific object, but they all united to form an organization whose executive committee had the power to claim their services whenever by concerted action they could advance any worthy cause. They hoped to bring about some needed reforms in the District of Columbia.

The National Council of Women invited the League to become a member of the organization in a letter dated October 9, 1894, and addressed to the corresponding secretary, Mrs. Anna J. Cooper. The League was also invited by the president, Mrs. May Wright Sewall, to be represented in a convention which was held in Washington from February 17, 1895, to March 2. Only national organizations were invited to participate.

In the 1894 November issue of the *Woman's Era* the following notice appeared:

The National Council of Women, which convenes in Washington, D.C., in February, has invited the Colored Women's League of Washington to be represented at the Convention. The Washington League, with broad minded courtesy, has made its committee so large as to be able to include delegates from other colored women's leagues, and has invited such leagues to send delegates.

Unfortunately, a majority of the members of the Woman's Era Club of Boston did not see the advantages of being represented, and voted not to send a delegate. In spite of this fact, which we regret very much, we hope to see the colored women of all sections represented by their best women at the coming council. In any event, Washington is prepared to ably represent the race.

The *Woman's Era* magazine was founded by Mrs. Josephine St. Pierre Ruffin, president of the Woman's Era Club, in March, 1894. The departments of the magazine were conducted by the following women: Mrs. Victoria Earle Matthews, of New York; Mrs. Fannie Barrier Williams, Chicago; Mrs. Josephine Silone Yates, Kansas City; Mrs. Elizabeth P. Ensley, Denver; Alice Ruth Moore, New Orleans (later Mrs. Paul Lawrence Dunbar); Mary Church Terrell, Washington. The writer of this article is the only woman among those whose names appear on the above editorial board who is living.

About this time something happened which caused the colored women of the country to meet to consider what should be done about a foul slander hurled against them. In a letter dated March 6, 1895, James W. Jacks, president of the Missouri Press Association, sent a scurrilous attack on colored women to Miss Florence Belgarnie, of London, Honorable Secretary of the Anti-Lynching Society of England, and a well-known friend of the race. In this letter Jacks declared that the Negroes of this country were wholly devoid of morality, the women were prostitutes and all were natural thieves and liars. Miss Belgarnie forwarded this letter to the editors of the *Woman's Era* for publication. It was not published in the *Era*, however, but it was printed and sent to leading men and women, particularly to those in the South, for an expression of opinion.

On the editorial page of the June, 1895, issue of the *Woman's Era*, and article entitled "Let Us Confer Together," the following notice appears:

We, the women of the Woman's Era Club of Boston, send forth a call to our sisters all over the country, members of all clubs, societies, associations, or circles to meet with us in conference in this city of Boston. And we urge upon all clubs, societies, associations and circles to take immediate action, looking towards the sending of delegates to this convention. Boston has been selected as a meeting place because it has seemed to be the general opinion that here, and here only, can be found the atmosphere which would best interpret and represent us, our position, our needs and our aims. One of the pressing needs of our cause is the education of the public mind to a just appreciation of us, and only here can we gain the attention upon which so much depends.

It is designed to hold the convention three days, the first of which will be given up to business, the second and third to the consideration of vital questions concerning our moral, mental, physical and financial growth and well-being, these to be presented through addresses by representative women.

Although this matter of a convention has been talked over for some time, the subject has been precipitated by a letter to England, written by a southern editor, and reflecting upon the moral character of all colored women. This letter is too indecent for publication, but a copy of it is sent with this call to all the women's bodies throughout the country. Read this document carefully and discriminatingly and decide if it be not time for us to stand before the world and declare ourselves and our principles. The time is short, but everything is ripe; and remember, earnest women can do anything. A circular letter will be sent you in the meantime. Let us hear at once from you.

As a result of this call, what is designated as "The First National Conference of Colored Women of America" was held in Boston, Massachusetts. It opened its session on Monday, July 29, 1895. Mrs. Josephine St. Pierre Ruffin called the meeting to order at 10 A.M. Distinguished people spoke; representative women read papers; the convention went into secret session to discuss Jacks's letter; resolutions were passed, and finally, the convention discussed forming a national organization.

Mrs. Helen Cook, president of the National Colored Women's League, was present and, according to the *Era's* August, 1895, report of the meeting, "Mrs. Cook was allowed time to make the necessary explanations regarding the National League." It was "proposed that a national organization be now formed, with its own laws, officers, constitution, etc." This motion prevailed, and a committee on organization, consisting of one delegate from each delegation, was appointed. A discussion followed as to the clause looking to a union with the Colored Women's National League. A committee was appointed to perfect the organization. Names of the candidates for whom the delegates should vote for offices, were given to the convention. It was voted "to frame the constitution, that the *Woman's Era* be made the organ of the national organization," and "that the name of the new organization be laid over." It was also voted that "the officers and Executive Board of the National organization should confer with the officers and Executive Board of the Colored Women's National League for the purpose of effecting a union." The meeting was adjourned "subject to call of the Pres., Mrs. B. T. Washington." The names of the other officers who were elected at that meeting were not given in this report.

In this "the First National Conference of the Colored Women of America," said the 1895 October issue of the *Woman's Era*, "for the first time in American history, could be seen an audience of several hundred women, in dress, manners and general public appearance, fully up to the average presentation of a similar assembly of their sisters in white."

In this same issue there was a "CALL TO THE NATIONAL FEDERATION OF AFRO-AMERICAN WOMEN, organized in Boston, Mass., July 31, 1895," the President, Mrs. Booker T. Washington, Tuskegee, Ala. In an editorial, reference was made to the fact that many were disappointed because the President of the Woman's Era Club, who called the meeting, had not been elected president. It was also stated that "the convention unanimously voted that from the delegate body a national organization be formed looking to a union with the Woman's League of Washington, which in order to meet an emergency and grasp an opportunity to make a creditable showing for themselves, their race, and the cause they were invited to represent, had been obligated to call themselves 'national,' to be eligible to membership in the Council held in Washington in March last. This action had been taken hurriedly and nothing but praise is due the Washington League for rising to the opportunity and using any measure to make the most of it. The convention held in July was the first one ever held by our women, and as most of the states and territories were represented, either by delegates or letters, can honestly be termed national in its scope and the only legitimate source from which a national organization could spring."

The members of the League were greatly shocked, that their organization had been accused of calling itself national before it had actually acquired nationality and an unfortunate misunderstanding between the two groups ensued. The article which appeared in Ringwood's *Afro-American Journal of Fashion* in the May-June issue of 1893 had stated that the Kansas City Club with a membership of 150 women had joined the League and never held a convention. There is no doubt whatever that other clubs had united with it. But the League had that the Woman's Era Club of Boston has the distinction of calling together the first national convention of colored women in the United States. Shortly after that the Colored Woman's Congress met in Atlanta, brought together many progressive women and gave an additional impetus to the woman's movement.

In the 1896 May issue of the *Era* it was stated that the "National Federation of Afro-American Women had taken every step consistent with dignity and self respect to effect a union with the Woman's League," but that a definite reply which had been promised by the League had not been forthcoming. One of the Federation officers went to Washington, May 1st, she reports, and was informed that in its issue of April 25th, the *Colored American* announced that the League would hold a convention in Washington in July. It was then decided that the National Federation of Afro-American women would hold a convention there also "on account of the cut rates to that city for the month of July."

And so it happened that on July 14th, 15th and 16th, 1896, the First Annual Convention of the National League of Colored Women was held at the Fifteenth Street Presbyterian Church, and what was called the Second Annual Convention of the National Federation of Afro-American Women was held in the Nineteenth Street Baptist Church July 20th, 21st and 22nd. It was the consensus of opinion among women of both groups that it would be impossible successfully to maintain two national organizations at that stage of our growth and it was decided to unite them.

On Monday, July 20, 1896, the first day of the Federation's convention, a committee of seven was appointed to confer with a committee of equal number from the League, with a view to uniting the two organization. The Federation's committee was composed of Victoria Earle Matthews of New York, Selina Butler of Atlanta, Rosa D. Bowser of Richmond, Josephine St. Pierre Ruffin of Boston, Libbie C. Anthony of Jefferson City, Mo., Addie Hunton of Richmond and Mary C. Terrell of Washington, D.C.

The committee from the League consisted of A. V. Thompkins of Washington, D.C., Coralie Franklin of West Virginia (now Mrs. George Cook), Anna Jones of Kansas, Julia F. Jones of Philadelphia, Fannie Jackson of Kansas City, Florence A. Barber of Norfolk, Va., and E. F. G. Merritt of Washington, D.C. The Joint Committee elected Mary Church Terrell as its chairman.

On the second day of the convention, July 21st, the Joint Committee reported as follows:

It is hereby stipulated

That we do consolidate under the name of the National Association of Colored Women.

That officers shall be chosen on a basis of equality by the Joint Committee.

That neither association shall assume any of the liabilities of the other incurred prior to the consolidation.

That the new association shall support the work already planned by each of the old organizations.

That the joint committee shall draft a constitution and elect officers for the ensuing year.

Considering the difficulties encountered, merging these two organizations into one was accomplished with comparatively little friction. But it was not easy to "name the baby." The Federation wanted to have its name adopted and the League felt the same way about its name. After considerable discussion it was finally decided to call the new organization the "National Association of Colored Women."

Then the most difficult task of all confronted the joint committee. Who should be the first president? That was indeed the question! It is safe to assert that while we were in the throes of electing the president, the name of no colored woman who had achieved success or prominence anywhere in the United States failed to be presented for consideration. To begin with, the name of every member of the Joint Committee was mentioned, not once, but several times during the day. When a member of this committee was nominated, the result of the poll showed that every woman on her half of the Joint Committee voted for her, while every woman on the other half voted for somebody else. Over and over again the tellers would report that Miss A had 7 votes and Miss B had 7. And this went on indefinitely, so that most of us had little hope that anybody either in the United States or out of it could ever be elected.

Several times during the committee meeting prayers were offered by the members who sought divine guidance in accomplishing the task they were trying to perform. Like the other members of the committee, I had been nominated early in the day and had met the same fate as the others. Finally I was nominated the second time, the deadlock was broken, I received a majority of the votes cast and was elected the first president of the National Association of Colored Women. It was nearly six o'clock in the evening when this occurred. The Joint Committee had been in session all day long and had to return to the church for the evening session at eight o'clock, although each and every one of us was worn to a frazzle. I shall never forget the sensations I experienced while presiding over that Joint Committee. It was the hardest day's work I have ever done.

I presided over three conventions—one in Nashville in 1897, the year after the Association was formed; the next one in Chicago in 1899, and the third in Buffalo, New York, in 1901. Each of these earlier sessions was successful from every point of view.

This is the story of the manner in which the National Association of Colored Women was organized. It was not founded by any one woman or by any particular group of women. Owing to conditions which confronted them and obstacles which they had to surmount, colored women had reached a point in their development where they decided they must work out their own salvation as best they could. They realized they would do this more quickly and more effectively if they were banded together throughout the country with heads and hearts fixed on the same high purpose and hands joined in united strength.

Needed:
Women Lawyers

Noted educator regrets she
didn't study law to serve race.

If I had my life to live over again, I am sure I would do exactly what I have been trying to do for nearly fifty years. I have been trying to present the colored man's case clearly, strongly and tactfully to the people of the dominant race. By talking with them I have discovered that many who are well-educated, broad-minded and justice-loving have no idea of the efforts colored people are making to help themselves in spite of the almost innumerable obstacles they have to overcome.

I would want to repeat the public work of various kinds which I have done, to represent colored women, not only in Europe and England, as I have done three times, but I should want to present the colored woman's progress and the perplexing problems confronting her here all over the world. It is a wonderful story and reads like a fairy tale. I should want to repeat the work I have done on the lecture platform, before Chautauquas, in the churches, in the forums and in organizations of various kinds, multiplied many times by still more glorious opportunities to tell our thrilling story everywhere from a colored woman's point of view.

In addition to writing articles for magazines and newspapers I would somehow force myself into the ranks of successful short story writers. I believe the deplorable conditions under which many of us live can be pictured more vividly and can be improved more quickly and more surely through the medium of the short story than in any other way.

Concerning the trade or profession I would follow I can say that I might

Originally published in *Negro Digest*, September 1943, 57-59.

be a lawyer. I am sometimes sorry that I did not study law when my late husband, Judge Robert Heberton Terrell taught in the Howard University Law School. But it seemed difficult, if not impossible, for me to do so and to discharge my duties and obligations at the same time. If I were younger I should be tempted to study law now in the Robert Heberton Terrell Law School here which was named for my husband. The women of our group can render excellent service as lawyers.

I would join as many organizations established to promote the welfare of our group as I could, and I would always pay my dues. I would encourage those I could not join by speaking a good word for them and attending their meetings every now and then.

I would never use the word Negro when I can avoid it. If a man is a Negro, it follows as the night the day that I am a Negress. I will not allow anybody to call me a "Negress" if I can prevent it. "Negress" is a term of reproach which the colored women of this country can not live down for thousands of years. In fact, they can never live it down. Those who handicap and persecute us always call us Negroes (usually with a little "n," when it is not changed into an uglier word). But those who are friendly and try to help us generally refer to us as "colored people."

There are no Negroes in the United States, no matter how dark the individual's complexion may be. Every one of us has white blood in his veins. If I could live my life over again I would start and maintain a vigorous crusade against the use of the word Negro. Our group will never receive the respect and consideration to which we are entitled so long as we allow ourselves to be designated as *Negroes*.

Colored people will succeed in business whenever they learn how to conduct it properly. Those who have earned the reputation of being good business men and who have made money have proved that their race does not militate against success.

The political future of our group is bright in the North if we will only discharge our duties and obligations as citizens, faithfully, honestly and wisely. It is a sin and a shame that so many neglect to do so.

If I were young I would go through the North, East and West urging people to do everything in their power to enforce the provisions of the Constitution which have conferred citizenship upon us. I would try to impress them with the fact that they are partners in the crime of disfranchising millions of colored people, so long as they wink at these disgraceful conditions without uttering a word in protest. I would show that the congressmen, who come from that section where the majority of colored people live and are not allowed to vote, sit in the Senate and House illegally, and let them judge for themselves whether the business these Senators and Representatives transact is done legally.

In the labor movement our prospects are brighter today than they have sometimes been in the past. Honest, earnest efforts are being made by those in power to give employment to our group and to remove the ban which has often prevented us from earning our daily bread. If I were young I would do everything I could to impress upon our group the necessity of training and fitting ourselves properly for whatever trade or occupation in which we want to engage.

I would work hard and continuously to remove the many injustices of which we are the victims and to make it possible for colored people to reach any height of human endeavor to which by our ability and industry it is possible to attain.

MARY CHURCH TERRELL was the first colored women in the U.S. to serve on a board of education. She was a member of the D.C. board for eleven years. She was also the first president of the National Association of Colored Women and later named honorary president for life. She was a speaker at the International Congress of Women in Berlin, Germany, in 1904 and later was associated with Jane Addams as a delegate to the International League for Peace and Freedom at Zurich, Switzerland, in 1919.

Dr. Sara W. Brown

Those who are cognizant of Dr. Sara W. Brown's innate ability, her high ideals, and her strong determination to finish what she started are not surprised at her many outstanding achievements or the valuable services she rendered to her own racial group in particular and to her country as a whole.

I was well acquainted with her for many years. I taught her in my second year class in the High School in Washington. When she was a pupil in my Latin class, I was impressed with the sterling qualities which she possessed. She gave indisputable proof of the fact that she not only wanted to understand everything discussed or read in class, but there was no doubt in my mind that she definitely intended to do so. It was easy to see that she would leave no stone unturned to satisfy this desire. I do not recall having taught any student who seemed to enjoy improving her mind more than Sara Brown did. In the experience of every teacher there are students who stand out distinctly in the mind many years after they recite in class because of the satisfaction and pleasure afforded in teaching them. Such a student was Sara Brown, when I recall the time I taught her. Persistent were these qualities when I remember Sara Brown as a teacher when she lived in my home.

Sara attended Hampton Institute and was graduated with honors. Later, she entered Miner Normal School and distinguished herself by the fine record she made. After teaching here for a while she entered Cornell University and received the A.B degree in 1897. The benefit derived from her course in Cornell was greatly increased by her extra-curricular activities. She became a member of three societies, two of them literary—the Wayside Club and the Aftermath Club, and one of them biological—the Jugatae. After receiving the degree of A.B. from Cornell, Miss Brown returned to Washington, resumed teaching biology in the public schools and began the study of medicine at

Originally published in *The Journal of the College Alumnae Club of Washington* 30 (Memorial Edition, April 1950), pages 17-19.

Howard University, from which she received her M.D. degree, in 1904. Having enjoyed such perfect academic preparation, Dr. Brown devoted much of her time and strength to practicing medicine and to discharging her duty as a good citizen by assisting the various social projects designed to benefit the community at a whole. Not content with her unusual scholastic record. Dr. Brown decided to study sociology under Professor Giddings of Columbia University and anthropology under Professor Boaz, and then added to her fund of knowledge by attending lectures at the Sorbonne during one of her trips to Europe.

It was natural that various important organizations should call upon a woman who had availed herself of such exceptional educational opportunities as Dr. Brown had to assist and serve them. For instance, the Women's War Council appointed her a member of the "Flying Squadron" which was composed of fifty women physicians. The American Red Cross appointed her a relief worker in the flooded areas of Mississippi and Louisiana in 1927. She was appointed a medical official to accompany the Gold Star mothers to France in 1930. Under the auspices of the National Board of the YWCA Dr. Brown was appointed a lecturer on health. In 1924 Dr. Brown enjoyed the distinction of being the first woman graduate trustee of Howard University. At the time of her death she was serving as trustee with two other women, Mrs. Eleanor Roosevelt and Mrs. Dorothy Canfield Fisher, the writer.

Among the organizations in Washington which were assisted by Dr. Brown may be mentioned the Freedman's Hospital Nurse Committee, the Lend-A-Hand Club for unmarried mothers, the first social settlement in Washington, and the National Association for the Advancement of Colored People. She was affiliated with the St. Luke's Protestant Episcopal Church in Washington.

But no attempt to give an outline, however brief, of Dr. Brown's achievements, services, and activities would be complete without referring to the important part she played in founding the College Alumnae Club. She and I talked about forming it for a long time. But we both knew there were difficulties connected with it and discussed the arguments for and against it many times. Neither one of us advocated or favored segregation. And yet we knew that many of our women would not graduate from accredited colleges, and that they would be unable to become members of the American Association of University Women. Therefore, if a club for college women to which colored women could belong were not formed, many of our women would be deprived of the benefits, opportunities of various kinds, and the pleasure which membership in a college club affords. After discussing the matter thoroughly Sara and I decided to go ahead and do something definite about it. I asked her to arrange for a meeting in our house, 326 Tea Street, N.W., on March 10, 1910. She complied and on that date four women, Sara Brown, her sister, Fairfax Brown, Mary Cromwell, and I met to discuss the reasons why we should form a college women's club. We decided to form one then and there. Of the four women who met on March 10, 1910, at 326 Tea Street, all are living except for one who was so genuinely, deeply, and enthusiastically interested in forming the College Alumnae Club.

All of us promised to invite all the college women we knew to attend a meeting at an early date, so that the club could start work as soon as possible. The importance and significance of what had happened impressed me so deeply that I recorded in my diary what we four women had done before I retired that night. A photostatic copy of that record from my diary was made for the College Alumnae Club a few years ago.

The invitations extended to our college sisters were cheerfully accepted. The first meeting was well attended and the founders were greatly encouraged. In the twenty-fifth anniversary number of the *Journal of the College Alumnae Club*, under the title, "The Day Before Yesterday", Dr. Brown gives some of the reasons why the Club was founded. After stating the "Through the haze of twenty-five years, some vivid recollections of the things we tried to do come to memory.", she tells what some of these things "we tried to do" were. In referring to the pioneers she says, "Do you ask what of them today, these pioneers?" She answers her questions by saying, "Not one has marked time. All continued to grow and become leaders of women." Then she proves this statement by giving a list of the important services these pioneers have rendered.

In giving a sketch of Dr. Brown's life it would be an unfortunate omission to fail to state that she belonged to a remarkable family. Sometimes one member of a family, or maybe two distinguish themselves by the service they render or the lofty heights they attain. But each and every member of Dr. Brown's family has a record of which each might be proud. Dr. Brown's parents lived in Winchester, Virginia, where she was born on July 12, 1868. Mr. and Mrs. Brown were held in high esteem in this community and had the reputation of being experts in handling business affairs, a trait inherited by Sara and their other children. There were eight children, seven living to adulthood to distinguish themselves in rendering valuable service to their communities. Of the surviving members, Dr. James Erroll Brown is a professor in the University of Pittsburgh, Dr. John W. Brown is a retired physician of Winchester and Pittsburgh, and Dr. Fairfax Brown is a retired teacher and pharmacist.

On November 12, 1948, the citizens of Washington were shocked to hear that, while crossing a street on a green light, as she should have done, Dr. Brown was struck and fatally injured by a Capital Transit bus which was making a left turn. This appalling accident suddenly closed the remarkable career of a woman with high scholastic attainments and fine training, who for many years and in various ways had been actively, eagerly promoting the welfare of her group, and demonstrating a democratic way of living to thousands of citizens throughout the United States.

I Remember
Frederick Douglass

90-year-old fighter for civil rights
tells of her friendship with abolitionist

It is 58 years since Frederick Douglass, that most illustrious Negro leader and to my mind the greatest of all Americans, died of a heart attack in his home, Cedar Hill, in Anacostia, D.C. The passing of the years, far from diminishing his importance, has made Douglass an even greater figure in his country's history.

I knew Frederick Douglass well and was his friend for 16 years. It seems more like 60 than 16 years, because so much happened of such great importance in the time that I knew him.

Before I met Douglass I knew practically nothing about his career. I did not know the story of his stirring struggle from slavery to freedom. I had heard his name spoken by my parents and by other colored people whom I knew as a young girl. I think the only thing I ever read about him before I left college concerned his marriage to a white woman. Most of the comments I read on his second marriage were extremely hostile. But from all that I had heard and read I knew that Douglass was a very great and distinguished leader of his people.

Meeting Frederick Douglass was an unforgettable experience. When I was a freshman at Oberlin College in 1881 my parents permitted me to accept an invitation extended by Senator and Mrs. B. K. Bruce to attend President Garfield's inauguration. Senator Bruce of Mississippi was the only colored member of the U.S. Senate at the time, and as far as I know there has been no other since.

Originally published in *Ebony*, October 1953, pages 73-80.

After reaching Washington Mrs. Bruce arranged a friend to take me out sight-seeing one day. As we were walking down the street I saw two men talking a short distance ahead of us. One of the men was tall and distinguished, of magnificent, majestic proportions. Immediately, intuitively, instinctively, I knew that he was the great Frederick Douglass. Fortunately, for me, my friend knew him and introduced me to him. Thus began a friendship which I dearly prize because I derived so much inspiration, information and pleasure from it as long as Mr. Douglass lived.

From the moment I saw him for the first time until the day of his death, not one of his words, not one of his deeds ever caused me to regret the high estimate I had put upon him as a man or the value I placed upon him as a popular friend.

He was a perfect Chesterfield in manner, cultivated and gracious. It was hard to believe that a man of such culture and refinement could ever have been a slave with no formal education. He was a brilliant conversationalist. His English was faultless without being pedantic. He had had such wonderful experiences and could relate them with such force, vividness and charm of manner that it was a delight to listen to him. Very few people cared to say much when Douglass talked. Although he did not care to occupy the center of the stage in a small group (for he was a very modest man), if he felt like talking, even the most garrulous individual was perfectly willing to be silent.

Douglass was no sedate, long-faced, solemn personality. He enjoyed having fun and being in a merry company, listening to jokes and telling funny stories himself. He liked to laugh.

During the summer Douglass used to invite a few of his friends, myself included, to come to Cedar Hill to play croquet with him. He enjoyed the sport and was very skillful at it. Many times my late husband and myself had the pleasure of playing croquet with Douglass on the lawn. I cherish the recollections of those delightful afternoons, so full of pleasure, which usually ended with a stimulating exchange of views and opinions on the questions of the day.

Both Mr. and Mrs. Douglass were very hospitable people who enjoyed entertaining friends in their home. Judge Terrell and I were often invited to Sunday tea at Cedar Hill. On these occasions Douglass would hold forth in the living room, telling fascinating stories. I now regret that I did not keep a diary in those days so that I would have a record of his wit and wisdom. During those Sunday evening sessions there was a "feast of reason and a flow of soul." Sometimes Douglass took out his fiddle, sang Scottish songs of which he was very fond, and played a few tunes. Then he and my husband would usually get up and dance a few steps, entertaining us immensely.

When the World's Fair was held in Chicago in 1893, to celebrate the 400th anniversary of the discovery of America by Columbus, Douglass was the commissioner in charge of the exhibit from Haiti. He employed Paul Laurence Dunbar, the poet, to assist him. Douglass entertained his friends at the Fair by taking them to see the exhibits which he especially liked. One afternoon he invited me to go with him to take in some of the sights.

As we walked along through the grounds and the buildings Douglass was continually stopped by admirers who begged the privilege of shaking his hand. Great homage was paid him, especially by white people who recognized him. Mothers with their children would stop him and say, "You are Frederick Douglass, aren't you? Please shake hands with my little boy, because when he grows up I want him to be able to say that he once shook hands with the great Frederick Douglass."

When his patience slackened Douglass suggested, "Let's get on the scenic railway so that we may have a chance to talk a little. Nobody can get us there." But we had no sooner settled ourselves on the little scenic railway than a man reached over two seats to touch him on the shoulder and greet him. "Well, we'll go up on the Eiffel Tower," chuckled Douglass. But just as we started to ascend a man in another cage shouted: "Hello, Mr. Douglass! The last time I saw you was in Rochester."

Douglass was a man of infinite patience, tact and graciousness. He was never rude and was careful to do or say nothing that would hurt anybody's feelings. To me he was a practical Christian. Judged by his deeds there has been no better Christian in the United States. He enjoyed helping others.

He encouraged and aided promising and talented young Negroes. As an example, he had become deeply interested in Paul Laurence Dunbar, the poet, because of his bitter struggle for existence and recognition. I first heard of Dunbar from Douglass. One day by appointment I went to see Douglass in his Anacostia home. After we had finished our business, Douglass, who was widely know as the "the Sage of Anacostia," asked me, "Have you ever heard of Paul Dunbar?" I told him I had not. Then Douglass told me Dunbar's story.

"He is very young," he said, "but there is not doubt that he is a poet. He is working under the most discouraging circumstances in his home in

Dayton, Ohio. He is an elevator boy and on his meager wage of four dollars a week he is trying to support his mother and himself. Let me read you one of his poems." Douglass left the room and returned with a newspaper clipping from which he began to read Dunbar's *The Drowsy Day*. When he had read several stanzas his voice faltered and his eyes grew moist. He was deeply moved. "What a tragedy it is," he said, "that a young man with such talent should be so terribly handicapped by poverty and color." I shall never forget Douglass's reading of that poem.

I remember a delightful dinner with Douglass and his family one summer on Chesapeake Bay. Shortly after our marriage, my husband and I were invited by Major Charles Douglass, one of Frederick Douglass's sons, to take dinner with his father, his wife and himself at Highland Beach, which is about five miles from the U.S. Naval Academy in Annapolis, Md. Major Douglass had bought a large tract of land on Chesapeake Bay, which he intended to convert into a Summer resort for colored people. Frederick Douglass selected a corner lot facing the Bay and asked us to take the one next to his. We decided to buy it and built our Summer home there. I think Douglass would today be pleased indeed if he could see what a great success his son's plan of establishing an ideal colored Summer resort has proved to be.

After dinner we decided to take a stroll to the Bay. As we walked over the land in front of Major Douglass's house he told his father that the following year he intended to have a fine garden on the plot. It was a sandy patch of ground, and his son's idea of having a garden there seemed to amuse Douglass very much. "Why Charles," he said, laughing. "Do you really think you can raise vegetables on this ground? I don't believe you can raise an umbrella on it."

The first time I went to the White House to see a president of the United States was with Frederick Douglass. Douglass went to urge President Benjamin Harrison to speak out boldly against lynching in his annual message to Congress. I was thrilled, entering the White House for the first time in the company of such a great man. I accompanied Douglass into the president's office for an interview and listened spellbound while he eloquently pleaded the case for anti-lynching legislation. He implored President Harrison to act immediately against the lynching evil. I remember urging the president to comply with Douglass's request. "Please Mr. President," I said. "Do something at once to stop the lynching of Negroes in the South." President

Harrison listened attentively, but so far as I can recall, took no action against lynching.

But Frederick Douglass never ceased to fight vigorously against lynching and all the wrongs of which his race was the victim.

I went to hear Douglass speak whenever I knew he was going to deliver an address. Each time I heard him I was more convinced than before that he was the greatest orator in America. When Douglass went to England to urge the British to help abolish slavery in America it was the consensus of opinion that this ex-slave was the greatest of all the abolitionist orators they had heard, including Wendell Phillips and William Lloyd Garrison. And the English were not prone to bestow undeserved praise.

Douglass spoke with great warmth, conviction and depth of feeling. He spoke in a rich, resonant voice. I think it was the most perfect speaking voice I have ever heard. His command of the language was masterful. He had the quality of moving audiences. The beauty and power of the language used by this ex-slave was truly a miracle of modern times.

People believed in him. He made people believe in him by his conduct and by what he said. On the platform he had an imposing presence. He was dramatic without being theatrical. No one who ever heard him could possibly accuse him of exaggeration or uncertainty. He could make a person feel what he said.

Once, after hearing Douglass deliver an impassioned unprepared speech, I said to him, "Oh Mr. Douglass, woman though I am, I would give everything I have to be able to speak extemporaneously as perfectly as you do." Douglass laughed. "Once I said the same thing to Wendell Phillips, after a speech I heard him make which I thought to be extemporaneous," he said. "I praised him for it." ' "Extemporaneous?' Phillips laughed. 'Why, I've been thinking about that for 50 years.' "

While I was a student at Oberlin College I first became interested in interracial marriage when Frederick Douglass married Helen Pitts, a white woman who lived near his home in Anacostia. She was a senior clerk in the office of the Recorder of Deeds for the District of Columbia during the time that Douglass was Recorder. In the reading room of Oberlin's Ladies' Hall, where I lived while in college, I read editorial comments on the marriage appearing in many newspapers and magazines. Many of these comments shocked and disgusted me. Few approved of intermarriage, while most of them bitterly attacked it.

A great outcry was raised against Douglass's marriage to Helen Pitts because it defied the customs and traditions of the country. Many Negroes criticized Douglass because he married a white woman. These same critics were continually clamoring for equality. But when Frederick Douglass, the foremost representative of their race, actually practiced equality by choosing a white woman as his mate, these very advocates of equality attacked him bitterly and condemned him.

Incidentally, it is entirely due to the thoughtfulness and determination of this white woman that Cedar Hill has been preserved as a memorial to her husband. In making his will Douglass neglected to have it signed by three witnesses, a procedure necessary at that time in order to transfer real estate from one person to another. Because of this Mrs. Douglass had to purchase the interests of the other heirs in order to retain control of the property. This was a big, heart-breaking task for Mrs. Douglass, but she succeeded, and as a result Cedar Hill is now "a perpetual memorial to my late husband," to quote a phrase from her will.

I must refer to some of the falsehoods told about the lowly position which Mrs. Douglass was said to occupy in her own racial group. Some colored people declared that they did not object to her solely because she was white, but because she was "a poor white woman" with no social standing whatever, who had married a Negro because he had a good job and was known as a distinguished man. The charge that Helen Pitts was "a poor white woman" was entirely false. She was a well-educated woman from a good family, and was the first president of the National Kindergarten Association.

When the various women's organization held their conventions in Washington the leaders invited Mrs. Douglass to their special functions and it was her custom to invite a few friends to luncheon or dinner at Cedar Hill. On such occasions Mrs. Douglass would usually invite Mrs. B. K. Bruce and myself.

When the 60th anniversary of the first woman's Rights Convention ever held was celebrated at Seneca Falls, N.Y., in May, 1908, Frederick Douglass's contribution to that cause was strongly featured. The descendants of the people who called the first meeting to demand equal political rights for women were asked to represent their forebears. I was asked to represent Douglass.

There is certainly a very good reason why Douglass should always be honored at an anniversary celebration which woman suffragists hold. When

Elizabeth Cady Stanton presented a resolution demanding equal political rights for women at that Seneca Falls meeting in 1848, it seemed doomed to defeat. Even dear, brave Lucretia Mott, who for years had courageously championed the cause of woman's suffrage, begged Mrs. Stanton to withdraw her resolution. "Lizzie," she pleaded, "thee will make us all ridiculous if thee insist upon pressing this resolution through the meeting." But Mrs. Stanton refused to withdraw the motion.

And so there was not a white man or a woman at that meeting who had the courage to second Elizabeth Cady Stanton's resolution demanding equal political rights for women. But it was the incomparable Frederick Douglass, a runaway slave, upon whose head a big price had been placed by his master, who had the courage to rise in that meeting and second Mrs. Stanton's resolution. And it was largely due to his masterful arguments and his matchless eloquence that the resolution passed in spite of the fierce opposition of its powerful foes.

The women of this country owe a debt of gratitude to Frederick Douglass which they can never repay. At the risk of doing an irreparable injury to himself personally and to the cause of abolition, he did everything humanly possible to secure the elective franchise for women.

It was a proud and happy moment in my life when on May 27, 1908, I witnessed and participated in the unveiling of the bronze tablet which was placed on the wall of the Opera House in Seneca Falls, now occupying the site on which stood the Methodist Church in which the first Women's Suffrage Convention was held. This tablet shows in relief the figure of a woman supporting a shield on which is inscribed "On this spot stood the Wesleyan Chapel where the first Women's Rights Convention in the world's history was held July 19 and 20, 1848. Elizabeth Cady Stanton moved this resolution which was seconded by Frederick Douglass: 'That it is the duty of the women of this country to secure to themselves the sacred right to the elective franchise.' " This bronze tablet makes it impossible to withhold from Frederick Douglass the credit due him for his heroic stand on Women's suffrage.

A few years ago I was shocked to read a report of a speech made by a Congressman Stevenson from Wisconsin in which he said that Elizabeth Cady Stanton's resolution demanding equal political rights for women was seconded by Frederick Douglass, "a Scotsman." I promptly wrote letters of protest to two Washington newspapers setting the record straight.

While I was a member of the Washington Board of Education in 1897, I introduced a resolution which was unanimously passed—to make February 14 "Douglass Day" in the Negro public schools. For many years Douglass Day was faithfully observed in the colored schools of the District of Columbia, but comparatively few schools observe it now.

Douglass lived a long and fruitful life. He enjoyed life. He was a gourmet. In fact, he loved the best of everything. He was a modern man in every sense of the word.

He won the admiration of countless women, yet throughout his life there was never a word of scandal heard about him. He lived an honest, upright life.

His second wife, Helen Pitts Douglass, absolutely worshipped him. Many times at Cedar Hill I saw her kneel at his feet while he sat in his favorite armchair. She would look into his face with adoring eyes and when his shock of white hair would fall across his forehead, she would lovingly put it pack in place.

Fate decreed that I should be with Douglass a few hours before his death on Feb. 15, 1895. Shortly before noon that day he had attended the second triennial meeting of the National Woman's Council. The meeting was held in what was then called Metzerott Hall, but what is now known as the Columbia Theatre. When one of the Council officers saw him entering, she announced from the platform "Frederick Douglass is in the house," exactly as she would have said "The president is here." A committee was immediately appointed to escort Douglass to the platform, and when he reached it, those white women gave him a royal Chatauqua salute, waving their handkerchiefs vigorously in the air.

When the meeting adjourned and the admiring women ceased paying homage to Douglass, which I enjoyed from a distance, I came forward and greeted him. He and I left the hall and walked together to the corner of 12th and F streets. There he stopped and asked me to have lunch with him. But I was not feeling very well and declined the invitation. Lifting the large light sombrero which he often wore, Douglass bade me goodbye. That was the last time I saw him alive.

About seven o'clock that evening a friend, Walter Hayson, a high school teacher, came by our house to tell me and my husband that Frederick Douglass was dead. He had died suddenly at dinner while telling his wife about the great ovation tendered him that day by the National Woman's

Council. I deeply regretted that I did not go to lunch with him, that I had been unable to spend another hour in the company of a great man.

His funeral was held at the Metropolitan A.M.E. Church, of which he was a member. It was one of the biggest and most impressive funerals Washington had ever seen. People of all classes and colors attended in thousands. Susan B. Anthony, the famous women's leader, was there, along with many other notables of the day. I almost did not get into the church. It took me over an hour to get inside, so great was the crowd come to mourn the passing of Douglass.

I remember the funeral as though it happened yesterday. Mrs. Douglass entered the church wearing not mourning attire but a brown fur cape. She did not believe in mourning. In not wearing black she knew she was giving offense to many present, but she followed her convictions.

Judged by any standard or test Frederick Douglass occupies a distinguished place among the greatest Americans. To have known that great man and to have been honored with his friendship I consider a priceless privilege, and one of the most cherished memories of my life.

Index

Black Women in United States History: A Guide to the Series

PUBLISHER'S NOTE

The sixteen volumes in this set contain 248 articles, in addition to five monographs. This *Guide to the Series* is designed to help the reader find *every* substantive discussion of a topic of interest in the articles. Included in the subject index are general topics such as education and family life, as well as individuals to whom articles are devoted. Geographical locations are included when they are an important part of the article. Professions are also included. Thus, one can look up Fannie Lou Hamer (three articles), Kansas (two articles), or nursing (four articles). The more than 200 authors represented in the index to authors are a who's who of contemporary scholarship.

For topics in the five monographs and for specific discussions in the articles, please see the comprehensive indexes for every title. The more than 10,000 entries in these indexes make this series a virtual encyclopedia of black women's history.

Contents of the Series

Volumes 1-4, continued

24. Foster, Frances Smith. *Adding Color and Contour to Early American Self-Portraitures: Autobiographical Writings of Afro-American Women.*
25. Fox-Genovese, Elizabeth. *Strategies and Forms of Resistance: Focus on Slave Women in the United States.*
26. Fry, Gladys-Marie. *Harriet Powers: Portrait of a Black Quilter.*
27. Goldin, Claudia *Female Labor Force Participation: The Origins of Black and White Differences, 1870 and 1880.*
28. Goodson, Martia G. *Medical-Botanical Contributions of African Slave Women to American Medicine.*
29. Goodson, Martia G. *The Slave Narrative Collection: A Tool for Reconstructing Afro-American Women's History.*
30. Gregory, Chester W. *Black Women in Pre-Federal America.*
31. Griggs, A. C. *Lucy Craft Laney.*
32. Gundersen, Joan R. *The Double Bonds of Race and Sex: Black and White Women in a Colonial Virginia Parish.*
33. Gutman, Herbert G. *Marital and Sexual Norms among Slave Women.*
34. Gwin, Minrose C. *Green-eyed Monsters of the Slavocracy: Jealous Mistresses in Two Slave Narratives.*
35. Hanchett, Catherine M. *'What Sort of People and Families . . .' The Edmondson Sisters.*
36. Harris, William. *Work and the Family in Black Atlanta, 1880.*
37. Hartgrove, W. B. *The Story of Maria Louise Moore and Fannie M. Richards.*
38. Hartigan, Lynda R. *Edmonia Lewis.*
39. Hine, Darlene Clark. *Co-Laborers in the Work of the Lord: Nineteenth-Century Black Women Physicians.*
40. Hine, Darlene Clark. *Female Slave Resistance: The Economics of Sex.*
41. Horton, James Oliver. *Freedom's Yoke: Gender Conventions Among Antebellum Free Blacks.*
42. Jacobs, Sylvia M. *Three Afro-American Women Missionaries in Africa, 1882-1904.*
43. Johnson, Michael P. *Smothered Slave Infants: Were Slave Mothers at Fault?*
44. Jones, Jacqueline. *'My Mother Was Much of a Woman': Black Women, Work, and the Family Under Slavery.*
45. Kennan, Clara B. *The First Negro Teacher in Little Rock.*
46. Kulikoff, Alan. *Beginnings of the Afro-American Family.*
47. Lawson, Ellen N. *Sarah Woodson Early: 19th Century Black Nationalist 'Sister'.*
48. Lawson, Ellen N. and Merrell, Marlene. *Antebellum Black Coeds at Oberlin College.*
49. Leashore, Bogart R. *Black Female Workers: Live-in Domestics in Detroit, Michigan, 1860-1880.*
50. Lebsock, Suzanne. *Free Black Women and the Question of Matriarchy: Petersburg, Virginia, 1784-1820.*
51. Mabee, Carleton. *Sojourner Truth, Bold Prophet: Why Did She Never Learn to Read?*
52. Massa, Ann. *Black Women in the 'White City'.*
53. Matson, R. Lynn. *Phillis Wheatley—Soul Sister?*
54. Matthews, Jean. *Race, Sex and the Dimensions of Liberty in Antebellum America.*
55. Mills, Gary B. *Coincoin: An Eighteeenth Century 'Liberated' Woman.*
56. Moses, Wilson Jeremiah. *Domestic Feminism Conservatism, Sex Roles, and Black Women's Clubs, 1893-1896.*
57. Newman, Debra L. *Black Women in the Era of the American Revolution in Pennsylvania.*
58. Obitko, Mary Ellen. *'Custodians of a House of Resistance': Black Women Respond to Slavery.*

Volumes 1-4, continued

59. Oden, Gloria C. *The Journal of Charlotte L. Forten: The Salem-Philadelphia Years (1854-1862) Reexamined.*
60. Parkhurst, Jessie W. *The Role of the Black Mammy in the Plantation Household.*
61. Perkins, Linda M. *Heed Life's Demands: The Educational Philosophy of Fanny Jackson Coppin.*
62. Perkins, Linda M. *The Black Female American Missionary Association Teacher in the South, 1861-1870.*
63. Perkins, Linda M. *The Impact of the 'Cult of True Womanhood' on the Education of Black Women.*
64. Perkins, Linda M. *Black Women and Racial 'Uplift' Prior to Emancipation.*
65. Pleck, Elizabeth H. *The Two-Parent Household: Black Family Structure in Late Nineteenth Century Boston.*
66. Porter, Dorothy B. *Sarah Parker Remond, Abolitionist and Physician.*
67. Quarles, Benjamin. *Harriet Tubman's Unlikely Leadership.*
68. Riley, Glenda. *American Daughters: Black Women in the West.*
69. Reiff, Janice L., Michael R. Dahlin, and Daniel Scott Smith. *Rural Push and Urban Pull: Work and Family Experiences of Older Black Women in Southern Cities, 1880-1900.*
70. Schafer, Judith K. *'Open and Notorious Concubinage': The Emancipation of Slave Mistresses by Will and the Supreme Court in Antebellum Louisiana.*
71. Sealander, Judith. *Antebellum Black Press Images of Women.*
72. Seraile, William. *Susan McKinney Steward: New York State's First African-American Woman Physician.*
73. Shammas, Carole. *Black Women's Work and the Evolution of Plantation Society in Virginia.*
74. Silverman, Jason H. *Mary Ann Shadd and the Search for Equality.*
75. Sloan, Patricia E. *Early Black Nursing Schools and Responses of Black Nurses to their Educational Programs.*
76. Soderlund, Jean R. *Black Women in Colonial Pennsylvania.*
77. Sterling, Dorothy. *To Build A Free Society: Nineteenth-Century Black Women.*
78. Sumler-Lewis, Janice. *The Forten-Purvis Women of Philadelphia and the American Anti-Slavery Crusade.*
79. Tate, Claudia. *Pauline Hopkins: Our Literary Foremother.*
80. Terborg-Penn, Rosalyn. *Black Women Freedom Fighters in Early 19th Century Maryland.*
81. Thompson, Priscilla. *Harriet Tubman, Thomas Garrett, and the Underground Railroad.*
82. Tucker, David M. *Miss Ida B. Wells and Memphis Lynching.*
83. Vacha, John E. *The Case of Sara Lucy Bagby: A Late Gesture.*
84. Wade-Gayles, Gloria. *Black Women Journalists in the South, 1880-1905: An Approach to the Study of Black Women's History.*
85. White, Deborah G. *The Lives of Slave Women.*

Vols. 5-8. BLACK WOMEN IN AMERICAN HISTORY: THE TWENTIETH CENTURY, Edited with a Preface by Darlene Clark Hine

1. *Votes for Women: A Symposium by Leading Thinkers of Colored America.*
2. Anderson, Karen T. *Last Hired, First Fired: Black Women Workers During World War II.*
3. Anderson, Kathie R. *Era Bell Thompson: A North Dakota Daughter.*
4. Blackwelder, Julia Kirk. *Quiet Suffering: Atlanta Women in the 1930s.*

Volumes 5-8, continued

5. Blackwelder, Julia Kirk. *Women in the Work Force: Atlanta, New Orleans, and San Antonio, 1930 to 1940.*
6. Brady, Marilyn Dell. *Kansas Federation of Colored Women's Clubs, 1900-1930.*
7. Brady, Marilyn Dell. *Organizing Afro-American Girls' Clubs in Kansas in the 1920's.*
8. Breen, William J. *Black Women and the Great War: Mobilization and Reform in the South.*
9. Brooks, Evelyn. *Religion, Politics, and Gender: The Leadership of Nannie Helen Burroughs.*
10. Brown, Elsa Barkley. *Womanist Consciousness: Maggie Lena Walker and the Independent Order of Saint Luke.*
11. Bryan, Violet H. *Frances Joseph-Gaudet: Black Philanthropist.*
12. Cantarow, Ellen and Susan Gushee O'Malley. *Ella Baker: Organizing for Civil Rights.*
13. Carby, Hazel V. *It Jus Be's Dat Way Sometime: The Sexual Politics of Women's Blues.*
14. Chateauvert, Melinda. *The Third Step: Anna Julia Cooper and Black Education in the District of Columbia, 1910-1960.*
15. Clark-Lewis, Elizabeth. *'This Work Had a End:' African-American Domestic Workers in Washington, D.C., 1910-1940.*
16. Coleman, Willi. *Black Women and Segregated Public Transportation: Ninety Years of Resistance.*
17. Ergood, Bruce. *The Female Protection and the Sun Light: Two Contemporary Negro Mutual Aid Societies.*
18. Farley, Ena L. *Caring and Sharing Since World War I: The League of Women for Community Service—A Black Volunteer Organization in Boston.*
19. Feinman, Clarice. *An Afro-American Experience: The Women in New York City's Jail.*
20. Ferguson, Earline Rae. *The Women's Improvement Club of Indianapolis: Black Women Pioneers in Tuberculosis Work, 1903-1938.*
21. Ford, Beverly O. *Case Studies of Black Female Heads of Households in the Welfare System: Socialization and Survival.*
22. Gilkes, Cheryl Townsend. *'Together and in Harness': Women's Traditions in the Sanctified Church.*
23. Gilkes, Cheryl Townsend. *Going Up for the Oppressed: The Career Mobility of Black Women Community Workers.*
24. Gilkes, Cheryl Townsend. *Successful Rebellious Professionals: The Black Woman's Professional Identity and Community Commitment.*
25. Gunn, Arthur C. *The Struggle of Virginia Proctor Powell Florence.*
26. Guzman, Jessie P. *The Social Contributions of the Negro Woman Since 1940.*
27. Harley, Sharon. *Beyond the Classroom: Organizational Lives of Black Female Educators in the District of Columbia, 1890-1930.*
28. Harley, Sharon. *Black Women in a Southern City: Washington, D.C., 1890-1920.*
29. Haynes, Elizabeth Ross. *Negroes in Domestic Service in the United States.*
30. Helmbold, Lois Rita. *Beyond the Family Economy: Black and White Working-Class Women during the Great Depression.*
31. Hine, Darlene Clark. *The Ethel Johns Report: Black Women in the Nursing Profession, 1925.*
32. Hine, Darlene Clark. *From Hospital to College: Black Nurse Leaders and the Rise of Collegiate Nursing Schools.*
33. Hine, Darlene Clark. *Mabel K. Staupers and the Integration of Black Nurses into the Armed Forces.*
34. Hine, Darlene Clark. *The Call That Never Came: Black Women Nurses and World War I, An Historical Note.*

Volumes 5-8, continued

Volumes 5-8, continued

68. Woods, Sylvia. *You Have to Fight for Freedom.*
69. Woodson, Carter G. *The Negro Washerwoman: A Vanishing Figure.*
70. Yancy, Dorothy C. *Dorothy Bolden, Organizer of Domestic Workers: She Was Born Poor But She Would Not Bow Down.*

Vols. 9-10. BLACK WOMEN'S HISTORY: THEORY AND PRACTICE, Edited with a Preface by Darlene Clark Hine

1. Aldridge, Delores. *Black Women in the Economic Marketplace: A Battle Unfinished.*
2. Allen, Walter R. *Family Roles, Occupational Statuses, and Achievement Orientations Among Black Women in the United States.*
3. Allen, Walter R. *The Social and Economic Statuses of Black Women in the United States.*
4. Armitage, Susan, Theresa Banfield, and Sarah Jacobus. *Black Women and Their Communities in Colorado.*
5. Biola, Heather. *The Black Washerwoman in Southern Tradition.*
6. Bracey, John H., Jr. *Afro-American Women: A Brief Guide to Writings from Historical and Feminist Perspectives.*
7. Brown, Minnie Miller. *Black Women in American Agriculture.*
8. Collier-Thomas, Bettye. *The Impact of Black Women in Education: An Historical Overview.*
9. Dickson, Lynda F. *Toward a Broader Angle of Vision in Uncovering Women's History: Black Women's Clubs Revisited.*
10. Dill, Bonnie Thornton. *Race, Class, and Gender: Prospects for an All-Inclusive Sisterhood.*
11. Dill, Bonnie Thornton. *The Dialectics of Black Womanhood.*
12. Fox-Genovese, Elizabeth. *To Write My Self: The Autobiographies of Afro-American Women.*
13. Higginbotham, Evelyn Brooks. *Beyond the Sound of Silence: Afro-American Women in History.*
14. Hine, Darlene Clark. *An Angle of Vision: Black Women and the United States Constitution, 1787-1987.*
15. Hine, Darlene Clark. *To Be Gifted, Female, and Black.*
16. Hine, Darlene Clark. *Opportunity and Fulfillment: Sex, Race, and Class in Health Care Education.*
17. Hine, Darlene Clark. *Lifting the Veil, Shattering the Silence: Black Women's History in Slavery and Freedom.*
18. Jackson, Jacquelyne Johnson. *A Partial Bibliography on or Related to Black Women.*
19. Katz, Maude White. *The Negro Woman and the Law.*
20. Katz, Maude White. *She Who Would Be Free—Resistance.*
21. King, Deborah K. *Multiple Jeopardy, Multiple Consciousness: The Context of a Black Feminist Ideology.*
22. Ladner, Joyce A. *Racism and Tradition: Black Womanhood in Historical Perspective.*
23. Lewis, Diane K. *A Response to Inequality: Black Women, Racism, and Sexism.*
24. Marable, Manning. *Groundings with my Sisters: Patriarchy and the Exploitation of Black Women.*
25. Palmer, Phyllis Marynick. *White Women/Black Women: The Dualism of Female Identity and Experience in the United States.*
26. Patterson, Tiffany R. *Toward a Black Feminist Analysis: Recent Works by Black Women Scholars.*

Volumes 9-10, continued

27. Reagon, Bernice Johnson. *My Black Mothers and Sisters, or On Beginning A Cultural Autobiography.*
28. Reagon, Bernice Johnson. *African Diaspora Women: The Making of Cultural Workers.*
29. Rector, Theresa A. *Black Nuns as Educators.*
30. Render, Sylvia Lyons. *Afro-American Women: The Outstanding and the Obscure.*
31. Scales-Trent, Judy. *Black Women and the Constitution: Finding Our Place, Asserting Our Rights.*
32. Shockley, Ann Allen. *The Negro Woman in Retrospect: Blueprint for the Future.*
33. Smith, Eleanor. *Historical Relationships between Black and White Women.*
34. Snorgrass, J. William. *Pioneer Black Women Journalists from 1850s to the 1950s.*
35. Strong, Augusta. *Negro Women in Freedom's Battles.*
36. Terborg-Penn, Rosalyn. *Historical Treatment of Afro-Americans in the Woman's Movement, 1900-1920: A Bibliographical Essay.*
37. Terborg-Penn, Rosalyn. *Teaching the History of Black Women: A Bibliographical Essay.*
38. Thornbrough, Emma Lou. *The History of Black Women in Indiana.*
39. Walker, Juliet E. K. *The Afro-American Woman: Who Was She?*
40. Yellin, Jean Fagan. *Afro-American Women 1800-1910: A Selected Bibliography.*

Vol. 11. **Daughters of Sorrow: Attitudes Toward Black Women, 1880-1920,** by Beverly Guy-Sheftall

Vol. 12. **Jane Edna Hunter: A Case Study of Black Leadership, 1910-1950,** by Adrienne Lash Jones; Preface by Darlene Clark Hine

Vol. 13. **Quest for Equality: The Life and Writings of Mary Eliza Church Terrell, 1863-1954,** by Beverly Washington Jones
including Mary Church Terrell's selected essays:

1. *Announcement* [of NACW].
2. *First Presidential Address to the National Association of Colored Women.*
3. *The Duty of the National Association of Colored Women to the Race.*
4. *What Role is the Educated Negro Woman to Play in the Uplifting of Her Race?*
5. *Graduates and Former Students of Washington Colored High School.*
6. *Lynching from a Negro's Point of View.*
7. *The Progress of Colored Women.*
8. *The International Congress of Women.*
9. *Samuel Coleridge-Taylor.*
10. *Service Which Should be Rendered the South.*
11. *The Mission of Meddlers.*
12. *Paul Laurence Dunbar.*
13. *Susan B. Anthony, the Abolitionist.*
14. *A Plea for the White South by A Coloured Woman.*
15. *Peonage in the United States: The Convict Lease System and Chain Gangs.*
16. *The Disbanding of the Colored Soldiers.*
17. *What It Means to Be Colored in the Capital of the United States.*
18. *A Sketch of Mingo Saunders.*
19. *An Interview with W.T. Stead on the Race Problem.*
20. *The Justice of Woman Suffrage.*
21. *Phyllis Wheatley—An African Genius.*
22. *The History of the Club Women's Movement.*
23. *Needed: Women Lawyers.*
24. *Dr. Sara W. Brown.*
25. *I Remember Frederick Douglass.*

Vol. 14. **To Better Our World: Black Women in Organized Reform, 1890-1920,** by Dorothy Salem

Vol. 15. **Ida B. Wells-Barnett: An Exploratory Study of an American Black Woman, 1893-1930,** by Mildred Thompson

including Ida B. Wells-Barnett's Selected Essays

1. *Afro-Americans and Africa.*
2. *Lynch Law in All Its Phases.*
3. *The Reason Why the Colored American is not in the World's Columbian Exposition.*
   Chapter IV. *Lynch Law*, by Ida B. Wells
   Chapter VI. *The Reason Why*, by F.L. Barnett

4. *Two Christmas Days: A Holiday Story.*
5. *Lynch Law in America.*
6. *The Negro's Case in Equity.*
7. *Lynching and the Excuse for It.*
8. *Booker T. Washington and His Critics.*
9. *Lynching, Our National Crime.*
10. *How Enfranchisement Stops Lynchings.*
11. *Our Country's Lynching Record.*

Vol. 16. **Women in the Civil Rights Movement: Trailblazers and Torchbearers, 1941-1965**

Edited by Vicki Crawford, Jacqueline A. Rouse, Barbara Woods; Associate Editors: Broadus Butler, Marymal Dryden, and Melissa Walker

1. Black, Allida. *A Reluctant but Persistent Warrior: Eleanor Roosevelt and the Early Civil Rights Movement*
2. Brock, Annette K. *Gloria Richardson and the Cambridge Movement*
3. Burks, Mary Fair. *Trailblazers: Women in the Montgomery Bus Boycott.*
4. Cochrane, Sharlene Voogd. *'And the Pressure Never Let Up': Black Women, White Women, and the Boston YWCA, 1918-1948.*
5. Crawford, Vicki. *Beyond the Human Self: Grassroots Activists in the Mississippi Civil Rights Movement.*
6. Grant, Jacquelyn. *Civil Rights Women: A Source for Doing Womanist Theology.*
7. Knotts, Alice G. *Methodist Women Integrate Schools and Housing, 1952-1959.*
8. Langston, Donna. *The Women of Highlander.*
9. Locke, Mamie E. *Is This America: Fannie Lou Hamer and the Mississippi Freedom Democratic Party.*
10. McFadden, Grace Jordan. *Septima Clark.*
11. Mueller, Carol. *Ella Baker and the Origins of 'Participatory Democracy.'*
12. Myrick-Harris, Clarissa. *Behind the Scenes: Doris Derby, Denise Nicholas, and the Free Southern Theater.*
13. Oldendorf, Sandra. *The South Carolina Sea Island Citizenship Schools.*
14. Payne, Charles. *Men Led, But Women Organized: Movement Participation of Women in the Mississippi Delta.*
15. Reagon, Bernice Johnson. *Women as Culture Carriers in the Civil Rights Movement: Fannie Lou Hamer.*
16. Standley, Anne. *The Role of Black Women in the Civil Rights Movement.*
17. Woods, Barbara. Modjeska Simkins and the South Carolina Conference of the NAACP.

Author Index

Boldface indicates volume numbers and roman indicates article numbers within volumes.

Subject Index

Boldface indicates volume numbers and roman indicates article numbers within volumes.